Arctic Crossing

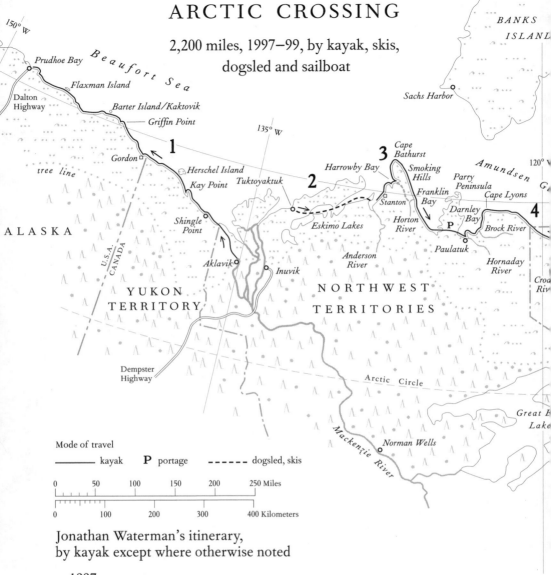

ARCTIC CROSSING

2,200 miles, 1997–99, by kayak, skis,
dogsled and sailboat

Mode of travel

——— kayak   **P** portage   - - - - - dogsled, skis

0   50   100   150   200   250 Miles

0   100   200   300   400 Kilometers

Jonathan Waterman's itinerary,
by kayak except where otherwise noted

1997

1   July–August: Aklavik to Prudhoe Bay

1998

2   April: Tuktoyaktuk to Anderson River on skis with Elias

3   Late June–mid-July: Anderson River to Paulatuk

4   Late July–early August: Paulatuk to Kugluktuk

5   Late August–early September: Kugluktuk to Umingmaktuuq with June Duell

1999

6   May: Cambridge Bay to Umingmaktuuq by snowmobile with *Inuk* companion;
return to Cambridge Bay by dogsled with *Inuk* companion

7   July–August: Elu Inlet to Gjoa Haven

8   Late August: crossing Rae Strait on the *Ocean Search;* then by kayak to Taloyoak

9   September: Taloyoak to Gulf of Boothia

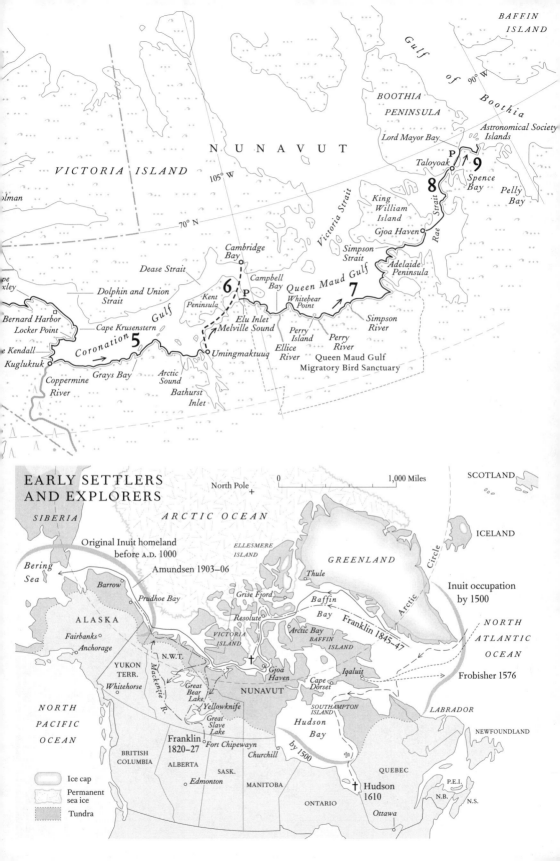

BAFFIN
ISLAND

Gulf

of

90° W

Boothia

BOOTHIA
PENINSULA

Astronomical Society
Islands

Lord Mayor Bay

P

Taloyoak ↑**9**

8

*Spence
Bay*

*Pelly
Bay*

N U N A V U T

105° W

VICTORIA ISLAND

*King
William
Island*

Rae Strait

olman

70° N

Victoria Strait

Gjoa Haven

*Simpson
Strait*

*Adelaide
Peninsula*

Cambridge
Bay

Dease Strait

*Campbell
Bay*

*Simpson
Strait*

Kent
Peninsula

6
P

Queen Maud Gulf

7

→

*Whitebear
Point*

*Dolphin and Union
Strait*

xley

Elu Inlet
Melville Sound

*Perry
Island*

*Perry
River*

*Simpson
River*

Bernard Harbor
Locker Point

Cape Krusenstern

Coronation

Umingmaktuuq

*Ellice
River*

Queen Maud Gulf
Migratory Bird Sanctuary

pe

Gulf

5

e Kendall

Coronation

Kugluktuk

→

Grays Bay

*Arctic
Sound*

*Coppermine
River*

*Bathurst
Inlet*

EARLY SETTLERS
AND EXPLORERS

North Pole ✛

0   1,000 Miles

SCOTLAND

SIBERIA

A R C T I C   O C E A N

*ELLESMERE
ISLAND*

GREENLAND

Arctic Circle

ICELAND

Original Inuit homeland
before A.D. 1000

Thule

Inuit occupation
by 1500

*Bering
Sea*

Amundsen 1903–06

Barrow

Grise Fjord

*Baffin
Bay*

Franklin 1845–47

N O R T H

Prudhoe Bay

Resolute

ATLANTIC

ALASKA

*VICTORIA
ISLAND*

Arctic Bay

*BAFFIN
ISLAND*

O C E A N

Fairbanks
Anchorage

✝

Gjoa
Haven

Iqaluit

Frobisher 1576

YUKON
TERR.

N.W.T.

Mackenzie R.

*Cape
Dorset*

Whitehorse

Great
Bear
Lake

NUNAVUT

LABRADOR

NORTH

Yellowknife

*SOUTHAMPTON
ISLAND*

NEWFOUNDLAND

PACIFIC

Great
Slave
Lake

*Hudson
Bay*

OCEAN

BRITISH
COLUMBIA

Franklin
1820–27

Fort Chipewayn

by 1500

QUEBEC

P.E.I.

ALBERTA

Churchill

✝ Hudson
1610

N.B.

SASK.

Edmonton

MANITOBA

N.S.

ONTARIO

Ottawa

☐ Ice cap

☐ Permanent
    sea ice

▨ Tundra

Also by Jonathan Waterman

The Quotable Climber (editor)
A Most Hostile Mountain
Kayaking the Vermilion Sea
In the Shadow of Denali
Cloud Dancers (editor)
High Alaska
Surviving Denali

Arctic Crossing

A Journey Through
the Northwest Passage
and Inuit Culture

Jonathan Waterman

THE LYONS PRESS
GUILFORD, CONNECTICUT
AN IMPRINT OF THE GLOBE PEQUOT PRESS

The Lyons Press is an imprint of The Globe Pequot Press

Grateful acknowledgment is made to Stuart E. Jenness for permission to reprint an excerpt from his father's diary, *Arctic Odyssey: The Diary of Diamond Jenness, Ethnologist with the Canadian Arctic Expedition in Northern Alaska and Canada, 1913–1916* (Canadian Museum of Civilization, 1991); and to the government of the Northwest Territories for permission to reproduce the chart of Inuktitut syllabics found at their Web site (www.gov.nt.ca/kids/school/inukcar.htm).

Printed in the United States of America

10 9 8 7 6 5 4 3 2 1

Library of Congress Cataloging-in-Publication data is available on file.

Stone Art also serves to give identity to the Eskimos. Having deprived him of his heritage, and even the memory of this heritage, we offer him a substitute which he eagerly accepts, for no other is permitted. And so he takes his place on stage, side-by-side with the American Indian whose headdress comes from a mail order catalog, who learned his dances at Disneyland, and picked up his philosophy from Hippies. He knows no other identity, and when he is shown the real treasures of his culture, when he hears the old songs and reads the ancient words, he aggressively says, "It's a lie, a white man's lie. Don't tell me who I am or who my ancestors were. I know!"
— *The anthropologist Edmund Carpenter in 1970*

The impressions which we have imbibed regarding the polar bear's ferocity are due more to old notions of what it ought to be rather than what it is.
— *The botanist Robert Brown while collecting lichens in the Arctic, 1867*

The great sea
Has set me adrift.
It moves me
As the weed in a great river,
Earth and the Great Weather
Move me,
Have carried me away
And move my inward parts with joy.
— *Sung by the ancient shaman Uvavnuk after a meteorite hit her*

Contents

Arctic Crossing

Introduction to The People

Rite of Passage

Before I began my journey across the Arctic, I learned that Inuit ("The People") have long preferred their original name to "Eskimos." The latter ("eaters of raw meat") was given to them several hundred years ago by their southern, Native American enemies. Those subarctic people, the Montagnais tribe, lived below the tree line in Quebec and were able to cook their meat because of an abundance of firewood. They too refer to themselves as People (*Innu*).

While passing through Inuit hunting camps and villages, I was obligated to obtain permission for crossing or camping on private lands, to get consent before exposing photographs of Inuit activities and to tell them my business. Most Inuit answered my questions. Some graciously hosted me while remaining silent. I have omitted or changed the names of those few people whose actions weren't flattering. Since I was autonomous and unaffiliated with any institution, I have shared observations openly; I'm an observant writer rather than a trained anthropologist.

According to one ethnologist, Louis-Jacques Dorais, the root *inu* refers to "what one has, that corresponds to the center." While Chinese cosmology similarly places all nonhumans (non-Chinese) at the edge of the world, Inuit philosophy—concerning other races as well as animals—lacks ethnocentricity. If they see themselves at the center of the universe, they do not feel superior to other races that are not. Inuit don't pass judgment, as I realized again and again while traveling through the Arctic. Unlike the racial epithets heard in our world, being called a *Kabloona* (also *Kapluna* or *Qallunaat*) did not mean that I was inferior or that I had a different skin color. It merely tells of my bushy eyebrows.

In 1979 the Inuit Circumpolar Conference in Barrow, Alaska, announced their real name to the world. The Canadian government officially adopted "Inuit," but the United States stuck with the old name, accepted by most Alaskan Iñupiat. *Webster's Encyclopedic Unabridged* defines "Eskimo" as "characterized generally by short stature, stocky build, light-brown complexion, broad, flat facial structure," while "Inuit" is "a member of the Eskimo peoples." Apparently the original name doesn't carry the weight of "Eskimo." It may be that U.S. citizens (and, to a lesser extent, Canadians) simply prefer the mythical and romantic use of old names. In 1922, Robert Flaherty's Eskimo hunting film *Nanook of the North* became one of the most celebrated documentaries of the century. No matter that Inuit at that time had begun collecting welfare and eating canned food. As the world was swept up in a wave of industry and technology, polite society preferred being marooned in the past, in remembrance of a Noble Savage still living off the land.

Like many public school children growing up in the 1960s, I was taught that Eskimos were still hunting polar bears with spears. Two decades later the cerebral best-seller *Arctic Dreams* used the word "Eskimo" repeatedly while "Inuit" was strangely absent. Today New York's American Museum of Natural History displays exhibits of nineteenth-century Eskimo living conditions with present-tense explanations—as if the Eskimos continued to live in *iglus* and sod houses. Even anthropologists argue that "Eskimo" is still a useful name for both The People and their language, which Inuit call Inuktitut ("in the manner of a person"). The syllabics and varying dialects that put their language into writing are shown in Appendixes C and D. Appendixes A and B show Wildlife Observations and a Canadian Arctic Cultures Timeline. I use the archaeological "Paleo-Eskimo" to describe the cultures that lived in the North before Inuit did.

Kabloona children still eat Eskimo Pies (modeled after Eskimo ice cream, a mix of seal fat and berries, unpalatable to anyone living below the Arctic Circle). Proficient Caucasian kayakers learn Eskimo rolls. Moreover, seeking northern pride, the Edmonton Drillers football team renamed themselves the Eskimos. The word, at least to my way of thinking, seems a xenophobic epithet.

You can imagine my confusion, while crossing the Arctic, when Inuit referred to themselves as Eskimos. Children shout the word often (along with curses) while playing with one another. It may be simple self-deprecation, yet Inuit are also incredibly sophisticated and fond of teasing *Kabloona*. It may be analogous to those African-Americans who have adopted the "N word" as their own, diffusing the epithet's power. Most likely, as The People continue to trade in their former tools and traditions while modifying their technology and society, they enjoy evoking a mythical name that we once knew them by.

Dialogue in my book that was not re-created through the sound track of video cameras or my microcassette recorder is recalled, through the best of my memory and journal notes, as it was spoken. I wrote the book in present tense in deference to both Inuit speech patterns and their free-floating perception of time. Similarly, as a bird lover I repeat their calls (and the inexplicable hum of the Arctic) as I heard them, phonetically.

I was in the Canadian Arctic from 1997 to 1999, and I refer to that country's dollar as equivalent to two-thirds of an American dollar (not counting the inflation rate of remote Arctic living in either country). Also, even though Canadian Inuit have converted to the metric system (infinitely more useful than degrees and minutes when one plots a global positioning system [GPS] course), I have shown distances, speeds and temperatures with the old-fashioned U.S. units of measure. I can't fathom paddling at six kilometers per hour or being warm at 20 degrees Celsius.

Along with the kayak—an English transliteration of the Inuit *qayaq*—many of The People have lost the umiak (skin whaleboat), the *iglu*, the *angekok* (shaman), kamiks (sealskin boots), *qilliq* (the soapstone seal oil lamp) and *Qimmiq* (the sled dog). Now, sadly, most Inuit children can no longer speak their parents' language. Fortunately, many old words, such as *kamotik* (sled), *Inuksuit* (stone cairns resembling a man) and *tuktu* (caribou), are still commonly used. I have used the Inuktitut language names remaining in the daily northern vernacular. Because of varying dialects throughout the Arctic, it would be difficult to record proper spellings and pronunciations. There are several Inuktitut-English or Eskimo-English dictionaries, but just one includes two dozen dialects; its author labored for decades only to complete the A's.

I also learned about Inuit culture from the works of Franz Boas, Jean Briggs, Hugh Brody, Edmund Carpenter, Norman Chance, Richard Condon, Colin Irwin, Diamond Jenness, Robert McGhee, David Morrison, Richard Nelson, Knud Rasmussen, Vilhjalmur Stefansson and George Wenzel. Other popular writers—Jared Diamond, Peter Freuchen, Sam Hall, James Houston, Barry Lopez, Ernie Lyall, E. C. Pielou, Gontran de Poncins, Duncan Pryde, John Strohmeyer and William Vollman—helped me understand other aspects of both culture and environment. (See Bibliography.)

During my travels through Inuit villages, I saw a level of poverty and despair that is strangely omitted from most modern Arctic literature. Although many Inuit still eat seals, whales, caribou and bears, their villages are not dissimilar to Harlem, Little Havana, backwoods Appalachia or the average Native American reservation. I chose to use candor in chronicling both the anguish and the joy that I observed among these humble people. Presenting the truth of their dilemma in changing times seems the fairest perspective for the new millennium. No sense propagating folklore masked as fact. Any misinterpretations of their complex culture are my fault—

caused by the limitations of my transient journey, the roller coaster ride of my emotions during a challenging adventure or my own cross-cultural near-sightedness. What *Kabloona* really knows what Inuit think?

If inexplicable at times, many Inuit still have magical and surreal lifestyles. They often showed me how to let go of goal-oriented distractions. Extended periods of solitude during my trip allowed me to adopt their ritualistic coping mechanisms: to revere wildlife, forget about time and value animal souls as equal to my own. I learned how to watch (rather than *identify*) birds solely for pleasure and how to let time wash over me as it does The People. I began to think of my Arctic crossing as an *Inuk* (Inuit person) would, in present tense, as if time no longer mattered. Consequently, my story does not have a strong allegiance to physical destination, chronology or daily movement. (Please see the endpaper map.) By the end, the ambitious demands and linear aspects of my journey were subverted by the myriad beauties of the Arctic and its People. Environment and culture—interspersed with isolation—transported me internally and so far altered my perceptions that finishing each grueling segment began to feel like being awoken from a dream.

My paddling so wide-eyed and alone, out of vast stretches of wilderness and into hunting camps, may have allowed The People to share their lives with me. Still, they trusted a total stranger, even though my own culture historically has not done them justice. They gave me food, shelter, route information and safety advice and offered me rides, yet they rarely inquired into my business. They showed me forbearance; they were quick with curative laughter. I learned that they possess a quiet grace and humility that almost certainly derive from suffering. In the face of global assimilation and a world turning into one market, as toxins waft into the Arctic and become absorbed by its inhabitants, the gentle selflessness and tolerance of Inuit should be a model for any culture. They are the most friendly and generous people one could ever hope to meet.

Prologue: Along the Smoking Hills

On July 5, 1998, I am running across the wind into Franklin Bay, Northwest Territories. A sail flies tight on the mast above my sea kayak, wobbling in the Beaufort Sea gusts. Rocks rattle down the cliffed shore. Natural underground seams of coal ignite upon exposure to air and waft out to me in bilious white clouds of choking air.

I'm sailing a folding Klepper kayak copied from the original Inuit design. In 1907 a German tailor, Johann Klepper, reinvented the kayak. The Klepper is fifteen feet long, half my own weight empty or twice my weight loaded with food and equipment. The frame is an ingenious skeleton of folding ash rods and ribs that tautens the insides of a rubber and canvas hull. Borrowing from the Inuit design of legend, the Klepper's wooden frame and canvas rubber skin also bends, creaks and flops softly over waves. Although my boat is not a speedy molded resin or high-tech plastic craft (surfing in Fiberglas or plastic boats feels like galloping bareback), the Klepper has advantages over the featherweight skin-and-driftwood kayaks used to hunt beluga whales. For one, it is as stable as a loaded canoe. It can be filled with provisions for over a month and then sailed like an umiak whaling boat. It can be taken apart, folded up, stuffed away into two duffel bags and portaged.

While watching the insect swarms along the wind-sheltered shore, I lean hard to windward to counteract heeling. Under most Arctic conditions, sailing without safety outriggers lowers me down the evolutionary curve with the vanished Neanderthals. But going ashore right now to inflate sponsons and assemble outriggers is equally hazardous. Along with the rock fall and noxious smoke, the mosquitoes would cover me like a blizzard.

I haven't seen another person for fifteen days. Although crossing the Northwest Passage is my long-held dream and I have covered 650 miles over the last two summers, plunging into solitude still freaks me out. Most days I feel lost in the sea of my own ambition. I haven't dared speak, let alone whisper, for days now. In this humbled state, I feel an acute and almost painful new level of awareness toward all my actions.

I compromise by sailing my kayak a hundred yards from shore, riding the edge of the wind envelope just outside the choking smoke and within swimming distance if I should capsize. Five minutes in this 39-degree water would stiffen my limbs into cordwood.

I recently learned that the most frequent cause of accidental death to

Smoking Hills' clouds of burning coal

Inuit is drowning. While the Coast Guard and the Royal Canadian Mounted Police (RCMP) insist that boaters wear personal flotation devices (PFDs) and take swimming lessons, trying to swim in the Arctic Ocean only hastens death. Even an Olympic swimmer's limbs would lock up after a quarter mile—and the shore is still a half mile away. Wearing a PFD in the hope that another boat would come by might prolong a nonswimmer's life for a few minutes, yet I haven't seen a boat for weeks. While the Arctic officials call these deaths drownings, I know that they're caused by hypothermia.

I steer in another quarter mile and nervously review the consequences of capsizing. My mind spins into a whole scenario:

My PFD vest is tightly cinched around my chest, and even though a surge of adrenaline would allow me to reboard the kayak, I would be sitting in ice water with wet clothes. First my lips would turn blue. Since the body cools up to twenty-five times faster in water than in air, it would only take a few minutes before my plummeting body temperature would begin to shut down the flow of blood to my legs and arms. The first defense against hypothermia would manifest itself as violent shivering to counter the heat conducting out through wet clothes and water. In this losing battle with heat loss, acid metabolite waste products would build up in my legs and arms, the shivering would stop and muscular rigidity would begin. As my body temperature dropped toward 90 degrees, the painful ache of the cold would relent. Then my stiffened arms would no longer allow me to pump out the water or find the muscular coordination to paddle. Now both my respiration and heartbeat would drop, and my core organs would begin to plummet toward Beaufort Sea temperature. (As I plunge deeper into these imaginings, my real-time heartbeat begins rising, making me sweat.)

After fifteen minutes—without the ability to change into dry clothes as the water continued to refrigerate my numbed legs and crotch—my slowing heart would reduce the flow of oxygen-rich red blood cells to my brain. As it cooled, cell metabolism would slow. I would no longer feel the cold. I would probably experience a rush of giddiness. Since the thermoregulation center of my brain would now be impaired, the water below my waist would feel like that of a warm bathtub. This false flush of heat would cause me to try to force off my wool hat, but I wouldn't be able to because my fingers would be too stiff and bloodless.

On land, death does not come so quickly to hypothermia victims. In the sea, an ice water–cooled *Kabloona* like myself, past the point of releasing adrenaline, would lose all sense of panic and drift into pleasant-seeming unconsciousness in less than twenty-five minutes. While I would be passed out in a kayak in the sort of waves I'm now experiencing, the loss of balance would no doubt cause another capsize. By then I would be too far gone even to hold my breath, and I would probably reawaken just long enough to experience the final nightmarish panic unique to drowning victims. I would probably open my eyes wide to confront a blur of bubbles and worry about how stupid everyone will think I am for dying like this. Breathing would probably cease shortly after my lungs filled with seawater. In all probability, I'd be history.

At this point young humans and animals experience the mammalian diving reflex. The heart, if it hasn't gone into complete arrest or ventricular fibrillation, might slowly keep pumping blood, which can preserve brain tissue for nearly an hour, a space of time that bears little relevance to a middle-aged kayaker submerged along some of the most isolated ocean in the world. The only guesswork to such a rapid exit is what would happen to my body.

Most Inuit bodies lost in boating accidents are not recovered. After a few days, fermenting gases trapped in the stomach and intestines tend to bring waterlogged bodies floating back to the surface. The distorting effects of bloating, hungry bears, scavenging foxes, pounding surf, furring seaweed and jellyfish tentacles render most floating cadavers in the Arctic unrecognizable. Here in the western Arctic the ice pack is never far out, rumbling like thunder on the northern horizon. If the north wind happened to break the current's pull and surf the body to land, the ice pack wouldn't be far behind, scouring body and shoreline to the bone.

The ice pack, along with wind and tide, makes it difficult for large animals to survive in the intertidal zone. The oceanic muscle of this slow-moving frozen surf crunches up ancient driftwood and sod houses, lifts boulders and creates perfectly furrowed fields of gravel push ridges. Eventually—in the next southern wind, moon tide, or maybe not until next summer—the ice pack withdraws, leaving great bulldozer gouges and an assortment of compressed blue ice chunks that take all summer to melt.

If I drowned, my body would probably not be found. Half of Sir John Franklin's 128 men never were during their attempt to cross the passage 150 years ago, and the bodies of the other half were torn apart by starving men, foxes and bears. Even my kayak would disappear into the vastness. Yet my pulse calms as I find consolation to this long and paranoic inner monologue: Having my remains picked clean to sustain the spacious Arctic is far preferable to feeding worms in a crowded graveyard.

The wind gusts first reveal themselves below the cliffs, cloaked with coal smoke, then flattening the wave crests. At each hit I loosen the sheet and let the sail swing safely to the lee. As the wind slows, my speed drops, so I sheet the sail back and lean into the wind, speeding me up again.

While I round a point, a rogue gust surprises me. Before I can release the sail, it's filled with a blast of air, rolling the kayak over and throwing me into the water.

I'm dead, I think. But it doesn't seem cold because of all the adrenaline pumping through me. I have to choose. Reboard the kayak? Abandon it? Or swim it in? Within seconds I grab the kayak stern line and begin kicking madly toward shore. The quicker I get there and get out of the water, the better my chances of beating hypothermia. It never occurs to me again that I won't make it.

Thirty yards out my arms stiffen. My legs drop. In an instant I realize that I can touch bottom; my chin comes just above the water. With new determination, I sprint onto the bouldered shore and up to a vent pouring out warm coal smoke. I watch, strangely detached from all that surrounds me, as my last week of food bobs in the shore surf next to the kayak. I'm elated to have survived. I begin laughing. The mosquitoes have been quelled by the coal smoke.

Within minutes, as the shivering relents and I change into dry clothes, I grow angry. This was a stupid mistake. I know better.

What am I doing here anyway, trying to solo the Northwest Passage?

Knud Rasmussen's book *Across Arctic America* put words to my quest. In

1922, while the Danish anthropologist prepared to set out on his dogsled journey, he met an *Inuk* (Inuit person) named Iyjugarjuk, who fasted for two weeks at a time to understand the meaning of life. The elder *angekok* (shaman) told Rasmussen: "All true wisdom is only to be learned far from the dwellings of men, out in the Great Solitudes; and is only to be attained through suffering. Privation and suffering are the only things that can open the mind of man to those things that are hidden from others."

This raison d'être for my journey would have seemed a mere abstraction if I hadn't learned about an elevated awareness on past expeditions, while hungry and pushing my limits. Ask any high-altitude alpinist or blue-water sailor. Discomfort and isolation can lift you beyond your mere physical being into a state of tolerance, a semblance of natural order.

The Dakota Sioux isolated their young men, naked and hungry, in the wilds to await animal spirits and visions that would show the unity of nature and the wholeness of the world. Of course, if the young men didn't come back alive, their vision quest wouldn't benefit them in the afterworld. Danger was courted only as a carefully calculated enterprise to be safely overcome.

Although the uninitiated commonly assume that danger is sought after as an end in itself, rewarded by mastery and adrenaline, risk taking is just a small step along a greater path. It is an important step too, one you try to dispense with as quickly and efficiently as possible.

I begin clipping together the aluminum outrigger poles, inflating and attaching the sponsons, rehauling the dripping sail eight feet up the mast. Assembling gear is therapeutic because fear dissipates if you can just move forward in logical, familiar sequences, as if you intended an act of mastery. I know that my actions are merely a preliminary to reach the greater understanding of which the shaman Iyjugarjuk spoke. Any committed adventurer eventually learns that equipment and performance are just a means to that greater end of finding your place in the natural world.

I can't afford any more dim-witted mistakes if I want to survive the next eighteen hundred miles. My thoughts drift back to last year, when I started out on the Mackenzie River, and to how much I've learned since then.

PART ONE

Testing the Waters

Fiery-Looking Birds

I am paddling the western channel of a dozen rivercourses, running at maybe 2 miles an hour. Honey brown and quiet as slow wind, it is more tilted swamp than river. My eyes flit between the maps and the mudbanks, trying to figure out where I am on the Mackenzie River. Maps are deceiving here in these shifting channels. The delta is 45 miles wide and a sweltering 75 degrees—too hot for 150 miles north of the Arctic Circle.

It is mid-July 1997. I am not exactly lost because I know that I'm three days below the village of Aklavik ("place of the grizzly"). I'm alone and trying not to be scared. Fortunately there are other distractions to keep me occupied.

If I step out of my kayak without probing the bank with a paddle, like testing the texture of a baking cake with a knife, I will plunge deep into dry-looking ground. Still, I can't help myself when I spy another potential bird's nest: wispy strands of grass lying in a depression on sage-colored tundra several yards above the river.

I paddle along the shore and feign indifference to being absorbed by the brown cloud of mosquitoes waiting in the riverbank lee. I plant my paddle behind to span the cockpit and then pry myself up and out. As soon as I step out in my rubber boots, I sink up to my thighs in mud while a blinding mass of thirsty insects brandish their probiscises.

I lever up and out of the black silt by pushing down, handstand style, on a driftwood trunk. While perched like a frog on a log, contemplating the leap to dry ground, I unwittingly open my mouth and inhale a crunchy mouthful of mosquitoes that will keep me blowing my nose all night. While trying to clear my throat, waving away the cloud to see, I discover that the nest is merely a caribou print, squashed grass.

During my first outings twenty-five years ago, I started using insect repellents containing the virulent and unpronounceable chemical combination called DEET. Now I've given it up, thinking it might be responsible for my receding hairline; wearing a head net makes me claustrophobic.

Local Inuit also scorn head nets. Aside from hindering one's vision, Inuit think that trapping anything but fish inside a net is the mark of a fey *Kabloona*. Still, no race is immune to aggressive swarms of mosquitoes that shoot up your face at each step on the tundra, like bits of ax-splintered wood. One story of an unattended baby "eaten by the mozzies"—the autopsy determined the baby had been "exsanguinated"—cannot be dis-

The broad Mackenzie River delta, from Inuvik toward Aklavik

missed as fable. A scientist here recently removed all of his clothes to show that "the mozzies" are as bad as Canadians say. An assistant stood by counting with the aid of a video camera. The scientist took nine thousand bites each minute, showing that a grown man's blood could be removed in less than two hours. This northern species is prolific because of their ability to reproduce without drawing blood and unlimited egg-laying groundwater.

I am no stranger to bugs. Alaska, whose state bird is the mosquito, used to be my home. Now I live in Colorado, where it's too dry for such aggressive clouds of insects. Accepting such things as bug bites seems a fair trade for my favorite pastime, exploring stretches of remote wilderness.

Although I've planned this trip for too long to remember, I'm not sure how to handle being alone, totally alone without another human soul for many miles. During the weeklong drive north I wanted to turn around every day. Now that the trip has really started I can hardly paddle back against the current. To add to my misgivings, yesterday I sawed the cast splinting a torn thumb ligament off my right hand because it interfered with my paddle strokes. Now I am tremble-fingered about how quiet and huge my undertaking is. It seems that the path of least resistance is to try to become a conduit for all that I will experience in this trackless wilderness.

Downriver, a bevy of least sandpipers appears. The light is brilliant yet soft enough that I don't need to pull on my sunglasses. As the kayak skims soundlessly, the sandpipers alight like flies, barely rippling the water's surface tension. Their buff primaries are lit cleaner than in Audubon's perfect lilting brushstrokes. Their eyes are black orbs. I blink and hold my eyes shut to dispel the illusion that the sandpipers are on fire. When I open up, they are still burning, twittering and bobbing in the warming light. They cavort just in front of my bow. They move their heads together, collectively, like soldiers marching in parade review. But *Calidris minutilla* will not fly off as the current pulls me past close enough to touch them. It's still too early for them to migrate. As the birds twitter in primeval and measured joy under the spongy light, I honor the moment by holding still, keeping my hands belowdeck and whispering, "Hello, everyone."

I'm crazy, I know.

On this, my third day into solitude, approaching the ocean, I am learning to shut down all the emotional noise in my head and exist quietly and without complaint. After all, I can't lose my center. So, lacking birds to watch, I turn to anxiety-reducing tasks. Pitching the tent. Cleaning the stove. Immersing myself in a novel. Then, when all else fails, I lie down and breathe deeply until sleep carries me away from the stress of absolute silence.

Hours later, my dream of a Great White Bear is interrupted by a barren ground grizzly tripping over a tent line and snorting with surprise. Before I can zip down the tent door, I hear his bowels erupt wet berries. His claws throw gravel as he sprints away. Looking out, I can still smell his sour, fishy breath.

The tundra sweeps south in an infinity of green swells, not dissimilar to the blackened ocean to the north. In an early-morning mirage, distant pack ice is undulating like an accordion (Inuit call such visual phenomena *puikartuq* ["rising up for air"]). I catch myself holding my breath as the sun's thick saffron glow brings to life otherwise inanimate objects: oblong stones, bleached driftwood and the distant British Mountains. The landscape is as untouched by civilization as several millennia ago, when the first Paleo-Eskimos wandered past with their stomachs clutched by hunger.

I am now north of the trees, just south of an immense ice pack that slides across the sea like grease in a hot pan. If one were to spend enough time alone here, one's thoughts could similarly slide off into the mysterious waters of Inuit myth. Linear thinking holds little coin to those who linked their souls with animals and never had their own written language. Many Inuit still do not understand banks, credit cards, or forty-hour workweeks; I often feel the same way.

This is all too much to grasp while half asleep at three in the morning. So I stand up and bow to the bear's hindquarters disappearing into the vastness. I don't normally bow. I am emulating the author Barry Lopez, who used this technique to show his respect, and to cope with all that is infinite and enigmatic. The bear, and the landscape, demand no less from me.

Inuit back in the village of Aklavik had scolded me for not carrying a gun or a radio. When I showed them my bear deterrents—air horn, flares and pepper spray—they laughed long and hard. Like many adventurers, I am indebted to Inuit for the kayak, the feathered and double-bladed paddle, the dry top and the *iglu,* to name only a few of their innovations. So I listened, even though I believed they had lost their shamans and their nomadic lifestyle.

They told me that bears might not respect an unarmed *Kabloona,* that grizzlies were more dangerous than polar bears and that dreams about polar bears were really dreams about sex. One *Inuk* described three knocks out on the door of his hunting shack along the ocean. He found a polar bear, eight feet tall, "asking" for food. He handed her a frozen fish.

I lie back in the tiny tent and try to sleep, my mind spinning. I would like to look into a wild polar bear's eyes, without holding a rifle. But what would I have done if this morning's visitor had been a polar bear, whose huge footprints litter the beaches? On the basis of no personal experience and few statistics, I am trying to believe that polar bears won't harm me.

In Canada during the last two decades only a half dozen people had been killed by polar bears, while people "in defense of life and property" had destroyed 251. In Alaska, from 1900 to 1985, bears (mostly grizzlies) killed only twenty humans. Although a polar bear caused one injury in that time period, they caused no fatalities.

The Russian biologist Dr. Nikita Ovsyanikov lived alone in the high Arctic and used only a driftwood stick to rap several bears on the nose during hundreds of polar bear encounters. This is the sort of polar bear story that Inuit tell.

Inuit carvings feature *Nanuq*—the Great White Bear—as an animal above all beings. Two-thousand-year-old ivory carvings (as well as modern soapstone pieces) feature the polar bear flying through the air as if it had supernatural powers. Often small, but incredibly detailed, the carvings are engraved with lifelines and anatomically precise skeletons. You can hold one of these tiny bear amulets in your hand and sense the supernatural power behind it, the carvings as robust as fifteen-thousand-year-old European works.

In Aklavik, an *Inuk* described to me how a lone bear boxed a twelve-foot-long beluga over the head, hooked its paws into the blubber and dragged the half-ton whale up out of the water onto an ice floe. Another day he had seen it on the sea ice kicking a child's rubber ball back and forth.

From the *Kabloona* perspective, the polar bear sits on top of the animal kingdom. *Ursus maritimus* fears nothing and is adept on both land and water. Pilots have reported bears swimming more than 100 miles from the nearest land or ice. They dog-paddle on top of the water at several miles an hour and cavort underwater like seals. They can sprint at 30 miles per hour, and mature boars stand over 10 feet tall. Mothers will fight to the death to save their cubs, and "sportsmen" shooting the bears with high-powered rifles have reported eerie screams that these hunters, when pressed, will concede sound like those of terrified women.

In 1988, in the Alaskan village of Kaktovik, I had seen a skinned polar bear. It had been prepared for a *Kabloona,* decapitated and emasculated, nailed by its forearms to a high meat rack. Soot-colored clouds rushed above the two-by-fours bracing this crucifixion against the sky. Years later I still feel embarrassed for having looked at it, like a voyeur interrupted, and not just because the body seemed obscenely naked and vulnerable. The white fat belly, distinctive rear end, red-muscled biceps and bulging quadriceps looked remarkably human.

The only intact wild polar bear I have seen was in the living room of an acquaintance in Alaska. The eleven-foot mounting typifies the disrespect (and perhaps fear) with which we commonly regard the animal. Its mouth leers unnaturally, displaying two-and-a-half-inch canines. The hunter has the sort of close-set eyes and aquiline nose you might expect in a cartoon caricature of such predators, and if you spend enough time in the North, it is surprising how many *Kabloona* you will meet who are like him. Along with polar bears, this particular hunter finds sport in shooting wolves from his airplane. He told me that he had no choice but to shoot *his* bear (while braced on his Super Cub wing strut) before being ripped from limb to limb. No matter how many times I heard or studied these bear stories, they always seemed false. *Kabloona* myths surrounding the bear just didn't make sense. It was no better than trying to understand the animal by watching the overweight and diseased polar bears in most zoos.

In a balmy dawn I pull down the tent and try to find inspiration to continue. I reassure myself with the knowledge, from previous expeditions, that I still have not tapped my limits. I can go for a week without food and perform lucid, route-finding decisions. I have learned how to avoid frostbite and hypothermia. I have also figured out one essential, if forgotten, truth: As a species we are still able to draw on remnant instincts to avoid natural dangers. I finish packing the kayak and jump in, batting at the growing crowd of mosquitoes.

On the cusp of a new century ruled by machines and technology, I want to do something unequivocal, by myself, something that will leave me satisfied into old age. I want to perform a journey utilizing instinct and soul, combining my love of sub-zero mountaineering, backcountry skiing, sea kayaking, dogsledding and ocean sailing. A week ago, just in case I was making a mistake, I handwrote a will that included instructions for wildlife officers not to destroy the bear that killed me—if this is how I meet my fate.

In a half-serious way I think of the polar bear as the animal that I seek in my modern-day vision quest. It seems that if I keep this inquisitorial dream going—like my fantasy of seeing an Eskimo curlew (an endangered shorebird, with a long downcurved bill and cinnamon wing linings, last seen on this delta in the 1980s)—then my hoped-for crossing of the Northwest Passage will mean far more than covering two thousand miles.

Out in the shallow delta I turn west toward the distant Prudhoe Bay. If I can handle the solitude and obstacles of this summer's shakedown cruise, next year I'll come back to the Mackenzie and spend the next two springs and summers traveling east.

The river's flood is so extensive here in the ocean that I can pot a breaking wave and still drink fresh water from Canada's interior. With no warning at all, a mile from shore, I ground out in two inches of water. I check my map location: Shoalwater Bay. Then I lever myself out and begin dragging the kayak through the mud. Anyone watching from the distant shore will think, initially anyway, that I'm walking on water.

Being alone, harried by mosquitoes and then flushed into the Beaufort Sea by this country's mightiest northern river give me pause, particularly after telling friends that I am attempting this long solo voyage to see a polar bear and watch birds. On a grant application, I suggested that identifying *with* (rather than simply *identifying*) birds might lend a new viewpoint on adventuring. My application was rejected. It's never easy finding sponsors.

Being called a birder is reductive. I have been admiring birds for decades, perusing bird books and taking photographs, even writing a column for *Wild Bird* magazine. It's not unusual to find species hundreds of miles from their supposed range. If nothing else, watching birds makes the monotonous kayak paddling go by quicker and steals away loneliness by providing me with a sense of familiarity. Birds I have seen before feel like old friends; previously unseen species become new friends. There are other minutiae too: the whisper of wings against air, the countless colorful markings and the delightful quirks of movement and mannerism. Best of all, during moments of doubt, the sight of a small bird defying gravity has always inspired me. I can't find anything in our ornithological literature that allows me to put this into words because it's something I feel inside that soars beyond the mere pleasure of identification and is subverted by envy yet comes close to empathy. For as long as I can remember, like the myths of Inuit shamans and polar bears in flight, my dreams have always been filled with flying.

Lost in these thoughts, I suddenly plunge in over my waist. I push the kayak back, dump the water out of my boots and then sit down. From the edge of Shoalwater Bay, dropping off into the depths, the Beaufort Sea looks like any other southern ocean—until you dunk a hand in and watch the white ice pack riming the northern horizon and realize that a minute more would freeze your fingers solid. The pushy wind might die at any moment, then whistle alive again from the opposite direction. There are jellyfish trailing mauve tentacles as long as my kayak, a beached beluga whale carcass feeding a golden eagle and uncountable jittery ducks.

With a soaking wet rear end, I wonder how to define the Northwest Passage. Although five different water routes pass through Canada's northern islands, most are locked in sea ice year-round. I have chosen the most southern and ice-free passage, hugging the warm and silted roof of North America. As I begin paddling out into the ocean, I decide to impose only two conditions for continuing each day: I have to be able to handle being alone psychologically, and I have to be safe.

History of the Passage

The Englishman Martin Frobisher, seeking gold as well as a shortcut to the Pacific, first attempted the Northwest Passage. Despite three attempts between 1576 and 1578, sea ice thwarted him. In 1610 Henry Hudson beat past the ice by crossing into the huge bay now carrying his name, only to die in a mutiny. The search for and crossing of this elusive transcontinental channel became a grail—at least for Europeans.

Inuit and their Paleo-Eskimo predecessors (Thule, Dorset and Pre-Dorset cultures) had already made this migration—from Siberia to Greenland—as early as 2700 B.C. But like most Native American history, the crossing of the passage is generally first credited to European explorers.

In 1789 the Scotsman Alexander Mackenzie couldn't find it and ended his trip here on the delta named after him. Three years later Captain George Vancouver sailed up North America's Pacific coastline, under Royal Navy orders to prove that the Northwest Passage was a fable. He could not.

Thomas Jefferson's first goal in his orders to Meriwether Lewis and William Clark was to find the Northwest Passage. They found the Pacific in 1805 by crossing mountain passes and floating significant rivers. But during the president's first public announcement about the expedition to Congress, he half apologized that Lewis and Clark did not find a water route across and "had all the success which could have been expected."

Jefferson's regret was that they had not discovered the Northwest Passage. It was decided that a waterway between the two great oceans did not exist below the Arctic.

After defeating France in the Napoleonic Wars, Britain ruled the seven seas—with the notable exception of the Arctic Ocean. Although it was by then known that the icy Northwest Passage was an impractical trade route, completing the fabled route promised great prestige and promotion to peacetime officers languishing on half pay. By the mid-nineteenth century steam engines had been fitted into two of the Royal Navy's stoutest bomb ships. Sir John Franklin took command and sailed *Erebus* and *Terror* into the passage with all the pomp and glory of a military battle. Within two years Franklin and his 128 men had disappeared.

When Franklin was lost, the Northwest Passage gained a macabre allure. Finding Royal Navy corpses and ships' papers was more the goal than sailing through to Alaska. Although Inuit were found wearing brass buttons and carrying Franklin's silverware, to date fewer than seventy British corpses have been uncovered—perhaps starved to death or accidentally poisoned by botulism and lead solder from their food cans. Their deaths remain the greatest mystery of the Arctic.

The Norwegian Roald Amundsen finally completed the Northwest Passage in 1906. It wasn't crossed again for forty years. While climbing the highest peaks and reaching the poles has consumed thousands of adventurers, fewer than twenty people have completed the passage without using engines.

Crossing the Northwest Passage will never become the grail that it was in Elizabethan times. Most modern adventurers can't afford to spend the time waiting for unpredictable sea ice to go out, dealing with bears or sprinting through short summers. Now expeditions mostly go searching for new clues to Franklin. Although I lack side sonar for finding his ships or metal detectors for scanning the ground, I have plenty of time on my hands. Traveling slowly in a kayak might allow me to discover graves or relics that icebreakers would pass by.

Many kayakers have attempted the journey. One Canadian, Victoria Jason (who advised me selflessly), linked together most of the passage over four summers. Martin Leonard of Alaska raced across the roof of North America in a record-breaking two summers, teaming up with Victoria for one difficult stretch. Most impressive of all was the Spanish team, spearheaded by Ramón Hernando de Larramendi. The men, in their early twenties, spent three years crossing from southern Greenland to Alaska. They covered 8,400 miles by dogsled and kayak.

Another two men quit after being attacked by a bear. One couple, depressed by the knowledge that the trip would take years, gave up after several hundred miles of rowing through ice. A devout solo kayaker, Bill Delayney, began paddling from Prudhoe Bay to Boston to promote both God and his homemade kayaks. He was rescued by helicopter on his second day out after trying to sneak around the five-mile-wide ice pack only to be swept out to sea when the wind changed.

Several dozen adventurers have made it by sail, powerboat or dogsled. One septuagenarian has even walked alone, two thousand miles, across the frozen sea ice.

Most instructive is the crossing of Don Starkell, already famous for kayaking south to the Amazon. As he wrote in his journal, he, like many others, believed that his willpower would allow him to "conquer nature." The middle-aged Starkell set out with minimal winter camping skills, carrying gear more suited for a temperate climate.

Experience proved a great teacher throughout his first two summers as he paddled up Hudson Bay, accompanied by Victoria Jason. In 1992, trying to finish at the Mackenzie River, Starkell left Victoria, ignored Inuit advice and braved an early winter. He broke his foot while climbing a cliff. He also made several risky crossings in big seas, oblivious of calm-water portages that would have saved him more than two hundred miles of paddling. By the time he was frozen into the sea ice in mid-September—within two dozen miles of his final destination—he was finished. Only the chance passing of an airplane saved his life. Most of his frozen fingers and toes were amputated.

I studied Starkell's book *Paddle to the Arctic.* Then I telephoned him to double-check my assumptions. He yelled, over the blare of a game he was watching on television, that I sounded too young for the Northwest Passage. I told him I was forty. I asked him if he had any insight about polar bears. He said, "Take a big rifle."

His whole tone gave him away. The message I got was that this trip would kill you if you didn't take your time and listen to Inuit. There's no margin for error as a soloist. If I could hold true to my own adventuring philosophy, I wouldn't feel right about accepting a 360-mile ride on a snowmobile (as Starkell did from Hudson Bay to Taloyoak). Also, getting injured and needing a rescue would equal failure to me.

Ice bobbing in the surf near Shingle Point

I've marked a 2,500-mile line from Prudhoe Bay, Alaska, to Hudson Bay, Northwest Territories, essentially connecting Pacific and Atlantic waters. If I took a similar amount of time and energy and applied myself to more popular goals, I could try climbing several Himalayan peaks or attempt skiing to the poles. Instead I have come here to be alone and to follow the more obscure tracks of history while admiring birds and looking for a polar bear. For the trip to be a success, of course, I cannot progress aided by engines. Muscle power is how the Inuit once migrated across this coastline. I might learn something by following their lead.

For the last two hours the wind has been filling my right ear and lifting the shoreline water into long rows of clapping foam mixed with ice. I avoid the noisy surf and confusion by paddling farther and farther out in less roiled water. A mile north of the mudbanked shore, the water is merely big black rolls of energy, lifting the Klepper up and letting me utilize the latent physics of waves by accelerating into the black troughs until I am floppily raised and softly slingshotted sideways by the next swell. Periodically beluga whales break the black swells with their otherworldly white backs and disconsolate, gasping breaths. I am two days west of the Mackenzie Delta. My bow is aimed toward the tip of Shingle Point's two-mile-long sand peninsula, dotted with indiscernible white bugs. Will I be welcome there?

Inuvialuit of Shingle Point

As I get closer to Shingle Point, the white dots morph into the tents and shacks of an Inuit camp. At first I hold my eyes there, like watching a seal, so I don't lose it all.

I have not seen or spoken to a soul for several days, and the idea of my paddling into an Inuit whaling camp is unsettling. Greenpeace environmental activists, whom most Inuit say that they would shoot on sight, are rumored to be protesting animal cruelty up here this summer. Other *Kabloona* also warned me that the area was off limits to our kind during whaling season. I will find out soon enough if this is true. For now I keep the Klepper aimed toward the distant spit, curving east out of the south-trending surf as the only dry exit from a growing sea of whitecaps.

Distant banks of snow beneath the mudbanks fume with mist, while the land rises south into a dusty chain of hills. The mud bluffs are dotted with tawny caribou backs, bowed over and worrying the green spongy tundra, gathering their energy before fleeing south. A ringed seal raises its smooth head and looks into my own eyes with anxious soulfulness. Then the specter of a giant floatplane trailing a plume of exhaust flies up off the sea and transforms into a flock of several hundred black guillemots, fading into the vastness as spewing smoke. Red-necked phalaropes are twittering along the lee shore, plucking and probing krill from the water with their long bills in a flurry of movement, like mosquitoes working tent walls. Seeing birds against such a huge landscape allays my fears and leaves me in appreciative rapture more quickly than anything I know.

How often have we seen books or films describing such exquisite environs with the cliché "Words don't do this place justice"? Such thoughts are not necessarily inarticulate excuses, I realize, while trying to orient things from my kayak: mosquito-birds, a distant mirage of icebergs transformed into minarets *and* dwarflike people appearing on the sandy spit ahead.

As I brace for a landing among a people of different gene pools from my own, a race that once crossed from Siberia, it is helpful to remember that they might think me rude if I ask too many questions. Or so I've heard.

Suddenly the line of dwarfs running toward me aligns into children when a man twice their size emerges from a shack and yells, "Welcome to Shingle Point!"

Darcy Gordon pulls the bow of my Klepper up onto the sand and announces, "My son supposed you were a Russian spy kayaking in from the North Pole."

His diction is perfect, I think, not at all what people had led me to believe.

Darcy is tall, with his black hair neatly parted. His movements show a natural athletic grace. He could easily be mistaken for a brown-eyed, broad-cheeked Tibetan. Like most Inuit men, he has learned to shake hands, but he does not attempt to grip my hand tightly as is customary down south. He and The People encamped here refer to themselves as Inuvialuit ("the great human beings par excellence"), from the Mackenzie River region of the greater Inuit nation, stretching from Siberia to Greenland.

Darcy has been to Washington, D.C., to lobby against proposed oil drilling in Alaska's Arctic National Wildlife Refuge. Every year the herd of 180,000 Porcupine caribou runs up from the southern tree line to the coast and then across the Alaskan border. He says, "The caribou are our lives, and our people know that oil wells will change their migration patterns and leave us eating frozen hamburger."

Along with being surprised to meet someone as articulate as Darcy living in the middle of this wilderness, I am bewildered by the surrounding landscape. I squint to try to view it all in perspective. At an undetermined distance along the west shore of the peninsula there is either a herd of muskoxen or a row of the ubiquitous fifty-five-gallon fuel drums. At a similar distance to the south what appears to be a grizzly or maybe a ground squirrel stands up on a bluff. Without a pair of binoculars in constant reach, Arctic distances and the flux of mirage air can make "tree squeezers" (in Inuit parlance) like me disoriented.

Darcy's family has long since adapted to the vastness of their backyard. When they travel south to visit family—in Whitehorse, the Yellowknife penitentiary or the Edmonton hospital—it is not unusual to see them glued to the airplane windows while passing the first forests, a hundred miles away from their Banks Island home. They gape at birch and spruce and fir that they only see normally as stripped pieces of driftwood carried north by the Mackenzie.

Living in a wilderness without trees or tall buildings alters the way we see the world, the way we talk and the way we perceive passing time. When tundra dwellers alight in a city, claustrophobia sets in. Clocks and whistles and car horns tell them to hurry. Darcy's grandmother referred to this as "trees stealing your spirit." Whatever the case, modern Inuit don't prolong southern visits if they can help it. When they return to the Arctic clutching new boom boxes, essential snowmobile parts or greasy McDonald's bags, they are as disoriented with the land and seascape as a mountaineer returning to ten thousand feet. With no trees or man-made architecture as a field of reference, with the clarity of unpolluted air and with the mirage bending of light waves that appear to lift objects below the horizon up into view, it takes days to readapt.

To account for the confusing vastness of space surrounding my kayak on Shingle Point, Inuktitut language is built around the Arctic field of view. If I could speak Inuktitut, I could precisely locate the mysterious-looking grizzly or muskox by choosing a single word that means "those there, these here, close to you and visible, above your eye level and not visible, below your eye level and not visible, or above your eye level and visible." Most western Arctic Inuit younger than fifty have been forced to substitute a comparatively imprecise English, loaded with "um" and proper nouns, for more than ten thousand Inuktitut root words and several hundred suffixes. These roots and suffixes can be made into an endless number of meanings that change inflection or elongate wordplay. One former trader and linguist frequently asked Inuit what they would do with money from fox skins. They answered, "*Atukkiqpallaaqtaillitiginiaqara,*" meaning "I'll use it to prevent getting into too much debt."

Watch an English-speaking person speak, gesturing with his hands and varying his facial expression to make his meaning clear. Then watch an *Inuk* speak; the precision of Inuktitut allows him to keep his hands in his pockets and his face still. Even when Darcy speaks English, he carefully chooses words that allow him to stay poker-faced, without pointing. While English is built around our concept of time, Inuktitut is built upon the complexities of space. Consequently, it cannot be fully learned in a classroom or inside a village because these formerly nomadic people wrapped their language around land and sea and wildlife, all blanketed beneath the soft vastness of Arctic space.

Instead of embarrassing myself by asking Darcy the obvious, I pull out the binoculars and scan the mud bluffs. I see a ground squirrel, not a grizzly. Then I peer across to the western shore and view fifty-five-gallon drums, not muskoxen. I leave the wavering minarets be.

Rather than scold the half dozen children who are crawling all over me, asking questions and exclaiming, "Holy boy!" Darcy uses a kind voice— "Oh, look at that sea-stained cigarette butt!"—to redirect their energy toward picking up the litter on the beach: soda cans, oil cans and browned tissue. They comply quickly, throwing the litter into a trash bag that Darcy carries.

The children are fascinated with the Klepper, so I give them some paddling tips. To judge by the slicing precision of their strokes, learning to paddle is easier for them than it was for me. For the next few hours, while their parents laugh, they all take turns paddling the kayak far enough out among the wind and whitecaps to make me nervous about their safety.

I watch, stupefied, as children too young to paddle—or run—are dumped into the cockpit by their brothers. The older boys then line the youngsters along the shore by whipping the kayak lines back and forth, as the youngsters beam from their new vantage points like miniature Buddhas upon watery thrones.

I am escorted into a ten-by-fifteen-foot plywood shack, heated by a fifty-five-gallon drum blazing with Mackenzie River driftwood. I strip off my jacket, then my outer shirt. Darcy introduces me to his wife, Lucinda, and father and baby. They all wear sweaters, as if they were storing up the heat, camel style, to make it through the next long crossing of winter. Ninety years ago the anthropologist Vilhjalmur Stefansson recorded indoor temperatures of the Eskimo houses around here as hot as 90 degrees Fahrenheit.

The children are not reprimanded as they sprint in and out of the shack and leave the door open to an Arctic wind. Darcy gently reminds them to don my PFD vest before getting into the kayak. They regularly come running in and interrupt the adults' conversation, spilling sugar into their mouths and onto the table. To my horror, I look out the window and see the youngest children stripping off their clothes and jumping into the icy bay to wade after one of the fastest paddlers. The adults shrug when I point this out through the window.

One eight-year-old pokes me in the stomach, knocking tea onto my chest. The adults laugh. The boy asks, "What is a kayak?"

"A boat your ancestors invented hundreds of years ago," I reply.

He seems shocked by this information.

"Are you carrying a gun?" the boy asks.

As I shake my head no, I see the elderly Peter sit up in the corner, eyes suddenly opened wide.

Children in 40-degree Beaufort Sea, Shingle Point

"No gun," Peter says, as a statement rather than a question, so I show him the bear rounds and a spring-loaded flare device that I wear around my neck to scare bears away.

He is not amused. "No gun," he says again.

I explain that I also have a can of bear Mace and an air horn in the kayak. I try to change the subject to whales. Peter speaks up as though he has awoken from a long sleep. "Polar bears will eat you alive up here."

He talks slowly, and like most elders who still speak Inuktitut, he chooses his English words carefully.

"I have watched *Nanuq* eat my dogs. I have had *Nanuq* sneak up on me. A man without a rifle in this country is as good as dead."

Everyone's eyes are on me now. Peter is so concerned by my incautious behavior that he breaks Inuit etiquette and asks a question, carefully assuming no stupidity on my part. "Have you ever seen a polar bear?"

I shake my head no, and he replies, "I bet they been seeing you plenty," which brings a round of laughter from everyone, including me.

Peter continues, "The problem is that people don't listen to their elders anymore."

Lucinda pulls off her nursing baby and lowers her sweater. The baby lies back on the large foam pad bed shared by him and the Gordons and several nephews. Then he begins waving his arms in paddling motions, as if he too wanted to take the Klepper to sea.

Lucinda pours me another cup of tea. She has waist-long raven-colored hair, is slender and moves like nobility with her head held high and her fingers spread wide. She could join in this conversation without interrupting the men if she weren't as shy about talking to a *Kabloona* as most Inuit women. The light in her eyes says that she has been listening carefully and has a lot on her mind. Instead she passes me the plate of fried bannock. I smear it with her homemade blueberry jam. To avoid offending her with a direct question, I ask the room if there is work for women on Banks Island. Darcy replies that Lucinda is the breadwinner and has been employed for years as a warden for Parks Canada. Inuit men often prefer to go hunting. Although Inuit women are still traditionally relegated to domestic roles, they are also more inclined to show up for work on time and keep their jobs.

Before I can take a second bite of bannock, Peter asks, "You carry a radio?"

I shake my head no. Most of the several dozen plywood shacks and canvas tents on this peninsula house battery-powered high-frequency Spilsbury-Tyndall sets. Trappers' radios are a lifeline for Inuit. Over distances as far as several hundred miles they negotiate business, carry out rescues, share the whereabouts of whales or caribou or geese, then, most important, fling gossip—in Inuktitut, in case bushy eyebrows are listening. This time, however, since Peter is from a preradio era, he approves of my minimalist style of adventuring, and says, "The only difference between me and a white man I've met anywhere else is that they have to carry radios everywhere they go."

"I want to be as far away from the rest of the world as possible," I tell him. Peter replies, "You have come to the right place then."

He is seventy-five years old and has seen changes in the Arctic that he cannot abide. Peter grew up in a shack next to a Hudson's Bay Company trading post in another abandoned Inuit settlement like dozens more across the Arctic coast. It's marked "Gordon" on my map, so named after a white trader who married Peter's grandmother. The last of its driftwood shacks and sod houses fell into the sea several years ago. Peter fished through holes in the ice and drove dog teams and used slitted bone goggles in the bright light of reflected sea ice so that he would not go snow-blind. Peter's grandfather taught him how to shoot a rifle. He learned that men no longer had to use spears to kill *Nanuq,* which roamed Demarcation Bay and stole the whales or seals that his family ate. The rifle, then later the outboard engine and the snowmobile, like his grandfather's amulets, kayaks, bone spears and bows and arrows, were Peter's survival tools.

As early as 1957 anthropologists like Margaret Lantis began speaking with compassion and trying to explain The People's evolution: "Eskimos are trying just as hard today to adapt as they did 500 or 900 years ago; the difficulty is that they are adapting not to the Arctic but to the Temperate Zone way of living."

While their culture is undergoing radical changes, the environment is also changing. According to an automated government weather station nearby, Shingle Point's summer temperatures have risen by two degrees Celsius since 1957—probably because of the disappearing Arctic ozone layer. In those years scientists have shown that the Arctic ice has thinned by an average of 40 percent; since 1978 the sea ice has shrunken about 3 percent a decade. Many scientists say that within fifteen years the ice-choked Northwest Passage will be navigable by regular ships all summer (rather than icebreakers). The ramifications for commercial transit—and a change in Inuit lifestyles—are huge: European ships bound for Asia must sail 12,600 miles via the Panama Canal, but through the Northwest Passage it's only 7,900 miles.

Peter doesn't need scientists to tell him that the North is warming up. He talks about his island many miles north of the mosquito-infested mainland. "On Banks in 1967 there no mosquitoes then. Now there plenty. There used to be sled dog races on first of July. Now we have no snow left on first of July."

Peter may have watched television programs about global warming and pollution, but he makes no assumptions and speaks only of his own experiences. "We used to dip our frozen whale meat into seal oil, but now we no longer do this because blubber in seals and whales is polluted. I don't know why polluted, but our people no longer eat the seal and whale oil. I do."

Peter is referring to industrial chemicals—hexachlorobenzene and polychlorinated biphenyls (PCBs)—that have wafted north and precipitated into the cold Arctic, absorbed into the blubber of sea mammals and Inuit mothers' milk. In the 1980s researchers discovered that Inuit have ten times the levels of these chemicals in their bodies than southern Canadians. Consequently, Inuit children often suffer from ear infections and possibly serious immune system deficiencies and neurological disorders.

In Peter's first tongue, *niri* is a root word that is used for both food and eating. *Nirimarik* means the real food or meat from wild animals. So his dismay is mostly about substituting processed foods for *nirimarik*. One hundred years ago his people found a whaling ship aground west of here, and rather than eat the flour, they dumped it all so that they could use the cotton sacks for fish and whale blubber.

Recently tourists aboard a motorboat were allowed to visit Shingle Point for an afternoon. They were invited into one of the family's hunting shacks for a meal. One of these visitors asked why Inuit were not eating vegetables or potatoes for dinner. Peter believes that *Kabloona* think of him as some sort of unhealthy caveman because he doesn't like the same food that the rest of the world eats. Studies have shown, however, that raw or lightly cooked meat provides all the necessary vitamin C for good health (which eluded Franklin's men and many of the early *Kabloona* whalers dying from scurvy). Since Peter has eaten *nirimarik* all his life, he has also avoided diabetes and heart disease.

The children outside on the spit have now exhausted the novelty of the kayak. No one seems particularly cold, even after plunging into ice water under a wintry wind. I help the Gordons pull up their fishnet, filled with two dozen herring, cisco and char. Darcy grabs the biggest, writhing Arctic char, knifes open its belly and plops a row of orange eggs into his mouth. Although I would not argue that the char's cooked flesh is tastier than any salmon I have caught, I pass up Darcy's offer to sample some eggs. He again anticipates my thoughts and heads off my amazement at his gulping raw fish parts by smiling, wiping his mouth clean and gently reminding me that he is a man of sophisticated tastes: "Caviar is free here."

We carry the fish back to the shack. Darcy mentions that no one has gotten a whale for nearly a week and that many of the children would rather be at home watching television. He also says, shaking his head with regret, that the two beached whale carcasses I saw a few miles back were probably belugas that sank because they had been rifle shot before being harpooned with a line.

I hand the Gordons several pounds of cheese. Peter chucks me an orange piece of oily-smelling whale blubber wrapped in cellophane. Then two of the children pass me a present that leaves me speechless. The five-inch carving has a detailed cockpit and an upswept bow, and it must have taken unusual discipline, or an instinctive sense for the way space fits around shapes, for a ten-year-old with a driftwood stick and a penknife. It is a replica of my boat that they have just learned to paddle. Actually, it is a replica of their boat, the kayak.

Kilalurak, the White Whale

Ulus

That afternoon every radio operator and listener on Shingle Point with his or her "ears on" hears that somebody got a whale. People gather on the beach awaiting the boat. The gaiety is infectious.

After introductions, my presence seems to be tolerated, probably because I came alone in a kayak, a mythical, albeit forgotten, tool. One surly woman won't look at me until I say, "I'm not with Greenpeace, and I'm not a tree squeezer," which transforms the shucked-walnut lines of her face into a smile of such bright fullness that I have to laugh with her. Laughter is suddenly contagious. Even the silliest puns bring a round of hearty backslapping.

The hunt is obviously important to these people. It replaces ego, identity and power, values that many white hunters feel about hunting. The mood here also lacks the usual remorse that *Kabloona* hunters have expressed to me about killing a beautiful animal. Rather, The People are celebrating the dead whale.

It is difficult to relate to the joy, so I struggle for objectivity. For the last two days I have heard the white whales breathing and chirping alongside me. They are gentle and curious beings, stretching no longer than my Klepper. They communicate with echolocation squeals, moos and croaks, which bounce back to them underwater to identify fish, motorboat or kayak.

Delphinapterus leucas (meaning "white-shielded dolphin without a dorsal fin") is not a dolphin. To those eighteenth-century men who gave animals Latin names, it was much smaller than other whales and had a dolphin-shaped head. Although these two sea mammals are from the same Cetacea family, the beluga is not a dolphin, because of its size and its cold-water habitat. Russians (and recently, Western scientists) call the whale *belukha* (Белуха) to distinguish it from the sturgeon fish of caviar fame (Белуга). French Quebec colonists mistakenly called it *marsouin*, after the other dorsal-finned cetacean the porpoise. French call the caviar *béluga* and the whale *le bélouga*.

Among all this confusion over the animal identity, only Inuit named it precisely. Their *kilalurak* means simply "white whale."

Kilalurak are known to help one another give birth and are noted for traveling in large and playful schools, called gams. Their five-pound brains are remarkably similar in appearance to ours. Their flippers contain humerus, radius and ulna bones. They are the only whales that can turn their heads. Their thick lips are capable of an array of smiles, frowns, and the mischievous curling grin of a cat hiding a mouse head in its mouth. Their melonlike foreheads can be compressed or expanded to receive underwater sounds. Their ten-pound hearts' large right atriums and extra blood vessels allow them to make mile-deep dives.

Although I have been startled on dozens of occasions when they have unexpectedly surfaced next to me, exhaling fecund blasts of carbon dioxide, and then sucking in lungfuls of air, a beluga has never hurt a human. Aside from lacking killer instincts, the beluga simply doesn't possess the sort of powerful jaws or sharp teeth to do us any harm.

Scientists like E. C. Pielou have observed them rubbing off old skin against sand or gravel beds—"no doubt pleasurably." Their rubbery and snow-white skin, through the tactile wonder of nerve endings and an underlying sonar reception circuitry, is arguably more sensitive than our own. Environmentalists have proposed that the barbed harpoon produces a fiery agony as it is jabbed through drum-tight skin, making the whale dive in an attempt to escape the electricity burning up its back and into the connective tissues of an echolocation system gone awry. Then the barb is pulled back tight and held up against the underside of skin, lodging like an angry fist, compressing and lacerating the blubber. Wounded belugas, like many whales, are often nudged or coddled by family members, confused by the uncharacteristic screaming and writhing. The ensuing rifle shot through the wounded beluga's brainpan is indeed merciful in comparison.

It would also be fair to consider the traditional Inuit viewpoint. The former delta communities of Kittigazuit and Gupuk hunted *kilalurak* here for hundreds of years. Archaeologists have determined that the beluga was the primary food source of Inuit, feeding them throughout the year, despite their skill at harvesting fish, caribou, muskoxen and waterfowl.

Kilalurak hunts were conducted by as many as two hundred kayakers, spaced a hundred feet apart and following a hunt leader. The hunters chanted or slapped the water with their hands and paddles, scaring gams of the kayak-size whales up onto shoals, where they were speared, cut up with their rounded ulu knives, then divided among the village.

Traditional Inuit believe that whales, walruses and seals were cut from the arms of an ancient girl by her father. This girl (who was to become the sea goddess Sedna) repeatedly tried to reboard their boat as her father hacked off more and more of her arms. She finally sank to the bottom of the sea.

Inuit believe that sea mammals, *uumajuit,* have the same souls as human beings. When killed, the beluga's soul departs the body. If the hunter shows disrespect by verbally insulting the animal or wasting any part of the body, the soul will not pass on to its next life and will remain to haunt the hunter. Nor will Sedna send up any more seals or whales to be eaten.

While Inuit believe that they are at the center of the universe and that they may be more clever than the whale, they also believe that the whale's soul is equal to their own. This clashes with modern Christianity, which espouses man's dominion over animals and was introduced to the region by whalers in 1870. Christianity radically changed the spiritual relationships of Inuit and animals.

Shingle Point became awash with death. At first *Kabloona* whalers grew rich from selling the baleen of the larger bowhead whale for corsets and umbrellas. The blubber too was in high demand for lamp oil, so as the huge bowhead was being thinned out of the Beaufort Sea, the whalers turned their harpoon guns toward the numerous belugas for blubber. Inuvialuit who complained about their dwindling food source, or the disrespect shown to the whales, or Inuit women's becoming prostitutes, were bought off with whiskey, which rendered them into apathetic stupors because their bodies lacked the enzyme to digest alcohol. Many picked up pidgin English and shrewdly learned to bargain for furs, meat and women. Unlike southern Native Americans who fought such invasions, Inuit were inherently gentle and indisposed to warfare while looking for food and surviving the harsh climate.

The bowhead and beluga have survived in the western Arctic because of the discovery of fossil fuel and electricity, and because corsets (built out of whale baleen) went out of vogue. In 1906 the value of baleen dropped from five dollars to forty cents a pound. A single bowhead's baleen had once fetched $10,000. In 1906 it dropped to $800. Whaling schooners continued to ply the western Arctic, taking in the odd whale and trading whiskey, firearms, sugar, tea, flour and tobacco in exchange for Inuit-hunted furs.

The 1960s introduced a new environmental consciousness. Before elephants or wolves, endangered whales evoked the compassion of the world. Commercial whaling was banned, and Inuit too stopped hunting. In the eastern Arctic the bowhead whale had been depleted from nearly thirty thousand to less than one thousand, an eighth the size of the Beaufort Sea population.

In the western Arctic the beluga and bowhead populations recovered. The clamor for protecting whales made people mistakenly lump the beluga and the bowhead together, while confusing the eastern Arctic's depletion with the western Arctic abundance. Over the course of several thousand years Paleo-Eskimos and Inuit had never hunted any animal to the brink of extinction. Nonetheless, the public perceives the hunts for these endangered creatures as unnecessarily cruel. So the public has ignored the fate of The People.

In 1996 the government gave the bowhead hunt back to the eastern Inuit. Various journals reported the controversy, often misreporting the number of whales in the Arctic. While environmentalists thoughtfully place whale preservation bumper stickers on their cars, a humanitarian "Save Inuit" slogan or its equivalent is unheard of. Nor would these proud people accept such sympathy, much less admit that their culture has degraded.

In 1991, after seventy years of abstinence, Canadian Inuvialuit were allowed to hunt one bowhead. Their Alaskan Iñupiat neighbors are allowed to take more than forty. Here, on Shingle Point, a thirty-seven-foot whale was landed, then split up among the villages of Aklavik, Sachs Harbor, Inuvik and Tuktoyaktuk. Inuit could finally say that the old way had been restored.

Most American schoolchildren can recite how whales were slaughtered a century ago, but few know about the diseases that whalers left Inuvialuit. They lay in driftwood shacks, skin tents and sod houses, doubled over with measles and tubercular coughing. (Through an extraordinary irony, at least to a birder, the fatal diseases came at the same time that the Eskimo curlew started disappearing, blasted out of the sky by the millions.) Tuberculosis was known at the time as galloping consumption because of the speed in which the infection colonized organs of the human body in seedlike masses. Most of its Inuit victims wheezed and coughed so steadily that they could no longer take a breath in which to eat. Many cracked their ribs, choked on their own blood, lost bowel control and became paralyzed. Others simply starved to death while lying on blood-spattered caribou robes. The RCMP quarantined them. Anglican and Roman Catholic priests performed last rites while berating their shamans. Of the original two thousand Inuvialuit living in Kittigazuit and Gupuk, only thirty survived *Kabloona* measles and galloping consumption.

An Inuvialuit survivor named Nuligak testified about the epidemic:

> During that time two of the Eskimos spent all their time burying the dead. . . . Corpses were set on the ground uncoffined, just as they were. Since I could not count at the time I shall not attempt to give a number; but I know that when The People left . . . they were but a handful compared to the num-

ber they had been. . . . Winter came, and one day we saw a huge pack of wolves out at sea on the ice, heading east. There were so many of them that the last ones were still in front of us when the leaders had disappeared on the eastern horizon. It was said that they had feasted on the bodies left on the Kittigazuit land.

Today most Inuvialuit would no sooner stay in these former villages than they would confront a polar bear with a spear. Many of The People camped here on Shingle Point are from families that migrated in from Alaska during the 1920s, repopulating the diseased landscape and selling furs to white traders.

Inuit villages are now given yearly whale harvest quotas by a Canadian government agency called Renewable Resources. Greenpeace and other environmentalists continue to rattle their sabers. Yet neither the bowhead nor the beluga is endangered in the western Arctic, and their Beaufort Sea populations are estimated at 7,800 and 11,500, respectively.

The beluga now being towed in toward me is in grave trouble in the eastern Arctic. In the St. Lawrence River, beluga blubber absorbs high concentrations of industrial toxins. The beluga carcasses have to be disposed of as "hazardous waste" in isolated dumps. No one can presently say how the mercury and cadmium and organochlorine compounds recently found in belugas in the Beaufort Sea will affect both the animal and Inuvialuit. It goes without saying that Inuit are not responsible for the pollution.

Every June in the Bering Strait the belugas wag their flukes eastward. The Beaufort current pushes Mackenzie River sediment, fish and toxins around Shingle Point, into the Yukon, along the Alaskan coast and into beluga mouths. Each day the food they swallow (more than chew) equals up to 4 percent (or sixty pounds) of their body weight. They stop to scratch themselves and bottom feed from shallow estuaries and sand peninsulas. Inuit everywhere consider the white skin and orange blubber, called muktuk, a delicacy along the lines of foie gras, sushi, caviar and Rocky Mountain oysters.

To my taste buds, muktuk is more like peanuts and overcooked cube steak than crab or fish flesh. The rubbery texture is unlike anything I have ever eaten before, and if you weren't hungry enough, if you merely stopped in to such a whaling camp without any particular caloric need to stay warm while living out-of-doors, your gastrointestinal tract would go into a state of overload. Still, eating muktuk, like throwing oak into the woodstove, has more caloric value than anything I could carry in my kayak. Fifteen minutes (and hours) after eating it, out of sight from any Inuvialuit in case my *Kabloona* stomach might embarrass me, I feel a flush of warmth flooding my face. I have to cool down by unzipping my jacket.

The long-awaited seventeen-foot skiff is roped up to a ghostly-looking blur in its wake. As the hundred-horse Evinrude throttles down, the crowd stands ready. The skiff grinds up onto the beach, and a score of arms soundlessly pull the dead whale toward the water's edge. You can't help but notice what looks like a thick-lipped smile.

A woman finishes sharpening two ulus—picture oversize brass knuckles, with steel blades replacing the brass—and hands one to her cousin. Three men grab the whale's tail fluke, brace their legs and drag it half out of water onto Mackenzie-browned sand. Two women slice off the two front fins with the best muktuk and hand them carefully to two boys. They carry them like holy scrolls up to a driftwood rack above the dogs. The men stand back smoking cigarettes as the two women continue deftly cutting a line around the beluga's neck, several inches deep, then carve back in several straight lines toward the tail.

"Holy cow!" one boy shouts as purple intestines droop onto the sand.

The older woman stops, grabs her cousin's ulu, and grinds the two blades against each other for a minute to bring back an edge. They finish their job by cutting out several dozen two-foot squares of orange muktuk and peeling it back off the black meat with their fingers. The boys make trips back and forth to the racks and drape it until from a distance the gray camp blazes alive in a Halloween orange of beluga blubber.

After two days the chair cushion–size pads of muktuk will be folded into

Using ulu knives to butcher a beluga whale on Shingle Point

several dozen five-gallon buckets. Some will be eaten raw, hacked off with pocketknives, while most of it will be boiled in seawater. Some elders will insist on removing the skin from the blubber, then boiling it down into oil so that they can continue to dip caribou meat in it, regardless of Health Canada's industrial toxin warnings.

The whole job takes a few hours, including scraping out the black and soft meat below the blubber, then scooping out the brains. Children splash bloody water up onto the dark sand, brightening it cerise. An elder named Danny Gordon reaches into what little guts remain, down into the warm innards of the cow, extracts a two-inch-long form, and holds it up for the children. They stop their splashing and stare. It is shorter than my hand, curled pink, with appendages that resemble arms. The children crowd closer. The beach smells of copper.

A seven-year-old missing a couple of teeth sports a wolverine-ruffed parka, unzipped to reveal a Mickey Mouse sweatshirt. He looks up into Danny's toothless face. The boy is trying to figure out whether he should stop being elated. The elder's face is hard to read. So the boy looks at me, and I nod solemnly back at the embryo.

Danny thoughtfully holds the tiny beluga up closer for me to smell. To me, at least, it is odorless. The boy and I can tell that Danny is really not smiling; this is only the illusion created by cheeks being lifted into bare gum lines. "That is enough pictures now," he says, in muffled English, so that we will respect the spirit of the unborn whale he is cradling in his fingers.

I lower the camera and put it away. Earlier one of the elders gave me permission to take photographs. Exposing these people engaged in a sacred ritual or any activity without first seeking their consent would be equal to a crime.

Although the tiny whale is dead, Danny lifts it as gently as he might an eider chick. He trusts me through his own innocence and instincts. He trusts that my camera's images won't appear in *Greenpeace* magazine. As he looks into my eyes, I think I understand what passes between us: the idea that life is never as simple as we want it to be.

The Summer's First Sunset

Later that evening, at the landward end of the spit, I meet a uniformed Renewable Resources *Kabloona,* who lives in a planked (rather than plywood) cabin. It is too windy to paddle on past the peninsula. Even though Inuvialuit here have already explained that strangers are welcome in their camp and that no one would mind my tenting on the spit, the uniformed man feels it his duty to go ask permission.

Some children guide me to a spring on the mainland. To get there, I must climb over an electric fence installed by Renewable Resources to keep out the bears, but the children explain that the fence never holds electricity. By the time I arrive back at my kayak with several gallons of tannin-colored water as cold as permafrost, I am again granted permission to stay. The Renewable Resources man seems unhappy about this decision.

"What is it that your agency does here?" I ask over his four-wheeler's growl.

He yells back, "We make sure that The People don't waste anything," and he roars off toward the seaward end of the two-mile peninsula to examine the whale carcass and Darcy's notes about the whale.

As soon as he disappears, I am invited into another tent, characteristically thick with cigarette smoke, where everyone already knows my name. Since Peter Elanik is not shy about asking me where I'm from and where I'm going, I ask, "What does Renewable Resources do?"

Peter, nearly four hundred pounds and battling heart disease, replies, "The job of Renewable Resources is to count fish. Period."

This brings knowing smiles from his wife, Mary, and another elder. Jacob is not introduced with his last name (Archie) because he was born with only one name.

Peter craves muktuk even though, he explains, the blubber, livers, brains and kidneys of belugas have recently been found to be laden with PCBs, the same talk that is bringing everyone down on Shingle Point. The irony is that the blubber also contains the healthy fatty acid Omega 3, which counteracts heart disease, unlike the polyunsaturated fats contained in the margarine and two different jars of processed cheese on the Elaniks' table.

The introduction of these foods, along with alcohol and tobacco, have wreaked havoc upon Inuit health. With the exception of worn-down teeth (from chewing animal skins), precontact Inuit skulls show no tooth decay.

Now it is not uncommon for Inuit elders like Danny Gordon to wonder how he can afford dentures.

After the whalers arrived with sugar and rifles on Shingle Point in the late 1800s, followed by the movement into settlements, Inuit physiology underwent remarkable changes. Children started growing faster and taller and reached puberty sooner. Antibiotics, vaccinations and flights to southern sanatoriums quelled diseases. By midcentury many Inuit had been weaned off their all-meat diet. They began contracting gallbladder problems, diabetes, emphysema, obesity, and heart disease, all of which were unknown to a culture that previously worried only about starvation and breathing in too much smoke from the seal oil lamps.

By the 1960s, when Peter was a teenager, nutritionists estimated that Inuit like him had increased their sugar consumption from 26 to 104 pounds per year. Because of lowered amounts of protein with these increased sugars, Inuit girls now reach puberty sooner and the traditionally short and stocky boys became taller and thinner. Acned faces suddenly became common. Customary infanticide was prohibited. Along with vaccines and antibiotics, improved medical care saved many children. The introduction of bottled milk allowed women to begin bearing more babies (at the same time, women began suffering from breast cancer—previously unseen—and bottle-fed children were hit by autoimmune diseases). Inuit birthrates jumped 50 percent. It was the greatest population increase of any developing nation in the world. Peter Elanik is part of a population explosion that outstrips the postwar baby boom. It is unusual today to meet an Inuit family, camped on Shingle Point or elsewhere, that doesn't have a dozen or more members.

Peter grabs another biscuit and, in lieu of whale oil, dips it into the jar of liquid orange-colored Kraft cheese. He mentions that people from his village of Aklavik don't like eating processed bread available from the distant town of Inuvik. "But everyone"—he smacks his lips and licks his fingers—"loves homemade bannock."

Peter refers to a recent survey of Aklavik (population ninety). In order of importance, their favorite fifty foods include caribou meat, bannock (fry bread), caribou tongue, Arctic char and muktuk. He talks with gentle, twinkling eyes, wiggling half-inch-thick ears.

"On the bottom of this list of foods are seal, hamburger, chicken, pork chops, canned tuna, hot dogs and white bread—we call it white man's bread."

He lists this last item with a great smile because I have already told him that I like whole wheat bread. Peter is an *Inuk* of unusual curiosity, conversationally skilled and pleasantly humble. When he asks me how to set the barometer (a gift given to him, no doubt, by an *Inuk* who also had no use for it) nailed to his shack wall, I explain that he needs to radio the Inuvik airport to calibrate it.

One of the skills of Inuit like Peter is their ability to perceive life as a circling destination, rather than a linear or time-imposed one. Eighty years ago Stefansson complained about how his Eskimo companions would not row his umiak out of Shingle Point because it was a Sunday. Stefansson was late for a meeting at Herschel Island, and a missionary had admonished his rowers not to work on the Lord's Day. Stefansson wrote: "The attitude of an Eskimo towards a contract seems to be about the same as the attitude of a sovereign state towards a treaty—it is an agreement to be kept if it suits you to keep it and to be abrogated whenever you feel that your interests are better served that way."

They continue to struggle with contracts, Christianity and quantitative values imposed upon them by *Kabloona* (such as setting a barometer, keeping nine-to-five jobs and measuring miles). They also appear well versed in modern North American culture (wearing Colorado Avalanche caps, citing their favorite foods from surveys and naming children after television soap opera stars). Still, their former traditions and the sweep of the landscape have left men like Peter Elanik better equipped than I for the abstractions of, say, quantum mechanics. My own culture and upbringing leave me more suited for such minutiae as memorizing baseball statistics.

Typical of many Inuit, Peter phonetically substitutes English declarative for interrogative sentences. He shakes a cigarette out of his pack on the table, then politely asks (although to most *Kabloona* ears it would sound like a declaration), "I can smoke."

"Sure, it's kind of you to ask," I say.

Peter changes the subject again by asking me, "What are you doing up here really?"

"I am hoping to see a polar bear and maybe an Eskimo curlew."

This is not disingenuous, and besides, telling him that I am trying to cross the Northwest Passage, with more than two thousand miles to go and winter coming, will not earn me much respect. Peter stubs out his cigarette and declares, "You're not a bird-watcher, are you?"

"I like to watch birds, yes."

"But you're not a tree squeezer?"

I can only laugh.

Along with today's beluga kill, there is one more item of great interest to everyone on Shingle Point: The sun has not set for two months. "The sun will fall sometime early this morning," Peter informs me.

I look at my watch. It's nearly 1 a.m., July 22, times and numbers that I had thought were of no importance to men like Peter.

"What time?" I ask.

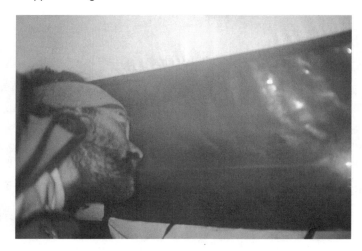

Watching the sun set early in the morning from my tent

"I do not know. But it will come up again quickly."

"Do you know when I should look for it to set?"

"Your watch will not tell us. Just pay attention."

He pushes open a veil of mosquito netting, suspended from an otherwise empty doorframe and hanging to the plywood floor by the weight of several tattered and filthy white socks filled with sand. Once outside, Peter fires an aerosol can of Off! toward his face, then lowers it downward with the routine efficiency of taking a shower. I wave away his offer to take the can with me or accept a quick hosing. As he escorts me toward my tent, he presses on me a paper bag filled with bannock, processed cheese, and an apple.

He tries again to give me the Off! can. "I guarantee that it will be as useful as a shotgun." Somehow, maybe from over the radio, everyone seems to know that I am unarmed. Then two children accost Peter with their golf clubs carved from driftwood. As he nods good night, the boys club a red ball toward the first of nine holes marked by driftwood sticks, flagged with orange survey tape. "Pay attention," Peter shouts to me, pointing toward the destination of this morning's sun.

I wait for an hour in my tent. Mosquitoes tapping on the nylon walls sound different from raindrops. While rain is a fluid and reassuring patter that puts me at ease for dry shelter, the dance of mosquitoes is like hollow twigs being clicked together on the drum-tight nylon walls. My imagination is further amplified by the appearance of these stick figures cast through the wall by the eerie northern light, pushed and bent by its long, sideways traverse through the atmosphere. Through these tricks of sound and light, it comes as an epiphany that the mosquitoes are rubbing their front legs up and down against their proboscises like the sharpening of knives.

At precisely thirteen minutes and fifty-nine seconds past 2 a.m., children shout along the water, at the impromptu golf course and from inside nearby shacks and tents. I peer north through the front panel of my tent's mosquito netting as the Beaufort Sea swallows the yellow ball of sun. While the mosquitoes click on heedlessly, a bearded seal plops into the water and a yellow-billed loon stops its braying. When the sun rises, maybe ten minutes later, I am probably the only soul asleep at Shingle Point.

Into the Yukon Territory

I sail west at 8 a.m. on July 22 with a breeze on my back. I am now 50 miles west of the Mackenzie Delta, and eight days out from Aklavik, having recently crossed from the Northwest Territories into the Yukon. The Alaskan border is 150 miles ahead.

While running under the wind in a sea kayak might seem novel in the Arctic, Inuit have been catching the wind with animal skins on their umiaks and *kamotiks* (sleds) since before Columbus or even the Vikings reached North America. While I hold the sheet, watching the water for sudden gusts, the Klepper shivers on past the last shacks. There is no movement anywhere on the spit. In a land where the sun will be shining for most of the night and day, this hour in the morning is thought to be unnecessarily early. There will be no more "great human beings par excellence" until I reach Herschel Island, nearly a week's worth of paddling and sailing to the west. I stow my wristwatch in a cockpit pocket. With an eye out for polar bears, I begin trying to pay attention.

The days lose their relevance as markers of time. Although getting scared slows things down, mostly there is no way to check the passage of time; the continuous light has a way of corrupting what you normally expect in a day. In the Arctic, summer is simply so short that every creature is hustling to make the most of things all day and all night. Unlike most North American places, the Arctic has no one commuting to and from work, so there is no noise for the beginning or end of a day. Birds sing at all hours. There are no jet paths overhead. The sun flies a circle course around the entire horizon without displaying evening or dawn. Time simply loses meaning, while the constant light produces chemicals in my brain that speed me into a birdlike metabolism.

The sun flows out like yellow honey from under a bank of altocumulus clouds, sticking to the land and bouncing off the slick black sea. With no trees or buildings to stop this liquid force perfusing the air, my red jacket seems aglow. Even the wind is given color as sea salt molecules drenched with light rush past in the wind. Birds ride back and forth in a state of hyperexcitement, as if they might fill the vacuum and stop time altogether.

Although Inuit seem indifferent to this light, it is a startling reminder about how the rest of the earth's air used to be, post-Pleistocene volcanoes and pre–industrial pollution. The three-thousand-mile-wide Arctic coast of

North America has no industry, a few hundred automobiles on less than a hundred miles of roads, and a clarity akin to the gelatinous lens of a baby's newly opened eyes.

With no warning the wind dies and the sea goes as flat and dark as pond ice. I drop sail. A loon takes flight in some immeasurable distance out toward the North Pole. It croaks manically. Its webbed feet and wings awkwardly splash water into what appears as prolonged points of ellipses— splashing white against the inky tablet of sea—until gravity and water tension release the straining outstretched head of the loon and its legs fall back behind: a sliding horizontal exclamation point. The loon, *Gavia pacifica* as it turns out, circles and disappears.

A mass of caribou undulates along the shoreline near Kay Point. They glide along with no particular leader in a wave of tawny rippling fur, seemingly guided by the same fluid and collective energy propelling the birds. I paddle behind a thousand animals for no determinate time. I am drawn west by the cacophonic slipstream of ticking hoof ligaments and swarms of mosquitoes so dense that the air darkens above the forest of waving antlers. Following so much concentrated movement feels effortless, as if I were being pushed by wind rather than pulled by my own deltoids and triceps. At the edge of the point the herd stops and balks as if tormented by mosquitoes, unwilling as yet to turn around or climb the steep bluffs above the beach. They have stopped en masse before a blond boulder that stands up and becomes a grizzly, sauntering along the water's edge as though each step should shake the earth. The caribou turn as one contiguous wheel, with shaky-legged calves and two cows waving tiny hoofed legs out of their wombs and uncountable barrel-chested bulls smelling like a collective barnyard, as they splash and click and run in wide-eyed terror past me to the east.

With so much animal musculature I had expected to hear the sound of the earth being trampled and drummed upon. I turn and watch them disappear. Their cloven hooves hit the shoreline as softly as dog paws, while their ligaments click against their bones and the ocean parts noisily before them: *ka-chunk, ka-chunk, ka-chunk.* . . .

The wilderness is never as simple as my expectations or imagination construe it. In the Arctic, if you are paying attention, animals express familiar emotions with remarkably human timing. As the caribou fade down the beach, there is the distinct impression that they are as off-balance and as scared and out of place as I feel right now. That, fortunately, makes me feel just a bit more at home.

I have lost whatever cockiness I began the trip with. More pressing than anything else, I haven't talked to anyone for two days. So, feeling a bit lonely, I paddle straight toward the barren ground grizzly, nearsightedly crouching in wait for my arrival. From a stone's lob away I say, "Hello, Mr. Bear," and without hesitation it bolts straight up the cliffs and beyond the bluffs with its forelegs throwing dirt behind its hind legs, now marked by two dipping and screeching glaucous gulls, circling south into the verdant and domed hills of the deserted Ivvavik National Park. It rolls uphill into a squirrel-size ball of fur, wavers into a brown dot and then vanishes into the immensity of space surrounding us.

In the mornings, curious and bright-eyed and feeling freed by the day's potential, I revel in this cloak of immensity. But by afternoon it has become hard to look around if only because the stretch of horizon is so overwhelming. As the bear disappears, I feel intimidated by it all.

It is not hard to imagine why Inuit turn to despair during winters in their villages, feeling the weight of this suddenly lifeless land and seascape and still further depressed by the lack of sunlight. Nor is it hard to see why their culture is so acceptant and humble. So much of the Earth and Its Great Weather—or Sila, as they refer to it—are utterly unchangeable, so they shrug their shoulders, smile and say, *"Ayornamut"* ("It cannot be otherwise").

Since I lack this level of tolerance, I turn to known quantities, labeling things to feel familiarity. The caterwauling blue jay falsetto from somewhere ahead identifies *Buteo lagopus*, the rough-legged hawk, before I can even see him with the binoculars. It's probably a male, judging by the multi-banded brown-and-black tail and aggressive swoops above his hidden nest.

As the dust of this small band of the larger Porcupine caribou herd settles over my head, a cloud of misplaced mosquitoes joins me out in the water. As if I were not terrorized enough by the mosquitoes, a bumblebee-size warble fly alights on my forearm and begins working its hind end. I plunge my arm elbow-deep into ice water, then head straight out to sea as fast as I can paddle, creating just enough wind so that the mosquito cloud whines behind me like a hive chasing its queen. Looking back once is enough to know that I cannot stop.

The cloud follows me two miles out by hanging to my back, unable to bite through my thick jersey or hat and unable to fly around me through the envelope of apparent paddling wind. I settle in to travel for as long as I can without stopping, knowing that calm water never lasts long and imagining how the firepower of Off! could drop the whole swarm.

The wind appears in the west as a steadily approaching white line, like a distant snowplow, so I turn directly back south into the hairy cloud and settle for a few bites on the left side of my face until the wind arrives, nearly capsizing the Klepper and blowing the bugs back toward the Mackenzie River. Now I just have to make it to shore.

Capsizing here would spell trouble. Unlike a skin kayak, my Klepper is too loaded down to perform an Eskimo roll, even if I did know how. But while swimming alongside, I could flip the kayak back up by jerking the gunwale from below. Then I would swim to the stern and reboard by mounting the kayak like a horse, *à cheval*. The Klepper has air sponsons and would stay afloat. Then, while I sat in the cockpit, a vigorous session with the bilge pump would allow me to drain enough weight so that the boat could be paddled. Practicing down south, I figured all this could keep me alive.

I run broadside to the wind, trying to minimize my drift east while maximizing my forward motion by paddling frantically toward shore. Nothing like a bit of fear to coax out your best performance. My legs are damp from errant waves, and my hands are numb. Seasoned sea kayakers in lightly loaded kayaks, who wisely frequent the protected waters of Mexico's Baja California peninsula, Washington's San Juan Islands or the Carolinas' barrier islands, are usually capable of performing an Eskimo roll. Such cognoscenti would undoubtedly laugh at my poor technique or my sloppy and splashing paddle strokes. Still, fear has a way of transcending technique and creating speed. More than a few people would think it foolhardy to be paddling so far off the Yukon's shores, particularly alone and without a radio, but these people have probably never experienced a cloud of Arctic mosquitoes. For all the so-called rules that I've broken in the last couple of weeks, there have been ample rewards.

Long-tailed jaeger perched on driftwood

Several hundred yards out from shore, the Klepper's bow caroms left and right in the wind waves. A long-tailed jaeger, *Stercorarius longicaudus,* appears ten feet above, hovering soundlessly. The bird is unaffected by the crash of wind and water and gives me peace of mind. Since I despise moments of adrenaline and fear that make me try to muscle through stressful moments like this, instead of *gracing* through them, I visualize myself as the jaeger, helping elevate me beyond the situation at hand. The bird's wings stroke the air powerfully, while its distinctive yellow face and black crown glide back out away from the breakers, as if to lead me away. Its tail feathers drift a half foot behind, prayer flags wavering in the wind.

Paddling for the shore through the surf might cause a capsize. I follow the bird and keep moving west. There must be a safer place to land. Deep breathing through my nose and picturing myself in flight keep me calm and allow me to indulge my imagination.

If I were an *Inuk* kayaker battling through such seas, having been plagued by otherworldly mosquitoes sent by the caribou and the bear, I would look for signs of having offended some animal spirit. Perhaps the photograph I took several days ago stole the unborn whale's spirit, and this—a sea of whitecaps and a line of surf guarding the shore—is the goddess Sedna's payment for my lack of respect.

As I crane up to keep the jaeger in sight, a wave breaks into the cockpit and floods the boat, forcing me to make my way through the surf. I toe the left rudder pedal for shore and take the next breaking wave over the stern and across my back. While I ride this wave, the bow plunges underwater, nearly flipping the boat stern over bow, until I brace the paddle across the cockpit and lean straight back. The wind blows my hat off. My heart pounds in my ears. I think: *If only it were warm water sloshing over my thighs, this might be fun.* Suddenly I'm halfway up the beach surrounded by clapping waves, so I roll out into the shallow surf, grab the bowline, and run for dry land.

The jaeger is nowhere to be seen. My teeth are chattering. There's no driftwood for a fire, so I put on a dry sweater and jog up and down the beach to warm up. The sand is dented with the size fourteen prints of a grizzly or a small polar bear. *Great,* I think.

It takes me two candy bars and twenty minutes of sprinting, while constantly looking out for bears, to break a sweat. I place my fingers in my crotch to bring back the circulation. I add out loud, "Six times seven equals . . . forty two," to verify that the blood supply to my brain is not shunted.

After draining the Klepper dry with my invaluable three-pound bilge pump, I push the kayak back into the water, line it back beyond the breakers with thirty-foot leashes on bow and stern, then begin walking down the

Lining a kayak along the shore is useful in rough water or when the kayaker gets tired of sitting.

beach while steering it through the waves with my arms spread wide like a kite flier. Lining a kayak is not exactly fun, but it's a good way to stay warm and still make miles in rough water.

Camping here amid the bear prints is not an option. The peninsula south of Herschel Island seems safer. At 9:30 p.m. I pull my watch back on to keep track of the time and to keep my mind focused. I can't afford to get dreamy-headed or hypothermic.

Hours speed past. I eat some cheese (my closest substitute for muktuk) and try paddling through the surf until I get wet again. To keep warm, I continue jogging along the shore, pretending that I'm kite-flying, with the stern line in my right hand, bowline in my left.

By midnight I am in a cold fog, still walking in the opposite direction of fresh bear tracks while looking for some sort of reprieve. Four different times I coax myself into another hour of walking by promising to go only another fifteen minutes.

A shack shows its square geometry looming out of the fog. Such squareness is alien to the Arctic. This unnatural form interrupts space in a landscape that otherwise allows air and light to flow evenly. Unlike the rounded and gradual forms of the earth, the shack throws hard shadows, even though the light is fading. Most of all, it offers something conspicuously absent along such a wild coast: shelter.

I pull the Klepper in through the surf, yank my sleeping bag and stove from the bow, and flip the hull over, thirty feet from the breakers.

My hands are almost too numb to unscrew the hasp behind a padlock. In most other circumstances—without fresh bear sign and hypothermia knocking on my defense system—I would sleep outside. Strange, I think, that a cabin out here would be padlocked at all. It takes a lot of discipline not to put my shoulder through the door. Desperation sometimes breeds a strange and enduring patience. After ten minutes I am inside.

Sleep comes immediately. I dream of guardian jaeger angels and a party of friends waiting for me on Herschel Island. Even in my dreams, the crossing grips me.

In the morning I leave most of my food, a $20 bill and a note on the table: "Sorry to break in, but it was a cold night. I am leaving everything just the way I found it and I hope it was all right that I drank some of your coffee."

Herschel Island

I paddle toward Herschel Island to test the furled water. Knowing that people (and food) await a dozen miles away is too tempting to resist. The mile-wide crossing looks risky. I decide to break one of my cardinal rules—avoid whitecaps—since I am starving for companionship. I set up a ferry angle, turning my boat at forty-five degrees into the wind and current to prevent being pushed out to sea. As I paddle, I make minute adjustments with the rudder pedals to maintain my course. Halfway out, it takes all my strength to keep forward momentum and keep from slipping out to sea. Tendons click in my arms. The torn ligament in my thumb throbs.

The current is running like a river, splashing up over the cockpit and swaying the kayak. Other than stealing quick glances at the Virginia Slims pack–size global positioning system (GPS) lashed to the spray deck, I stay focused on the far shore. When my forward speed drops below a mile per hour, I tap the right rudder pedal and allow the current to push my bow. Then, as I slip farther away from the spit on Herschel Island, I toe the left pedal and resume battling the wind and current. I try not to consider what might go wrong. Were I to capsize here, I could not swim through the current to shore.

It takes an hour to fight my way to the island. I miss the beach by half a mile, but it's easy to paddle once I am inside the circling eddy current behind the sand spit. Then, with no warning, fifty yards from shore, the pedal cable snaps, and the rudder flaps uselessly behind me. Since I have often practiced paddling without a rudder, it isn't terribly difficult to feather and stroke my way in.

I pull the Klepper up onto the sand and immediately remove the repair kit from its dry bag. It takes half an hour to install a new rudder cable. Once the job is done I stand up, stretch my sore shoulders, wiggling my swollen thumb, and look out at the wind stirring the water white.

This time Sedna must've been looking after me.

It's five miles to park headquarters on the other side of Thetis Bay. The paddling is mostly protected from the wind by huge snowbanks running down into the sea.

Halfway across I spy a pond in an ice-dammed stream. I stop and strip for a bath. Although I carry all the essentials for repair and first aid, I've left out soap. Too much weight. Sand scrapes the dirt off quite nicely, making me smile at my barbaric resourcefulness.

It helps to get out of the kayak, stand up and think. The adrenaline from the crossing has subsided, and as I consider the chances of capsizing that I took in the wind and current—probably 95–5 in my favor—it seems a bit dodgy. I wonder how to continue without risk. In addition to those lapses in judgment I might commit, there are all too many sudden unpredictables out here.

Twenty years ago in India I met a Hindu monk who found nirvana in a cave, living alone and fasting for weeks without physically endangering himself. His time in the cave irrevocably changed him. He had gained placidity and wisdom there. He waved his fingers like wands through the air as he spoke.

I surrounded his holiness among a throng of respectful pilgrims who came to worship and fast at his temple above the headwaters of the sacred Gangotri. My three companions and I were the first Westerners allowed into the region in a quarter of a century. After we had sheltered for two nights in a storm, the man gave our Anglo-American team his blessing. We walked off on a shepherds' trail toward the unclimbed mountain above, towing our porters in the wake of a snowstorm. The monk told us that we would climb Thelay Sagar safely. I felt that he approved of our risk taking, that he understood that we too were following the path of enlightenment.

While rappelling off the mountain, we all were lucky to survive rock falls. Our ropes were cut; I was woozy with high-altitude sickness. Since that experience I have always tried to put risk taking in its proper place as an element to be avoided or at the very least as a sometimes necessary evil that shouldn't overshadow the greater ends of a trip. Looking out at the whitecaps in the bay, I can't help pining for the constitution of that monk, for a path around the physical risks—and into the realm of sheer spiritual discipline.

To reach Herschel Island Territorial Park, I cut across Thetis Bay. It's an acceptable maneuver with the wind at my back. Besides, people are watching me from the far shore. If the kayak should capsize, I can always swim in. Still, the wind is driving the Klepper so fast that the bow begins submarining. As the boat sways to and fro, I find myself wishing for outriggers. I lean back and reef the sail down repeatedly during gusts, until I am flying the equivalent of a T-shirt above me in the wind. Thirty yards from shore I let the sail out entirely—lest it be ripped apart—and the rubber bow grinds half out of the water up onto the sand beach.

As I pull the boat up, a uniformed warden for Herschel Island Territorial Park greets me. Richard Gordon pulls out a citations book and, scribbling aloud, tells me that he is issuing me a ticket for unsafe speeds across Thetis Bay.

"Sorry," is the best rebuttal I can give to his joke, after mostly having talked to myself for the last week.

"Would you like some muskoxen stew?" he asks, knowing that offering such foul-tasting meat to other Inuvialuit would be met with howls of derision.

"Do I look that hungry?" I reply with a smile, and he shows me toward his cabin.

"Do you know if my cache of food got flown in last week?" I ask.

Richard holds his hands several feet apart. "The bag that used to be like this?"

"Yes"—I nod enthusiastically—"that's it."

"Well, sorry, we were hungry; it is now like this." He holds his hands a half foot apart. I look at him more closely and realize, to my relief, that he is smiling broadly.

The paradox about Herschel Island Territorial Park, given how the resident *Kabloona* whalers destroyed both whales and culture, is that it is a park at all. Of course it has its history, but the abandoned villages of Kittigazuit and Gupuk have histories that predate the destructive and relatively short visit of the whalers by centuries. The Inuvialuit wardens who work here—Richard, his uncle Colin (brother of Danny from Shingle Point) and their boss, Park Superintendent Andy Tardiff—are proud of their park. More important, perhaps, is that they have jobs that allow them to be out upon the land all summer long.

The wardens and I peer through our binoculars as a gleaming red ice-breaker anchors a half mile east, issuing a final puff of white from its smokestack. Then Zodiacs begin whisking in scores of tourists. The wardens take deep breaths and brace themselves.

Americans, several Canadians, two Japanese, Germans, French and Australians each pay $19,000 to cross the Northwest Passage in a mere two weeks. A shorter version of their journey will take me ten months spread over several years and cost me only several thousand less (even with exorbitant airfares to and from remote villages). While I devour dried food, the Northwest Passengers pick at fruits and vegetables and croissants and filet mignon. Like me, they come ashore for prescribed rest stops and to expose film. Few passengers lack cameras. If you close your eyes and listen to this particular herd splashing out of the water, the recurrence of shutter clicking (although not the metallic frequency) is comparable to that of frightened caribou running the shoreline.

They repeatedly expose pictures of wardens. Finally Richard blithely announces that he will begin collecting $100 per photograph.

One *Inuk* who has somehow retained title to an abandoned whaling house poses in front of the cameras. He is wearing an anorak parka carefully embroidered with mystical and colorful creatures. His hand is held by a two-year-old daughter wearing brand-new hand-sewn kamiks. He takes $5 per photo.

I tag along for a tour with Richard and twenty tourists, beginning with the RCMP barracks. Our guide cracks jokes about hungry polar bears lurking in the corners, then takes us to the storeroom to show us a three-foot-long curved bowhead eye socket. Richard wagers a Japanese man—with a sumo wrestler build—ten dollars that he cannot pick up the bone. The man shrugs rather than try.

At the abandoned Anglican church, Richard is happy to announce that the pews have been painted white by nesting guillemots. He points up, and their red webbed feet are just visible, clownishly knuckling out over the rafters. I linger for an hour, cooing upward, trying to urge one all the way out for a photograph. As usual, I utterly lose myself in the company of these birds.

Richard will not accompany any tourist to the graveyards. The *Kabloona* graveyard is enclosed behind a whitewashed fence with carefully inscribed wooden markers. On lower ground nearby is a sprawling field of unmarked and casketless Inuvialuit graves. Runoff water is washing the tawny skeletons out of the tundra like newly emerged avens. A long-tailed jaeger hovers above, hunting lemmings rustling through a field of northern water carpet and grass of parnassus waving in the wind. Here the ground sucks wetly at my shoes, and I can feel the layer of permafrost below, cold as tubercular death.

Gordon invites me over to their quarters for more caribou stew. I don't normally smoke cigarettes, but the air is so thick with smoke in most Inuit homes that it's more polite to accept a cigarette, get the taste in your mouth,

Herschel Island Kabloona *graveyard*

and then not worry about having to breathe secondhand smoke. It is rare for an *Inuk* to offer a visiting *Kabloona* alcohol, if only because drinking is a private act among a people who are largely devastated by its effects. In the words of Norman Chance, the ethnologist who knows these people and their Iñupiat cousins to the west, "those who drank were not responsible for their actions—and thus couldn't be held accountable. That is, 'being drunk' was not only an explanation for damaging behavior, it was also a justifiable excuse."

I then make the mistake of asking Richard how hard it might be for someone to drain the flooding Inuvialuit graveyard, at which Colin Gordon gets up and walks out. Richard, his nephew, explains, "Colin will pick up cigarette butts and empty the honey bucket, but you will not catch either of us working the graveyard."

"Why not?"

"Would you want to mess with the bones of your relatives who are dead from bad whiskey and whaler bullets and strange diseases?"

Later, in their library, I find a book with this comment written about *Kabloona* diseases by one of Colin's relatives, Hope: "There were lots Inuit people there at Qikiqtaruk [Herschel Island] long ago. In the summer they went and waited for the ships to come there. Most of them died and every day they would bury someone. My dad was helping with the funerals digging graves, there at Qikiqtaruk, long time ago in 1902."

Inuvialuit wardens are clearly professionals. Colin Gordon complains of having to pick up American cigarette butts. He claims that Canadians smoke only unfiltered cigarettes, and he doesn't have to pick up their litter. Picking up litter is something so foreign to most Inuit (except those who have traveled extensively south of the tree line) that Colin is mystified by the whole concept. Once something has served its purpose, it is simply tossed over a shoulder, no questions asked. If trash is brought back to their village, it then trashes out their homes or village. Landfills seem little different to most Inuit from leaving the trash out on the land. Still, this park is run with better humor and as much expertise as any south of the Arctic Circle, including those parks I've worked in as a rescue ranger.

As the Zodiacs begin shuttling the Northwest Passengers back to the icebreaker–cum–cruise ship, the Japanese man asks me for a photograph. He poses me next to my kayak, and I smile for him. He is dressed in a hooded down parka, while I am hatless and wearing a fleece sweater.

"Are you cold?" he asks.

"You get used to it."

"I wish I was doing the Northwest Passage your way."

"Right now I'm so worried about making it the next hundred miles across the Alaskan border to the next village that I wish I were doing it your way."

Colin Gordon (far right) showing Herschel Island tourists an umiak

The lee shore is strewn with broken-up boulder-size icebergs. Grimy clouds race above snowflakes. I meet a young man named Sheldon Brower, clad in short pants, flip-flops and T-shirt. Turns out that his grandfather is the famous *Kabloona* Charles Brower, who wrote *Fifty Years Below Zero* and opened up trading in northern Alaska. In the wake of the whalers, as northern Alaskan Inuit lost traditional skills, Brower retaught them how to build umiaks. The more time I spend upon this coastline, the more evident it becomes that Inuit share both the mechanical skills and blood ties of those *Kabloona* explorers a century dead.

Sheldon Brower has just emerged from the steam house built by the wardens. Following his directions, I throw two pieces of driftwood into the fifty-five-gallon woodstove, strip down, soap myself up and then sit on a pine bench for as long as I can stand the heat. I continue my Inuit fantasies by sprinting out of the sauna down the sand beach and straight into icy Thetis Bay as if I lived here. From a back float, as yet unaffected by the cold, I spit out water more fresh than any ocean I have tasted. I wonder what it would be like to live here, bathing myself with ice water and fingering traditional food into my mouth. My flesh—to a polar bear anyway—might taste as peanutty as the whale. Gamboling naked in this inky sea, with my heat receptors still fried from the sauna, I know that the great anthropologist (and, some say, propagandist) Stefansson was truthfully giving his own opinion of this environment when he titled his book *The Friendly Arctic*.

I dry off, change and escape the wind by ducking into another oven-hot shack to visit several elderly Inuvialuit. The women share traditional bead-work and embroidery, the sewing of kamiks and fishnets, old-style dancing, throat singing and the forgotten art of language with several fifteen-year-olds flown in from distant villages. The elders speak mostly in Inuktitut, rarely taught now to children, but everyone happily answers my questions in English.

Rosie Albert tells me about how she was prevented from speaking Inu-vialuktan (the local dialect of Inuktitut) in school.

"But the elders like us"—she gestures to the two other women in the room, her pointing hand making up for English-language inadequacies—"never stopped."

"What about the phone books I saw in Inuvik printed half in English and half in syllabics?" I ask.

"Most of Inuvialuit cannot read them, you know, because those letters were invented by priests only a hundred years ago. Eskimos never had books or written words. Even until the 1960s the only things printed in Inuktitut were a book of prayers and government brochures that explained social assistance."

"Is Inuktitut hard to learn?"

Rosie replies with a series of guttural throat noises, earlier described to me by one of the Northwest Passengers as the language of spitting out mosquitoes.

"Excuse me?"

"In Inuktitut I said, 'Not if you are willing to pay attention.'"

Then Rosie announces that she is the grandchild of a famous *Kabloona*. No doubt she has told this story before to Inuit, but because I have expressed interest in her past, she lights up a cigarette and begins deciding how much she should tell me.

Recently widowed, she is employed part-time as a language teacher by Aurora College in Inuvik. She has dark skin, brown eyes and unusually curly, graying hair. She sees me looking and says, "You know that you can always tell a full-blooded *Inuk* by their straight hair."

She pats my thinning head and gets a round of laughter from the other women by saying, "Inuit never bald."

As she runs into an adjoining room, Peter Elanik's twenty-three-year-old nephew, Kelvin, pulls off his ball cap, bends over and tousles his full head of straight hair, before good-naturedly coming by to pat the top of my head. Big egos, I have noticed, would not last among these fun-loving people.

Rosie then drops a photograph of a curly-haired *Kabloona* and a younger version of the same man in my lap.

"Who is this?" I ask.

"My grandfather Vilhjalmur Stefansson. And my brother, Frank Stefansson. They are grandfather and grandson, not two different men. The famous Stefansson did not want the world to know that he had Eskimo child."

I am amazed. In all of Stefansson's books and several biographies, a child is never mentioned. Rosie verifies the story by showing me an article from *North/Nord*. Indeed, the anthropologist did have a son, Alex, from the liaison of Stefansson and his *Inuk* seamstress, Pannigabluk, but Stefansson actively denied, even to his later *Kabloona* wife, that Alex belonged to him. To a race-conscious and celebrated *Kabloona* anthropologist who built his whole career around the study of Inuit, acknowledging Alex, amid the Victorian sensibilities of the East Coast society he lived in, would have been anathema. What impresses me most is that Rosie, like Stefansson's son and most of her people, doesn't hold a grudge.

That night I can't sleep. It's not just the bizarre Stefansson story. I have to get back to the mainland somehow.

Pygmies Across the North Atlantic

Muskox horn and whalebone carving of Sedna, the sea goddess

I leave in a fog that night of July 28, hoping that my crossing several hours to the mainland will be calm. This is the first trip in which I have used a GPS. I wouldn't think of attempting a blind crossing without it.

A GPS does miracles in a fog. I place the one-by-four-inch unit on the spray deck, next to my map, and use it like a compass. In the Arctic compass needles are pulled off true north by the magnetic north pole, and compasses often give erratic readings. The GPS allows me to place myself precisely on the map by showing my longitude and latitude.

Occasionally a sand reef or a limb of driftwood floats past. Otherwise I am riding the surface of a great onyx lung, heaving at half the rate of my own shallow respirations. If the GPS batteries should go dead in this fog, I still have options. My hearing orients me toward the ocean's mouth, sighing against the distant mainland. Without dead-reckoning skills that have little to do with technology or equipment, the GPS could easily lead you astray.

In my head I am as unruffled as the surface of the sea. At times like this, my intuition and love of navigation helps overcome my fears.

After ten miles the icy fog penetrates my jacket until paddling is no longer possible without my shivering. I pull onto a high spit of sand near an old mound of driftwood. Nearby the unmistakable size seventeen prints of a polar bear sow step easily over a log I have to jump over; two sets of cub prints, half the size of my feet, trail around the log. Fifty yards from the woodpile I light two small fires and curl up between them, hoping that the heat will not draw bears. Last summer, here on the Firth River delta, a rafting client was awoken by a polar bear poking its head into the tent. She screamed, and the curious bear vanished.

Although the biologist Ian Stirling, known to northern researchers as Dr. Polar Bear, says the big bear comes ashore only in winter to den, I need to be careful. As Inuit say, "No one knows the way of *Nanuq*."

As the flames lick all around an old piece of fir that once floated on the

Mackenzie, I close my eyes and imagine the fire burning through the dense cloud above. I reassure myself with the notion that any polar bears lurking in the fog are as frightened of me as I am of them.

In the morning sun I lay my sleeping bag out to dry, flip my Klepper upside down and towel the rubber hull dry with a spare shirt. As the boat air-dries in the sun, I walk around the woodpile and find a pile of stones, a fuzzy gray pile of down holding green eider eggs and the protruding bones of a human foot. There would be a tombstone or a cross with *Kabloona* remains. This *Inuk* was buried next to the sea that supported him. I touch nothing and circle away.

Kneeling above the Klepper, I pry open the lid of a rubber cement can. I smear glue onto a palm-size patch that will cover a gouge beneath the kayak's center, earned while scooting across a shallow gravel bar.

Although the used kayak cost $1,800, it gives me more pride than the $30,000 sailboat I once owned. I run my hands along the chine above the flat keel and think about how many places the boat has taken me, about how many planes and boats I have thrown it from over the years, about how many miles I have sailed and paddled it. As the grave glows pumpkin orange in the eerie light, I imagine how The People might have regarded their own boats. While I can merely patch my hull, Inuit had to replace their hulls every other spring because the sealskin rotted and cracked over the winters. I paint the Klepper with rubber cement, thinking about how they dabbed on seal or whale oil. Caribou oil would have offended Sedna.

The kayaks of this region were unsurpassed as feats of engineering and environmental adaptation. Beginning A.D. 900, Inuvialuit boatbuilders lit smoky fires to keep the mosquitoes down. They painstakingly bent several dozen willow ribs, notch fitted, and then lashed them with sinew onto a

Patching the Klepper kayak hull with rubber cement

skeleton of fir keel and gunwales. The finished frame looked like that of a skinny beluga, sixteen feet long. Other less developed kayaking cultures in the Arctic forbade women from working on the boats, but here by the Mackenzie River the kayak was so central to its survival that the entire village celebrated in the crafting. Women and children chewed on the edges of sealskin to squeeze the water out, then expertly stretched and stitched it over the flush-edged frame. They laid strips of bone over the edges of the cockpit to prevent chafing, and after drying overnight, the boat was seam-sealed with whale fat.

Many kayakers adorned the bow of their boat with the webbed feet of the yellow-billed loon, *tullik,* the wisest and most agile of all sea ducks. The kayak was so lightweight that it could be carried with one arm to a high driftwood rack so that sled dogs wouldn't eat the hull.

The Mackenzie Delta kayaks were graceful, but their narrow beams made them fast, tipsy and thrilling for amateur paddlers. Sticks or gravel inside the boat wore holes in the fragile skin hull. Paddlers learned their rolls and balance in the warm river while stringing out fishnets. The kayaks were also distinctive for their Aleutian or Greenland-style upturned bow and stern stems, which were used to tie off and tow belugas.

Although the heavier seagoing kayaks of far-off Greenland had a slightly different design, the two kayaks were as similar as the dialects of Inuktitut. Within 150 years, paddling its umiaks and kayaks, the new Thule Culture's boat designs had spread three thousand miles east.

In Greenland today a handful of Inuit continue to hunt beluga and narwhal from skin kayaks. In the rest of the Arctic, most adult Inuit stare with instinctual recognition and respect at modern polyester and resin kayaks. Skin kayaks have not been paddled on the North American coastline for half a century. Mechanical-minded hunters saw the obvious advantages of motorboats and never looked back.

Kabloona rediscovered the seaworthiness of newly modified kayaks by making lengthy trips. In 1956, Hannes Lindemann crossed the Atlantic alone in a Klepper. Modern plastics, Fiberglas and rubbers have allowed entrepreneurs to redesign Inuit kayaks into German Kleppers, American Eddylines, French Nautiraids and Canadian Feathercrafts, to name just a few. Still, the high watermark of engineering occurred a millennium ago, when Inuit craftspeople built kayaks for survival rather than sport.

The testament of both kayak and Inuit paddlers' endurance came from northern Scotland as early as 1420. Before European sailing vessels were crossing to Greenland, Scotsmen wrote of "pygmies" being washed ashore in skin kayaks. These early and mysterious crossings of the North Atlantic were Inuit hunters, boldly seeking out new horizons.

In 1698 a Scottish vicar described an Inuit paddling near Aberdeen:

"They have this advantage, that be the Seas ever so boisterous, their boats being made of Fish Skins, are so contrived that he can never sink, but is like a Sea-Gull swimming on top of the water. His shirt he has is so fastened to the Boat, that no water can come into his Boat to do him damage, except when he pleases to untie it, which he never does but to ease nature."

Two years later an *Inuk* kayaker paddled up the Don River but promptly dropped dead from exhaustion. His kayak, displayed in the University of Aberdeen's museum, was the heavy style of boat known to Nuuk, Greenland, and not dissimilar from the Mackenzie River kayak. In a feat of navigation that is even more remarkable than the Polynesian reed boats sailing across the Pacific, this sealskin vessel came more than fifteen hundred miles across the stormy North Atlantic. The brave paddler fought against the Greenland current, then bypassed Iceland entirely, ducking, rolling, bobbing over ten-story waves as skillfully as *tullik,* the yellow-billed loon. To survive the North Atlantic, a small boat could shelter along ice floes bigger than ships as well as the sort of tall iceberg that would sink the *Titanic.* A hunter could also stay alive by sipping ice melt and spearing seals. But to accomplish such a feat without losing his mind, a man would have to stake equal faith in both Sedna and his own well-designed boat.

These journeys from western Greenland to Scotland were remarkable yet strangely unheralded. In 1873 the *Inuk* Joe Eiberling performed a similar journey by riding eighteen hundred miles on ice floes from Greenland to Labrador while hunting for and feeding a dozen shipwrecked *Kabloona.* Of course, everyone knows about such *Kabloona* sea heroes as Sir Ernest Shackleton, whose ship *Endurance* was crushed by sea ice in 1915; he then led twenty-seven men across a thousand miles of the storm-tossed Weddell Sea.

Before the twentieth century began, kayaking was already a European pastime, thanks to Inuit. However, there were several small but sophisticated tricks that weren't copied by *Kabloona* for several decades. My feathered paddle, its two blades tilted perpendicular to each other, is an example. These feathered blades allow me to penetrate strong winds or breaking waves. While one blade pushes water, the other perpendicular-angled blade slices through the air without wind resistance. Although a modern European has claimed this essential paddle design as his own, the renowned archaeologist Robert McGhee has reported that these feathered paddles have been found buried in the Mackenzie River graves of old Inuvialuit kayaker wizards.

These medieval double blades also eliminated a debilitating kayaking injury, now called paddler's tendonitis. The syndrome is caused when undertrained or dehydrated kayakers push poorly designed paddle blades until the sheaths swell inside their arm tendons. The injured kayaker can feel this miserable creaking and grating like a rusted bicycle brake cable at each paddle stroke. Inuit artfully carved their paddles out of heavy driftwood with blades scarcely thicker than the handle and then feathered the blades so tendons weren't strained while pushing the blade through both wind and water. Small, thick blades also allowed the paddler to fend off ice chunks. The carvings were tested so that the blades dropped naturally into the water when slightly lifted. For long journeys, Inuit placed a piece of muktuk on the foredeck, gyrating (instead of lifting) the counterweighted paddle across the soft pad of whale blubber. Not unlike a modern secretary typing on a neoprene wrist pad.

Then there is the incredible Eskimo kayak roll: both innovation and technique. Most *Kabloona* kayakers didn't learn to roll until after the turn of the century, just as Inuit began abandoning their kayaks for motorboats.

Ten years before the Revolutionary War, a Moravian missionary, David Crantz, described the Eskimo roll: "He overturns himself quite so that his head hangs perpendicular underwater; in this dreadful posture he gives himself a swing with a stroke of his paddle, and raises himself aloft again on which side he will. These are the most common cases of misfortune, which frequently occur in storms and high waves." Crantz detailed nine more different rolling techniques. Waterproof jackets and spray skirts, made from loon skins, kept the paddler dry underwater.

I have yet to master the Eskimo roll in a heated swimming pool, so it's hard to imagine Inuit practicing in ice water. But any birder who has watched the yellow-billed loon catch a herring while ducking and rolling in the surf can imagine how Inuit invented the technique.

One *Inuk* from Greenland is still infamous for his film performance in 1959. The man is seen taking a long drag from his cigarette, then ducking his head underwater to the left like a loon, rolling the boat upside down while keeping the cigarette above water in his extended right hand, then transferring it across the bottom of the hull to his left hand, placing his right hand back underwater and rolling the boat back upright. When he places the lit cigarette back in his mouth for another puff, Inuit audiences everywhere laugh uproariously at their brother kayaker.

Orientation at the U.S. Border

The next day, July 29, while sitting in the middle of a flat sea of ice along the deserted beach called Komakuk, I light a cigarette that Richard Gordon gave me two days ago. I am grappling to understand mesmerizing distant objects, seen through a strange, bright cerulean foreground of ice. Perhaps nicotine will calm me down and give me better perspective.

For most of the morning I have been paddling around and under Byzantine-shaped pieces of ice that have been fired by sun and chiseled by surf into shapes resembling polar bears, swans, a walrus, a whale tail, loons and ptarmigans. Again and again I discover the inanimate come to life: clouds as heaving lungs, turreted cities upon the ice-packed horizon, sunset-colored lichens and boulders shaped like muskoxen. The ice appears to be mimicking the animate world. These forms are often sculpted with detailed eye sockets or textured fur, so that their creation seems more deliberate than coincidence. With enough time alone out here, contemplating both the hinge points of creation and the origins of Inuit mythology, a solo kayaker could easily find companionship in a place deep within his imagination: without linear constraints, sympathetic to Inuit perceptions of space.

The purest Inuit—or pre-European contact Dorset Culture (named after Cape Dorset on southern Baffin Island)—did not differentiate between time and space. They saw it all as part of one dynamic based upon a wary eye for detail, unlimited by enclosure or property. For instance, Inuit pay no attention to the Alaskan/Yukon Pacific time zone boundary, looming a dozen miles from where I now sit. To understand Inuit, one must understand both land and sea. It's like learning to speak Inuktitut outside a classroom.

It is helpful to put away my map, stop calculating how long it will take me to reach the Alaskan border, and look at how the land joins the sea, as Inuit would. Inuit do not make maps and instead rely upon their memories as well as oral traditions to inform them about how space fits over the horizon. The most memorable things were first seen and then heard, not measured by specific times or distances.

In Hudson Bay just after the turn of the century, a *Kabloona* asked the locals to draw their island for him. The Inuit were initially stunned by the request; why should they bother putting down on paper something that was locked in their heads? But the *Kabloona* insisted. Two Inuit sketched him a map from memory. Years later their map nearly matched the first aerial survey of Southampton Island: 200 miles long and 175 miles wide.

GPSs blunt the way the way traditional Inuit carry land in their collective memories. The anthropologist Edmund Carpenter believes that Inuit perceive space more from auditory cues than from the visual and measured cues that we apply to geography. While *Kabloona* eyes pinpoint a place specifically within a space and next to a background, Inuit ears can perceive sound coming from any direction.

More precisely, Carpenter believes that *Kabloona* sensory traditions mirror the first sentence of Aristotle's *Metaphysics,* telling us that sight, not sound, is "above all others." Our traditions continue with the Bible's "Seeing is believing" and on to modern physics, measuring light waves. Yet the parts of our brains that process sound or intuition are little used—unlike those of traditional Inuit.

These audible and remembered perceptions are useful because my modern map cannot possibly include all the details of the land and sea in front of me. The tide rises and falls, revealing uncharted sandbars. Currents then wash the sand away and create new sandbars in different locations. Or consider the ice pack, a dynamic presence sawing the coast apart and lifting away prominent landmarks, then falling back north, unmappable (even by the inaccurate weekly satellite sea ice maps) because of its hourly fluid and grinding mutations. Pingo ice hills, looking like miniature volcanoes, disappear as underlying permafrost melts. Floods carve new river channels out into the sea. Bays drain. Storms wash away whole beaches.

Inuit stories about a particular space were also helpful for preventing a phenomenon called *nangiarneq* ("kayak angst"). This anxiety attack occurs when a kayaker is far enough out from the shore that the water and ice assume a disorienting sameness, similar to being lost in a whiteout. The afflicted kayaker, without noises or story linking him to the land or his people, often hallucinates and grows dizzy to the point of capsizing.

Having been isolated for several days, I now experience, along with the disorientation of *nangiarneq,* a sensation akin to that of plunging over a waterfall. I have a sudden fear that I will either capsize or loosen my bearings of where I fit into the world so badly that I will never go home.

Just for the sake of making noise, I shout out loud, trying to have some effect upon this immense seascape and trying to exit the waterfall.

Lacking any cultural ties or remembered stories, I look away from my map and try to discern some detail about the earth and sea. It is the wind, with its noise and depth added to the water, that saves me from disorientation.

Wavelets begin whistling inside aqua blue iceberg chambers. The grass blurs into a soft mat of lime green, stretching south to the dusky British

Iceberg bird seen from under my sail

Mountains. Then the wind stands up, and the ice moves like a collective white-pistoned machine, thumping up and down against the sea as I haul my sail and flit past an ice alligator and under the upper jaw of a great alabaster hippo drooling fresh water onto my face. I emerge into a field of surf and steer for shore.

I comb surf-pounded beaches. At times the wind blows so hard that I have to lie in my tent, sheltered behind a pile of driftwood, to prevent it from being picked up and kited away. Mostly I read and write. It goes calm on the second night, so I pack up and leave while I still can.

Since leaving Herschel Island, I've been alone for five days. A few minutes past midnight on the last day of July, I paddle past a bluff holding a miniature Eiffel Tower–shaped iron radar beacon. It's the border of Alaska: 141 degrees west; 69 degrees, 40 minutes north. I am now more than two weeks into my journey.

Two ravens stir and release the radar beacon, their wings creakily grabbing air. A white beluga cow and her gray calf startle me with their sudden exhalations, heading west, several knots faster than I can paddle in the

Beaufort gyre current. Then, as if to defy all laws of motion, a distant iceberg swims east toward the Yukon.

I refuse to give in to every illusion, so I paddle out toward it, intent on solving the mystery. Two miles out, so lonely that I cannot even consider going to shore to sleep, I give the fifty-foot berg (shaped like the radar beacon) enough room in case it should roll over and inundate me. Then I stop paddling. The current continues to pull me west, but the berg still floats east.

I pull away as the yellowing disk of sun skitters into the sea at 12:59 a.m. Up comes a stiff wind. I continue paddling farther out, to where the land appears to meld with the sea, until swells scare me back landward. Along the shore I search for calmer water, surfing along the breakers, plying the lee of a sandbar and feeling for the gyre's edge with my paddle. The collusion of current and wind force me onto a high sandbar covered with Mackenzie River driftwood. The abandoned place I lay down my head is called Gordon.

Before sleep, I watch the sunrise at 3:59 a.m., then aim these words toward the sea: "Thank you, Sedna, for looking after me."

Sometime later I tilt my head up out of my matted sleeping bag into coruscating sunlight. I roll out, draw my knees up into my hands and wonder at the last few days of hallucination. As if unsure of sleep-encrusted eyes, I sniff flat air toward a tawny curl of *Inuk* fibula poking from its log crypt right along my own sleeping position.

I quickly pack to leave. I'm desperate to talk to someone. Being alone this long might be the hardest thing I've ever done. Although I've learned to talk aloud and ask myself questions to prevent any accidental impulsiveness, I constantly worry about some sort of transformation, about reaching a point where my mind simply floats north and I won't feel the need to go home again.

Iñupiat of Alaska

First Born

On my eighth day alone, sixty miles inside Alaska, two Inuit skiffs loaded to the waterline approach my kayak. As we rise up and down on the cold swell, I hear my voice hurl "hello" up and out of my throat. After one has been alone for a week, there is an almost supernatural quality to human voices, allowing me to analyze the silken yet glottal quality of Inuit speaking English.

Thomas Gordon smiles toothlessly at me and, with the distinctive Inuit singsong, a nasal whine inflecting end vowels, he says, "We thought you were piece of drift*wood*."

He then starts speaking in Inuktitut, spitting vowels up out of his larynx as if I too understood.

When I ask him to repeat himself, he says, in English this time, with the same high-pitched tones of Canadian speech, minus the interrogative eh's concluding his statements, "Please make yourself at home at our camp," then nods backward. "It is at the place where the land curves around again."

Coke cans and cigarette butts pebble the ground. From inside driftwood fish racks laundering reddened char, James Lampe holds out his hand, ushers me toward a wall tent and asks if I'm hungry.

The sea laps gently against the lagoon. A dozen ruddy turnstones, chestnut-backed with black-and-white bibs, pick bits of fish and krill along the tide line as I nod yes and say, "Yes, thank you."

I feel a flood of emotions and words that need to be expressed, yet Inuit men are minimal conversationalists. It is always best not to talk too much at first.

"We never ask how long anyone is going to stay," James says, "so we feed them, welcome them in. It is not that way everywhere." He referred to the unfriendly treatment he received while visiting Fairbanks (a $500 round-trip flight south).

I duck into the tent's cloud of cigarette smoke. Archie Brower, the director of nearby Kaktovik's Iñupiat Corporation, holds out a plate and motions for me to fill it with caribou steaks, smoked char and fried bannock steaming on the Coleman stove. There is margarine for the meat, and big bowls of salt and sugar and jam for the bannock.

The tent is scattered with clothes, a boom box, batteries, molding food, cans, gasoline containers and unwashed dishes. No one asks more than where am I coming from and where am I going. Out on the land this mind-your-business frankness is typical in the midst of such gracious generosity. All the modern complexities fall away here, the alcohol is left at home and everyone works together pulling in fishnets or butchering caribou.

In Kaktovik, Tuktoyaktuk or Paulatuk a *Kabloona* stranger stepping off into the village from the latest scheduled flight might perceive The People as shy and taciturn. At this camp The People are both kind and humorous.

Iñupiat ("human beings par excellence" or northern Alaska Inuit) elders speak both Iñupiaq (the regional dialect of Inuktitut) and English. They all are corporate shareholders. They are conversant in international news brought to them by their satellite televisions. They have also long debated with and advised both developers and environmentalists about the oil in their backyard, the Arctic National Wildlife Refuge.

In 1971, when President Carter signed the Alaska Native Lands Claim Settlement Act (ANCSA), indigenous people were deeded one-ninth of the state lands plus $963 million; half the money comes from oil revenues. Because Iñupiat residents all tax facilitation on oil-bearing land managed by regional and village corporations, their Canadian Inuvialuit relatives are comparatively poor.

In 1972 the 5,700 Iñupiat formed the 56.6 million-acre North Slope Borough. This Minnesota-size municipality encompasses the subterranean fossil fuel reservoirs north of the Brooks Range, from the Chukchi Sea to the Canadian border. Their first act was to assert the right to levy a real estate tax of $7 million on the oil companies. Initially, the oil companies refused to accept the fact that these former nomads could tax the Prudhoe Bay oil complex, along with every oil well on the roof of America. The oil companies fought the levy in the Alaskan courts until they were forced to pay the North Slope Borough, headquartered in Barrow.

This Iñupiat town, 225 miles to the east, became the richest city per capita in the United States. The borough gave jobs to any Iñupiat who would work. Schools and theaters and plumbing came to The People.

Then southern speculators began milking the guileless Iñupiat. During

Draining the ice water from my boots in Alaska

the 1980s two *Kabloona* garnished more than $21 million in hidden kickbacks from the Iñupiat mayor of the borough, Eugene Brower. This Iñupiat son of the famous Charles eventually plea-bargained and later served thirty days for accepting bribes (the use of an Anchorage house, phone and Cadillac, trips to Las Vegas with $1,000 wads of gambling change, $1,000 plane tickets to Hawaii, $45,000 worth of rings and a 27-foot dory worth $35,000).

Brower was educated, like most Iñupiat, by a lackluster Bureau of Indian Affairs school. He simply wasn't capable of such grand deception. The case was eventually investigated by the FBI and turned into the longest, most expensive criminal trial in Alaskan history. In an act of cultural patronization unprecedented in such a high court, the attorney representing the white-collar criminals claimed his clients were only honoring the traditional Eskimo *pamaq*. Such gift giving was usually performed for a starving or helpless member of the village. This defense was thrown out of court since no one could show that receiving more than $100,000 worth of cash and gifts had anything remotely to do with the traditional *pamaq*.

In 1989, after more than a hundred witnesses and thousands of documents were introduced, the jury found the two *Kabloona* guilty of more than forty counts of racketeering, accepting kickbacks, bribery and fraud. They both were fined $5 million and sentenced to seven-year federal penitentiary sentences. The Iñupiat will never recover all that was swindled.

I ask James Lampe if oil rigs and pipelines placed here on Arctic National Wildlife Refuge hunting grounds will scare off the caribou.

"Holy boy, that is such tree squeezer crap. Go to Prudhoe Bay and you will see caribou all over the place grazing beneath pipelines. Most people here want oil development because it will bring us jobs."

While he is unemployed, his wife, Vanessa Lord, works as a nurse practitioner. His father works full-time for the borough. His father (a vibrant Clark Gable look-alike) jumps into his four-wheeler and drives forty yards away to take a leak.

James was born here on Griffin Point in 1957 and, in the modern Christian tradition, named after his father. *Kabloona* teachers and missionaries forbade young James to speak in Iñupiaq while growing up. It is the experience that all former Inuit children shared, from Barrow to Greenland. James is now fit and unusually tall, just shy of six feet. He raises his voice and furrows his brow while describing the new bumper sticker displayed on many of the several dozen new pickup trucks around his village: I SPEAK IÑUPIATUN [like an Eskimo] TO MY CHILDREN.

"Now in Kaktovik you only get a job if you speak Iñupiaq. First they tell you not to speak it; now they say you are not culturally complete if you speak only English."

After eating, the full-faced elder Thomas Gordon offers me a cigarette from his pack of Marlboros. Because of his missing teeth, it's difficult to understand his pronunciation and his conjunctionless, dangling participle sentences. His grandfather and namesake (*atiq*) was a well-known white trader who put Gordon on the map eighty years ago. Now, out of respect, everyone listens to the elderly Gordon as he answers my question, in nasal singsong, about bears.

"September last year came thirty-seven polar bears next to village while we were whaling. I had to kill a cub right here too because it would not come out of the water where my fishnet is. Most people do not like polar bears, but I do."

He pauses, then asks, "Did you see polar bear ten miles back?"

"No. Where?"

"By the graves at Kuluruak. He was following you."

This shocks me. But I am not entirely surprised. The anthropologist Richard Nelson lived with Iñupiat and found that it was typical to hear seemingly exaggerated animal sightings, only to find out later that the Iñupiat never lied about seeing polar bears onshore during the summer. Or walrus swimming a thousand miles out of their range.

James's seven-year-old reaches over my plate to grab a mosquito, and neither his mother nor his father scolds the boy as he reaches a second time. Nor does anyone else here seem concerned about young Jules's whining.

Many Inuit traditions have been abandoned, but the art of raising children is still steeped in ancient culture. If Jules had been born a hundred years ago, his *atiq* would be that of a dead relative. Even in the days of customary infanticide, when parents killed female babies in favor of male hunters, a baby could never be killed after having been given its *atiq*. Thus named, the child is loved for both itself and the memory of the former relative. *Atiq* names were also genderless. The *atiq* helped Inuit see their lives as a cycle of renewal in which no one dies, at least in the cosmic view, and in which those wise and treasured members of the tribe provide an ongoing sense of cultural identity.

Since children are thought to share the adult characteristics of their *atiq*, male or female, it would be pointless for Vanessa to discipline her son. Would she scold her grandfather or grandmother for reaching over me? But the third time Jules grabs for a mosquito, nearly knocking my plate off the table, Vanessa speaks up. "Jules, stop it, please."

Jules stops immediately. Although Vanessa defers to James's indulgences toward his son, she grew up in Fairbanks and is largely removed from Inuit traditions.

Another former Inuit belief, *isuma*, may be deteriorating amid modern Western values. *Isuma* (rationality) is something that cannot be taught and is thought to grow with the child. Shouting at a child who has not gained his *isuma* used to be considered immoral and useless. If Jules follows the pattern of other Iñupiat boys, he will grow up more quickly than most *Kabloona*. He will not graduate from high school. He will remain in his parents' house until after they die. He will marry without ceremony, often after his girlfriend becomes pregnant. Above all else, he will honor his family.

I try to wash the dishes. Thomas waves me away. Wayne, a thirty-five-year-old *Kabloona* orphan, asks if I have seen any caribou. It is not the first time I have been asked to provide game directions, and I never refuse, because northern hunters would never dream of withholding information from me. They are observant enough to know that their outboard engines and high-speed boat trips are sometimes inferior to the stealth of a quiet kayak.

Wayne is interested in looking at my map, but the other Iñupiat in the tent prefer a verbal description of where I saw the caribou. Wayne wears designer jeans and speaks only English but seems to be an accepted part of the community—mostly, it seems, because he loves to hunt.

I put away the map. As Wayne walks out to prepare his boat, I ask James if Wayne is married to an American.

"No, he is married to a Native Alaskan, but I guess they are the same."

In search of caribou, James, Vanessa and Nathan Gordon motor off in

Wayne's eighteen-foot-long aluminum skiff, into a sea of whitecaps outside the lagoon. Jules is left to whoever cares to watch him.

Two hours later, in Beaufort Lagoon, while James puts down his 30.06 rifle, Wayne promptly raises his and shoots toward a scrawny-looking caribou in front of a small calf. The cow drops dead in the doorway of an abandoned distant early warning (DEW) station, shot through the heart.

As the hunters approach the cow, muscles still jerking, its calf runs off across the tundra. In front of their eyes, the bounding calf shrinks to the size of a mouse, then an ant, until it disappears amid lustrous green earth.

Wayne pulls a knife from his lanyard and proudly slices open the mother's belly, only to find the carcass full of pus and warble flies. He walks away in disgust. Inuit call this rancid-smelling and warble-infested caribou the same name as bacon, *tuktukiuk*.

James remembers his grandfather's great lesson: how hunting is a contract between caribou and man, how the animal soul, like that of the man, will not allow itself to be hunted if it is not respected. He runs back to the boat, grabs an ax and chops off the caribou's head. While their *Kabloona* companion scans the horizon for more caribou, James gently carries the head out away from the abandoned building. He sets the *tuktu* head down on soft tundra. He then opens his water bottle and drips water into its mouth so the *tuktu* will not go thirsty.

With their typical refusal to judge others, particularly *Kabloona,* no one criticized Wayne during the boat ride back to Griffin Point. But when Vanessa walked back into camp, she spoke several words to me that told leagues about the traditional respect shown to animals versus the *Kabloona* harvesting of meat: "Wayne is a bit trigger-happy."

There is a plethora of accounts from both *Kabloona* hunters and anthropologists trying to pin a trigger-happy syndrome upon Inuit culture. Eighty-three years ago, on this same stretch of tundra, the anthropologist Diamond Jenness wrote about accompanying the *Inuk* Fred Ailuat to Charles Thomsen's fox trap, which held a polar bear cub:

> We approached within 20 yards of her—or at least the captain and I did, for Fred and Thomsen were some 10 or 15 yards behind us on our right. The bear stood in front of its cub, facing us and growled two or three times. We agreed not to kill the cub, then fired a volley at the mother. She pitched on her head, and slowly fell over on to one shoulder, then began to roll down the side of the mound. By this time she had received another volley, but one bullet unfortunately went astray and killed the cub—piercing the lower jaw and penetrating the neck. Still the mother was not dead and several more shots were fired—about 18 altogether before we were absolutely sure there was no sign of life. Fred was very excited and blazed away at a great rate without taking much

aim, so that I, who was on his left and in front, was in far more danger from him than from the bear. There is little doubt but that it was a bullet from his rifle that killed the cub.

Jenness was trying to understand the abuse of the firearm, the tool that revolutionized Inuit hunting. Fred Ailuat came from western Alaska, where there were no polar bears and therefore none of the great respect that northern Inuit held for *Nanuq*. Jenness's journal continues: "It appears to be rather typical of Eskimo hunting—Capt. Nahmens and I both thought—to stand off some distance and empty the magazine into the object on the chance that one bullet at least will get home. It was rather a pathetic sight to watch the mother guarding her young one so anxiously. She had stayed by it for hours, and would not leave it even when attacked by four men. I greatly regretted that in the hurry of getting away I had forgotten the camera. One could have approached within 10 yards without much risk and secured a splendid picture. It was sheer butchery on our part, but necessary, for here at the ships they have had almost no fresh meat, but only salt beef all the winter."

Jenness spent that spring unearthing old sod and log houses on Barter Island, named for those Inuit who came from both Canada and Alaska to trade. He unearthed bone-handled knives with copper blades (traded with the Copper Inuit from six hundred miles east), fishhooks, arrowheads and Inuit skeletons. Stefansson had already stolen the skulls and shipped them back to eastern museums.

As Jenness paid the men $20 a month to hunt and dig for him, he made observations much more astute than those of missionaries and government officials. Later these cultural differences were used as an excuse for assimilation—Jenness spent much of his later career fighting to protect Inuit. He wrote: "They are unable, I suppose, to project themselves out of themselves—to love their neighbours as themselves. This perhaps explains their cruelty—or so it seems to us—to birds and animals—a child-like thoughtlessness which permits them to torment an injured bird or thrash unmercifully a dog which has provoked them."

A permanent settlement was not established on Barter Island until 1923, when Tom Gordon opened up a trading post for a San Francisco company. To relieve the famine caused by the decimation of bowhead whales, the Bureau of Indian Affairs introduced tame reindeer herds to the coastal plain south of the island, in spite of the large summer migration of the Porcupine caribou herd. When Kaktovik residents began starving in 1936, three thousand caribou were driven in from the western Arctic herd, but the animals quickly migrated away, drawing all the reindeer with them. In 1938, as fur prices dropped, old man Gordon died and the Barter Island trading post closed. Iñupiat were forced to trade with their Canadian cousins through the trading post settlement of Gordon, near the Alaska–Canada border.

In 1947 the U.S. Air Force ordered Kaktovik residents to relocate so that a runway and hangar could be built. In 1951 the cold war prompted the military to build huge radar dishes, and the island was transformed completely into a military base. This gave Iñupiat jobs on the military's distant early warning site (monitoring Russian movements in the Arctic), but their village had to be moved yet again. Since hunters could be confused for Russian infiltrators, the air force moved Inuit away from Gordon. The opening of forty more DEW Line sites throughout Canada and Alaska similarly brought the nomadic Inuit lifestyle to an end.

Kaktovik's population tripled to 150. The People were forced to relocate again in 1964, but this time the government, feeling generous about nearby oil reservoirs, deeded the Iñupiat title to their new village.

Kaktovik, Barter Island

While paddling through the night, I cannot see Kaktovik, ten miles across the semiprotected waters of Jago Lagoon. The bell-shaped Barter Island rings around the village on its northeastern corner, separated from the mainland by a quarter-mile-wide channel beneath its southern handle. In the half-light and ground fog, I can make out Kaktovik's DEW Line, a two-hundred-foot-high radar dish, which Inuit call white men's ear. These giant ears, surrounded by outmoded and dilapidated buildings and old radar devices for sensing Russian MiGs or missiles, stick up into the sky every 150 miles along the coastline. Technicians stopped manning the stations a half dozen years ago.

Fifty-five-gallon fuel drums strewn across the sites leak PCBs into the groundwater. Inasmuch as the United States subsidized the DEW Line sites throughout North America, the U.S. Air Force is now paying Canada millions of dollars to clean up the mess. On Barter Island the roundup of

Sailing toward a DEW Line site

more than twelve thousand discarded drums is costing taxpayers $2.8 million.

The ascendance of Kaktovik (population 200) is still heard in the hum of diesel generators from the automated DEW Line station, retrofitted with twenty-four-hour surveillance cameras and modern satellite technology. (The replacements for the DEW Line, built every 200 miles along the coast, are called the North Warning System.) A two-mile sand spit, curving back east toward the Canadian border 90 miles away, now protects the island. The fogged-in jet runway is also cruised by polar bears, strutting back and forth looking for bowhead whale scraps. The tops of aluminum aircraft hangars poke up out of the white mist. I double-check my course toward town with the GPS.

The harbor curls around the village. Even asleep, it all but breathes with blowing food wrappers and stray sheets of plywood that double for walk-ways, shutters, fences, meat-cutting boards, seats and tables. Halogen lights flicker against the incomplete gloom of the August dawn.

I pitch my tent on soggy ground next to the thirty-foot-long arching back-bone of a bowhead whale. It is flensed clean yet still tawny and rancid-smelling. The hail comes as a pattering gray wall just as I slide the last pole into the tent sleeves. I jump in, zip the door shut and fall asleep clutching my can of bear Mace.

At midday speeding four-wheelers and pickup trucks wake me. Familiar faces from Griffin Point and Canada—the Gordons, the Browers, the Elaniks and the Lampes—peer at me, until I can't tell if I'm looking at Canadians or Americans (at least a dozen Canadian citizens are awaiting naturalization here). They shout out, "Welcome to Barter!"

In hopes of placing myself squarely in time and space, I flag down a pass-ing police car and inform the uniformed *Kabloona* that I crossed over from the Canadian border about a week ago. But he isn't interested in customs work. He directs me to the town hall, where the *Inuk* woman manning the mayor's desk does not understand the word "customs" or even the idea that I have crossed an international border. Her baby is screaming, so she reaches into a drawer and presents me with a green and gold Kaktovik lapel pin. I attach it to my jacket and thank her as I leave.

A silver water truck winds down the web of a half dozen streets, filling up thirsty homes, then driving out to a reservoir on the north edge of town to pump in more water. On the south end of town, everyone (except the plumbed school and hotel) dumps his polyethylene toilet bags into a con-tainment pond that in turn draws polar bears and grizzlies from miles away.

The post office can't find any general delivery mail for me, but two strangers invite me to their homes for tea and ask when I'll be leaving for Prudhoe Bay. James is there too but shakes my hand quickly and runs out as if embarrassed to be seen with me. The rain falls in sheets, rendering the dirt streets into bogs. Somehow strangers know that I am alone and in a kayak, so they stop to smile and wish me a safe journey.

Even in the grocery store The People already know who I am. Before I leave, the owner insists I take a bag of canned food. I try to refuse, particularly when I learn that she will accept no money.

"You need it. Please take it. Safe journey," she says.

From previous experience, I know that no one will ever make so presumptuous a statement as wishing me good luck. After all, you must have only skill to paddle this coastline in a kayak.

Thomas Gordon's son Nathan picks me up in his truck while I am walking to the hotel. The Waldo Arms is a series of welded-together trailers run by a kindhearted *Kabloona* bush pilot and his wife. Locals drop in frequently, cadging free cups of coffee and french fries, but the burly and taciturn *Kabloona* construction workers from Fairbanks pay $150 per night, not including meals.

Since Nathan is driving an oil truck, I ask for his opinion about the controversial oil development on the nearby wildlife refuge.

"There is nothing I can do about it. I do not care. But if I did care, no one would listen. They are going to do it anyway. They have too many dollars to be stopped."

After this he begins driving recklessly, sliding across corners, his hands white-knuckled on the wheel. Nathan appears to be more broad-cheeked Cherokee than narrow-faced Inuit, and he wears his raven hair down to his shoulders like a 1960s war protester. His face in fact is unmistakable, and in a sudden flash I remember meeting him here ten years ago. He was walking out to a boat on the spit with a rifle to go seal hunting. I had made the mistake of wishing him good luck.

Nathan had turned angrily and said about his hunting heritage, "It is not luck. It is skill."

Today I want to avoid angering him again, so I open the oil truck door and say, "Thanks, Nathan."

He stares straight ahead. He won't meet my eyes or speak. It is as if he too suddenly remembered me. He waits for me to walk up the hotel steps and disappear from sight before he opens the truck door to begin his business.

I kick off my boots and place them next to the pile inside the door. The hotel smells of burning dryers and the unique bubbly-fat seared flesh of cow that I have not whiffed for the last month.

From a saddle-worn couch in front of a television playing a soap opera, the elderly James Lampe waves to me. He is dressed in coveralls, but he no longer looks like a movie star. The contrast in his appearance is so striking that I stop and struggle for words. I try not to stare, but I can't help myself. It occurs to me, with James slumped in repose, seemingly hiding out, his hair combed in a neat gray wave across his forehead, that something dies in these people inside villages. At Griffin Point he bustled with energy, as if he belonged, as if he had a mission, even while jumping onto his four-wheeler to take a leak outside camp. Here, lit pale from the fluorescent lights above, his face cast in pale blue television light, I could be looking at a different man. I open my mouth to ask him how he is but swallow my words when I notice, after he finishes his wave to me, that he is cradling his other arm. His hand is curled, withered and useless.

In Kaktovik, where the military has moved him so many times that he no longer has a will of his own, James senior is handicapped, literally and figuratively. Out on Griffin Point, upon the land where he conceived and birthed his children, among the wildlife and seascape that sustain his identity, his handicap seemingly disappears. Just two days ago I watched him heft a rifle and crank up an outboard engine like a young man. But here in the village, Lampe, like his son, seems hurt and displaced.

He looks up at me. His brown eyes are tired and searching. He looks down at his curled hand, then back at me before I can look away. I am certain that he knows my thoughts.

I have the feeling that it's time to go, just in case I'm not welcome.

Re-creating the Past on Flaxman Island

Needles and needle cases

It is August 11. Winter could shut me down any day now. I am several miles out from Brownlow Point. Kaktovik is nearly fifty miles away, back across Camden Bay.

I let my hand drift beside the kayak. A mysterious current is rippling through the blackness of the Beaufort Sea. I yank my fingers out of the water and slide them up into an armpit. A distant ice pack, falling and rising, bellows up into a white cliff, then drops down into the water, only to come bellowing up again. This aerial accordion could just as easily be two miles away or ten. At times like this it is helpful to know that envelopes of cold and warm air bending the light rays create a mirage. Lately the line between reality and illusion has been narrowing.

If I let my feelings take over when I'm alone and distant visions appear from across a huge ocean, they can overwhelm me. To quell these fears, I look for explanations for events like the mirages, which early Arctic sailors called ice blink. In my lonely state of mind it's easy to imagine this ice blink as a tsunami rearing up in the distance. I constantly refer to my thumb-worn copy of *A Naturalist's Guide to the Arctic,* because E. C. Pielou's down-to-earth explanations for northern phenomena give me no small comfort and real-time perspective.

I lean right, work the rudder to run with the current, pull my hand from my rubber shirt and brace the paddle against the pull of the water.

Flaxman Island is a half-mile-wide, three-and a-half-mile-long wedge of cotton grass and brownish yellow sand. In places, a hundred-foot-thick lens of permafrost shows through like a slip of underwear. Since Inuit once lived here, I want to see the world as they experienced it. They arrived here on what they called, simply, *qikiqtaq* ("island") long before Franklin named it after a British artist.

The coastal plain of the Arctic National Wildlife Refuge stretches out across the widening orb of earth to the south. This yellowing tundra is like a great sponge, leaking out permafrost and absorbing the runoff from glaciated peaks. Some call this lush plain the Arctic Serengeti, which comes true when hungry wolverines, foxes, wolves and grizzlies chase thousands of calving caribou. Now, with the exception of muskoxen, most wild animals have fled south over the mountains, following the Porcupine caribou herd, escaping winter. The land has become more desert than African plain.

As I round a long sand spit, the splashing of thousands of flightless and molting old-squaw ducks stretches for miles. Each bird sounds a turkey gabble, swallowed by a peculiar series of gasps as they dive into my bow wake, swim underwater for forty yards and reemerge as a great lake of masked paddlers.

From the shore a bevy of elusive male common eiders flash their white-and-green heads as they run into the water and burst into the air, awkward as loons, characteristically avoiding flight paths over land. I see the ordinary russet-colored female everywhere, its black bill shaped like a Roman nose, nesting on tiny islands and sand spits and running in small flocks for protection against marauding glaucous gulls.

With the aid of binoculars sweeping the island, I can see only a half dozen fifty-five-gallon drums and a few ground squirrels. I double-check to make sure they're not grizzlies. Beyond the bluffs, breaking the flat field of tundra, are a half dozen mounds. Grass grows high around the edges. Pieces of driftwood poke skyward. I steer for a mud gully below.

The sod houses are surrounded by bits of bowhead whale vertebrae too heavy to lift, pieces of caribou scapula and a pond (once flat ground) that the sod was mined from. Amid the astringent smell of rotting grass and stagnant water is a broad sea view that would reveal the spouts of passing bowhead or beluga whales. *Qiviut,* the soft muskox underfur, is lodged in one of the walls where a passing bull scratched its back. The sod walls are topped with driftwood frames. I pry out an old Remington rifle shell, hammered into a wall.

To the west is a cabin built from wreckage of the *Duchess of Bedford,* after sea ice crushed her timbers in 1907. The cabin is rotted beyond repair, but inside, I find a waterlogged newspaper and two ancient bottles of Listerine. There are no footprints in the mud or any sign of recent visitors. On the ground next to the cabin is a sign, limed by a roosting peregrine: LEFFING-WELL CAMP STATE HISTORICAL SITE. LEFFINGWELL ALMOST SINGLEHANDEDLY MAPPED ALASKA'S ARCTIC COAST DURING HIS STAY FROM 1907–1914. HE ALSO IDENTIFIED THE SADDLEROCHIT FORMATION, MAIN RESERVOIR OF THE PRUD-HOE BAY OIL FIELD.

As if the ice pack and the elements have not already vandalized things enough, there are a few more unnecessary remarks about removing the sign or damaging this national historic site. There are no signs near the former sod houses, inhabited for centuries before Leffingwell's arrival.

Leffingwell's cabin, built from his ship, on Flaxman Island

Aside from storytelling traditions, Inuit culture is also kept alive through the records of passing *Kabloona* scientists and ethnologists. Here on *qikiqtaq,* along the western edge of an intact ecosystem and just east of the industrialized Prudhoe Bay, there appears a border more distinctive than that of the United States and Canada, 130 miles east.

In 1906, Stefansson, Ejnar Mikkelsen and Ernest Leffingwell came to Flaxman Island to determine what landmasses lay north of Alaska. After learning the "Eskimo" language, Leffingwell complained in a letter to his father that he could not express himself. It wasn't just that the Eskimos were unaccustomed to numerical concepts; the language's lack of adverbs or adjectives showed the literal fashion in which they perceived the world. Leffingwell was a driven soul who devoted himself to the area while bearing the more innocent agendas of science that wouldn't allow him to corrupt The People. He did not bring whiskey or take Eskimo women, but along with guns, ammunition, tobacco, flour and sweets that would help wean Inuit off the land, he probably traded germs.

Mikkelsen was the first of his party to try a real kayak, barely managing to paddle across a lagoon without capsizing. When he got out of the boat, he lost his balance, reached out to an *Inuk*'s shoulder in a nearby kayak, and promptly capsized him. Mikkelsen wrote: "I had never before seen an angry Eskimo, but I saw one shortly afterwards when he stood dripping on the beach and pouring the water out of his skiff and using all the fancy words which the whalers had taught him. I got wet too, but not so much, and had nothing to give him but some soaked tobacco. This he did not like, and on his way home, as far away as I could hear him, he expressed his opinion as to white men's ability to use a kayak and their lack of generosity."

It was the forty-five-year-old man named Sachawachick who most impressed the scientists. Sacha was respected all along the north coast of Alaska for his hunting prowess and was one of the last Inuit to wear button-size labrets pierced into either side of his lips. In a rite of manhood, Sacha's father pierced each corner of his son's lips when he was ready for marriage. Over time, bigger plugs were inserted, until the holes became as wide as pencils. (Menstruating girls were tattooed on their chins.) After the turn of the century missionaries quelled these "vulgar" practices among Eskimo youth. Only intractable elders, with a continuous stream of saliva leaking out the holes in their cheeks, continued wearing labrets made from muskox horn or caribou bone. Sacha wiped his cheeks dry and squinted merrily into Mikkelsen's camera lens, braving the magnesium flash and resembling the 1970s movie tough Charles Bronson.

By the turn of the nineteenth century Sacha, like many other Eskimos, traded caribou meat for whalers' whiskey or food. While he was out hunting for a whaling ship anchored in Barrow, a *Kabloona* took his comely wife without asking her husband's permission. Sacha could have extended a form of spouse exchange (*nuliaqatigiit*), in exchange for trade goods, but the whaler violated the cooperative code by not asking and seemed to have no intention of returning his wife. Sacha hurried home to kill his wife and the whaler but they sailed off before he could catch them. It wasn't until they were a thousand miles south, along the Kenai Peninsula, that the newly eloped couple felt safe again. Sacha had chased them in his dogsled most of the way to Nome.

Sacha, who would have immediately shot both adulterers to uphold *nuli-aqatigiit,* eventually gave up the chase. At Point Hope he found another wife, Douglamana, and after having a child (and adopting Douglamana's children from a previous marriage), he moved his new family away from the disease, diminishing game, and rude ways of Barrow's *Kabloona.* Flaxman Island was a place still undesecrated, free of booze and disease. For the next several years Sacha worked as a guide and furnished fresh game for the scientists.

Mikkelsen lost several sled dogs after a long trip. Inuit in the sod houses traded him one dog for two sacks of flour, twenty-five pounds of beans, six pounds of coffee, twenty pounds of dried potatoes, twelve pounds of cocoa, one shotgun, hundreds of rounds of Remington ammunition and one broken tent. Sacha returned from a hunting trip so appalled by his people's greedy trade that he gave one of his best dogs to Mikkelsen for free.

Many of the adult Inuit came by Leffingwell's cabin to beg for food, even if they weren't starving. One woman grew angry with Mikkelsen after being reprimanded about stealing food and later kicked his favorite puppy to death.

Mikkelsen wrote about a family living on the mainland inside Brownlow Point, the filthiest people he had ever seen. While visiting their *iglu,* he saw an unaccompanied toddler playing with needles and knives. He wrote: "Now and then The People would stop playing, look serious for a second, and then start an eager hunt for one of the many lice which inhabited their ragged furs. . . . It was the mother's business to keep the head of her darling boy clean, and she had the remarkable but by no means uncommon way of putting the louse out of harm's way forever—by swallowing it!"

The scientists described how The People took care of one another, sharing out the meat from every hunt, and how the children would not beg for candy. They watched one boy who, completely unprompted, shared a piece of pie with a dozen others. When Mikkelsen inquired why a "naughty" boy was not punished, his parents looked up in surprise and explained that the child did not understand, and soon enough, when he grew older, he would behave.

Leffingwell wrote and asked his father to send plenty of chewing gum. He described how all the Eskimo jaws were going full speed, crackling like Gatling guns. This square-jawed, long-nosed geologist patiently cranked his Victrola phonograph and played classical music and opera, such as Eames and Melba, while Sacha repeatedly expressed his amazement by saying, "A-ka-ga," meaning roughly, "Oh my God."

As the wind tore at their former ship's walls and Leffingwell wiggled his toes to stay warm, Sacha wondered what relation his own rhythmic chant singing bore to the strange voices Leffingwell forced from the box with the crank. Outside the hut, braving the winds, the rest of the village crowded around, shivering and laughing at the strange *Kabloona* noise box.

Leffingwell showed Sacha magazine photographs of skunks, and pictures of airships and automobiles "filled him with wonder." Leffingwell wished he could bring Sacha back to civilization to fill his intelligent mind, even though other such arrangements with Eskimos had always ended poorly. But Sacha would never leave behind his family.

On September 26, 1907, ninety years before my arrival, Leffingwell wrote to his father about dispensing placebos, dressing cuts and curing boils. But some sicknesses he could not cure. Children died as they contracted white men's germs to which they had no antibodies. There was a sick baby whom Leffingwell was powerless to save. He wrote: "I have another patient now. Sacha's favourite boy (another) is down with diarrhea and fever, and I again suspect typhoid. As Sacha has been so good I shall delay my trip into the mountains for a few days until the boy is well, or dead."

Measles wiped out half the Eskimo population on the west coast of Alaska. In Barrow, the town that Sacha refused to return to, influenza had become endemic. As the demand for whale oil and corsets declined, and the whalers abandoned the Arctic and their temporary wives, venereal disease lingered. Leffingwell's party wrote that tuberculosis was the great plague of the Eskimos, knocking them on their backs in winter and then allowing them a brief recovery during the warmer summer months.

Disease became the story of the Arctic.

Omingmak, the Bearded One

I walk behind Leffingwell's shack and circle into the wind to approach six muskoxen that I had earlier perceived through my binoculars as fifty-five-gallon drums. They are the only Arctic animals whose guard fur drapes to their feet, hiding the legs. Mistaking them from a distance for inanimate objects is not uncommon. It might be a twisted notion of irony, but to me the muskoxen, because of their Asian origin and winter adaptations, represent something important in terms of both environment and culture. Each week, it seems, I discover something as vital as the missing Eskimo curlew. So I stalk these animals patiently.

I crawl on hands and knees and stand up slowly, peering into my camera to focus. The muskoxen startle suddenly and circle a calf, wagon-train fashion, offering a wall of ten curled horns and tatterdemalion shoulders, hanging clumps of tawny fur streaming in a rising breeze. Two of the adults duck their heads and brush their orbital glands against their forelegs, prompted by either fear or sexual excitement. I keep a high bluff and fifty yards between the muskoxen and me. Inuit know them as *omingmak* ("the ones with the bearded skins"). *Ovibos moschatus* is a member of the goat family, Bovidae, and it occurs to me that the bluff would be precious little defense against a muskoxen charge. Although mature bulls weigh as much as a thousand pounds, they have the cloven hooves and agility of the mountain goat.

The lead bull paws the ground, its mud brown eyes flashing. It lets out a long half growl, half burp. I drop back ten steps and bow from my waist in hopes of showing respect. The animals are deceivingly fast runners, and more than one *Kabloona* with a camera has been charged, usually by lone bulls.

Over the years, agrarian schemes, such as the herding of reindeer, the planting of various crops, or farming *omingmak*'s *qiviut* (underfur), have been introduced to the Arctic. Amid this long-established hunting culture, such profit-making schemes usually fail, with the exception of some Banks Island Inuit who collect and knit *qiviut*. These sweaters sell for more than a thousand dollars each. But most Inuit do not believe in owning or profiting from either land or wildlife; most Inuit communities still have barter economies. Successful *Kabloona* muskoxen farms exist only in southern Canada or Alaska.

Omingmak is also the only large mammal that Inuit will often abstain from eating. Although previous generations routinely ate the animal, muskox flesh is often permeated by a rank, almost sweet ammonia taste, caused by bladder leakage during butchering. Around the Mackenzie River, it remains a private joke among Inuit that white trophy hunters will mount such an unsavory head on their walls. Still, Inuit happily outfit and guide white hunters to find animals like the gang in front of my camera lens.

The muskox is unique to North America because it is the only ox, unlike the woodland and the shrub oxen, to survive the last ice age, eighteen thousand years ago. Fossil remains are spread from Iowa to New York, but never in the Arctic, where the muskoxen moved after the retreat of the continental glaciers. The shaggy ox's adaptations become apparent during the winter: *Ovibos moschatus* does not migrate south, hibernate or seek shelter. As blizzards sweep over the open tundra, the muskox simply stands still out in the open, letting its coat provide warmth, while remaining as isolated among other migratory Arctic mammals as Inuit in the tropics. Its thick underfur—beneath the coarse two-foot-long guard fur—is the warmest and softest of any animal coat on earth, including cashmere, down and the finest wools. Blizzards that leave a muskox serenely napping on a ridgetop will drive a ptarmigan beneath the snow, a fox into a den and caribou to southern forests.

For a *Kabloona* hunter, shooting such a passive animal is more a problem of investing the time to fly to the Arctic and then paying Inuit to find a herd. As I squeeze the camera lens open to procure my own trophies, it is hard to imagine how such a hunt could be sporting. Separating this animal's head from its robe of fur, bagging it up and attaching it to a wall reenacts the antiquated collector morality of the nineteenth century, when animals were killed and posed in museums to be appreciated.

Today's argument is that *Ovibos moschatus* is well managed by federal wildlife agencies in both Alaska and Canada. This wasn't always the case. The muskoxen's demise (like that of the plains buffalo) was mostly due to the arrival of the rifle, which allowed Inuit hunters, soused with whiskey or so far ingratiated to their new *Kabloona* masters' wishes, to shoot down whole herds with impunity. By the time the whalers arrived in greater numbers, muskoxen had all but disappeared from the coastline. Herds were decimated for European carriage robes and zoos. The sought-after calves (capable of surviving zoo captivity) could be plucked out of a herd only by gunning down every adult standing guard. In fifty years, nearly fifty thousand hides were exchanged with various furriers, until the Canadian government prohibited the hunt in 1917. By 1930 fewer than five hundred muskoxen remained in North America.

Thirty years later their population had tripled. Biologists are hard pressed to explain their survival, given that the animals don't reach sexual maturity

Alaskan oming-mak (*muskoxen*)

until they are several years old, and even then they are 75 percent less reproductive than deer.

By the early 1970s, after reintroduction of the muskoxen (from an inexplicably thriving herd on Banks Island) throughout Alaska and the Canadian mainland, *Ovibos moschatus* had come back. Today more than ten thousand roam the top of the continent. Another seventy-five thousand animals can be found on the high Arctic islands.

In light of the muskox's recovering from overhunting, let alone surviving the last ice age, some people might think of it as a resilient animal. Yet the greatest threat to its survival is Arctic warming, which causes rain instead of snow, icing over both its coat and winter grasses and preventing grazing. Random genetic testing among the muskox of the high Arctic has also shown that the animal is unusually inbred. The lack of genetic variation leaves it susceptible to diseases that are likely to spread as temperatures continue to rise.

Trophy hunts for the animal have provided needed income to many of the poorer Canadian villages. Some Inuit have told me that "stinky *omingmak*'s urine" is chasing away the caribou, which share the same grazing grounds. But hunting the animal to such a wasteful end only to procure a trophy, while leaving the meat and fur to rot, goes against everything Inuit once believed. It would be rare to meet an *Inuk* so disrespectful of tradition as to mount an animal head on a wall. But if *Kabloona* wants to pay cash for such an absurdity, Inuit figure, why stop them?

Anthropologic speculation about cultural origins exasperates Inuit, who believe what they can see and touch, versus carbon-dating techniques that might merely serve agendas of those book-taught *Kabloona* who do not understand the land or its People. Still, it is true that Paleo-Eskimos trailed muskoxen across the Bering land bridge from Asia. The animals later became extinct in both Europe and Siberia. In North America, Inuit followed the Bearded One's survival tactics. They made slitted bone goggles that mimic the muskox's horizontal slitted pupils to prevent snow blindness. They refused to migrate south during the winter. In addition, both Inuit and animal essentially stood defenseless out in the open as *Kabloona* decimated them. One hundred and twenty-five thousand years later the muskox has survived; two thousand years later—or five thousand years if the Inuit are proved to be ancestors of the first Paleo-Eskimo migrants— The People are still here. But both Inuit and muskox are still fighting for their survival.

Point Thompson Oil Camp

Cold rain lopes out of the sky, and except for dimpled water the passage five miles from Flaxman Island to the mainland is flat, calm paddling. I am now sixty miles from Prudhoe Bay.

I arrive an hour and a half later, with teeth chattering, at the oil-drilling site of Point Thompson. Thirty-seven trailers are stacked in rows. The contrast between the coast behind me and this camp is as sudden and unlikely as traveling by time machine into the future. It is not just the otherworldly aspects of diesel fuel and pipe and rusted metal in the middle of the Arctic wilderness. It is the change in the wilderness itself. The snowy peaks of the Brooks Range are fading out of sight, along with the rolling tundra of the coastal plain. I now behold the vast pond muskeg of the petroleum reserves, rent by water-filled tire tracks and discolored by pieces of flying plastic and foam. To eyes trained for such movement in the Arctic, the litter initially appears as low-flying falcons or jaegers.

I am shivering with the first stages of hypothermia, so I jump out of the kayak and put on another sweater. I walk briskly, putting the wind at my back to warm up. The drill pad beneath my feet is a yard thick with river gravel from Prudhoe Bay. Next to the trailers is an aluminum warehouse full of pipe and diesel engines. The drill rig is mounted over a test hole, centered in the quarter-mile-square gravel pad. Point Thompson Hole, like scores of other test holes spread across the next few hundred miles, is bereft of oil. The camp is abandoned.

Each of the dozen sleeping trailers has refrigerator-style handle doors and thermal-gasketed frames to lock out cold and wind. The various workers have abandoned clothing, newspapers, calendars turned to the previous month of July, western novels and magazines—*Soldier of Fortune, Hustler* and *Penthouse*. Until now it was more common for me to stumble upon Inuit camps than *Kabloona* enclaves, and an anthropologist might find it useful to compare the detritus that these two cultures leave behind in the Arctic. The only common denominators are the Louis L'Amour novels. Lewd magazines are not found in Inuit family camps. An unforgettable *Kabloona* from an Inuit village once explained to me, "The Eskimo has no interest in looking at naked white girls because he does not like hairy bodies found on our white girls. Somehow the Eskimo has evolved to live in a cold climate without hair."

This oil worker didn't know that hair is problematic in the cold. Beards ice up. Body hair causes perspiration. Short limbs and small noses and a high-fat diet (along with shrewd technique) are what really keep The People warm.

Otherwise, the very idea of reading *Soldier of Fortune* stories about men shooting other men would so horrify most Inuit that they would perceive the magazine as fiction. *Snowmobile Magazine* is commonly found at Inuit hunting camps because of its literal-minded presentation of machinery and parts that Inuit have a natural affinity to and dependence upon.

Unlike Inuit camps behind me, Point Thompson is also utterly separated from the environment. Close the trailer door and you enter a hermetically sealed world of fluorescent light, Naugahyde chairs, wood-veneered furniture, humming diesel engines and the clanking drill rig. A recent caribou migration along the beach on the edge of camp—shown by thousands of tracks and clumps of fur and rounded scat—must have so far startled those men who happened to be looking out their window as to make them question if they had plunged back in time. The clomping hooves and blur of long-limbed barrel-chested deer would make anyone drop a wrench and look on in childlike wonder at nature uncontested.

If ungulates failed to draw the oil workers' attention, there are three warning signs around this camp illustrated with polar bears: BEWARE BEARS. Three years ago, at a nearby camp, a polar bear wandered up to one of the trailer modules. A worker inside teased the bear by thumping a magazine against the window. The hungry subadult leaned both paws against the glass, as the bears do to sea ice to test its strength, then easily smashed it open and jumped in after the worker. He ran into the adjoining trailer and tried to shut the faulty door. The bear got into a shoving contest with the man and within seconds pushed the door open and leaped onto him. One of the man's last memories before passing out was holding up his hand to protect his face and seeing the bear's teeth slide through his hand like butter before grabbing his head, like a seal, to burst his skull. Suddenly a fellow worker placed a shotgun against the bear's side and pulled the trigger. The bear yowled, released its prey's now–powder-burned head and tried to escape back out the broken window. It took two more twelve-gauge slugs to drop and kill the bear.

Later a biologist said that the bear was a starving and remarkably light three-hundred pounder, crazed by impenetrable crates of muktuk that Inuit had temporarily stored near the camp. The bear perceived the man behind the window as a seal beneath the sea ice. The moral of the story to the oil camp was that bears were ruthless killers. Yet in my mind the polar bear had been goaded.

I spend two nights at Point Thompson Hole waiting for the icy wind to

Porcupine caribou herd migration on the national petroleum reserves

relent and keeping a close watch for signs of bear other than the three posted warnings. The sun has been setting for several weeks now. On August 13 it remains below the horizon for five hours, long enough for the first fall night. The camp becomes so thoroughly dark that I can't sleep. Surf thumps louder and icier in pitch. Something is really wrong, so I hold my breath and listen: The small birds have stopped singing.

All night long I hear brant, snow geese and Canada geese murmuring, gabbling and honking in the air above. This exodus, along with the robbery of light, produces an eerie feeling. A scared voice inside me tells me to flee while I still can, before winter comes.

By morning most of the flocks have departed, while the northern horizon bristles with the incoming ice pack. The mirages have also fled south along with the warm air. My position is precarious; if the ice pack locks tightly on the shore for the winter, I will have to cache the kayak and begin fording rivers and walking around bays and peninsulas for the sixty miles to Prudhoe Bay. None of this seems impossible: I have warm clothes, plenty of food, and large reserves of patience, along with several unread books in a dry bag.

Part of my agenda about being alone is to absorb those subtleties a partner might distract me from. Alone, for instance, I can approach wildlife more easily. Although a partner would increase the margin of safety—during a capsize, in the event of an injury, for lightening the load while increasing the man-days of food, or for scaring off bears—I want to experience the Arctic while alone to understand its vastness the way Inuit do, to hear things (birdsong, ice cracking, caribou clicking) that a companion might block with talk.

When you get to this point, seals look up and give you a glimpse of something behind their eyes. I have begun to identify and attribute meaning to the crying of different bird species. A yellow-billed loon wails forlornly, croaking, then braying out *GOHOMEGOHOMEGOHOME* from a swale somewhere behind the gravel pad. Despite soaking my feet in the muskeg, I cannot find the bird. Later a red-throated loon circles the exact perimeter of the oil camp, and without opening its short brown bill, it cries *Ohhhh-hhh, ohhhhhhh, ohhhhhh,* like a wounded child.

The eight days alone from Kaktovik to here seem like a long time, particularly while staying among the rusted leavings of a once-active oil camp. So when I hear the *whop-whop-whop* of an approaching helicopter, I run outside, anxious to reenter the exhilarating circle of human companionship.

The JetRanger sets down in the center of the gravel drill site, and the oil worker (wearing the unmistakable British Petroleum hard hat) in the passenger seat has a map spread out on his knees. I remove my wool cap and approach from the front, as the blade wallops out a vacuum two feet above my head. It is hard to control my excitement about being able to talk again after so long. When I gesture to the pilot with my hand for permission to approach his door, thinking that maybe I can give them directions on their map, the pilot shakes his head no, frowns, and motions violently with his finger for me to leave.

They take off, engulfing me in a dust storm. I have no idea of what they were looking for. Their unfriendliness is a startling contrast with the hospitality of Inuit.

Barren Ground Grizzly Surprise

Sitting in a kayak day after day is not, in and of itself, my idea of a great time. Or so I think as Point Thompson disappears slowly to the stern on August 14. Anyone who tells you that he likes paddling long flat-water distances might also tell you that he likes carrying a heavy pack, pulling a loaded sled or pushing weights in a gym.

Lost in this reverie, a half mile out from braided river channels, I mistakenly go aground. I step out gingerly away from my kayak onto ankle-deep sand shoaling. I probe the width of the bar with my paddle. Then I lift the binoculars from my neck and try to see how to pass the shallow delta.

I lower the binoculars an inch and spy a full frame view of the kayak floating fifty yards away. I begin running, fall off the bar into a mix of icy-warm ocean and river water and begin swimming. As if in a dream—my water-filled boots tugging downward—I grab the bowline and surge toward shore. This exercise in survival could be costing me anywhere from two minutes to a half an hour. Potential disasters scramble time. All I have left is shards of my former ego. I feel asinine for swimming myself into exhaustion, just as I realize that my feet can touch the waist-deep bottom. If I had lost the kayak, I'd soon be dead.

Snowflakes fall out of an apocalyptic gray sky. Ice water cascades out of my clothes. Yet I feel warm (maybe because of all the adrenaline pumping through me). Brants gabble past, veiled by the snow squall. Everything goes so quiet and leaden tight that I wonder if anyone else is alive in the rest of the world.

More hypothermically dumb than scared, I dump precious white gas onto a driftwood tangle and torch it with a lighter into crinkling life. I don't begin to shiver until the heat registers on my wooden fingers, as I spin around and around, cooking the steaming flanks of my body like sides of sacrificial beef.

I stand for hours, afraid to move away from the heat of the fire and resume the routines of setting up camp. I am angry, because I didn't come north to *survive*. I came to *thrive*. If the trip turns into a survival mission, I figure it will be a failure.

The arc of a fluent paddle stroke or the passage of hard-won miles is undeniably satisfying. Still, athletic mastery alone is not enough to sustain me. Nor do I have an *atiq,* or relatives living upon the land, or Inuktitut speech. I was born in a hospital in Providence, Rhode Island, only a thousand miles south of tree line but culturally light-years removed from the Arctic. My bloodline comes from those English pilgrims who converted the indigenes of New England. But guilt from those ancestors' mistakes does not motivate me. I empathize with The People because I understand the inexplicable value of living by instinct and sleeping on the ground and feeling icebergs collapse through the water tension palpating the hull of my kayak.

The ice pack blows in closer. Since it has stopped snowing, I sleep in shifts outside my tent so that I can open my eyes, turn my head and scout for polar bears. Inside a tent you can never know when a bear is coming. Despite my best intentions, I sleep through the four o'clock alarm and wake to the sound of crunching from beside my boat. I check my watch—5 a.m.—then jump to my feet and wave my arms in hopes of scaring off the invader. Instead of a polar bear ripping apart the kayak, a scrawny, rabid-foamed Arctic fox chewing an oil bottle is unimpressed by my performance and continues gnawing on the plastic. It takes half an hour of shouting and waving my arms to send the intruder skittering off onto the tundra.

I am tent-bound all day. That snowy evening I sleep inside the tent. Just before dawn a loud *WOOF* awakens me. I unzip the door, but the bear is gone. I roll outside and find grizzly (or immature polar bear) tracks sauntering to within ten feet of my head. Then, its claws dug deep, the prints show it galloping away. The bear has vanished, but I know what happened: It was frightened by my scent and will not come back. I try to go back to sleep. As usual, I am reduced to shaking.

Bears are a constant concern while I try to sleep at night. Although there are no records of a barren ground grizzly's stalking then eating a human, a curious grizzly could still rip up my kayak or tent because of food or tantalizing odors. Barren ground grizzlies rarely exceed eight feet in length, unlike ten-foot-tall salmon-eating brown bears in southern Alaska. Yet Inuit regularly observe grizzlies knocking char out of rivers, digging up tubers, stripping beached whale carcasses, killing and eating cubs and raking the tundra clean of berries, using their teeth like the jaws of a steam shovel.

It is rare to be attacked while traveling in a group of four or more people because grizzlies respect strength in numbers. A story keeping me awake right now tells of two men who attempted paddling the Northwest Passage three years ago. In all fairness, they were more prepared than I was, at least with extensive piles of new equipment and a firearm, but neither man had dealt with grizzlies before. Several hundred miles east of here, while they were committing the ultimate sin in bear country—cooking dinner in their tent—the smell of simmering meat drew in a hungry five-hundred-pound bear. It grabbed one of the men by his calf and yanked him out the tent door, past the stove. The terrified partner grabbed the rifle and fired a shot skyward through the nylon ceiling, scaring the bear across the tundra. A maintenance crew at a nearby DEW Line site radioed in a medevac helicopter. Even though the victim was not in danger of bleeding out, such a wound can quickly go septic. Barren ground grizzlies are famous for nightmarish halitosis; their breath stinks because they eat all manner of fermented, rotted and wormy food.

Yet another expedition fails, less than two hundred miles into the Northwest Passage. So why am I different?

Before setting up this camp, I scouted the surrounding land for bears. Island or peninsula camps minimize the odds of being stalked. I try to pitch my tent so that the wind will carry my scent over the sea rather than over grizzly habitat. If I am forced to camp among scat piles or tracks, I eat granola and wait to cook a meal until the kayak is mostly packed and I am ready to leave in the morning. While many bears are myopic, their sense of smell is likened to radar. With the wind blowing in the right direction, boiling food molecules can be lofted along in a gaseous state for miles across a landscape mostly devoid of such smells.

I have the small psychological advantage of having survived a dozen bear encounters in Alaska. After I was chased or stalked several times, it's clear to me that grizzlies have the stealth and cunning of cats. I have learned that they often run from unnatural noises: clicking off a gun safety (audible a

Barren ground grizzly along Beaufort Sea coast

half mile out to sensitive bear ears), banging pots, shooting a flare or blasting an air horn.

Grizzlies are drawn in by smoky campfires, which I save for emergencies. I also avoid fishing or carrying foods that aren't vacuum-sealed and freeze-dried. I cook quickly at mealtimes, forty yards downwind from where I sleep to keep the food smells out of my tent.

Bears can smell fear. The pheromones that both humans and animals emit when frightened signal "prey" to a hungry predator. Bears also interpret direct eye contact as a challenge.

Inuit insist that the smallish barren ground grizzly is more aggressive and dangerous than the polar bear that I am seeking. These men often liken bears to people: unpredictable and quirky, depending upon their mood or personality. Inuit hunters offer all kinds of advice about how to kill a charging bear. Some say to shoot for the hips, to knock the bear's legs out. Guides say aim for the neck. Elders show you how to parry with a knife or spear for the polar bear's heart; these men will chase grizzlies out of their camp with a mere pocketknife.

I have been "bluff-charged" twice, effectively tested to see if I'll run like prey. Standing your ground or backing away slowly while gently talking the bear down is always better than trying to shoot it. Yet talking a bear down takes nerve. Since I've done it only once (backing away while clutching a T-shirt cradling a disassembled handgun, which I was intently oiling when the bear snuck up on me), I can't say whether or not a loaded gun in my hand would make me project the wrong attitude and anger the bear. Bears can sense or smell the lack of respect exuded by an aggressive male clutching a firearm. Right now that bone-headed and pacifistic theory, while potentially true, is preventing me from sleeping at night.

Since grizzlies are famous for defending their territory, I take the trouble to pee around my tent at a hundred-foot radius. I also mark *my* territory by circling camp, spitting, and scuffing the ground. After two days in the same place, my scent is so infused into an area that I know the grizzly will concede me my small stretch of turf. If I wake up in the middle of the night to noises, I often say, "This is my camp. Please leave me alone."

If I hear something lurking out of sight, I roll outside, stand up tall and launch a flare skyward. Mostly this indulges my overactive imagination, scaring away foxes or ground squirrels.

Prudhoe Bay Finale

I give up on getting any sleep and start paddling west. It's now dark for about six hours of the night. Prudhoe Bay oil derricks separate gas from the liquid ooze of ancient fossils in a flare of yellow fire. The eerie light can be seen for miles. From behind, an orange gibbous moon, dimmed by the brilliance of the flares, shimmers against the blackened Beaufort Sea. A shiny white patina of snow covers the shores.

A snowy owl hoots, and when it goes silent, the drone that I have been hearing for weeks now resumes: *oyyyyyyyyyyy, oyyyyyyyyyy, oyyyyyyyyyy.*

This noise comes at all hours, and if you were to spend enough time alone here on the roof of North America, you could begin to question your very senses, let alone feel overcome by vertigo—best described, again, as *nangiarneq* ("kayak angst"). Day after day alone in such a place, banal sensory reception is scrambled by the vast land and seascape.

I am no longer in an Inuit place. At the Bidami refinery being built inside Mikkelsen Bay, the skyline is rent by towers and clanking, beeping D-9 Caterpillars and dump trucks. Several dozen men stop their work and watch me from a wharf as if I were some sort of balmy savage. No one waves back, and it occurs to me that maybe workingmen don't like the sight of playing men. I paddle over to a tugboat to say hi—too close, because a hard-hatted *Kabloona* leans over the railing and warns me not to get out of my boat. Apparently he has been instructed to treat strangers as oil terrorists.

That night I camp inside the peat moss delta of the Sagavanirktok River, watching bits of yellow, white and blue foam from the Bidami construction site blow by in the wind. The Brooks Range marches resplendently across the southern horizon, a ten-thousand-foot snow-covered patrol of soldiers camouflaged by sooty clouds. The tide rises higher and higher, pounding the littoral with surf, a comic book page, a rusty-nailed plank, three Valvoline bottles and two coffee cups. I shiver through the night to stay warm.

In the morning I paddle with my back to the waves and ride the river current out around a peninsula blackened with oil. I round the corner and spy Endicott oil field, built atop an artificial island several miles away. The stadium-size infrastructure of pipe and aluminum is connected to the mainland by a long causeway, buzzing with shrunken-looking pickup trucks.

I aim toward it, leaving the sheltered lee of Point Brower for a maelstrom of wind and water.

A snowy owl sitting high on a snag turns its head back and forth, seemingly nervous about my bravado. I bow my head in supplication, then say, "I know it's stupid, but I have to go for it in case it snows again."

I think about how Inuit befriended me as a total stranger and a *Kabloona,* how eating the char that Thomas Gordon pressed into my hands as I left Griffin Point still keeps me warmer than Power bars. I think about new friends and know that they will not return any of the letters I write, but they would not hesitate to watch over me, feed me and shelter me if I came this way again.

In 1826, John Franklin relied on his Indian hunters for game. His conscripted French voyageurs rowed him down the Mackenzie River to this point. Then, facing winter, he turned back. Although he had discovered Prudhoe Bay, he had no idea of the value of its black mud. He was a glandular man, also slow in both thought and action and uninterested in learning how to hunt or use dogsleds. He abstained from hiring or learning from the local "Eskimaux." Although his boat was nearly overwhelmed by the press of their kayaks in the Mackenzie Delta, he refused to let his men shoot their guns.

If he had been born a hundred years later, his gentle and plodding disposition would have made him a better bureaucrat than an explorer. But as a Royal Navy officer he was duty-bound to overcome the limitations of his own flesh. The governor of Hudson's Bay Company complained about how Franklin could not do without "three meals per diem" and how "with the utmost exertion, he cannot walk *eight* miles in one day."

Franklin had earlier succeeded in canoeing east from the Coppermine River to the Kent Peninsula. While wintered over, some of the men resorted to cannibalism. Ten died. Franklin later became famous in his best-selling book as "the man who ate his shoes."

By reaching Prudhoe Bay, he had mapped and crossed half of the Northwest Passage. He was knighted upon his return to Britain.

My own trip, 439 miles and thirty-two days west of Aklavik, has shown me what it means to be a discoverer. The foremost lesson is about letting go of my ego. As I battle through confused waves, it occurs to me that my Northwest Passage seems as hubristic and beside the point as searching for birds and polar bears. Looking inside myself, I realize that whatever cockiness and swagger I started with are now gone.

Waves churn over my bow. A contrary current tries to pull me out to sea, so I fight with all my strength to reach the causeway, hoping that I won't pull a tendon. My nose itches, but instead of stopping a stroke to scratch it,

Burning off gas at Prudhoe Bay, Alaska

risking a capsize, I lower my head into the next wave and make my whole face go numb, losing the itch.

I paddle beneath the sheltering causeway to lose the wind and current, while above, a security truck follows me at a slow crawl, its lights flashing, and then brakes to a stop. I pull onto the shore. Since Greenpeace has been running interference with seismic oil boats in the area, security clearance will be a problem. I get out, half hypothermic, and crutch my cramped legs with the paddle.

I am done for the summer. This is as far as I had hoped to come. It is August 18.

Next year I will come back to the Mackenzie Delta and try going east. Since Arctic summers are so short, I will start in the spring and travel with a sled atop the sea ice. This is how my mind works: roving over the future in order to defuse the anticlimax I now feel about ending my trip.

The uniformed man stands on the roadway above. It is not likely he will be offering me food or a place to stay. Still, I am happy to see him. He is tall, redheaded and clean-shaven. He is leaning the palm of his right hand on a holstered gun. Like me, he is shivering in the winter wind, so he will understand how cold I am. I smile up at him and shout, "Hi. I just paddled from the Northwest Territories, from Mackenzie River. Pretty wild out there today," glancing back out at the white-capped bay I just crossed and figuring it would be a stretch to mistake me for one of the Greenpeace oil terrorists (who travel in Zodiac boats).

I had already anticipated it, like the close of every hard trip, like the resounding ring of a gong reverberating inside my head. It comes with the guard's shout, reminding me that I have left Inuit hospitality and welcoming me back among my people, my world: "You know you're not allowed here, so don't you come out of the water!"

PART TWO

Into the Great Solitudes

Back to the Mackenzie

On April 12 I hire a Somalian cabbie to drive my dog, Elias, and me ninety miles to Tuktoyaktuk (Tuk). Our two sleds are lashed on top of the roof. We crest Inuvik's riverbank, whisk down into a foot-deep overflow pool and then slalom out onto solid ice. Driving the east channel of the Mackenzie River makes touring the infamous Dempster (which cost me three flats the previous fall) look like an interstate by comparison.

Inuvik is connected to the rest of the world by the 440-mile washboarded Dempster Highway, famous for shredding tires. Its lone gas station does a booming business in tire sales and flat repairs as the snow melts to expose the shale road surface. Driving the highway, for most people, is an adventure in itself.

Inuvik is party capital central. No mainland Arctic town features such a worn-out, bloodshot-eyed, cigarette-smoking, staggering, sweet-breathed populace. Midnight is lively on the main Mackenzie Road, as revelers traipse back and forth between two bars, shouting vague threats up into the aurora borealis while navigating huge slush piles. Most Inuit come to visit family; stock up on food, booze and sundry supplies; check into the hospital; attend art festivals; enroll in Aurora College; attend court; cash checks; or take temporary jobs.

Inuvik is also a town of red tape, built by and for the government. Mixed in with the drinking revelers is a placid and tolerant set of bureaucrats.

Townspeople do not complain when drunks shatter a restaurant calm. Anything's better than the traffic jams and congestion and madness of southern cities. Also, the RCMP are the most garrulous and helpful police imaginable. Still, there's something askew here, as if most of the white men and women had slipped a cog. It might be the recovery phase following another cold and dark winter, but the impression lingers, like a reverse phenomenon of Inuit's trying to adapt to the southern world, that *Kabloona* do not yet have the cultural tools to be living north of the Arctic Circle.

I am no exception. My home and my world are two thousand miles south, sheltered in the trees. To make things even more difficult, I fell in love with a woman while driving back south last fall. Three weeks ago I asked her to marry me. She accepted, and while hatching plans for a wedding next spring, I trained with Elias. Mostly we went out sled pulling. Elias learned her "right" (gee) and "left" (haw) commands, pulling me as I skated along on my skis (skijoring), while we both got fit.

Now, in addition to the usual dread of loneliness, I am gripped with anxiety about taking care of myself. If something were to happen to me, June would be wrecked. All my visions of independence and adventure are in danger of being drowned by the knowledge of my own selfishness. Although June was too kind to say it, I can imagine her thought as I left her in the Denver airport: *If he really loved me, would he be leaving me?* So now it's all I can do to look out the taxi windows at the intimidating immensity of the Mackenzie Delta. Pulling a sled across this frozen seascape is going to be a lot more work than paddling a kayak. At least I'll have Elias for company.

The river ice beneath the station wagon is several feet thick. According to local gossip, the river is opening up, so the cabbie drives in silent and nervous agitation. Elias's continuous barking doesn't help. I open the window (plunging the temperature 40 degrees), and she directs her barking outward, toward occasional orange barrel road markers, sawhorses over thin ice, snowplow berms and fox tracks ambling across featureless vanilla frosting. The road is one continuous traffic-free ice arena.

An hour downriver the cabbie announces, without removing his eyes from the barely discernible bulldozer tracks cleaving the ice in front of him, "We be on the ocean now."

White prevails here, now that the last gnarled spruce trees, willows and dwarf birches have disappeared in the rearview. The only relief to the monochromatic vista are aqua blue pressure ridges, frozen swells of the Beaufort Sea. Even Elias seems subdued, allowing me to roll up the window and shed my down parka.

I roll down the window a minute later because she still carries the acrid air of a skunk she chased during our last night in Colorado, despite my bathing her calico cat–patterned fur in vinegar. Her rottweiler–Australian shepherd heritage prompts her to growl at anyone approaching our sleds and to chase anything moving: cars, snowmobiles, deliverymen, joggers, bikers or wildlife. Elias will be pulling her own sled full of dog food, keeping me company and earning her keep as a bear alarm. Every little trick that I would like to claim as my own for safety or efficiency has already been figured out by Inuit, who were using barking dogs to warn them of approaching bears long before Lewis took his Newfoundland dog, Seaman, and before Clark hired Sacagawea. After relentless teasing by Inuit last year, I am also toting a brand-new nickel-plated marine shotgun. June insisted.

The hills that Elias and I can see to the east are pingos: ancient lakes drained into the ground. As the water and permafrost below expanded, the skin of tundra was pushed back upward like a great frozen boil.

Out beneath the next pingo is Kittigazuit, the site of the measles and

The village of Tuktoyaktuk in April

tuberculosis epidemic. After it was abandoned in 1902, an Anglican church opened, followed by the Hudson's Bay Company trading post. In 1934 Inuit moved farther down the peninsula, to a ship harbor that Inuvialuit named Tuktoyaktuk ("resembling a caribou"). Legend has it that an ancient shaman petrified a herd as it waded out past the shore. Today, during low summer tides, reefs resembling caribou are exposed.

The cabbie nervously accelerates as he first lays eyes on Tuk, causing more skidding sashays across the frozen Beaufort Sea. From eighteen miles out, we can't actually see the town, but we can discern what looks like a giant golf ball mounted on a tee, which proves to be the radar dome of Tuk's abandoned DEW Line site.

The cabbie hits the beach at full speed, to hydroplane us up over any weak ice, and suddenly we are driving up the shoreline and onto the main street. Most of the several hundred homes are square and prebuilt kits; the more expensive tar-papered homes are rectangles of cheap plywood, with several windows. Dogs are tied up beside houses. In place of cars, snowmobiles crowd Arctic double-entryway doors.

Elias is barking again. We tip the cabbie 25 percent of the $200 fare.

The Tuktoyaktuk Oil Boom

Ever since *Kabloona* arrived, the Mackenzie River Inuvialuit have been try- ing to survive cultural assimilation. While survival used to constitute merely long winters or diminished game, the twentieth century brought industrial whaling, foreign diseases, dropping fox fur prices, social welfare, banned sealskins and the false promises of big oil.

In the late 1970s, oil companies turned the former Inuvialuit hunting community of Tuk into a boomtown. Watching America's windfall at Prud- hoe Bay, the Canadian government rescinded a 1926 order called the Arctic Island Preserve: 450,000 square miles that belonged to Inuit. Before, when white men needed to get in, they had to be granted permission. When Inuit protested these lands' being opened up, Prime Minister Pierre Trudeau replied that all Canadians, regardless of their origins, should be equal.

He then gave the oil companies fat tax incentives to drill, causing a stam- pede into Tuk not dissimilar to that of the nineteenth century's Klondike gold rush. Thousands of exploratory drilling permits and 450 oil leases were released on the former Inuit preserve. The Canadian minister of energy declared that there was enough oil to power Canada for a millennium and gas for a third of that time.

Kabloona businessmen moved in to provide whatever services—hotels, meals, groceries, and entertainment—the locals weren't already providing. Many Inuvialuit cashed in on elevated wages and began driving new pickup trucks back and forth on a few miles of town road. Whaling, fishing, hunt- ing and trapping began to lose their appeal. Oil and gas rigs were drilling offshore, but the work crews were based in Tuk, so many hunting families simply stayed in town and took advantage of a full-bore cash economy.

Most Inuvialuit were unhappy about rampant development. Taking inspiration from their Iñupiat cousins (just as the Alaskan oil bonanza had inspired the Canadian government), Inuvialuit began fighting back. Begin- ning with their introduction to *Kabloona* whalers, the Alaskan Inuit who moved into the Mackenzie River region had long been aware of the power of money.

After the whalers left ninety years ago, Knud Rasmussen had nearly fin- ished dogsledding from Hudson Bay to Alaska. The anthropologist was charged $8 for a leg of caribou that would have been free farther east. Even though he spoke Inuktitut (with a Greenlander's dialect, pronouncing, for instance *t*'s as *s*'s), the locals here cut him little slack. In 1922 he wrote about their shrewdness: "The first Eskimo immigrants from Alaska, . . . like the white trappers, were now seeking their fortune in the country of their 'wild' tribal kinsmen. They were extremely hospitable, spoke fluent English, and soon proved to be thoroughly businesslike. We did not take long to discover that we were in the land of the Almighty Dollar."

Evolving with the times a half century later, Inuit formed the Committee of Original Peoples' Entitlement (COPE) and a brotherhood called Inuit Tapirisat of Canada (ITC). COPE and ITC found government grant money and tax incentives to fight the invasion of the 1970s. They also badgered the government through the media, making Prime Minister Trudeau and his minister of energy look like racist opportunists, which wasn't hard to do (leading *Kabloona* to accuse Inuit of becoming uppity). In 1977 COPE presented a formal land claim to the government.

Oil spills and industry could destroy the environment that Inuit depended upon. A huge gas pipeline slated to run up the Mackenzie River valley to Edmonton (like Prudhoe Bay's oil pipeline to Valdez) was quelled. By the early 1980s the price of the oil barrel had dropped. Businesses moved out of Tuk overnight.

Before big oil crashed, however, the government had been anxious to appease Inuit so that oil-rich reservoirs could be fully exploited. In 1978 an agreement in principle was reached. Inuvialuit surrendered rights to 344,000 square kilometers, much of it rich in oil. After the oil companies pulled out in 1984, the Canadian House of Commons had no choice but to pass its earlier agreement, the Western Arctic (Inuvialuit) Claims Settlement Act. Twenty-five hundred Inuvialuit were compensated with $152 million for economic development, housing and health care. Each elder was given $2,500 in addition to two payments of $500 per year. A regular dividend of $100 was paid out to every Inuvialuit. Herschel Island was made into a territorial park to be run by Inuvialuit (as a twist on the culturally insidious reign of American whalers), while most of the Yukon Territory's northern shore was closed to development and made into Ivvavik National Park. Inuvialuit were also given title to 35,000 square miles of land, of which they own full mineral and oil rights to 5,000. Inuvialuit money and land were put into trust so that they would not sell out. The Inuvialuit Regional Corporation, as it turns out, invested most of the money wisely.

This rise and fall of capitalism within their egalitarian community matched the earlier whaling scenario. Those Inuvialuit who had not been profiting from the oil companies continued collecting government social assistance checks, as they had been doing since 1953. Few returned to living off the land. Although the settlement act seemed a benevolent gesture, fourteen years later "Tuk," in the words of an Inuvik bartender, "is a hole."

(To show their generosity about granting permission for crossing their private lands, once Inuvialuit leaders learned that I was traveling alone and on foot they immediately acquiesced without asking for any fee.)

Most Inuvialuit within the six communities—Tuk, Sachs Harbor, Aklavik, Paulatuk, Inuvik and Holman—think they might have settled too quickly. Many of The People claim that the land reform has done little to improve their lives. Still, the Inuvialuit settlement act is more financially generous than any indigenous Canadian reform.

Staying in the Eskimo Inn, I learn that Tuk (population 918) has hit hard times. Most people here don't work. The optimistic calculations of the 1996 Labour Force Survey cite a 40 percent unemployment-to-population ratio (Kaktovik has 30 percent unemployment). Of the 605 residents who are fifteen years and older, 20 have university degrees and 25 graduated from high school. Most remarkable of all, according to the locals, no one under the age of fifty speaks Inuktitut. According to a recent government census, 705 of the residents speak English, 5 speak French and 200 speak "other languages" (other than the original Inuktitut tongue, that is).

Like many Arctic villagers, the townspeople have voted (by a very narrow margin) that they will not allow the sale of alcohol within town limits. This does not stop people from driving, snowmobiling or boating ninety miles

Pull-starting a Ski-Doo in twenty below

upriver to Inuvik's liquor store. In such a "damp" (versus dry) town as Tuk, it's not illegal for residents to bring in their own booze. In 1995 the Alaskan Iñupiat community of Barrow voted to ban the sale of alcohol in town. Drunk driving dropped 79 percent, fights by 61 percent and felony assaults by 86 percent. But the ban was overturned the following year because residents felt that they wanted the same rights as *Kabloona* without being made to feel like criminals for drinking in the privacy of their own homes.

It is common for the Tuk Co-op to prohibit the sale of certain products to known alcoholics. One of the Inuvialuit clerks tells me that aftershave, deodorant, even hairspray are commonly filtered down or inhaled for their alcohol content. Kids *and adults* inhale Lysol, glues and gas. But once a known drinker or huffer is refused these products, he or she simply stands outside the door and asks a friend to buy it.

Sledding East Through Eskimo Lakes

Pulling a Sled

At 9 a.m. most of the town is still sound asleep. Jim Elias drives up to the hotel in a ruckus of snowmobile treads churning gravel. First I explain my mission: dragging my sled twenty miles east across the Tuk Peninsula, then northeast along the shore ice of Eskimo Lakes, three hundred miles to the village of Paulatuk.

"Alone?"

"Well, I've got my dog."

"You got a firearm?"

"You bet."

"You want me to give you a ride?" He smiles.

I pour him a cup of coffee while he shows me a few pointers on the map. While holding a cigarette, he draws a line across the peninsula, zigzagging his pencil across the map's landscape at about the same speed—forty miles per hour—that he pushes his Ski-Doo (no *Inuk* calls it a snowmobile, and "to snowmachine" is the verb of choice). He describes the shape of hills, erases then redraws two sections he drew wrong, then decries the inaccurate mapping of this particular quadrangle. "Government never quite gets it right," he says.

While interviewing explorers, I have only seen one man—Dr. Bradford Washburn, who mapped Mount Everest, the Grand Canyon and Mount McKinley with laser-beam technology—describe a landscape with such accuracy. It is as if Jim too had majored in cartography. (I learn later that he didn't graduate from high school.)

For several years he worked for the RCMP in Kugluktuk, eight hundred miles away. When they transferred him back to Tuk, so he could live among his friends and family, he didn't last the year. His sister, Eleanor, proudly tells me it's because his natural leer earned him too many push-ups in training and made his superiors think that he was disrespectful. But the truth of it is that no Inuvialuit can police their own hometowns without losing friends. Sooner or later Tuk drinkers become victims of violent binges and have to be arrested.

Jim wears a red, white and black checker-flagged Sno Pro Racer snowmobile suit, Scott ski goggles, caribou skin mitts and blue jeans underneath. His preferred Ski-Doo is the Polaris because it is easy to change parts, which are readily available in Inuvik, even though the Polaris needs constant lubrication. His father, Jorgan, has always preferred Yamahas and has been driving an old model without having to fix anything yet.

Jorgan's white hair is shorn close to his skull; his cheeks cave to a narrow and jutting jaw. His eyes shine with a warm, regal gaze, which his sons and daughter share. He is missing some lower teeth, but his upper front teeth are inlaid with gold.

Father and son routinely put ten thousand miles a year on their machines while building new *kamotiks* (sleds) out of plywood and two-by-fours every other winter. They sprawl their legs out over their "mechanical dog teams" with the same sense of pride with which their relatives shimmied into kayaks a thousand years ago. Like the kayak, the Ski-Doo has allowed modern Inuit to climb another rung higher in their hunting culture.

Jim tells me that although cars have advanced my culture, they're useless in a town with so few roads. Even four-wheel-drive trucks won't help for hunting or checking a trapline. Dog teams give his family access to hunting lands, but at the cost of constant maintenance and frequent outbreaks of parvo or rabies. It takes more than an hour to harness a dog team to a sled. It takes less than ten minutes to fuel, preheat and hook up a *kamotik* to a Ski-Doo. In two hours a Ski-Doo can cover the same ground that takes all day in a dogsled. Jim adds with a leer, "You bet that they make a lot less noise too, eh?"

I leave that day, dragging my sled, depressed every time a snowmobile roars past. After eight hours of work I go as far as a snowmobile travels in a half hour.

Ski-Doos, Jim explained, travel faster than bears, wolves or caribou. Some hungry, impoverished, or rifle-jammed Inuit hunters simply chase these animals down until they drop from exhaustion. Jim claimed he doesn't condone this behavior.

There are disadvantages to snowmobiles that Jim didn't mention. Their noise frequently scares seals back into their sea ice *aglus* (holes). Parts break. Also, riders get into trouble because they travel large distances so quickly.

On my second day sledge hauling across the peninsula I meet Jim's fourteen-year-old son, Kurt, searching for an *Inuk* girl who lost the trail on her snowmobile; she radioed Kurt for help, then found the trail once the fog cleared. But more than anything else, the snowmobile, like the outboard engine—by its disorienting speed and alarming engine noise—has distanced Inuit from the land and wildlife that they love. Ask a walker what he sees out upon the land, and then ask a snowmobiler. The main difference is usually quantitative: The snowmobiler sees more land, a value (quantity over quality) that traditional Inuit used to deplore. Most Inuit say that wildlife is scattered so far and wide that only a Ski-Doo allows them the access they need. But arguing the aesthetics of snowmobiles, like asking how to distill alcohol out of Right Guard, will not bring me inside these good folks' heads.

That night I write in my journal: "Fighting back all the notions to retreat. Just have to give it 10 days or so and I'll fall into a grace. Today hard because of a headwind and thoughts of my June; my delightful June—who has transformed my world. Am I crazy to be here?"

Jim comes out for an afternoon ride across the Tuk Peninsula on my third day out. He is appalled at my lack of progress, let alone that I am still planning to ski several hundred miles to Paulatuk.

"You should take a Ski-Doo," he suggests again. He's not joking. Skis are not Inuit tools, and I am trying to deny that a snowmobile comes from my own speed-oriented culture.

After four days of sled hauling, my Elias is still growling at the amount of space surrounding us. The treeless horizon stretches on in every direction as far as we can see. Elias is verbalizing our unease.

I'm a mess. There is no way of communicating to June that I am alive. Every two hours, when I stop for a break, my thoughts turn south instead of remaining focused on the tasks in front of me. I try, forlornly, telepathically (I have no other options), to let her know that I am mostly okay.

*Jim Elias
showing me
a route
on the map*

My heels are bleeding raw from pulling 150 pounds on my sled. Small bands of caribou come trotting in off the sea ice to investigate us. Elias in turn chases them, pulling me and our two sleds for several hundred yards until she realizes that the caribou are slowly pulling away from us.

Ptarmigan explode out of the snow in front of Elias's nose, then squawk, croak and cry gutturally as their wings *thwock* them away from harm. Bear tracks litter the ice, and the horizon continues to yawn on all sides in a monotone series of rolling hills and endless white ocean. The wind often comes straight into my face, out of the northeast, and brings Elias sheltering behind my heels as I trudge forward with my face tucked into a windproof neck gaiter. Several times a day I take out one of two digital video cameras and film myself, hauling the sled or talking about how lonely I feel.

It has taken me three and a half days to ski thirty-five miles, a distance I could cover at home in several long runs. Sled hauling is the most grueling and boring work imaginable. Putting yourself into such a broad landscape, alone, in the interest of just making progress can make you feel as if you were walking on a treadmill. Ptarmigan, two scraggly foxes and scores of caribou offer needed distraction, as well as give some depth perception to the nearly featureless seascape.

Nor is there any navigational challenge. I merely follow the snowmobile tracks toward yet another abandoned DEW Line site, like walking on a deserted road. I have counted seven trashed *kamotik*s, countless cigarette ends, one oil can, four gas containers, a can of Spam and bread crumbs so petrified that Elias drooled them out.

We see our first ringed seal this afternoon, sunning outside its *aglu* in 50-degree heat. Aerial censuses estimate that there are a million of this species in Canadian waters. *Phoca hispida* has always been the foundation of Inuit socioeconomy—for skins, blubber lamps and food. Its Inuktitut name, *natiq,* is the root name for an array of descriptions: *tiggak* (breeding male), *netsilak* (adult), *netsiavinerk* (silver jar pattern of a molted pup), and *netsiak* (white coat of a newborn that has not yet acquired its insulating blubber). The seal has a pattern of white-ringed spots, like the inverse of a leopard and not dissimilar to Elias's mottled and soft coat; its shiny head is remarkably similar to a dog without ears. While this adult is probably too wary for a stealthy polar bear, its less experienced pups are easy game. To test this out, I let Elias pull us toward the sleeping seal, and it suddenly comes alive and plops headfirst back into the *aglu* with a hollow-sounding *koosh* of icy brine.

I suddenly realize that the ocean drops hundreds of feet deep. We slide away as gently as possible from the seal hole.

Minutes later a snowmobile's distant buzz transforms into a coarse, chainsawing whine. Buddy Gruben shuts off his Polaris. He is bound back to Tuk from the DEW Line site that he and a nineteen-man crew are dismantling.

In 1912 his grandfather moved from Alaska to the Mackenzie Delta. John Gruben married an attractive Iñupiat woman, built a house and lived "rather splendid for these parts" (according to a visiting scientist). Gruben was a Swiss-American trader known for his hospitality. Today in Tuk the Gruben house perches like Prince Bandar's in Aspen: high above town and built from varnished logs rather than cheap plywood. Inuvialuit Grubens now own barges and a gravel company—gravel being in high demand whenever a road or building needs to be placed on top of soggy tundra.

It comes as no surprise when Buddy Gruben mentions that Jim is his brother-in-law. Many people in Tuk are related, and it is not unusual to see intermarried cousins. He fiddles with his hearing aid (deafness is common among intermarried Inuit, not to mention the damage caused by two-stroke engine noise or the recent news of industrial toxins falling into the Arctic and causing ear infections). Buddy asks me if everything is okay. He then cautions me to put on some sunglasses and sun cream. Buddy smiles slyly as he explains that blue eyes and white faces like mine will burn up in the sun reflected off the ice.

His face is purple-polka-dotted with what looks like sun-cancer melanoma. An angry-looking welt on his neck might be a knife scar. Gruben is stockily built, I realize when he stands up. He looks a foot up into my eyes and asks where I'm from. Then he politely says that he would love to see the Rocky Mountains someday.

I reply, "You know, where I come from is okay, but I like the bigness of your backyard here."

"You got all your freedom here," he replies, waving his arm broadly across the horizon. He asks, "You got a firearm?"

I point to my sled, nodding. Gruben flicks his smoldering cigarette where Elias won't eat it, then yanks his old Polaris starter cord. It chuckles, once, twice, then catches. Roaring off, he yells back, "Sure you don't want a ride to town?"

Several minutes later the chain-sawing engine noise shuts down, then a single shot from his 30.06 hammers the silence with echoes, like the drop of a primordial tree: killing the ringed seal. Gruben leaves it there on the snowmobile trail so he can pick it up and give it to someone later or maybe eat it himself. For now he's rushing back to the Jamboree, a weekend celebration of spring, spread out among six different villages so that those Inuit inclined to travel will not miss a single party.

"Everyone in Tuk gets drunk," Gruben had said, "you cannot get around it."

Natiq, the Ringed Seal

Bringing Bearded Seal and Fish

Throughout the Arctic, the ringed seal, or *natiq* (pronounced *na-chick*)—unlike whales, caribou or any other animal—was prized sustenance for sea-based Inuit. *Natiq* were the fingers of Sedna. After epidemics wiped out villages, whaling died and the fox pelt market collapsed, The People still had *natiq.* One seal could feed a man for six days. After the snowmobile's arrival in the early 1960s, making seals an easier target for hunters, the sealskin sold for $14. It was not a lot of money, but it was the only cash crop left to many Inuit.

Inuit continue to share the meat of animals with everyone in the village, just as they believe that the animals are sharing their energy with the hunters. It is a system of high and treasured reciprocity. If a hunter betrays this system of sharing, this country food, then the community shuns the hunter. In turn the animals supposedly withhold themselves from being hunted.

Seventy years ago Stefansson met a blind *Inuk* on Victoria Island who confessed to having hidden seal meat from the rest of his people. The others had found the meat, distributed it among themselves and castigated him for not sharing. Within a year he had lost his sight. He begged Stefansson to pass the story on to others so that they would avoid selfish ways.

Many *Kabloona* today would perceive such tales as myth. Gruben, when I told him this story, said (in the laconic parlance of Inuit acceptance), "Must be."

Most *Kabloona* believe that the functional hunting, killing or consumption of animal meat is a biblically written right, that the animals were put on earth for man's dominion. Yet Inuit subsistence hunters, including those who attend church, are still attuned to an unspoken rite that expresses the equality of human beings and animals fulfilling obligations to each other.

Inuit hunter peering into seal aglu

Outside environmentalists, long nurtured by the traditional image of a harpoon-bearing Eskimo standing motionless for hours over an *aglu* hole with a dog team harnessed nearby, have judged the gas-guzzling snowmobile as an unfair shift in the Noble Savage's traditions. No matter that the Dorset Culture's technological marvels (umiaks, *iglus* and toggle-headed harpoons) similarly advanced northern culture more than two thousand years ago. This *"minimax* strategy," according to the anthropologist George Wenzel, has always allowed Inuit to make new adaptations to expend the least amount of energy for the greatest return. Since the kayak first plied its way into the waters beneath my feet, The People evolved because, as Wenzel writes, "more durable materials and tools meant less time spent in the manufacture of artifacts and more time for resource and social activity."

By 1976 (when Gruben was in his twenties) a sealskin fetched about $24, allowing Inuit to buy gas, bullets and new snowmobile treads and to resume their cultural hunting activities without relying on social assistance checks. That year sealskin sales brought over $1 million to twenty-three different Inuit communities. This cash crop gave many Inuit economic and cultural autonomy. Their 1976 yield of over three-million pounds of seal meat was free and more nutritious than the expensive beef imported into these communities. The ancient rite of hunting *natiq* also offered more prosperity than any modern, altruistic government reforms. Certainly Inuit, who had lived off the land and its animals for centuries, did not think that the growing animal rights furor would affect their own traditions.

The following year Greenpeace and Brigitte Bardot followed the lead of the International Fund for Animal Welfare and widely publicized the plight of the endangered harp seal. The snow-white pup was clubbed by *Kabloona* Newfoundlanders and sold for its fur coat, rather than eaten. Inuit paid no attention. For food and gas money, they shot and skinned adult ringed and bearded seals, whose populations remained healthy. Most Inuit figured that their practices had no relation to the anti–harp sealing war being waged down south. But they were wrong. The ensuing boycott included sealskin of any species.

In 1977 sealskin prices crashed. The prices rose several years later, but by 1983 Europe had banned importation of all seal fur. About the same time that the oil companies pulled out of Tuk and the Inuvialuit act was settled, the animal rights movement dealt Inuit a crippling blow. Although Inuit continue to harvest adult ringed and bearded seals for country food, sealskin sales for the Arctic have dropped from $1 million to $17,000 a year.

Now, when Gruben recovers from the Tuk Jamboree, he might come back to cut out the meat from this ringed seal and most likely discard its skin on the ice. Only a few Inuit still sew sealskin kayaks or kamiks when they can travel with outboard engines or Sorels. Now, Gruben says, kids will hang out at the co-op and get their friends to buy them hair spray or glue because they are bored and hunting is no longer their passion.

After the European boycott of sealskins, the president of Inuit Tapirisat of Canada told the Ottawa Parliament: "One of the disasters that has happened as a result is youth suicide . . . we have youth problems, drug and alcohol abuse, violence. There is very little employment and when you are hit with something like [the loss of sealskin markets] you are bound to see these problems come up as a result."

Another group of cultural preservationists, trying to repeal the sealskin ban, told the United Nations that Inuit culture had turned into "the most socio-economically depressed population in the world." In the same letter Greenpeace was accused of forcing Inuit off the land and into social welfare, causing deterioration in family and community lives.

In 1977 and 1978 suicide among Inuit males soared to .5 and .8 percent respectively, more than doubling the rate of any previous year. In 1978, .2 percent of Inuit females (who until then had rarely killed themselves) committed suicide. Social workers who did not understand Inuit traditions of course pointed to alcohol, social conflicts and bad weather, while those who did said that the victims were making an "effort to return to a traditionally accepted and respected death." Inuit pointed out that the sealskin crash began in 1977, just before the suicides.

Eleanor Elias, who believes that the sealskin boycott started their social problems, told me in a flash of passing anger, "I would like to take one of those Greenpeacers out on my trapline and put them out of their misery."

The Hunters of Anderson River

A week out, and the thaw continues. Creeks are burbling down onto the sea ice and pooling, forcing me to ski far out from shore or drag my sled above the gravel beaches across dry tundra. The Kevlar sled, designed for snow but now being dragged across rock and jagged sea ice, has popped several rivets. My ski bindings are beginning to wobble disconcertingly.

It is a scary thought that El Niño's warming might melt the sea ice before I can reach Paulatuk. My progress slows to less than ten miles a day.

Arching, bow-shaped clouds appear on the eastern horizon as the west holds a promising smear of blue. Later it goes white, and the fog rolls in. Just as suddenly the sun breaks through, and I doff my wind jacket. The temperature climbs to 50 degrees.

Arctic foxes cock their heads from nearby eskers as we yank our sleds through dwarf willows. Every hour I stop to eat some nuts and dump water out of Elias's sled. I notice that her prints across a snowbank are blood red, which sends my heart pounding until I check her paws and find squashed tundra cranberries.

Elias and I crossing frozen lakes toward Anderson River

Some days I put her paws in padded fleece booties so the sharper-edged sea ice won't cut her. After eight or nine miles she gets tired (like me) and looks up, whining. I pull off her harness and drop my pack attached to the sled, and she runs barking circles around our sleds, then rolls in the snow.

As Elias prowls a perimeter, I cook and set up or pull down camp. This takes two hours every morning or every night, no matter how fast I move. Every night, exhausted, I knead her paws, carefully checking for nicks or bruises. My blistered heels have scarred over in a smooth and shiny raised lump of old ivory tissue, which I brush nightly with antibiotic cream.

I wish I had had the courage to ask how Buddy earned the scar on his neck. A day south of Anderson River, I meet his cousin Roger Gruben, bouncing his snowmobile across bare tundra and ripping through willow thickets.

"Warm out, isn't it," he says.

"Ever seen it like this?" I ask.

"Never, not in twenty years."

Gruben was the director of the Inuvialuit Regional Corporation. He was voted out after being charged with tax evasion and stealing thousands of dollars. (The charges were later dropped.) Jorgan Elias told me, "This is what happens when you get educated men. They say educate the Eskimo, and I say no way because then they just steal and cheat when they get smart."

I asked about Roger's education, and Jorgan replied, "He graduated."

I asked, "From where?"

"High school, which is a big thing around here, particularly for Roger's age."

Gruben is in his mid-forties, and unlike many people from Tuk, he held a position that gave him enough money to see the world. After answering the usual question about where I'm from, he replies, "Very clean there in Colorado. I was impressed by how clean everything was."

Now he runs a guiding business. Behind him, on two more snowmobiles, are a barely recognizable plump and pasty-faced couple from Wisconsin. I last met these dairy farmers on the airplane to Inuvik, wearing flannel shirts and Levi's. Now they are wearing caribou mitts and white canvas anoraks smeared with seal blood. They are as surprised to see me fifty miles from Tuk as I am to see them.

Roger says, "Yesterday we snowmachined all the way back to the tree line. A really interesting transition that. From the sea ice here right up to the taiga forest."

"The trees are that close?" I ask.

"Yes, there are trees at the tide line in the Kugaluk River because of a biosphere shift that sends the tree line sweeping north. They say it happened during a warming trend about year 1000 A.D."

"That's only thirty miles from here?"

"That is correct."

Gruben talks as if he reads a lot, with a distinctive *Inuk* spin: He politely defers to me. Yet as a man with a degree he can't help his curiosity. After all, I am a *Kabloona,* whom he normally tows along behind. So he asks, "How can you possibly get enough food in your tiny *kamotik* to last all the way to Paulatuk?"

On my tenth day out, I spy the high bluffs of the Anderson River. Tuk is now 110 miles away. I am exhausted from having to pull my skis on and off while sledging across unseasonably dry tundra. My bindings are pulling out of the skis.

I have come to accept the selfishness of my mission here. June met me after I had hatched this scheme to solo the Northwest Passage, and although the ache of missing her is intensified by isolation, I have to own up to my dreams. My main promise to June is simply to make it home.

It takes another hour to tiptoe two miles across thin river ice, crackling out in disconcerting spiderwebs beneath our feet. We pass a snow-white lump of dog fur and flesh (bitten by a rabid fox, it was then shot before it could infect the other dogs). We climb up the riverbank to a red-roofed, five-room cabin. Two dozen filthy white dogs are clanking thick chains and howling like hungry wolves.

Jim Elias's brother Brian pokes his head out the door and announces, "Coffee's hot."

For the next week I wait for the thaw to play itself out. Brian is a soft-spoken, trusting nineteen-year-old with a ready smile. He cooks pork chops and potatoes while I rehydrate freeze-dried beans and rice. We play cribbage, hunt for ptarmigan, gather firewood from driftwood piles along the ocean and talk about books. His favorite is Louis L'Amour's *Last of the Breed,* about a Russian "native" moving to Alaska.

The cabin, I learn from its logbook, was built for government reindeer herders fifty years ago. Abandoned by Inuit hunters each spring, it is resettled by passing canoeists and biologists.

The cabin logbook starts in 1948. Most of the recent entries were from Tuk hunters, with concise and thankful descriptions of egg gathering and bird hunting. Occasionally *Kabloona* clients described polar bear hunting or biologists rattled off bird statistics. Throughout the years only one *Inuk* entry bragged (perhaps fictitiously), "Shoot 270+ Geese in a few days and it takes seven sleds to bring it all back to Tuk." Otherwise Inuvialuit entries lack boasting or quantitative accounting of animals; to do so, if I understand Inuit culture, would show disrespect for man and animal fulfilling their obligations to each other.

Kabloona entries are rife with measurements and vaunting:

> . . . shot a 9′ polar bear. . . .
> . . . killed an eleven foot bear out on Whale Point. . . .
> Banded over 1,000 whitefront, 1,000 canada Geese, and several hundred brant. . . .
> Saw two belugas 10.5 miles upriver!

Below a thankful seven-year-old boy's sketch of a gun and a caribou, a drawing shows a hunter standing with upraised arms on a huge pile of car-casses. The text that follows is staged, a *Kabloona* canoeist's parody on Inuit hunting:

> June 1 97 When I grow up I want to be a killer like my Dad. He kills lots of tings. He kild 500 geeze in one day. He killid a giant polar bear musta been 15 foot hi. He killid lotsa muskoxe an cariboo. I hear him say bout how much he killed. Thousand of em. He tell me to kill as much as kan when I kan cause later thre wont be any. Hees so smart.
> Wyatt Trash

I have to read the signature aloud to understand the final twist of self-parody. After reading it all to Brian, he only smiles politely. He is not inter-ested, or upset, about how *Kabloona* perceive him or his culture.

"Does it bother you what this guy was doing?" I ask.

Brian only shrugs. It doesn't occur to him to be offended, let alone judg-mental about someone who is slamming his culture.

I ask if he prefers to call himself an Inuit or an Inuvialuit, but he does not know the difference. Nor can he spell "Inuvialuit." I ask if he can speak his culture's original language, and he explains, "Most people in Tuk speak English and could not be bothered with the other."

Every day he rolls and smokes a half pack of Export tobacco, drinks a liter of coffee and reads one book from a library of several dozen left by summer visitors. Like most Inuit I meet in hunting camps, he is clean and well groomed, taking the trouble to heat water and sponge-bathe every morning.

We stalk the willows looking for ptarmigan. Brian has a potential shot or two, but before he can lift the gun to his shoulder, the ptarmigan squawk up out of the brush like airborne windup toys and fade out of sight. He turns around and smiles. His eyes are angelic. Thoughtful. And ego-free. He would rather be partying than hunting.

Back at the shack he tells me about a polar bear coming into camp once while his father was gone. When I ask if he had to shoot it, he looks exasperated. "I fired over his head to scare him away. He was starving and just grabbed some seal meat."

"How old were you?"

"Maybe ten."

Brian is here watching his family's dogs because he just finished a year in the Yellowknife penitentiary for assaulting an RCMP. He tells me quietly, his soft brown eyes falling to the floor with embarrassment, "I was drinking, and he kept bothering me, so I punched him out."

This is so uncharacteristic of Brian's behavior that it seems he could be describing someone else, which is how many Inuit think after being let out of jail following drunken brawls. They no longer feel responsible for their behavior, since alcohol so radically changes their personality. Brian mutters that his brother snowmachined him out here to keep him out of trouble in Tuk.

That night his sister and father, Eleanor and Jorgan, arrive on two snowmobiles, dragging *kamotiks* loaded with a dozen yelping sled dogs and their Cuban-American hunting client, Cephirano Machado. They have spent ten days out on the coast looking for polar bears. But the sea ice has melted so early that they found only old-squaw and eiders swimming on open water. No seals, and therefore no polar bears.

Jorgan sees me, a stranger, at the door of the cabin and asks, "Already. Another?"

(Later he explains that he thought I was another "mice trapper," or biologist, two months early. Jorgan becomes jolly at the idea of unarmed men roaming the tundra, counting lemmings or birds.)

It is no small coincidence that I named my dog after a saint with the same name as this family. At first they all think I recently renamed my dog to get a laugh out of them. Then Jorgan explains that the government could not pronounce his grandfather's last name. Nor does Jorgan seem to remember it. So his grandfather's first name became their family name: Elias. These names also hint that his grandfather may have been a Russian whaler, who had married his Alaskan *Inuk* grandmother. But if Jorgan is aware of this, he does not say.

Somewhat exasperated from all my questions, he explains that since The People his age did not know what day they were born, the government arbitrarily gave all the older people in Tuk the birthdate of January 1. He shrugs, graceful about those things that he cannot change.

"Which gave The People all the more reason to celebrate harder on New Year's Eve," he says with a boyish grin, showing where Jim got his smirk from.

Jorgan hands Cephirano a flask of bourbon but asks him to drink it out of sight from Brian. As their client retires to his own private room in exhaustion, Jorgan tells me, "I used to be a drunk but quit twenty-five years ago."

Wearing ski goggles has left pale rings around his eyes. The rest of his face is dirt brown from sun reflecting off the sea ice. He says his tan is caused not by sun but by the salt air. He also insists that the color of tea is influenced by whether the water is taken from a spring, a river or melted sea ice. Everyone listens politely when he talks, although his children—to judge by the blank looks on their faces—are not really sure how his old Inuit myths intersect with their own world.

Jorgan's faulty hearing makes for halting conversation. It takes a sharp ear and intuition for the context of his statements to fill in the gaps. If you close your eyes, Jorgan's (and his progeny's) muted talk, peppered with quick repetitions of phrases, sounds like that of schoolchildren singing half-forgotten choruses.

"I quit with none of those clinics or nothing just cold turkey, just cold turkey," he says. "Every few years most of The People get so mad about the drinking problem that they vote to keep liquor stores out of Tuk, which they done for sixty years. Sixty years. This is wrong."

I ask Jorgan why.

"Because town would clean itself up after a while, and people wouldn't be trying to hide their drinking or bootlegging it."

This prompts Eleanor to say that her dad owns a stun gun. Jorgan jumps up in excitement and runs to his duffel so that he can break it out and show me.

"Because he is old-fashioned and keeps his door unlocked in Tuk, and when someone comes knocking drunk, he always lets them in the door, and someday they might try and take him out," Eleanor explains.

The nine-volt prod's batteries are dead. Jorgan is still bouncing boyishly. He disassembles the stun gun (after his daughter finds him a screwdriver), studies each part in hopes of learning its secret, puts it back together and holds it against his arm and presses the trigger: nothing.

Periodically, he rolls DuMaurier smokes from a big can with the Canadian warning label, "Cigarettes cause strokes and heart disease." Eleanor makes him swallow diabetes and high blood pressure pills several times a day. He tells me, while turning the cabin's contents upside down for his missing pills (which Eleanor found later in his pocket), "Cigarettes are good for me, and lots of Eskimos like me are tough enough so that smoking do not hurt us."

"Have you read the label on the can?" I ask.

He asks me to read it to him. Immediately he replies, "That's baloney."

Eleanor rolls her eyes from behind her father. She is a plucky thirty-five-year old, wearing her hair in a shag and dressing in a white button-down blouse and fashionable jeans. Since Jorgan is too modest to say it, and she is nothing if not proud, she announces a non sequitur to change the subject: They are the only family left in Tuk still living off the land. And she is the only woman running a trapline in the western Arctic.

Jorgan relies upon her like a surrogate wife. She uncovers his cigarette lighter and prescription pills, fixes him coffee, cooks and washes dishes. Twice a day she calls Tuk on their trappers' radio—powered by nine D cell batteries and left on day and night, filling the cabin with white noise, which further mutes their shy sentences. When they're not looking, I turn the volume down; when I step out of the cabin, they turn the volume back up. On the radio she often talks to her mother, whose English is so garbled and bent by caroming radio waves that it might as well be Inuktitut to my ears. Eleanor also arranges the sale of animal skins for their client and badgers an Inuvik ski plane pilot to come in and get rid of Cephirano, whom she teases nonstop because he can't take care of himself.

Cephirano tells me that he escaped Cuba thirty years ago on a boat to Miami and has since set himself up as a successful building contractor. He is in his mid-fifties and shaped like a Mediterranean wine casket, and he modestly admits that he is out of his element in the Arctic. His glasses fog over. He has difficulty walking up the short river bluff. He is wearing so

Eleanor Elias on trappers' radio, Brian
reading in back

many layers of fleece and down clothing that it is hard for him to raise his arms above his head.

Cephirano is polite, soft-spoken and not altogether different from his Inuit guides. His limited grasp of the English language forces him to talk simply, while his Cuban roots were altered, if not assimilated, by a larger and more homogenized society. He has paid Elias $7,500 (U.S.) to guide him on a ten-day polar bear hunt. Last year he paid several times as much but complained to the Tuk Sport Hunting Association that Jorgan and his daughter took him out for only four days instead of the promised ten. This year Jorgan is compensating his client with a cheaper hunt to set things straight. While out of earshot from everyone else, Cephirano says he would never go with the incompetent Elias family again.

"A black man weel alwayz be a black man, an Indian alwayz an Indian, and Eskimo alwayz Eskimo."

"What about Cubans and whites?" I ask.

"You and me, mon, we are deefferent."

"How?"

"We are civeelized, mon," he pleads with an innocent-sounding whine.

Out of earshot from Cephirano, Eleanor says she does not trust him because he put a whalebone that she wanted in his pocket. Also, he plans on paying her friends with a personal check for bearskins instead of the cash he promised over the radio. This mistrust, however, is not really about her client as much as it might be the Elias family's naiveté toward operating in a service-oriented economy.

No one in the Elias family feels particularly frightened of polar bears, but they are fiercely protective of the animal. "It is ours," Eleanor insists, "just like the whalebones and dinosaur fossils on the beaches."

She says that if someone like me kills a polar bear without an *Inuk* guide, even in self-defense, he will be fined and deported. (I learn later that this is not true.)

Eleanor explains that since 1970 each Inuit community has been allowed a quota of polar bear kills, about five hundred total; Tuk is assigned fifteen for "cultural or economic purposes." Biologists have counted more than fifteen thousand polar bears roaming the Canadian Arctic. If Cephirano ever kills a polar bear, by shooting it from at least fifty yards away while bracing his scoped rifle over a dogsled, a recent repeal within the U.S. Marine Mammal Protection Act will allow him to bring the skin into the United States for $1,000. Since he has not yet killed his own bear, Eleanor arranges for him to purchase skins in Tuk: a wolverine for $300, two wolves at $500 each, two grizzlies for a total of $2,000 and a polar bear for $1,000. Cephirano plans to "live mount the grizzly and white bear locked in mortal combat" in his living room.

I cite the Russian photographer who had five hundred close polar bear encounters and never needed a gun. Cephirano, armed with three rifles and a handgun, loudly debunks this as fiction. He thinks that polar bears, like the African elephant he plans to kill this spring on a $30,000 trip, are "dangerous animals."

"I hunt for pride as a professional hunter," he says. "I am doing the world a favor. Polar bear animal who never change their path; ninety-nine percent of the time it kills whatever is in its path. If your dog is there, it eats your dog."

Elias is gumming my hand as he says this. Eleanor asks how much I will sell Elias for, explaining, "Its coat will bring a good price in town."

I wonder if she's joking because none of her family has patted Elias in the last few days. The lack of vaccinations in their team cost them all of their dogs during last year's parvo outbreak. A dog's life is cheap out here. They repeatedly warn me not to let "it" loose "because any of our dogs will make it dead meat."

I did not expect these people to be advocating animal rights. Yet at this moment it surprises me that this stuffy cabin, with Eleanor sitting cross-legged on the grimy floor beneath an empty chair, could be a scene from an old, blubber lamp–smoking sod house.

Brian is now engrossed in a book about the Hell's Angels, given to him by Eleanor. She talks at length about how the motorcycle gang has taken over Whitehorse, that many are rich, and how smart and tough they are, cutting off the official tattoo from the arm of anyone who is not a real Hell's Angel.

Jorgan chimes in. "These Hell's Angels would never make it in Tuk, though."

Eleanor tells me about a local who committed a revenge killing of two white men. He is now locked up indefinitely. "He is one of most dangerous men in Canada. And he is *Eskimo,*" her father proudly finishes.

He then recites the story about the former RCMP officer who had a reputation for cleaning up tough Inuit places like Cambridge Bay. "But when he came to Tuk, Tuk cleaned him out instead. Now he's just a prison warden in Yellowknife," Jorgan concludes, fluttering his hand down to show the man's career descent.

Eleanor says that criminals from Tuk are too smart to get caught and tells about a local who robbed the Mackenzie Hotel in Inuvik.

"That was never solved, that crime, even though a lot of locals know who did it. It's the same with bootlegging and drug dealing. No one from Tuk is going to turn anyone else from Tuk in. And Eskimos never get long jail sentences, unlike white men, so they have nothing to lose by killing someone."

I interrupt only so that they can clarify details. Both Jorgan and Brian have healed-over pinkish lacerations on their faces. This reminds me that knife fights were a featured entertainment on Barter Island during trading sessions between the Alaskan and Canadian Inuit at the turn of the century.

It is tempting to believe that this family has fallen on such hard times that they need some distinction, some pride, maybe even a perverse notoriety. The stories go on and on: about how their friends will offer a woman $30 for a bottle of hair spray while sitting in an Inuvik bar because it gives a better high than whiskey or how bottles of mouthwash that are 17 percent alcohol go like hotcakes at the Tuk Co-op.

By midnight the cabin is so torpid with the 90-degree heat of an ungoverned woodstove and billowing cigarette smoke that I can no longer breathe or think. I excuse myself and go for a walk. No one else is interested in joining me out in the cold. Even the elder hunter, Jorgan, has not walked out of the cabin for two days, preferring to look with binoculars through the windows for any caribou foolish enough to walk by a cabin with no less than eight loaded firearms and four crack shots.

As soon as I close the door and step around a blown-off window shutter bristling with rusty nails to discourage bears from breaking into the cabin, a polar wind sneaks up into my nylon jacket and past three layers of fleece clothing. I look up to the thin, creamy blur of a cloud-hung moon, tightening the sky around it like the skin withering around the scars of my heels. A splintering crack shoots off from the half-frozen river below. A husky rattles its chain as Elias pushes her cold nose into my hand. We retreat back inside.

In the face of it all, my ideals about the mythic Inuit persona have been altered, through no fault of The People themselves. It was my culture that taught me that they still hunt polar bears and seals with spears. Assimilation has wrought a world of change. I'm certain as I go to sleep that something of their original culture still remains. Even if they have changed, what culture, including my own, remains static?

In the morning Eleanor hands me a cup of coffee, so in Inuktitut I say, "*Cowanna.*"

In reply to my "thanks," Eleanor says that she learned more French in two years from her high school teachers than she learned Inuktitut in six years.

"They kept teaching me the same words over and over again. Like *tuk* for place and *tuktu* for the animal. Dad has tried to teach me, but it's too hard for me to make the sounds."

Jorgan, sipping his coffee next to the woodstove, says he understands the language, but ever since one of his elder friends died a few years ago, he no longer has any use for Inuktitut.

Our conversation is interrupted by the whine of snowmobiles. Outside the windows, Jim and his son, Kurt, are stretching their sore backs after a six-hour ride from Tuk. Brian's face visibly brightens at the sight of his admired older brother striding into the cabin with his Cheshire cat grin and a cigarette dangling Bogart style. Everyone lights up except fourteen-year-old Kurt and me.

Jorgan is peeved that his son Jim hauled some parts to the nearby DEW Line site for just $200 a day, instead of the $300 that he deserves. Jim sips from his coffee and tries to deflect his father's criticism by telling a good Tuk story: "Hoo boy, that was some Jamboree. I am not totally over it all."

"How come Buddy [Gruben] didn't come back out with you?" Brian asks.

"He's, uh, sort of sick," Jim stammers, then clarifies, "Well, he came by and started saying some bad stuff, so I punched his lights out and he's too fucked up to see straight and ride his Ski-Doo out here today."

Both his son and younger brother are hanging on Jim's every word, who tilts back his Indianapolis 500 cap and continues, "Yeah, I hit him real hard, hard enough to do some damage. Yeah, I hit him real hard all right." Everyone assumes, knowing Jim, that Buddy must've deserved it. But no one asks why.

I change the subject and ask his son, "No school, Kurt?"

Eleanor answers for her nephew, who is too shy to reply. "They promoted him two grades even though he can barely read, so we took him out and we are going to home school him this summer."

Although no one is interested in accompanying me with a dog team to Paulatuk, Jim volunteers that he might consider snowmachining me over for $1,000 plus the down jacket that I am wearing. I thank him, knowing I can't accept. Then Eleanor offers to sell me one of her dogs for $300. Big Boy might allow me to make better time than I have with Elias over the next 230 miles. Eleanor suggests a test drive.

Slipping Big Boy's head and lifting his leg into a harness is a wrestling match, which I eventually win but not before getting peed on. It takes all my strength to get Big Boy out of the dog yard without a major fight.

Hooked up to Elias and me, the 130-pound dog is so powerful that he yanks Elias off her feet repeatedly. But I can't get him to hold the trail; he's more interested in snapping up old dog turds and ripping out whole willows by the root system. His eyes are running goop that blackens his muzzle, while jaundice-colored fur is falling off in great clumps. He smells like rancid seal meat, and his nose is scabbed over. Out of sympathy I reach down to pet him, and seeing his advantage, he effortlessly bowls me down to the ground, then begins humping me as Elias snarls to my defense. Now I know why Jim was smiling more broadly than usual when I left the cabin.

Jorgan waits for me back at the cabin, concerned. It is the first time I have seen him outside in days. He scratches his head and smiles at me, "You know, if you continue to Paulatuk in these thaw conditions, next time we see you you will be in a grizzly bear scat."

This is all the inspiration I need. Until now things simply didn't feel right. Yet quitting only on the premonition that I would not make it would be a noodle-backed move, because disastrous foreboding is common on these sorts of trips. I have experienced these premonitions on several previous expeditions. In the end, skill and stamina carried my friends and me through. But this time I have an Inuit elder, descended from generations that have relied upon intuition and age-old knowledge of the land, passing me a tip. I would be a fool not to listen.

In case I didn't hear his warning, Jorgan adds that the Horton River has probably flooded over the sea ice, making it impossible to reach Paulatuk. Walking the shore, I would be exposed to an angry beehive's worth of barren ground grizzlies. Jorgan offers to share his flight out to Tuk. But it will cost me.

That afternoon the first ski plane lands Brian's supplies for the next month: hamburger, a case of Coke, white bread, cigarettes, chicken and bags of barbecue-flavored chips. Cephirano rides out alone on this plane, filled with his firearms and excess equipment, for a quick stop in Tuk, where he will further stuff the Cessna 185 with animal hides. Eleanor confides that he is paying the pilot $1,000, "white man's prices," while our flight, crammed with Elias, Jorgan, Eleanor and me, and flown by Willard Hagen, a Gwich'in entrepreneur, costs only $800.

From above, the land is a browned tundra carpet potholed by frozen white lakes. Nothing moves below. While Eleanor and Jorgan sleep through the hourlong flight, Elias and I stare below, wondering at the starkness of it all, an immense land and seascape that we managed to cross without accepting a single snowmobile ride. Nonetheless, I am haunted by shame and disappointment for quitting.

Back in Inuvik, standing on the frozen floatplane lake, Willard, the bush pilot, seems perversely excited by the opportunity to put a white man in his place.

"Trying to walk the Northwest Passage, uh-huh. I've heard it all before. Did not get too far, did you?"

"No, I didn't. A matter of ambitions exceeding conditions."

"Why did you turn back?"

"Because the sea ice is getting flooded by all the creeks, and it's likely that the Horton River will let go."

"The Horton never lets go until late May, and you can just walk around the creeks," he says, laughing.

"Maybe you can fly around flooded sea ice, but I can't walk around it."

"This country has a way of putting you in your place, doesn't it?"

"Yes"—I let out a long breath—"it does."

"Why did you turn back *really?*"

"Because Jorgan Elias said if I kept going, I would be history."

"What do those Eskimos know anymore anyway?"

I telephone June, figuring that she will have departed for a friend's wedding in Venezuela. To my great surprise, she picks up on the first ring. At the last minute, sensing that something was wrong with my trip, she canceled her flight south.

Elias and I catch a flight home the next day. Although I am overjoyed to go back, I am plagued with doubts about quitting. At night I lie awake with thoughts of what might have happened if I had kept going.

Several mornings after I get home, the television producer for the documentary I've been filming rings me up. He begins yelling over his speakerphone. He accuses me of coming home because of June, and he is not entirely wrong. "What's a little bit of water on the sea ice?" he asks. He threatens to sue me, while I gently remind him about the elder's warning about bears and that the contract I signed with him prohibits me from taking unnecessary risks.

I feel a great reprieve to learn that the Horton River really has broken out over the sea ice, flooding the bottom of Franklin Bay for miles, as a prolific band of barren ground grizzlies begin snuffling the tundra for ground squirrels and licorice roots. As April warms to May, Inuit hunters will neither walk nor snowmobile across thinning ice and deepening slush.

Ever since Inuvialuit have been moved into centralized villages, those former settlements between Tuk and Paulatuk—Kevorik Landing and Stanton and North Star Harbor and Baillie and Langton Bay and Letty Harbor—have been burned down or swallowed by the sea. This stretch of continent is now almost as abandoned by humans as it was before the Bering land bridge.

By May I am training on Colorado lakes with a detachable sailing rig for my kayak—sponsons, outrigger arms, leeboard and mast. My heart is with June, but my thoughts fly north, as I imagine millions of birds repopulating the deltas, trumpeting across the sandbars, web-printing the beaches and sliming the tundra ponds with gizzard-borne algae and southern seeds. Phalaropes and sandpipers and plovers are now picking for the larvae of the midges and crane flies that feed schools of arctic char.

Who knows? Maybe I'll finally even catch a glimpse of the elusive Eskimo curlew.

Searching for an Eskimo Curlew

On June 20, once the satellite sea ice maps show that the ocean has melted, I fly back north without June or Elias. I am so anxious to make up for lost time and miles that June nearly kicked me out of the house. From her perspective, it's better to have me gone than stuck at home pacing and talking incessantly about the Arctic.

North of Yellowknife, looking twenty thousand feet down from the airplane windows, I am happy to see that the ice has come off the lakes. Up north the ice pans are pulling out with thunderous cannon fire reports, releasing the land. I think of polar bears paddling and riding the ice pack, stalking seal pups.

From Inuvik I fly back in toward the Anderson River. Another bush pilot dispenses the usual cautionary advice to me, the southern greenhorn. For twenty-two years now I have listened to the warnings of these celebrated northern bush pilots, who have dropped me off or picked me up in the most remote places imaginable. For transportation they are indispensable. Yet it is rare to meet a bush pilot whose perspective isn't colored by the vastness he darts across. It's as if the land has become a private reserve that he alone gazes upon from the safety of a third-story window. I always listen to these men, if only to affirm those clichés that I am trying to escape in the wilderness. I listen to them as I would a cabbie: for folksy, thirdhand news about bears, river crossings, ski descents and mountain routes. This place that they pass by faster than migrating birds is a geography that Inuit families have lived in for centuries—a place that, to be understood, must be earned with sweat and muscle fiber.

As the pilot drones on, my eyes are locked below the wings, trying to gauge the blurred scrape of eroded bluffs being slapped by ocean. Lone pans of ice are so dazzlingly white against the royal blue sea that I pull on my sunglasses. I am interested in how far the deltas stretch, how many whales are out there, and, once I am plunged over into mind-numbing solitude, how I will stay sane.

Beneath the mudbanks of the deserted cabin, I watch the floatplane fade into a silver sparkle until I can hear only river caressing shore. I am alone. I will not let myself quit this time, and I am ready to let go of everything to realize my dreams. I must let go of all self-absorption and stop feeling belittled and pay attention.

Mosquitoes bounce greedily off my ears, caribou tracks dapple the mud in parallel crescent-moon script, and the river swallows a diving loon's yelp whole. I lift a cupped hand out of the delta and taste sweet ice melt with no salt. Tide's out.

There is no sign of the Elias family in the cabin, and although they had no use for the yellow, cigarette-smoked maps on the wall, Eleanor replaced the *Kabloona* map wall with new vinyl-coated quadrangles. The cabin is immaculately clean, stocked with food and conspicuously missing its cache of rifles. Grizzly claw marks decorate the ceiling.

I step outside and confront the windy vastness. My legs are shaking, and I am suddenly uncertain if I should cry about the mosquitoes or drop in fearful prayer. I want this land to reveal itself to me. All adventurers share this dilemma of trying to be appreciative while simultaneously setting ambitious goals. The danger of course is that you start seeing the landscape as an adversary or something you have to conquer. To get beyond this jock perspective, you have to banish your ego and seek out harmony. I want to feel all that surrounds me, as the poet Byron wrote, along the lines of my blood.

This is a place bedrocked with dinosaurs, as enormous as the sea, and older than the glaciers. But Inuit do not live here anymore, even in this cabin, in face of the psychological price to be paid.

I am scared shitless.

I paddle ten miles to the black mud outside the delta and gingerly step out of my kayak. Angry arctic terns swoop and dive, protecting a nest. A brant hen rolls off and waddles silently down into a mud slough. *Branta bernicla* is a shortened, plump cousin of a Canada goose. I stoop down and note in my journal that she is incubating three chicken-size ivory-colored eggs on a hollowed-out nest of silver gray down preened from her body.

The delta smells like a dried-out dog yard, while terns waver opalescent against the cloudless blue sky above. As far as I can see, the ocean shores are plastered with rich brown river mud and the distant white necks of nesting tundra swans and shimmering black water. I leave as quickly as I came, knowing the terns will guard the nest until the brant returns.

From somewhere close, I hear the two-tone *Cur-leeou! Cur-leeou! Numenius phaeopus,* the whimbrel, wings past like a boomerang. Its legs are flung behind, and its long bill curls downward, almost mimicking the brown Eskimo curlew. I know it is a whimbrel because of its large size and grayish color. Its wing tips are barred. The whimbrel cries, *Kew-kew-kew-kew-kew-kew!*, then disappears into a horizon wavering with the gray summer heat and memories of birds long gone.

Roderick MacFarlane, who named the Anderson River after his boss, found the last Eskimo curlew nest in 1866 and sent his specimens to the Smithsonian Museum. His Arctic collecting, which supplemented his fur

*Reaching for grizzly graffiti on the
Anderson River Delta cabin ceiling*

trading, stopped shortly after the measles hit. MacFarlane wrote that the
"Esquimaux" who had collected his curlew specimens "were carried off by
the fatal epidemic of 1865." Like most Hudson's Bay Company traders, he
left the Anderson River region when his fur collectors died off. A century
later the search continued for the Eskimo curlew.

In Massachusetts during the early 1970s, two different observers picked
out a migrating Eskimo curlew's distinctive pale cinnamon wing linings and
the lack of barring on its primaries. (A century ago, on the island of Nan-
tucket, riflemen bagged seven thousand Eskimo curlews during one afternoon's sport.) Also, there were the two unconfirmed sightings on the
Mackenzie River a decade ago.

Hunters in the Midwest used to knock more than two dozen out of the
sky with a single shotgun blast, and if the Eskimo curlew was fat from its
winter graze in southern Chile and Argentina, the still-warm birds hefted in
at about a pound each in a man's hand.

Numenius borealis was first classified in 1790 as one of four North American curlews. The bird had no less than forty names, but in the heyday of
late-nineteenth-century hunts, it was most commonly known as the doughbird, after its huge fatty reserves for migrations. Long before the Eskimo
curlew was so named in 1834, the Inuit had been calling it *akpingak*.

For me, seeing even one Eskimo curlew—it used to fly in sky-darkening flocks—would be like reaching the summit of an unclimbed peak. Flocks once wheeled in tight formation a quarter mile high, then dropped, skimmed the ground and simultaneously threw out thousands of four-toed feet, filling fifty acres of cornfield. The Eskimo curlew was easy to hunt, and Omaha hunters filled whole wagons with the birds in an afternoon of sport. One commonly held parable is that the eradication of an animal has to do with whether or not men like to eat it. Other birds removed from the endangered species list—the peregrine falcon, the osprey, the bald eagle and the brown pelican—are not so palatable. But of the doughbird one connoisseur said, "The flesh of the Eskimo curlew is said by all who have eaten it to have been exceedingly well flavored, and . . . the equal if not the superior of any of our large shore birds."

Its *tee tee tee* resembled an immeasurable tinkling of sleigh bells or, from far away, the wind whistling through a ship's rigging.

I don't want to dress out the skin or even photograph an Eskimo curlew; I just want to lay eyes on it. The bird would give me that same joy of the early voyageurs seeing nature unbound, as it was meant to be.

In the 1970s an ornithologist combed the ground from the Anderson Delta several hundred miles east. But after a decade of searching (playing recordings of the little curlew's cries and crisscrossing the summer nesting grounds on foot and helicopter) he found only whimbrels. It appeared that the larger bird had been able to chase out the overhunted flocks of timid Eskimo curlew. While half-hour tapes were playing, several whimbrels aggressively approached to within thirty feet of the little curlew recordings.

It occurs to me, as the abandoned Inuit settlement of Stanton appears ahead of the Klepper, that the ornithologist may have been similarly struck by loneliness out on these tundra shores. All the people had vanished. As he combed the deltas for a lost bird, named after those people, his tape recordings drew no response. The land seemed deserted.

Battling to Cape Bathurst

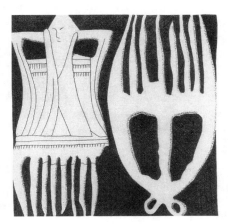

Two combs

At the former trader's post of Stanton, marked by a tilting cross up on the hillside, only one cabin still stands. All else has been carried away by the ice pack. I boot open the crooked door and enter a hive of grease and battery-acid smells. On a table, in an extraordinary coincidence, I find a note from some Montana friends, Jon Turk and Chris Seashore, two weeks out from Tuk, who attempted this same journey sixteen years ago: "Thanks for the roof. We caught a [fish] out in front. Bound for Pond Inlet."

They quit a few weeks later, whipped by the knowledge that the passage would take them three summers rather than one. The note is dated July 15, 1982, but folds as crisply as if it were yesterday. The brief glow of familiarity is overcome by my fear that history will repeat itself, that winter will shut me down as it did Jon and Chris in Paulatuk.

The cabin is filled with rusting snowmobile parts, a romance novel (marked "Property of Brian Elias"), hundreds of browned-over batteries and wall art. It's Brian's crayoning: a snowmobiler flying through the air above an upside-down airplane.

I sprint outside, thinking that I hear a barren ground grizzly rifling through my kayak on the beach. But there is only wind chattering against the spray skirt. I am making scant miles because of it.

Damned wind.

The stretched horizons have shaken me so badly that I can't write in my journal, lying snug under the waistbelt of my pants, clammy up against the small of my back. Journal writing, after all, is about being honest with yourself. If I record this sort of fear and sleeplessness, this sort of constant looking over my shoulder, then I will have to carry it with me in the kayak every day where these feelings might drown me.

I run up above the cross onto a hillside and look through my binoculars at the tundra rolling back to a boundlessness of distant cumulus. Out beyond my kayak, a flock of mergansers kicks by. To the south, a white-fronted goose escorts seven waddling goslings beneath a bluff. Too far away to hear, a flock of glaucous gulls worries a school of fish. It's all so sublime and still that my teeth ache, while somewhere in my gut I pine for a sense of belonging, some companionship, even some noise with which I can assert my presence. The limitless-looking vast horizons have reduced me. I aim the shotgun up toward the distant clouds and fire, pump and fire, pump and fire, until my ears are ringing and the chamber is empty.

Short of bawling some pagan scream, and inasmuch as I lack the vocal cords to howl, this will have to do. I reboard the kayak feeling Lilliputian. I am still too gripped and lonely to appreciate all that surrounds me.

My hands are so swollen with salt sores and tendonitis that I cannot make a fist. The cold water has wrecked me. Reaching inside the hull and pulling out food, stove and fuel hurts like bee stings every time my injured knuckles bump wood.

But I am not turning back again. I will tape the paddle to my hands if I can no longer hold it. Thinking this, I fight a more few miles north in the gale.

I would love to have someone to talk to. In lieu of a radio or satellite phone, I have quick-release strapped a brick-size personal locator beacon (PLB) onto the kayak deck. This tool is a concession to June in case plans go awry with a head injury, a bear mauling, a capsize, appendicitis or a life-threatening disorder. As a last resort only, I will extend the antenna on the PLB, unlock the switch and turn it on, signaling a Russian or U.S. satellite that will immediately transfer my distress signal and position to a Canadian military base. Then I hope the RCMP will figure out how to come get me.

If I broke a leg, I could probably paddle myself to safety without tripping the PLB. Signaling others to risk their lives and come rescue me from a vacation gone sour is not an option to be taken lightly. Almost every time I look at the device, my imagination gets the better of me. There are so many things that can go wrong out here.

The wind continues howling out of the northeast. I sleep fully dressed in the sandy lee of my kayak, ten feet from the surf, ready to jump in and paddle at the first respite. I have collected almost forty miles while walking knee-deep in broken waves, lining my boat out beyond the breakers. This five-mile-per-day pace is only half what I can make man-hauling a sled.

At dawn on June 27 I cross Harrowby Bay against a legion of whitecaps and against my better judgment. Like most days, it is about 60 degrees, but out on the water and in the wind it feels 20 degrees colder. Two miles out, the waves suddenly lose their predictable rhythm, and I am forced to muscle through a chaos of spumy blackness that runs up over my spray skirt, goose-bumping down my legs and puddling over my toes. I cannot afford to stop and don my PFD because any loss of momentum against the sea's pushiness will capsize me. I punch back at the wind and try to visualize the mile-distant shore growing closer. I am so certain that the waves will knock me over that I eventually go into a trance of focused fear, uniting every iota of balance and strength that I own just to put dry land beneath my feet again.

Once the arctic terns begin swooping by, turding on my face, screaming shrill ratchet notes into my ears and dragging their tiny talons across my pate, I realize that I will not drown. But waves continue to block my vision. Old-squaw gabble, common eider wings flurry and a red-throated loon's eye glows like a hot coal. I feel my way behind the lee of a peninsula. On a calm shore I roll out and splash up onto granular sand, lose traction, fall down with my numbed legs, then hug a polished boulder.

It was only a two-hour, five-mile crossing. Yet it felt as if a day had gone by.

According to the map, this bight of land stands west like the head of a striking snake coiling up the ancient riverbed of the Horton. If it were April, I would walk fifteen miles up the old riverbed, then portage five miles over the Smoking Hills cliffs onto the western shore of Franklin Bay. Twenty-five miles east the Horton has carved its new channel sometime since the last

Common eider nest, eggs and chick

ice age, punching through the Smoking Hills and doling out sand effluvium over Franklin Bay beaches.

Seen by the high-flying sandhill cranes, the Horton River curls southeastward up out of the giant bay, gouging out Precambrian granitic canyons—and watering dwarf birch, willow and heath. Forty miles upriver the first stunted spruce trees cling to its warm banks. The tree line then follows the river back south, paralleling the Anderson and Hornaday Rivers into undulating uplands, wrinkled with glacial eskers, littered with shale, polka-dotted with water and underlain with permafrost several hundred feet thick. All speckled, of course, with millions of birds.

The tree line curves from the Mackenzie Delta a thousand miles southeast, arcing long beyond the Horton headwaters, all the way down to the refrigerating mouth of Hudson Bay. This great wedge of tundra, called the Barren Lands by former explorers, is a riot of green summer bog.

Seen by an astronaut at night, this tundra roof of Canada would have only several points of discernible lights, generated by Inuvik, Kugluktuk, Cambridge Bay, Gjoa Haven and Churchill. Paulatuk, Umingmaktuuq, Pelly Bay and Taloyoak do not generate enough light to be seen from space. South of the tree line the capital cities of Yellowknife and Whitehorse, collectively thirty thousand people, glow like headlamps. But here, north of trees, fewer than nine thousand Inuit live amid these pinhole lights of human habitation that I am passing through.

There is no more isolated landscape in all the Americas. Kayaking above this balding continent, I would be foolish to risk a twenty-mile shortcut through cliffs and bears into Franklin Bay on the drying riverbed. So I place a string on the map's coastline: first west, then north to Cape Bathurst, and finally back south into Franklin Bay, for a total of seventy-eight miles.

Standing here as alone as I have ever been, I fold the map carefully back inside the vinyl case and then clip it to the gunwale. This frayed and waterlogged set of contour lines—with my penciled arrows, circled x's, and bird names—is what separates me from Inuit hunters. While they prefer an innate memory of the land as an animate and infinite force in their lives, I depend upon knowing where the river ends and the ocean begins. If I were to throw away this dependence upon maps, this security that the land is in fact finite, then I would think it unreasonable to even begin crossing the Northwest Passage.

Now, as I am surrounded by expansive earth and waves, it no longer seems within my power either. I need help.

I walk atop the nearest bluff, pull out my binoculars and patiently scan every direction. Out to the north I spy six shacks standing like tawny ghosts above the tundra: salvation. Even though North Star Harbor is abandoned, at least I can pretend. It takes half an hour to walk across soggy tundra, batting through sluggish clouds of tiny mating midges. Fortunately they don't bite.

I focus upon the dwellings ahead as hard as I did upon the wave-battered shoreline while crossing Harrowby Bay. Here in the Arctic I have the impression that if I don't fix a destination with my vision, it will disappear just like the vanishing swans and bears and people I regularly imagine along the shoreline.

North Star Harbor is lovely, albeit wind-torn and colored by rust. Plywood and bleached-out bones are scattered among dented-in snowmobiles and cabins. I take my time, unwinding each door's latchstring, ducking through the shortened entrances and trying to avoid cutting myself on broken glass or corroded nails.

I write down all that I find, like an archaeologist, and try to loosen my loneliness by sharing The People's former lives: "Oil cans (too many to count), caribou skin anorak for five-foot man (or boy), two combs, fleece blanket anorak, leather gloves, rusted 30.06, photograph of an Inuk woman, cans, gears, pots, teakettles, wash buckets, rust, snowmobile treads, snowmobile handlebars, 52 steel leg-hold traps, *Snowmobile* Magazine (1989, probably the Elias family's), calendars (mostly ending in the 1970s), tape cassette player w/ Slim Pickens tapes, and two pair of ice skates."

I leave smiling, with wind in my face and friendly midges in my slipstream. But I still have not reached the understanding of landscape that I desperately seek.

Every day is a waged battle into the northeasterly wind. My elbows and shoulders swell and click with tendonitis, while my eyes fill with grit, blown across the dunes of Cape Bathurst. I hug the shorelines trying to duck the wind. On June 29 I hit a new low when the wind tears my spray skirt off the deck and out to sea. Breaking waves flood across my stomach and into the cockpit. I would cry, but I'm afraid to reveal any weakness out here.

As the wind reaches its roaring afternoon peak and stops all paddling, I hunch over and trudge through freezing surf, lining my kayak out beyond the breakers with long leashes. I wonder if I'll ever make Cape Bathurst.

Eyes of a Wolf

Ninety-one miles and nine days out from Anderson River, I sail past snow-banks covered with watermelon-colored algae onto the most northerly shore of my journey, Cape Bathurst, 70°34'N, 128°00'W. A caribou cow and calf trot stiff-legged out to my boat, perceiving the mast as caribou antlers. Polar bear and wolf tracks meander up and down the spit. Distant black anvil clouds foreshadow Franklin Bay's naturally smoking seams of underground coal. Out beyond the shore breaks, countless beluga backs rise as illusory as surf until I confirm their spouts by looking through the binoculars.

In the morning, still trapped by surf, I walk back to the bluffs to gather drinking water from a tundra swale. Thirty-five molting Canada geese surprise me, running flightless down the edge of beach and up onto the tundra like a herd of miniature caribou. They run in the same chevron formation as they fly.

At the caved-in rickety shack walls marked on the map as Baillie, the Elias and Gruben families have left their initials and dates—all in midwinter, but not for several years. In lieu of sifting through more traditional artifacts, which have already been plundered or buried by collapsed sod walls, I kick plastic two-stroke-engine oil cans and ubiquitous fifty-five-gallon drums. While walking back to camp, I stop and confess in my journal: "What a heartbreaking effort it has been to get here between doubts about continuing and wanting to go back home to June. Headwinds all the time. Bouncy water. Setbacks like losing the spray skirt. I've hit an all-time low of misery and loneliness. Backaches. Mosquitoes. No time to relax. How can I continue?"

I get up and begin walking back to the tent. A mile to the south, through distances that waver inside my binoculars like liquid smoke, I see a blond wolf trying to outfox a caribou standing knee-deep in water. The wolf runs straight along the beach toward the young bull until it splashes out of the water, and the wolf cuts away east up a side draw. The caribou stops and looks back, bewildered. Several moments later the sly wolf emerges from the tundra in front of the bull, nearly hamstringing it until the bull puts on a sprint. The chase is again on, the caribou easily outrunning the wolf as the two recede into the horizon, bent-over twitches of knotted energy.

I spin north and spy the whitening curls of whale backs, moving in gams, then alone, rising and falling to scratch their bellies on the seafloor as I rub sand across my own belly in self-conscious wonder at how it must feel. Krill lines the beach in a fetid orange banner. A long-dead caribou—hide and bones—lies flat as a blanket on the sand. Lost to the contemplation of animal souls that seem more and more like my own, I close my eyes and lightly finger the size seventeen tracks of a polar bear. When I open up, movement catches my eye to the east along the sand bluffs.

I sit down. Ready for the ultimate confrontation, I push the gun out of reach, compose myself and wait for the animal to crest the dunes and come into sight.

It's the wolf! Trotting half sideways, in that half-braking stance of submission so unlike domestic dogs, while fixing me with only a peripheral glance, the wolf runs up to me, then on past. It stops twenty feet away, unmistakably male with its sharp-shaped muzzle, hunching down to get my scent and sex me on the wind. There is no reason for the wolf to be here other than me: I am camped on the end of a two-mile-long, fifty-yard-wide peninsula. I hold myself back from trying to pat him, knowing full well that this would show disrespect. In obeisance to his not violating our space, I mimic his sidelong glance and stay seated; staring directly into his eyes would only send him away. We both remain silent.

For the first time in ten days I have suddenly lost both fear and loneliness. This is all I have been looking for. The wolf has acknowledged that I belong out here in this conundrum of sand, wind and water. As he turns and lopes back toward the bluffs, watching me with a cocked-back head, I stand up and bow my appreciation.

There was something in his eyes. I grab the binoculars to try to see it again.

Polar bear tracks next to my size twelve bootprints

If I can have only a glimmer of Inuit religiosity—in spite of clinging to maps and being focused on linear concepts as a *Kabloona*—it is just this: Something has passed between me and the wolf. It has little to do with fear or hunger or being bluff-charged to see if I would run like prey. What I have felt here is totally unscientific. Most people will think that I have been alone for too long, that I have loosed all things rational, but so be it.

I have seen wild wolves before: in dens, swimming rivers, howling pups away from danger, bluff-charging grizzlies and running down other caribou. So mine is not the enlightened perspective of a wilderness neophyte. After all, wolves are killers in those rare places that still retain a primitive order.

But here for the first time, I finally know *amaruq* as I hope to know the bears. The Sioux boys out on their vision quest waited for weeks until this sort of thing happened. It's not every day that a wild animal runs up to you. Unlike the bear (which scares me half to death), I have always identified with the wolf, thinking that if I were an *Inuk*, the *amaruq* would be my spirit animal. At home, above our living room hearth, Robert Bateman's framed painting *Midnight Black Wolf* hangs prominently. Now I am powerfully affected by the notion that the wolf and I are not dissimilar. We're both loners. Playful, but fierce when the need calls for it.

I am not the only maverick American male drawn to the wolf, but while sitting face-to-face with my wild counterpart, I felt all of the warm, fanciful dreaminess of our culture's Disneyesque notions being replaced by the coldness of hair standing up on my neck.

I now know something that both the Dakota Sioux and Arctic Inuit believed. I realize that no matter where our souls may fly or descend upon our mutual ends, once our flames have been lifted from our antithetical carapaces of fur or flesh, we all burn alike, as bright and similar to one another as the day on which we were born.

I know this because I felt it in his eyes. It was like looking into a mirror.

Loneliness has all but vanished; I felt as if the wolf merely came by to give me the courage to continue, showing me a reflection of who I really am.

Owning Up to the Near Miss

Sailing across the wind into Franklin Bay on July 5, I pass through noxious clouds. My map shows, erroneously, that I still have miles to go before the Smoking Hills. The smell is like driving into a paper mill town, and the sight of hillsides billowing white smoke is surreal. I blink my eyes to make sure I'm seeing it all correctly. I can only hope that these natural underground seams of coal, which ignite upon exposure to air, will thin the mosquitoes.

I haul my sail and lean to leeward without taking the time and trouble to go ashore and inflate my outrigger sponsons. My next food resupply is still more than one hundred miles away in the village of Paulatuk, and I have already begun to fast on those days that are too windy to paddle. Cape Bathurst trapped me for three days in surf, so I can't waste another day or night.

It's not difficult to sail a kayak, but it is dangerous without outriggers because the boat has a natural tendency to roll. I compromise and sail a few hundred feet from the mainland's lee, riding out in the wind. The cliffs are now close enough to swim to should I capsize.

The east and north winds carry the airborne weight of frozen ocean water, but this warm western wind rushing over sun-heated land makes me forget I'm in the Arctic, until I remove my gloves and dip a hand into water as cold as an ice bucket.

I stay focused on the land's gullies and bluffs so that I can watch the wind. The gusts first reveal themselves below and outside the cliffs, rushing sideways like water shooting from a faucet. I gauge the oncoming wind strength by the whitecapping, then I loosen the sheet to let the wind out of the sail. As the wind slows, my speed drops to about four knots. I sheet the sail back and lean into the wind. This speeds me back up to about eight knots.

The next gust punches me while rounding a point. Before I can release the sheet, I am thrown into the water.

The cold doesn't bother me. I am strangely calm while swimming toward shore. Intellect tries to take over with a myriad of choices as I trade the kayak stern line for the bow line. I switch from a breaststroke to a crawl. Shore is a long way off.

The weight of water in my clothes and boots is pulling me down. My

PFD is holding me up. As my arms stiffen, I try touching bottom. It works! I rush the burning, bouldered shore.

Shivering wracks a body that feels as if it were no longer my own. I dump out the boat, then pull it in. I strip and grab a waterproof bag full of dry clothing, the thermos and dried fish. I run forty yards to the nearest smoke vent. As I change, the plastic-bagged shotgun bobs to shore.

I drink hot tea and towel myself off with a dry shirt. The smoke is acrid against the back of my throat, but it seems worth the risk to breathe this foul air in exchange for its heat. I tie a bandanna over my mouth. It takes several minutes to dress. I grow angry as I wonder what I'm doing here.

I have to get back in the boat immediately. Staying here only invites asphyxiation. Also, pausing for contemplation will just make me rue my mistakes or make me more frightened than I already am. *Why am I so constantly scared out here?* I think of the shaman's wisdom of the Great Solitudes; I think back to when I started on the Mackenzie River.

I pump my boat dry, assemble the safety outriggers, haul the sail and jump in. My kayak accelerates smoothly in the wind. The shoreline fades as I head out to sea, giving the katabatic winds plenty of leeway. I swear to never again sail without outriggers.

A golden eagle, a hundred miles north of its supposed habitat, soars a thermal above the white clouds. I make the identification initially because

Sailing fully rigged with main, jib, outriggers and sponsons

of its wing profile, held upward in a dihedral, the way only vultures and goldens fly. The bird is too tawny and large to be a bald eagle. To me, *Aquila chrysaetos* is not a particularly exciting bird; it is easily identified and often overglorified. But seeing it here, wandering out of its range, gives me a glow of empathy; we are both far from home.

Several miles above the golden eagle, I see a shiny airplane in front of a contrail, shortcutting over the top of the world for Scandinavia. This is the closest I've come to seeing people since the pilot left me at the Anderson Delta two weeks ago.

By early evening I have sailed twenty-six miles to the delta of the Horton River, my longest day yet. I want a cigarette, but my rolling tobacco is ruined from the afternoon swim. I've never been a habitual smoker because it's counterproductive to being fit. But after last summer in Inuit camps or feeling strung out while alone offshore, I have found nicotine to be a useful distraction—at least until I finish the trip.

Instead of contemplating how close I came to disaster, I get busy. I spread my maps on the floor to dry. The nickel-plated shotgun is already stiff from its dunking, so I disassemble it, and while mosquitoes tap-dance on the tent walls, I oil all the moving parts until the pump action slides smoothly again. Periodically I look through my binoculars and the vinyl tent windows for bears.

I know that these tools—shotgun, maps and binoculars—are mostly psychological crutches. Eighty years ago Stefansson introduced rifles to Inuit. One particular band was nonplussed; they hammered their rifles down into knives. He tried to impress another band that had never witnessed rifle fire before by shooting apart a distant stick, but the shaman replied that he routinely killed caribou on the other side of the mountain. As for Stefansson's binoculars, they asked, "If you can see caribou today beyond normal eyesight, will they allow you to look at caribou into tomorrow?"

The failings of my map reveal themselves once again as I peer up out of the tent through my windows to "Maloch Hill." White smoke spills down through the air to the sea like a great waterfall. Yet the Smoking Hills are marked as being twenty miles south of here on the map.

The Elias family relies more upon instinct, hearing and oral traditions than on one-dimensional maps. (Eleanor reported dinosaur bones here but became vague about showing me where to find them on the map.) Space after all is not static, as the map would have us believe. Right now these ideas make a lot more sense to me. Alone, in the middle of a wilderness, on the verge of sleep and wondering if I have bent my mind or become half Inuit, I find it easy to discard scientific logic.

To prevent further mishaps, it's essential to identify my dysfunctional parts. I repeatedly do this to prevent any small (and perhaps subconscious) mistake that would bury me so quickly that I wouldn't have time for regrets. Without full disclosure while isolated in the wilderness, you're doomed. So I confess out loud that to save time I have been taking shortcuts, which may have caused the capsize. As I close my eyes, I know that I have to get my head together and somehow minimize impulsive risk taking.

In the morning I'm wasted. I try to stand up, but dizziness swirls the sand and surf and smoke into a blur. Somehow I have to use more discretion. Another fifty yards of swimming would have killed me, but the adrenaline buzz from yesterday's near escape is undeniable. The sirens of risk are more addictive than nicotine. I load the kayak reluctantly and turn back to the tent to cook a second breakfast of oatmeal and tea, a luxury I can barely afford with dwindling rations. My body is so numbed from yesterday's capsize that I'm too tired to stand up. I can't make a fist.

It's time to leave. But I'm so exhausted I plunge back into sleep.

I dream of Cephirano Machado's live mount, a grizzly and a polar bear fighting over a seal in Franklin Bay. Jorgan told me the story about how the big polar bear knocked the grizzly down dead onto the sea ice with a final head punch. The polar bear walked away for a bit, lay down as if he wanted to think it over and died from blood loss.

I wake up anxious, looking out my windows. Jorgan said that no place in the world has such a bear population as this.

As I stuff my tent into the kayak, it occurs to me that if this otherworldly concentration of bears and seams of underground burning coal were in Siberia, the bears would be destroyed and the hillsides lit up and mined. In Alaska it would be a protected national park, lined with asphalt roads, radio-collared bears and friendly rangers. But here in Canada it's a poorly mapped and mystical backwater—the way it should remain.

Bear Aggression

A peregrine flies over the water with swift and sure wingbeats, lowers its talons and clenches and unclenches them, readying itself for a kill. I continue paddling east, eyes agog. Charred shorelines are snuffed by the weight of the sea as smoke pours out of fumaroles laced with a frosting of burned sulfur. I stop several times to fill my water bottle, but the streams run black and taste of rotten egg. Rattling rockfall noises are followed by the sound of scalding steam as vents open and close. In a sudden and unexpected delineation like the discovery of paradise, these alkali-yellow and ocher tousled mounds of smoked cliffs give way to gently sloping verdant hills, covered with lupine and whistling ground squirrels. These hills stretch south for untold miles, striped as if plowed by a combine driver and dotted with the distant curved backs of nodding caribou, bear and muskox. Higher still, this green tableau is dappled with moldy snowfields.

Canada geese run as fast as I can paddle along the shoreline. One gaggle suddenly stops running and turns back to look at me, as a grizzly stands seven feet tall in their path. The geese bolt into high grass and the grizzly passes them up, distracted by my presence off the shoreline.

Two dozen more grizzlies ply the tide line, digging up bear root and ground squirrels, occasionally watching me pass by. Curious about the barren ground grizzly reputation, I fire a spring-loaded flare from my kayak. When it explodes in the sky, two cubs jump while their mothers merely glance up, yawn with aggressive indifference and then continue unearthing their roots. To these coastal bears, the explosion (which would have sent most inland grizzlies running) merely resembles the familiar crack of parting sea ice.

It is not until midnight that I find a shoreline without a grizzly. I point in toward the calmest-looking breaks showing the least amount of white surf, then paddle as fast as I can down the face of a gathering wave. In a rush of wind, I jump out up to my knees in water, snatch the bowline and run straight up the beach to pull my kayak out from under the next wave.

Fifty yards above the tide line, I scoop two quarts of water from a scummy foot-deep pond indented with countless caribou tracks. Behind the windbreak of a driftwood log, I light my stove to a throaty burst of yellow flaring gas and then carefully observe the horizon for visitors. As soon as I lower the binoculars to pick out a flat tent site, a dark bear, the size of a large Hereford, ambles into the foreground, snuffling its nose and looking for food. I step atop the log and stand up high to project a more frightening height. As if to fake me out, he turns and runs straight south to circle back into camp. I run over the ridge behind the pond and watch him galloping uphill, a rolling, jiggling ball, his dark fur waving like grass in the wind.

He's gone, but there will be others.

I gulp down my freeze-dried spaghetti and push off into the surf, soaking my salt-crusted nylon pants again. Two belugas wag lazily, their breath whistling like a bellows, while swimming twice as fast as I can sail. An arctic tern swoops in low to investigate me, shivering its wings as if freshly awoken from a nap. I too feel invigorated.

Suddenly, as I sail tightly around a corner, a grizzly saunters in front of a hill pockmarked with ground squirrel holes. Since I'm lonely, I can't help myself. I sail in closer, keeping a respectful forty-yard distance, and attempt my first conversation in weeks—"Hello, Mr. Bear"—bringing him straight into the surf without a change of speed. He slams through two breaking waves and stands up to look me over. As if curious, he pushes off the bottom and swims after me, his ears wiggling in concentration. He holds his head high above the water with his fur ruffed out to appear bigger than he already is. The bear is strangely beautiful and harmless-looking, like a child's stuffed animal.

A glaucous gull swoops by, screeching. The bear startles and turns his head with a sudden snarl, a split second from curiosity to ferocity.

I sheet the sail against the wind, kick the rudder pedal and paddle for all I'm worth. But this isn't good enough. He appears to be gaining on me. I paddle harder. Finally he gives up and turns back toward shore. By splaying his paws wide, he catches a gathering wave and rides it up onto the beach. He steps out gracefully, in slow and measured movements, without losing balance. There is no shaking off. It was as if the whole chase had never happened for him. I'm shaken, but he simply continues walking north, wagging his head to and fro while inspecting the sand.

I watch each of his lumbering steps. He never looks back.

I can't stop. It would be asking for trouble to tent here. I realize that I was taunting the bears by greeting them aloud and firing off flares. They deserve more respect.

Although the bear's aggression is still palpable in my pulse, I feel as if I were on the verge of breaking through to some previously unattainable connection, a more tangible proof that these animals and I share the same soul—as Inuit believe. Maybe I am just lonely, vying for companionship, but I am convinced that there is a way to reach out to the bears. I want affirmation that I am not prey, that like the wolf, the bear and I hold some common ground. It could be that I am misguided, that the barren ground grizzly

Bearded seals often expressed great curiosity about me

is just a bully that you don't mess with. But I'm going to try. Giddy with this hoped-for kinship, I glibly christen my kayak *Swims with Bears*.

A few miles later five proud caribou bulls trot down the beach. They loft their antlers ahead like Olympian runners baring the ceremonial torch. Water flies up from their sure hooves while the sun paints their flanks golden. They stop as I draw close. Their eyes are dark, opalescent planets. Their muscles are quivering, their nostrils steaming. They turn to watch me float past and become stone-still statues as I crane my head back and drift along in a vestige of wind and current. The caribou do not move.

Enough time alone out here, reduced to simple survival among the animals, and one could surely reach an Inuit understanding. I now feel no more or less important than a nearby snowshoe hare, mimicking the grizzly by standing on hind legs with forelegs dangling and ears tuned up, revolving through incremental adjustments like satellite dishes.

For days now distant driftwood has been morphing into people, while ice chunks appear as kayaks and snowfields become sailboat hulls. I have aimed toward all these visions until they assume their actual forms. Then I steer away, alone and disappointed.

The midnight wind dies as the sun scalds the edges of the sea beneath the clouds. Utterly exhausted, I pull down the sail and paddle into Langton

Bay. The sun is now heating the land, which will settle the grizzlies down so that I too can get some sleep.

Out on a narrow sand spit that sticks into the bay, I unroll my tent on a fetid-smelling beach with three bearded seals. The steel blue matriarch of the harem swims back and forth watching me. I am surrounded by a brown halo of mosquitoes and plunged into such low-headed loneliness that I would scream if not for the seals' splashing companionship.

I dive into my tent and spend half an hour slapping and brushing away mosquitoes. The walls become splashed with blood: my own.

Suddenly a woman's voice sends a chill up my spine: "Everything is all right, Jonathan, you can sleep here without fear."

I half expect it be a bear, so I grab the gun and zip open the tent to find no one here. No tracks either. "Maybe it's the bearded seal," I say aloud.

I drift off into a half sleep, concluding that the seals are too earnest to tease me. The voice must have come from one of several female common mergansers, floating by with their crimson punk hairdos, gabbling away and trying to put the fear of Sedna in me.

Even in the morning, nothing can convince me that the voice was not real. I have been alone too long. I need to get focused, to get psyched for the coming portage.

Portaging the Parry Peninsula

It took me three long days to drag my kayak between lakes and up creeks across the Parry Peninsula. I followed a line traced on my map over the least land, connecting blue dots of water. Each time the lakes ended, I staggered across bogs with three loads. I lumbered along in two separate trips with seventy-pound duffel bags on my shoulders, taking care not to sprain my ankles. Then I went back for the empty hundred-pound kayak, looped its bowline around my waist and began heaving like a sled dog.

By the third day I have finished seven portages. I dropped my invaluable pump somewhere, but I can't afford to go back for it. Fifteen miles of portaging is drudgery, but when it's stacked against 160 miles of paddling around the peninsula, I have no choice. I'm almost out of food. Most of all I need to talk to people again, soon.

On this third afternoon of portaging, while backpacking down to the ocean, I watch a caribou mutate into a sandhill crane. I am careful to write this off as a mistake, assuring myself that it was a crane from the beginning, and I excuse the imagined caribou as a trick of the featureless tundra, spinning time and space together into a web of apparitions that are devoid in depth or distance. I close my eyes to let hearing verify that the animal is not altogether imagined. Its clacking cry, like the clattering of a bag of bones, is

Hauling the Klepper between lakes

followed by a hollow-sounding luff of feathers shuddering against air. It is a bird. I am not losing my mind.

I pitch my tent just beyond a spray of whitecaps beating into Argo Bay. A black-bellied plover (*Pluvialis squatarola*) runs back and forth across the tussocks and bearberry, wildly crying out, *pu-eee pu-eee pu-eeee,* and hobbling with a feigned injury to divert me from its nest. Unlike its cousins the golden plover and the Eskimo curlew, this species has eluded destruction by some Darwinian urge that tells it to fly in smaller flocks so that hundreds can't be blasted from the sky as they migrate back and forth to the Arctic through the United States.

Just after I hop inside the tent, the drone of a four-wheeler arrives. I dash back outside to talk to the first people I have seen in twenty days, Andy and Millie Thrasher. It is so good to see people again that I am all but jumping up and down. I suppress the urge to hug them both. Nervous about my excited movements, they back off a bit. I force myself to say slowly, "How are you?" and instead of listening to their reply, I watch their mouths to see how they shape their lips while speaking.

They explain that it is only a couple of hours' drive to Paulatuk. Since Andy—curly-headed, broad-beamed, constantly smiling—has the weekend off, they're going fishing. Millie is reserved, and like many shy Inuit women, she is careful not to address me directly or look me in the eye. They leave me an apple and a bagel and volunteer to bring me trout if they catch any.

Since people are expecting me in Paulatuk by today at the latest, Andy promises to let the authorities know that I'm okay. I am greatly relieved. If June doesn't get word, she will call the RCMP and start a search.

Their four-wheeler whines into the distance, and I am comforted that I can still talk coherently. After being alone for so long, I thought complete sentences would fail me.

In the morning I battle the surf for half an hour until it becomes apparent that leaving the protected bay to cross over to Paulatuk will only be asking for another capsize. At a lagoon in the lee of Greens Island, I camp behind a sand dune and settle in with a novel. I am a captive of the wind.

Trapped Again by the Wind

On my second day stuck in the wind, Rueben Green pulls his seventeen-foot Lund ashore, inside the narrow, protected envelope of water to the lee of Greens Island. He shakes my hand warmly and says, "Come on out to the island so I can introduce you to The People." I jump in.

Rueben is forty years old, with a black mustache boldfacing his long, narrow features. In January he was elected chairman of the Paulatuk Inuvialuit Council, entitling him to attend sessions of the Parliament in Ottawa (costing several days' travel and thousands of dollars in plane fare) as a representative of his village. He claims that his position just pays travel costs and benefits, but with the lack of employment for Paulatuk's 190 residents, Rueben isn't complaining.

He has six daughters and sons, whom he regularly takes hunting and fishing. Rueben does not contradict his twelve-year-old, Angus, about the incoming tidal current lugging against the seventeen-foot aluminum skiff; the boy informs me that it's going out. His dad merely nods his head respectfully, without interrupting or embarrassing Angus in front of a stranger. He lets his other son pull the throttle off plane, dropping the bow back down to the water. Angus jumps out and snatches the bowline as the boat grinds up onto Greens Island. We laugh as the small boy braces his legs and tries to drag the boat up the beach the same way his father does.

Angus throws his soda can down onto the sand, and none of the surrounding crowd corrects him. To judge from the abandoned campsites I saw during my portage, littering is perfectly acceptable here. When their elders' possessions were bones and wood and skins, they were dropped where they belonged, then naturally absorbed by the land and sea. Now that they are saddled with nonbiodegradable containers and tools, everything they throw away lies conspicuously about the landscape.

After I ask how things are going in Paulatuk, Rueben replies, "The fucking government has given us a socialization program that gets us fucking nowhere because once The People see that they do not have to work for a living it opens up a whole cycle of social problems."

I don't ask what these problems are, because we both know that some Inuit villages are hurting. I try for a positive note: "This Nunavut will be good for Inuit to the east anyway."

"We're not ready for something like that yet here."

"Why not?"

"Because we have a lot of outsiders, such as the southern Gwich'in tribe and whites in places like Inuvik, so the Inuit would be a lot harder to represent."

Rueben kneels to the sand and brushes it smooth, as if he has done this before with lost *Kabloona*. But instead of drawing a map of the coast, he charts the Gwich'ins, Inuit and whites, treed off to their three political representatives. Rueben says, "If you go to the white representative instead of the Inuit representative, he might be able to look into your problems, but he will be pissed off about it because he is only supposed to help the white people."

"Kind of screwy."

"Yeah, welcome to the modern Arctic."

"What about the 1984 settlement act?"

"That was just another load of bullshit that amounted to nothing."

"What about the hundred million dollars and land given to the Inuvialuit?"

"The money's mostly gone, but the land is still a messed up deal, and right now we are fighting with the government so that we can get some mining jobs going for our people in Darnley Bay."

It's hard to talk on an empty stomach, and although I have kept this to myself, Rueben takes me to his father's big white wall tent. After a brief introduction to eighty-one-year-old Sam, twelve years a widower, Rueben disappears. The elder Mr. Green fixes me with an iron stare, then asks, "Want a chair?"

He hands me a five-gallon jerrican with a spigot on top.

The smoothness of his face and his smiling demeanor make him look a dozen years younger than his age. He wears an old wool shirt and pants, neatly, without the de rigueur Inuit ball cap or synthetic garments. He may also be the only *Inuk* here still wearing a full set of original worn-down and brown teeth—if only because he was not weaned on sugar like many younger Inuit.

He hands me a cutout gallon white-gas can that he sees me staring at, one of hundreds that I have seen littering the tundra. It has been neatly cut and filed down into a washbasin. Another can has been cleanly cut open to hold knives and forks.

"Nobody does this sort of thing anymore except me." He shrugs about the wasteful, throwaway world he is expected to live in.

Although the five-gallon jerrican spigot is embossing my rear end, I am more comfortable than I have felt in weeks: The canvas wall tent has no mosquitoes, I can sit up straight, and the air is warm, albeit thick with carbon monoxide from the purring Coleman stove. Most of all, I am delighted

Sam Green and daughter at his tent, Greens Island

to have company. Sam continues to stare at me, and although neither of us has anything to say, for once I am aware that not talking is more polite than riddling an elder with questions.

In traditional northern culture, it is helpful for *Kabloona* to remember that the *Inummarit,* or a real *Inuk,* must exhibit strength, honesty and goodness. All over the North it is commonly accepted that the ideal personality is not inquisitive, does not interrupt and is not moody or given to anger. Wisdom (*silatujuq*) is shown through silence. Typically, *Kabloona* like me show up in Inuit camps and lose respect from the elders by interrogating them. But traveling alone across the land, in Sam's eyes anyway, may act as compensation for my curiosity.

For the time being, I honor his peace by asking no questions. Although I am determined not to mention my hunger, he sees me looking at a pile of freshly boiled moose ribs on the floor.

"Like some moose meat?"

"Yes, please."

"We have not see moose here for ten years, and at first it seemed he was a caribou until he would not run away, so we shot him quick in the willows over on the creek. He is not tasty, so I boiled him for two hours just like you do bear meat."

It is a delicate balance here, filled with potential pratfalls of Inuit etiquette, and although the wrong statement will earn his scorn, I decide to be honest: "I am a vegetarian, except for fish."

For a few seconds he sucks in his lips tightly and then narrows his eyes, trying to get a bead on me. He lifts ten pounds' worth of stinky ribs from the floor and onto a plate, then passes it to me along with a bowl of salt and a tub of discolored margarine. I smile at him, pick up the biggest rib, a foot long, dip it into the margarine, then rip off a piece of gray and leathery meat with my teeth, careful not to look away from his eyes. My qualms about eating inhumanely raised and slaughtered animals are more about living in a shrinking southern biosphere. Explaining this to an Arctic elder, unfamiliar with vegetable gardens, might be difficult. Besides, a gurgling belly knows no moral qualms.

Sam suddenly bursts into deep laughter, rolling back his shoulders and holding his stomach. He reaches up and wipes tears from his broad face.

I put down the first cleaned-off rib, gently, wipe my hands on my pants, and reach for another rib. The meat is as tough as anything I have ever sunk my teeth into, and if I were not so hungry, the smell of this livery, boiled flesh would be enough to make me sick.

Sam regains his composure. "You are a vegetarian, eh? That's the funniest thing I have heard in weeks. A man paddles into our whaling camp from wilderness and says he does not eat meat."

He stands up, a foot shorter than I am, his knees so bowed out that his legs form a giant O, and reaches over for eating utensils in the cutout gas can. "Like a fork?"

"Would you be offended if I continue eating with my hands?"

That brings another round of deep belly laughter. He manages to choke out, "That is just how I eat them."

Sam next passes me a plate stacked with sugared bannocks (he calls them Eskimo doughnuts): fried dough half an inch thick and ten inches wide. He motions for me to wipe my face with it. Then he passes me a jar of jalapeño peppers to wash down the third rib, insisting that I use a fork to get the peppers out.

To my surprise I see that Angus has slipped in and is sitting behind me eating a rib. He smiles at me and says, "Please pass the jalapeños."

Sam offers me some sauerkraut for dessert, explaining that when he was a boy, a German ship took on so many whales that it was forced to dump fifty cases of sauerkraut out on the shores of Langton Bay. Paulatuk, he says with a smile, has since become the only village in the Arctic addicted to pickled cabbage.

Sam is already somewhat famous, at least to me, from his opening quote in Hugh Brody's book *Living Arctic: Hunters of the Canadian North*: "I have sat down many times and thought over the differences or the distinction between my people's way of life and your way of life. . . . Your way of life down south as white people is a way of life I myself would not want to live. We are people who are free to go hunting every day."

I ask him about the book. He has never heard of it, but for all I know, he doesn't read. He also denies that the island we're on has been named after him.

"Your map is wrong, because we have always called this place Egg Island."

"What happened to the eggs?"

"We ate them all."

Sam seems ready and willing to answer my questions. After all, every *Kabloona* he has ever met is full of questions, so why should I be different?

I learn that his family moved out to the Parry Peninsula from Alaska when he was three years old. After the epidemics had wiped out all the local Inuvialuit, the Alaskan Iñupiat, suffering from caribou declines, hurried in to exploit the plentiful fox and wolverine for their pelts. Although there were many wooden motor schooners then, Sam remembers no kayaks.

The people of the area became renowned for their skill in trapping. While Eleanor Elias baits her traps with fish, and central Arctic trappers use seal, men like Sam in Paulatuk have yet another preferred bait. Before rebaiting a set of traps spread over the land surrounding his village, Sam would go outside with an ax and chop a twenty-pound chunk of human turds from one of many frozen, bucket-shaped piles stacked outside the houses like cordwood.

Back then, he mentions, one shaman regularly commuted back and forth to the village of Kugluktuk, four hundred miles east.

"How did he get there?" I ask.

"He flew"—Sam holds out his arms to show exactly how the shaman traveled—"like a bird. But our missionary soon stopped all of that."

"Do you believe he really flew?"

"I do not believe in things. I just knew how to fear them," he replies, lowering his eyes.

By the time he was in his twenties, a band of Inuvialuit moved off the peninsula to present-day Paulatuk at the behest of their shaman, to take advantage of better caribou hunting. Sam has been there ever since. He is one of the last men here still speaking Inuktitut.

I am suddenly struck by an epiphany; my stomach is full for the first time in weeks, and I have found a fast friend in Sam. "You know, I often dream of flying," I tell him. "But the closest I can come to this while I am awake is by sailing my kayak, and there are times when it really feels like I am flying over the water."

He says nothing, bobbing his head in slow affirmation and watching me. "I am going to sail to Kugluktuk next."

"That is a long ways away, you know."

"And I get there in much the same way that you travel by listening closely to the wildlife and respecting the land and trying to learn from all things."

Seemingly changing the subject, Sam suddenly asks, "What is that hanging around your neck?"

I slip off the leather satchel, tied around my neck with a silk cord, and pour seven colorful stones out into my palm. I pluck out the most important one. "A howlite, polar bear fetish for protection," I say, and hand it to Sam.

Angus grabs the rest, and Sam suddenly looks pale. He makes Angus hand back the stones. I try to ease his mind. "I don't really believe in these stones, but I don't disbelieve in them either. My fiancée wears the same pouch around her neck."

"You know shamans used to do this. They used to carry stones," he says, pointing to the pouch. With his eyes on the muskox robe bed in the corner he announces, "I am going to take a nap now if you will excuse me. It has been good talk with you, and I hope you come visit tomorrow."

He reaches back to grab what looks like a pile of red sticks and drops them into my hands. "For the vegetarian." He smiles. "Moose jerky. Don't get sick now, okay?"

"*Cowanna*," I say, before stepping out the tent flap.

There are a dozen more wall tents like this one spread around the island. It is a sunny 48 degrees until I step out of the tent's lee and into the wind, a transformation as sudden as opening the door of a walk-in freezer. Surf purls the long, narrow wedge of island, and the sound of thrumming water fills the air. Paulatuk is just visible as a salt-sprayed blur of buildings thirteen miles east. In this northeasterly wind—for both Inuit powerboaters and *Kabloona* kayaker—town might as well be a hundred miles away.

No one has seen any beluga all summer with these winds. Last year they managed to shoot four. There are several brackish ponds out beyond the outhouses, and half a dozen children are towing a small wooden boat, carved from a piece of driftwood, through the surf. Above their heads a peregrine falcon swoops by with powerful and precise wingbeats, combing the shore for unwary ducks.

Suddenly one of Sam Green's daughters steps in and tries to identify the bird: "Arctic tern. A good sign because they always follow the whales."

Liz is stumbling from home brew. She ducks in front of me, collecting cigarette ends from the ground and shaking out the tobacco into her hand. After several minutes she has recycled enough to roll a thin cigarette. The island ran out of smokes several days ago.

"You know that anywhere down south you woulda been charged for a meal like one my father just fed you."

Liz blows out a smoke ring, and we watch the wind carry it away. She is single, nearly sixty years old and happy to tell the story of being sent to the Aklavik residential school as a child. It was there that, like most Inuit, Liz was forbidden to speak Inuktitut. By the time she was boated back to her family each summer for two months, many of her traditional family values had been lost. She is accepting of all this, as most Inuit seem to be, and although she is slurring her words, she still holds her head high.

She mostly wants to know about all the big driftwood logs lying on beaches to the west of the Mackenzie River. When I tell her they do indeed exist, she looks over at her fire, barely glowing under a few gaunt-looking pieces of willow. A blackened teapot lays on top, tilting into the fire, its steam clouds flying south at thirty knots.

"Wood's a commodity that we don't take for granted 'cos we need to keep tea going and meat smoking. We spend all of our time looking for more wood on days like this when there ain't nothin' to do."

I take the hint and go comb the beaches for more driftwood.

Every day Rueben ferries me back and forth from the mainland to his father's namesake island. No one talks much, and I try to hold my questions and ideas until I am near to bursting with the need for conversation, my own specific cultural response to having been isolated. On the third day I insist to Rueben that I'm okay staying alone on the mainland (it's difficult sitting silently inside fumed wall tents filled with interesting people, politely not speaking and learning how to overcome my curiosity and not ask questions). Rueben insists. He says that The People on the island are worried about me. So I give in.

That afternoon Rueben begins trying to tenderize some raw moose meat by beating it with the back of a knife. His taciturn wife, Lily Ann, provides directions from the bed, where their five-month-old is sleeping. Rueben sautés the meat in lard with a load of potatoes and canned peas. The tent fills with hungry kids, and we eat on the plywood floor, silent except for the polite "please" and "thank you" from various children. When one teenager pulls up short of his hunger, Rueben gently suggests that he go next door to eat more supper with his aunt. The apples and cherries are rotten from being banged around on too many boats and planes, but no one complains. As the adults light up, the kids fight over a palm-size beeping Nintendo game. When they begin shouting too loudly, Rueben respectfully suggests that they head outside and let the baby sleep.

Lily Ann plays cribbage with me. I honor their customs and remain silent, trying to find the answers to my questions by simply watching, rather than asking questions that they might perceive as rude. After she has won three silent games in a row, she overcomes her shyness and begins talking. I couldn't be more surprised. She announces, apropos of nothing, that her grandmother in the diseased village of Kittigazuit used to talk to sandhill cranes.

"She climbed atop the pingos and sang in a beautiful voice to the cranes. After a while the cranes came closer and began dancing"—Lily Ann puts her hands in her armpits and flops her elbows back and forth—"jumping up and down and clacking and listening to my grandmother sing as they danced closer and closer."

She is animated, the worry lines on her glowering face replaced by joy as she pushes back a strand of black hair from her eyes. It is the first time in days that I have seen her smile.

Rueben, logical-minded, explains, "It was probably just mating season, and the cranes got a little crazy like they sometimes do."

Lily Ann's face returns to narrow-eyed anger. Rueben apologizes about the paperback Louis L'Amour lying on the floor. He prefers to read history, and there are so few books in Paulatuk that he is forced to reread "stupid westerns." He is well read in Arctic history, but he has a bone to pick.

"You know that the Eskimos are rarely given any credit in any of the literature. No one talks about the Eskimos who taught Amundsen how to survive the Northwest Passage or the Eskimos who helped all those people get to the North Pole, let alone how all the whalers got fed when they were here. There is one book called *Give Me My Father's Body: The Life of Minik, the New York Eskimo*. It was written by Peary's Eskimo and puts it all straight. You have to read it."

The Inuvialuit of Paulatuk

I sneak-paddle into Paulatuk during a brief respite in the winds. It is July 13, three days later than June was expecting me, and Andy Thrasher forgot to let people know that I'm safe. Fortunately the RCMP has not yet started aerial searches for me. June, meanwhile, has just jumped on a plane to Inuvik to begin searching for me.

Within an hour of arriving in town, I hop a ride on an empty plane back to Inuvik to surprise June. The scent of her skin and the light behind her eyes leave me giddy. I try to gain back lost weight—with fresh food, beer and ice cream—and catch up on old news. I replace my spray skirt and pump. Twice I break down and cry because I'm no longer fighting the wind and water and uncertainty. With June, unlike when I'm alone in the wilderness, I can show all my weaknesses. After five days, the last month's suffering falls into distant and somehow pleasurable memory.

I fly back to Paulatuk on July 19, ready to resume my trip east to Kugluktuk. I have found my center, even though I'm sure the hardest part of the trip is yet to come. From the air above, the town appears on an ancient sand delta inside a small bay, connected to the Hornaday River by Sauerkraut Passage.

Less than ten inches of precipitation falls here annually, making the region nearly as arid as the Mojave. In the winter, temperatures drop as cold as Siberia. The locals also report cyclones, spawned by warm summer zephyrs colliding with icy northeasters. Since the area is so far from any legitimate weather bureau, the storms are dismissed as Eskimo myth.

Another violent phenomenon has hit a dozen houses in town. These are not events that any Inuit on Greens Island would mention to me: During drunken rampages the subsidized housing, for which the owners pay $32 per month rent, have had their windows broken, their furniture burned and their inner walls torn down. Other than forcing families to cram into another already crowded house while the damaged one is repaired, destroying a welfare house does not penalize the owners. Because of the difficulty of transporting labor and materials, it costs $180,000 to build a small box-house here.

Several years ago Paulatuk's *Inuk* mayor, known to *Kabloona* as the Godfather, became famous for flying in planeloads of booze during the holidays. The chartered Twin Otter cost $4,000, and the liquor, which filled the entire plane, came to at least that much. Since the Godfather had a monopoly on construction contracts and was thought to be siphoning off the Inuvialuit Regional Corporation money, he looked after everyone in town.

The reign of the Godfather came crumbling apart when a *Kabloona* nurse discovered a prepubescent girl with venereal disease. Accompanied by two RCMPs, a social worker moved in, and she spent a month interviewing everyone in town. Eight men eventually pleaded guilty to various rape charges. The Godfather was accused and convicted of raping various women in his family—aunt, mother, grandmother, granddaughter and daughters. One girl was a mentally retarded twelve-year-old. Two women had to be taken from town; after they had accused the men of rape, the Yellowknife judge was warned that their throats might be cut before they could testify. In accordance with Inuit culture (in which nonconsensual sex was not uncommon), the judge sentenced the Godfather to one day in jail. Southern women's advocates later appealed the sentence. The Godfather eventually served three months. Today the convicted men carry no guilt or shame, and with the exception of a dozen *Kabloona* in town, most villagers attach no stigma to these crimes.

Although the RCMP used to be stationed in Paulatuk, cutbacks have shut down the local station. As Rueben Green's cousin put it, when the uniformed, sidearmed men first arrived thirty years ago, "We were so scared of them. They were so big, they looked like moose and muskox to us."

In 1997 the RCMP flew from Inuvik into Paulatuk at 4 a.m. during a drunken shooting. No one died, but the sixty-year-old *Inuk* shooter was sentenced to three years in the Yellowknife penitentiary.

The last time RCMP lived in town, the sergeant walked outside in circles trying to find the source of an inhuman screaming. The sergeant was so perplexed that he radioed his wife (a devout Christian) and asked her to look out from their home's second-story window with the binoculars. She spotted the source of the noise in a nearby dog yard. Her agitated voice came over the radio to her husband, describing a man bent over a spread-legged husky.

In court the *Inuk*'s lawyer said that his client's behavior was a tradition that had gone on in Eskimo society for hundreds of years. The accused was sentenced to thirty days in jail, while the sergeant moved himself and his wife out.

Paulatuk's 140 adults compete for thirty jobs: administrators, truck drivers, teachers, grocers, minister and clerks. *Kabloona* fill half these positions. The unemployed People collect about $900 per month in social assistance. There is little self-employment, such as carving, here, and I am likely to be one of only a few tourists who will pass through Paulatuk in 1998.

I visit the jam-packed grocery store—twenty by thirty feet short—and buy a liter of milk for $3.75. In Yellowknife it would cost $2. The round-trip plane fare to Inuvik, where milk costs $2.50, is $400. Since alcohol is not sold in Paulatuk, the locals fly there to buy vodka at $1 per ounce, the same price as in Yellowknife because of government subsidy. (Rueben is one of several people in town who remain bitter that the government subsidizes liquor but not milk.) Also, Inuvik hoteliers refuse to rent rooms to groups of Paulatuk Inuvialuit, who routinely party so hard that their hotel rooms are trashed.

The average Paulatuk *Inuk* consumes about twenty-four cases of soda per year at $2 per can; it's $1.25 in Inuvik. As for vegetables, I can only find three browned-over cucumbers, selling for $3.75 each.

I get directions to Rueben Green's house from young Angus, who seems strangely subdued and refuses to walk back to his home with me.

Rueben is surprised to find me knocking at the door. He is bare-chested, and his abdominal muscles ripple like a high school gymnast's. His black eyes seem awash with blood.

I hold up a gift, a bag of meat, for him. He invites me in, and the smell of fish is strong enough to make me gag. I kick off my runners (as Inuit refer to them), then quickly regret it when I see how filthy the floor is.

Lily Ann is sprawled on a foam pad in the middle of the living room, next to their baby boy. She looks away from the television and up at my hello, slowly, silently, until deeper disdain (almost a look of horror) knits her brow for my intrusion. She remains prostrate, watching television. After our laughter and talk together on Greens Island, this hostile reception surprises me.

There is no furniture other than a kitchen table; no stereo; no light. Two parakeets fly out of the back bedroom, and I duck in surprise. One takes a quick perch on an unframed portrait of Jesus and Mary, coloring the otherwise bare wall, then wings past a broken window and into the kitchen.

Rueben ushers me into the kitchen, to get away from the gunfire and screeching tires from a satellite-transmitted cop show. Caribou blood dapples the linoleum floor. Bowls of fish bones and guts litter the kitchen counters and floors.

"Sorry for the mess," Rueben says. "Let me get you some char."

Clearly I have erred by coming; although I had been warned about the weekend parties, it seemed that a Saturday afternoon might be safe. Now Rueben is red-faced, but he is not going to let me leave without returning a gift—as if he could actually afford to be giving me something. But it would be bad form not to accept it.

He swings open the door of a new Frigidaire that holds a jar of mayonnaise, one of mustard and a liter of milk. His body blocks my view into the main compartment, so I peer around it and identify two fully feathered white-fronted geese, a Canada goose and two huge char—unwrapped, lice-ridden and as comely as the day they all were shot and netted from the Hornaday River. The shelves are otherwise bare.

Rueben grabs the biggest speckled fish and plops it onto the kitchen table. He takes a huge cleaver, chops off the glistening char's head and slides the body into a trash bag, leaving the blood and head for a later cleanup. He invites me back for coffee in the morning, as I carefully try to lay my stocking feet on dry bits of floor for ten yards back to the front door.

I mention the dog food I left for his sister at the hamlet building, as well as an application that I have asked the Inuvik library to mail to him so that he can receive books on interlibrary loan. (Later a phone call verifies that he has not filled out the application.) Lily Ann looks too sick to say good-bye, but in her husband, who shakes my hand tightly as he has learned from other *Kabloona* in the halls of Parliament, I have undoubtedly found a lasting friend.

If I had grown up here, I would be lucky to have come as far as Rueben. He has found an education despite poor schools. He has a loving family despite his ruined village; he's thoughtful and passionate. While sitting in his rocking boat by the lee of Greens Island, he spoke to me about animals, the fishy flavor of loons and the taste of wheat and alfalfa in the flesh of white-fronted geese that had roosted in farmers' fields down south. He told me that he liked to travel by his taste buds, that he appreciated how rich and broad a place the world really is. He said that Inuit never have to leave the Arctic because they already have everything they need.

As I stroll to the Thrashers' house with more gifts, I am surrounded by a gaggle of children screaming my name and grabbing my camera and asking for money. A rank smell pervades the streets. I ask the nearest kid if he knows what it is, but he just looks at me silent and wide-eyed, as if I had just landed from Mars. Until recently no one had showered or flushed a toilet in Paulatuk. Now that plumbing has been installed, I'm hoping that the honey-bucket remains have been removed from the houses. The kid, who must've realized that he had always taken the smell of feces for granted, then volunteers, "They pump shit three times a week with sewage truck. Now can I have your camera?"

Andy Thrasher, who invested in a water truck half a dozen years ago, runs the second busiest operation around. On the opposite side of town from where the sewage truck pumps out its effluvia, Andy pumps in lake water. Then, on the opposite side of the houses from the sewage truck, he pumps out lake water, three times a week, charging the hamlet five cents per liter.

Andy Thrasher's grandfather was a Portuguese crewman who jumped ship, named *The Thrasher,* just after the turn of the century in Langton Bay. Millie Thrasher likes to kid her husband that he wouldn't like red wine so much if he weren't half Portuguese. A local *Kabloona* claims that Andy is the only *Inuk* in town who can hold his liquor. They are also the first Inuit couple I have met who don't smoke.

Millie, whose grandmother died in the epidemic in Kittigazuit, is a fifty-five-year-old grandmother. She still turns men's heads, with wide cheek-bones curving out to pouting lips and with the cordial manner in which she dissuades me from leaving her house after visiting for a half an hour. Still, she won't make eye contact with me.

Her husband is engrossed in a boxing match in the television room, so she plies me with tea and fresh-baked bread from the dozen loaves cooling on the kitchen counter. Andy runs out during the commercials, and in a high-pitched nasal whine characteristic of Paulatuk men, he tries to get me to eat more bread or join him in watching the fight.

Unlike the Greens, who live in a welfare bungalow, the Thrashers own their two-story house. Their stereo is beside a large collection of country-western music. Swallowed up in a plumped-out living room chair, I gaze over a collection of slim encyclopedias and family portraits. Framed and autographed portraits of Wayne Gretzky, posed with two of the Thrashers' sons, are placed more prominently than the framed likenesses of Jesus and Mary. From inside this could be a house of Alberta farmers.

The Thrashers outside their home

Millie is answering my questions about their recent vacation to Edmonton, where they travel to several times a year, stay in motels, eat Chinese food and shop. When I ask if she has ever considered moving to Inuvik, she shakes her head and says, "It's so-o-o-o expensive there."

The heat is really getting her down. It climbed to 90 degrees today, a temperature that she calls awful. She croons with great envy about her husband's truck, the only place in town with air-conditioning.

"Andy had it turned on high all day long."

I mention that it's late and that I should go, although it doesn't seem to bother Millie that our conversation is uncomfortably halting. I suspect that she hasn't fielded as many inquiries as I've thrown since her final exams in high school. Most of all, I am self-conscious because, as if by a knee-jerk reaction, I could not stop myself from polite and repeated attempts to keep the conversation moving. As I wave good-bye to the couple, standing arm in arm on their porch, I suspect that they will perceive my talkative curiosity as mere rudeness.

Fighting out of Darnley Bay

July 20. It takes a long day to paddle a few miles east of the Brock River. I look for a quiet landing near the browned-over skeleton of a beluga whale. But instead of stepping clear, I trip over the gunwale and fall face first into a wave, filling the kayak with surf. It's wet work pulling the heavily laden boat out of the surf, and I am angry because this is a beginning kayaker's mistake, not mine.

I wring out my socks and pants and hang them on a driftwood snag, hoping for some heat from the tepid midnight sun. Since the wind has quelled the mosquitoes, I'm able to lie in my sleeping bag without a tent and fall asleep to the sound of yellow-billed loons neighing like horses. Cotton grass swishes back and forth. All night long the wind circles the log, flattening the sleeping bag and caressing my legs.

The next day I continue fighting the wind until midafternoon, when it seems silly to risk going farther. I surf up onto a steep shore, and the kayak unexpectedly rolls as the bow catches on a boulder, and a wave capsizes me. I'm soaked again. I can't help but laugh in despair.

It feels desperate paddling into isolation, particularly when the miles are so hard won. I allow myself to cry, beating the shoreline with my fists, hoping to purge my doubts. At ten o'clock, like every evening, I spend the agreed-upon half an hour to send my thoughts south to June. But it doesn't seem to work. And how would I know if it did?

Partly to imagine where my spirit might go when my corporeal being dries up, I throw sand up into the air and wonder what it would be like to bury my kayak and stop fighting the sea: just walk out into the water, relax and let the goddess Sedna end the misery of days like this.

Some Inuit elders still believe that every person possesses two souls, known as *turnqaniq*. The human soul is thought to embody the external and visible signs of strength within each individual Inuk. This soul lives only one life on earth before passing on to the next world.

The name soul (*atiq*) hangs invisibly around each person. Generally the *atiq* is given at birth during the naming ritual, and both animals and humans can share it. But once the flesh dies, the *atiq* floats in limbo until another naming ritual.

Turnqaniq may provide less thoughtful Inuit with justification for rape, suicide and even murder. Plus, an afterworld of pain and suffering was never even imagined until Christian missionaries scared Inuit into believing it; before, they had only one continuous afterlife, shared with all the animals, up through the stars, through the night sky's illuminated portal holes. After all, the desperation wrought from everyday survival was thought to be a kind of purgatory. Indeed, in midwinter severe wind-chill factors actually make exposed flesh feel as if it were burning. In such a harsh environment, believing in *turnqaniq* gave meaning to otherwise desperate and difficult lives. If there is an equivalent to hell for Inuit, it is often the here and now—this world, not some afterworld.

Were I an *Inuk,* would my name soul slither off as a seal and my human soul whiz wraithlike through the clouds to an afterworld of peace?

I cannot indulge such self-destructive thoughts for long, if only because of what my disappearance would do to June. Still, the urge to vanish out here makes me feel as if I were pulled by a powerful magnet. It's as if the lack of boundaries and the vastness of horizon has begun to blur everything that I formerly trusted as reality. Soon enough I'll talk to the animals again, I'll hear voices, and everything that I trusted as real—twelve hours of daylight, the hum of machinery and the solace of companionship—will be subverted. Almost like the Inuit vision of the world.

I am not afraid of being alone again, if only because fears are based upon the unknown. Solitude is less intimidating now that I've lasted twenty days to Paulatuk. Nor do I mind failing in this trip, as long as I give it my best shot. Quitting, I keep reminding myself, might have something to do with surviving. But the idea of not accomplishing anything—of getting soaked every night, of being stormbound, of being so late to Kugluktuk that another search is initiated—keeps me going.

Yet breaking through to true cultural understanding has eluded me. I now

Seal skeleton beside the Beaufort Sea

fight the temptation of thinking poorly about Paulatuk. This sea change occurs most every time you spend too many days in a poor Arctic village, just as it does to Inuit plunged into a *Kabloona* city. Too much time amid a strange culture, and you risk losing your tolerance. It's helpful for me to remember that my culture's roots—amid competition, achievement, biblical values and skills orientation—makes it an easy mistake for *Kabloona* to have false expectations of The People. Undoubtedly those cultures who have experienced bigotry would have more empathy for Inuit lives. The danger in making any conclusions about these humble people is that I don't know how they think or what they expect of themselves.

Still, I can't help enumerating all the negatives about Paulatuk. In the 90-degree heat wave, thick-furred huskies were chained up for days at a time without food and water. Rumors abounded of adolescents being sexually abused; as many as five twelve-year-olds were pregnant in the middle school classroom. Few people were awake by noon, nor was anyone working or hunting. One of the best hunters in town was asking *me* if I had seen any belugas. Kids were begging on the dirt streets with the same sort of canny desperation of open-palmed children in third world countries.

While I'm beginning to understand the former traditions of Inuit, figuring out who they are now is more difficult. Part of the challenge is letting go of the idea that they should subscribe to my modern work ethic. While it is one thing to criticize those *Kabloona* in inner-city America who've become self-indulgent because of welfare, Inuit have never been interested in work as I know it. Welfare (called social assistance in Canada) was originally foisted upon them in hopes that they would eventually enter the working world, but their work ethic is still different from mine. Inuit collect social assistance checks as a means to continue hunting.

The RCMP, Hudson's Bay Company traders, and missionaries introduced social assistance to Inuit in 1923. Originally the idea was to prevent starvation, but by the end of World War II the Canadian and American governments had already so far corrupted traditional culture by moving the nomadic hunters into villages that they had to continue protecting them. Numbered Eskimo disks, one and a half inches wide, were worn around their necks like dog tags or sewn into their clothing and presented to traders each month as identification for food and supplies. Unlike the former system of checking in by name only, this allowed the Canadian government to keep track of its "aborigines" and prevented The People from taking someone else's share of credit (although some people shared an *atiq* or changed it if they were having bad luck, confusing bureaucrats to no end). It may have been akin to ticking off heads of cattle, but the government, in addition to whatever acts of compassion it felt obliged to perform, wanted to prove its sovereignty over its northern coasts by counting their residents.

For centuries, healthy hunters provided country food for those people who could not hunt for themselves. Shamans tended to the sick. Elders essentially retired. Every Inuit somehow gave back to the community, even if he or she did not provide food. Elders provided invaluable advice, old women made clothing, and those who could not help committed suicide so that they would not become burdens. When the government started giving out social assistance checks or credits at trading posts, it was tantamount to telling Inuit that they should not work for the community in return. This disoriented Inuit; they always gave back somehow. As The People began living their own, newly separated lives in small houses, social assistance corrupted their sense of community.

It is useful for me to keep in mind the attitudes of colonizer versus colonized. O. Mannoni wrote: "Civilized man is painfully divided between the desire to correct the errors of the savages and the desire to identify himself with them in his search for the lost Paradise (a Paradise which at once casts doubts upon the merit of the very civilization he is trying to transmit to them)." Mannoni could have been writing about me. I am alone in a paradisiacal wilderness, full of respect for the traditions of Inuit but then confused when I find these people caught in a depraved limbo, somewhere between paradise and the ugly side of modern civilization.

Into Amundsen Gulf and Nunavut

I glide north beneath bulbous and ashen cliffs that rise in columns like the legs of ancient, petrified elephants. Behind me to the south lie the waters of Darnley Bay. Soon I will turn east into the open Amundsen Gulf. It is July 21.

I cinch the spray skirt before rounding Halcro Point into the full force of the wind. I emerge into the spin cycle, fighting for my life to keep the boat upright and paddling so hard against the headwind that my tendons clench all the way down to my calves. The surf froths wildly against granite ledges, and I feel the water-borne vibration of boulders clunking below. Spray covers my face, and I call it quits at a protected cove, preparing myself for more northeasterly wind.

On the plain a hundred feet above sea level, the tundra has absorbed an old sod house. There are chunks of coal and whalebone, unlikely dandelions and tall grass, wooden sled pieces and a triangular sandstone skin-flensing tool indented with human fingerprints. I wrap my fingers over the palm-size reverse arrowhead, predecessor to the ulu, and find that my hand fits perfectly. Sod houses like this are reputed to be from the early Dorset Culture.

In a five-mile radius there is no further trace of these ancients. I spend two days as this former family might have: walking around with all my clothes on in the hope of drying them in the wind and scanning the horizon for bears.

Surf-battered jellyfish pulsate beyond the shore breaks: dinner plate–size, pink-rimmed orbs of translucent plasma, trailing ropy tentacles as thick as human umbilical. *Cyanea arctica* can grow to be six feet wide, with tentacles as long as a hundred feet. "If toxicity is related to size," E. C. Pielou wrote, "the arctic jellyfish is an animal to fear." Although it may have been just the alcohol talking, a Paulatuk *Inuk* told me that jellyfish were disembodied vaginas cut from Sedna, who birthed the seals, walruses and whales.

In 1914 Stefansson counted thousands of belugas surfacing between here and Victoria Island. In a similar range I have seen only one brown skeleton. From the site that later became Paulatuk, Stefansson counted four hundred seals in several minutes. So far I've seen only a half dozen, one floating belly up in the delta. Whereas Stefansson described the Parry Peninsula as limit-

One of many abandoned sod/wood houses

less swan-breeding grounds, I've seen only a dozen. Were I to wax scientific like a *Kabloona,* I would say that wildlife is declining. But Inuit don't bother counting because they know that wildlife comes and goes in an unpredictable and cyclical fashion.

Out on an isolated sand spit, removed from marauding foxes, a colony of arctic terns springs up and down. There, to my great delight, in the midst of the swarming, screeching terns, a Sabine's gull (*Xema sabini*) pecks the shoreline for krill, while two chicks—fluffy gray balls hung with unlikely red beaks—rest beneath a driftwood log. Sabine's gull has the same black-capped head and forked tail as the terns, who tolerate the gull as one of their own. Without warning the gull pounces toward the chicks but is beaten back by a surprised cloud of terns helicoptering up and down with minute tail feather adjustments.

I nap frequently. Out of the wind in a hollow on the tundra, I open my eyes to the sight of the grass moving in the wind, as if the earth were shaking its shaggy-maned head. At a small spring, dappled green on the edges with goose scat, I cup slightly acidic and bitingly cold, clean water in my hands and drink deeply.

When the rain sheets horizontally across the sky, I retreat to the tent and watch the temperature fall to freezing. I no longer feel the fear of plunging over some abyss into loneliness. By mimicking the families who lived here

Arctic tern flying above Sabine's gull

for several months of the year, I have found a small sense of belonging. I try to absorb all, as if I were an *Inuk* moving across the land in search of food: looking for tracks, noting the passage of birds and closing my eyes to listen.

A ptarmigan clucks past, and I open my eyes to find the sun wrestling with the clouds. Aside from a mysterious outboard engine noise that I can't locate, I follow a clattering to a cliff above my camp and observe rocks melting out from gray permafrost ice exposed to the sun. On the cliff's edge, overhanging a narrow beach 150 feet below, is a scuffed-down circle of tundra beside an unnatural pile of boulders where hungry Inuit hunters once stoned passing caribou.

By singing each morning to the bearded seal that investigates my kayak, or dancing with my arms lofted antler style above my head to lure a caribou into camp, I have found a sort of companionship. But I am losing patience with the weather. Inuit used to believe that storms are caused by death. Picking up seaweed is said to create wind. Killing a spider will cause rain or fog.

If winter comes early, I will walk overland to Paulatuk, sixty miles away, when the ocean freezes up. If the wind stops blowing, I will jump in my kayak and continue east.

On the third day of waiting, July 24, the wind spins from east to west. I take a gamble and sail around Pierce Point, past an abandoned DEW Line site and the blown-down shacks of House Point. I can't bear to stop; the ruins would only provoke loneliness. Nothing is permanent here.

Dark clouds fly out of an angry sky as I invoke whatever gods might be listening to let my bouncing kayak pass through unscathed, if only so that I can later warn others not to come here. Wind whistles through dried-out planks and snowmobile oil cans and rusted engines. Wooden bows, copper-tipped arrows and bone-shafted harpoons rot into the tundra, while sod houses slump into the green hillsides.

I fly, like the shaman of yore, past flesh-colored limestone bluffs. Wind furs the wave tops, while surf bursts in high clamor against steep walls. The kayak skims across the water faster than I can run. I reef the sail and lean windward. Sedges and cinquefoil riffle atop blond-pebbled cliffs. Every mile or two, coves break the limestone walls, with surf breaking loudly up onto chocolate-colored sand beaches and oozing down out of the hills.

I point into a protected cove, pick a wave and ride it in. Seconds before the wave lets go, I loosen my spray skirt and throw my paddle ashore like a harpoon. As my kayak begins to slide back into the next wave, I leap out and snatch the bowline, promptly slipping on a wet rock and into the oncoming wave. Two more waves fill the boat as I crawl up the beach, cursing and heaving five hundred pounds of waterlogged Klepper.

It is two in the morning. I have kayaked forty-two miles in fifteen hours. It is late July, but it feels like early November. I'm soaked. My hands are numb and shaking so violently that it takes me an hour to pitch the tent.

Over the next twenty-four hours I drag the tent inland, twice. The storm roars louder and louder into the cove, as the tide, normally two feet, eventually creeps ten feet higher. I drag *Swims* uphill and repitch the tent a third time above the inundated cove on top of the cliffs. Rain sheets the tent windows, so that inside, it's like trying to peer out from a car wash.

As the rain stops, the wind continues to throw in black clouds from the distant Bering Sea. I walk east, then south and finally back north, chased by wheeling glaucous gulls protecting their broods above limestone walls. Errant caribou flicker on distant hillsides, and various microbial life forms fill the rain puddles. Yet this particular landscape is so devoid of smells that I wonder if it's all going dead.

When I discover the postcoital smell of rotting kelp—heaped high by the storm tide—or the fennel sweetness surrounding the green grass of a ground squirrel colony, I sit down, close my eyes and inhale deeply. While curled up in sensory delight, listening to the amplified *sik sik sik sik sik sik sik sik sik sik* of ground squirrels burrowed below, I recall the rancid smell of a polar bear carcass hanging from a meat rack in Tuk.

Right now a battle is raging about the bear. No one can agree which territory will keep the coveted polar bear–shaped license plates next year when the Northwest Territories is split into the new territory of Nunavut. The two-dollar coin, the *toonie,* also features a polar bear.

I sit just outside the boundary of Nunavut. In April, a fifth of Canada will be made into the new territory, giving its residents ownership of 136,000 square miles, a tenth of which they own mineral rights to. The Canadian government will also give $1.148 billion to the 23,000 Inuit within the new territory.

Nunavut's borderline begins halfway up Hudson Bay, zigzags northwest into Amundsen Gulf, several miles east of me, then cuts back east, splitting Victoria Island in two and taking the 110th meridian until adjacent with the northern tip of Ellesmere Island. Nunavut will include most of the twenty-five major islands west of Greenland. Anyone seeking solitude here can find it quickly, as the population density rounds out to one person per thirty-nine square miles. Even good hunters in Nunavut will be hard pressed in this vast space to find one of a million roaming caribou, a hundred thousand muskoxen, a hundred thousand whales and walrus and millions of visiting birds.

An explicit part of both Nunavut and Inuvialuit agreements is that Inuit "surrender" those areas that they do not own subsurface or mineral rights to. Nunavut negotiations were called "friendly," another way of saying that the government may have carefully hoarded much of the oil, diamond and gold potential. According to the Nunavut "royalty cap," Inuit will collect 5 percent royalties of the federally owned mineral developments but are prohibited from earning royalties exceeding the average Canadian income.

Nunavut is only one of numerous Canadian indigenous land claims. While the international media are celebrating this as the largest land reform, the uncelebrated and more financially generous Inuvialuit Final Agreement (for Tuk and Paulatuk) has been forgotten. The government's *Statistics Quarterly* shows a "metals" extraction of nearly a million dollars per year from the Northwest Territories since the IFA was signed, most of which tithes the federal (rather than territorial) government. Hardly any of the region's diamond and gold mines even employ Inuit. Ask the average Inuvialuit what he thinks of the IFA and he'll reply that nothing has changed.

I've already seen enough isolated Inuit villages to realize that a benevolent land reform might mean nothing to The People. In their hunting camps they lead noble and happy lives for several months a year, but in their villages, full-time disenchantment and unemployment demoralize even the strongest people.

By the time I reach the Croker River, another hundred miles closer to the village of Kugluktuk, I am ready to go ashore to break down my outriggers

While waiting three days for sea ice to subside from Perry Island, I was mesmerized by the surreal Arctic light. (Snow geese and old-squaw ducks appear along the shore.)

After three weeks alone, I found a special peace during a midnight sunset on Adelaide Peninsula.

Caribou migrate across the continent's roof like the bison that once filled the Great Plains.

Muskoxen guarding a calf on Flaxman Island. The muskox preceded Paleo-Eskimos across the Bering land bridge and survived extremes that killed off all other North American oxen.

Red fox kits napping outside their den, Prudhoe Bay

Launching from a white shell beach into Queen Maud Gulf, I knew that I would not see people for several weeks.

It was inexplicable good luck for me to hitch a ride across Rae Strait on the Ocean Search, *the first cutter to cross the Northwest Passage in a decade.*

In Gjoa Haven harbor, my new French friends raised me in a bosun's chair, then hauled the sails—sheer bliss.

Rough-legged hawks take over an abandoned Alaska airstrip floodlight—nature often prevails over such Arctic encroachments.

Snowy owl hunting in midnight light

King eider circling Amundsen's wrecked ship, the Bay Maud, in Cambridge Bay

Tens of thousands of snow geese like this one crowd the remote Queen Maud Gulf.

I was glad to be alone under this rare sun parhelion outside Umingmaktuuq.

Escaping satellite TV in Elu Inlet, mid-May

My down parka was no match for this man's caribou jacket in Melville Sound.

The soulful David Amagainik contemplating bones in an ancient stone house, Elu Inlet, mid-July

wo barren ground grizzlies lurked outside the ence while this Kugluktuk woman butchered her inter caribou supply near Coronation Gulf.

At Shingle Point, after a beluga whale was stripped of muktuk. Inuit confront life and death at a much younger age than most North Americans.

Meeting a polar bear—known to northern Inuit as Tôrnârssuk (The One Who Gives Power)—became more important to me than anything else.

In the Gulf of Boothia, 2,100 miles into my journey, the September wind and six-knot tides pushed icebergs faster than I could paddle.

and sails in the dying wind. The hillsides are waving with lupine. Although driftwood lines the shore, the river isn't shown as starting from the tree line on the map (another failure of government cartography that any *Inuk* would point out). Ground squirrels scatter and whistle. The small beach hidden below a bluff is blindsided, and something tells me not to go ashore. Around the corner I find a cinnamon-colored bear with blond stockings, lying in wait, head resting on paws. As I slide fully into view on the water in front of this bear, it hurtles up the hillside.

Around another corner appears the wreck of the *Nechiluk,* driven ashore by a storm in 1968. It lists slightly to port, hardly rusting, as though it had been abandoned just yesterday.

Gulls shriek as a long-tailed jaeger darts away, with batlike wingbeats, to search out nests with less wary hens. A molting Canada goose plops into the water in front of me, so I drop the sail and wait, but to my frustration, it seems to have disappeared. As I sit there mystified, two red-throated loons quack through the sky to the north. *Kabloona* would call the darkening clouds coincidence, but Inuit lore says that red-throated loons passing to seaward will bring rain.

I point to shore yet a third time, only to spy a hairy brown leg lofted above a nearby sand dune, stretching. I pull out the binoculars and see that it's a napping grizzly, only forty yards away. Three weeks without conversation, I paddle closer and say, "Hello, Mr. Bear."

Rather than run, the bear rolls upright, hisses, walks down to water's edge, tests the temperature with its right paw and calmly walks in after me. I view all this through the lens of a video camera. Through the zoom, his steady, splash-free movements are cocksure and hungry-looking. Even worse, it seems that he is within inches of my kayak. His head quickly fills the frame. A dollop of moisture hangs from his nostrils. His brown eyes flash in the sunlight. His yellowing incisors jut below the flapping gums. I drop the camera onto its neck leash and splash my double blade into action.

After a minute of paddling, I look back. To my great relief, there's plenty of sea room. But once again I have broken the aura of respect that these animals deserve.

Inuit Relocations

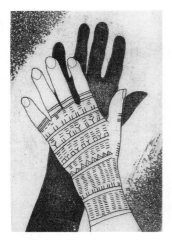

Beautiful Hands

I pull ashore just before midnight, at the ruins of an old hunting camp. Rather than rip my tent floor atop broken glass and rusted metal, I camp forty yards downwind. Curls of Canada goose excrement lay thick at my feet, reminiscent of a spring lawn aerated with dirt plug cuttings. Yet sleeping among the residue of *Branta canadensis* feels as natural as sleeping on my own front lawn.

The weather turns sultry hot after the sun drops into the sea, so I gather up abandoned fifty-five-gallon drums and roll them to the windward side of my tent to block the oncoming squall. As I wait for it to hit, I sift through enamel cups and bowls, silverware, a caribou jacket, a pickax, a chisel, vise grips, screwdrivers, hammers, dolls, a dory, jars filled with coffee turned to green moldy dirt, soap and unidentifiable old food.

Previously this culture tipped bone and wood arrows with copper and sewed caribou-skin anoraks. Many of the women were tattooed. If they wanted a drink, they cupped water in their hands. When enamel cups, stainless steel knives, glimmering mirrors and muzzle-loaders arrived, Inuit felt a new sense of power. But most families were caught in a paradox with these new possessions. They could not resume their nomadic lifestyle of following the animals. All their new heavy tools acted as ballast.

Even today it is easier for Inuit to leave things behind than it is to burden a boat or *kamotik*. Inuit are little different from most poor cultures throughout the Americas: Survival precedes environmentalism.

On the beach below me, a sleeping bearded seal's fur has gone ashen. It's as if the storm's vortex, plying its tentacles across the sky, had sucked us dry. The wind hits with a shudder of air being released from my open tent door. The water goes suddenly flat with the sound of pouring peas. The seal's coat wets to gunmetal gray.

I dive into my tent. Barrels clank in the wind above the rhythmic breathing of surf on sand. I fall asleep to this metallic symphony (which should keep bears away), thinking about how wind trips on sharp metal edges in contrast with how it merely flows across earth and water. No wonder animals avoid human camps.

I come awake an hour later, startled by silence. The squall has passed.

I unzip my tent. Out in the lagoon the seal plops its square flippers with all the playfulness of a child cannonballing into a pool. I distend my nostrils for whatever new smells the rain will wrest out of the ground and immediately smell feces more sulfurous than any goose shit. I must be camped above an old Inuit toilet.

In the morning I paddle up to a lone shack, increasing my pace and pushing the double blade ferociously. A man appears to be leaning against the door frame, and I'm desperate for conversation. But my eyes cannot discern movement, and I become frustrated. I look down for the last minutes, promising myself not to glance up until I get closer. In front of the beach below the shack, I finally look up and find that the shadow of the dark-room cabin has painted a black, humanoid form onto the door frame. It's yet another trick of the spacious tundra.

Shadows like this speak to the ghostly drift of life across this landscape. With the exception of a few birds and small mammals, nothing stays. Thousands of caribou, harried by wolves, bears and wolverines, have passed through and grazed the tundra dry, indenting the ground. Suddenly all are gone. Entire herds, along with clouds of insects, vanish or relocate. Even satellite telemetry collars leave scientists baffled about the inexplicable transit of life here.

The nearby abandoned DEW Line attracted this settlement. Many died from tuberculosis and influenza. The government relocated the survivors north to Victoria Island or east to Kugluktuk. Inuit abandoned their possessions and left like migrating caribou.

In 1953 the government made its most infamous relocation five hundred miles north of here, moving seventeen Inuit families to Ellesmere and Cornwallis Islands (where Inuit had never lived), beside the Grise Fjord and Resolute Bay DEW Line stations. At 58 degrees north, in Quebec, the families had never experienced three months of total darkness. At their new home, near 75 degrees north, more than a thousand miles from the tree line, the sun sinks below the horizon in late October and does not rise again until early February. Nor had these "people of the caribou" ever hunted polar bears or walrus. If not for the government's bringing in other Inuit walrus and seal hunters from Baffin Island, the Quebec Inuit would have starved.

The cold is a presence on Ellesmere and Cornwallis Islands. Winter kept everyone confined indoors. The wind brought instant frostbite to their cheeks. As the peculiar depression of Arctic night set in, and sea ice

One of many abandoned distant early warning stations

groaned the bays shut, the Quebec Inuit thought of their former home without ice beneath the ground. It was hard for these people not to dwell in the memory that the darkest part of winter in Inukjuak still held ten hours of daylight. Down south they lived off fifty-two local plants and animals. In Resolute and Grise Fjord they were forced to survive off half a dozen species.

Women were used for sex by *Kabloona* men, while Inuit men labored at the DEW Line site, which, along with the *Kabloona* housing, was too far away to walk to in winter. During the hungry months they sifted through the *Kabloona* dump for discarded food.

The government initially insisted that these relocations were to prevent Inuit from starving in Quebec, but by 1989 the government had agreed to move volunteers back south to their original homelands. The following year the Aboriginal Affairs Committee conceded that Inuit had been moved to support Canada's sovereignty. Inuit testimony referred to The People's being used as "human flagpoles." Correspondence and documents show that the cold war had sparked Canada's fears about Russian-educated infiltrators and the U.S. military's staking claim to uninhabited Canadian islands. By relocating Inuit, Canada staked its sovereignty and ownership to these northern islands thought to be rich with minerals. Quebec Inuit began to press for a $10 million "heritage claim" as compensation. By 1996 the government had quietly paid up, sans apology or any admission of wrongdoing.

The subject is still hotly debated. Although relations are typically cordial between Inuit and *Kabloona,* their Resolute townsites are still several miles apart, as if Inuit inhabited a northern ghetto. Books were written both for and against Inuit relocations, with claims of racial abuse and starvation versus claims that the starving Inuit had freely volunteered to move north. Through it all, Inuit are learning to distrust *Kabloona* motives. In the minds of most northern Inuit, seen as clear as meltwater atop sea ice, governments do not move bushy-eyebrowed folk from their homelands.

In my mind, it is no small wonder that Canadian Inuit question today's government. Even the groundbreaking benevolence of Nunavut is viewed askance by The People.

The Warning of Diamond Jenness

Appearances deceive in the Arctic. Blue lines that denote major rivers on my maps turn out to be only streams gurgling into the sea. In the warm afternoons the flesh-colored cliffs of Victoria Island appear in a heat mirage, stretching up into the sky and extending the normal horizon enough to make me contemplate a quick crossing—until I measure two dozen miles of open water on the map.

Swims with Bears skims several feet above rocks that look like submerged pieces of ice through the distorting pellucid lens of water. This ocean is indolent. When a wind comes, the metallic bright surface shivers, mimicking the textured sand furrows below in a strange parallelogram, and licking gently and rhythmically against the lurching bow of my kayak.

A fist-size loon chick, abandoned by its skittish parents, paddles along the shore and dives repeatedly away from my kayak. I stop to let the gray ball of fluff get away and lift up my T-shirt to pick out several weeks' worth of lint from my belly button. What I find (or rather can't find) shocks me: the hole on my stomach has vanished with the long days of paddling on a freeze-dried-food diet. I am burning up all of my fat.

Singed terraces above show no sign of life except for a caribou skull, dazzling white in the sunlight. I pull my sunglasses on and stare into shallow bays backed with basalt cliffs.

The heat from distant forest fires is carried to me on the south wind, like opening a sauna door. Even in the middle of a five-mile crossing to Cape Bexley, where the Dolphin and Union Strait pinches twenty miles between Victoria Island and the mainland, the air is stifling. With great relief, I find that the narrow strait is more tranquil than Amundsen Gulf behind me.

Back along the mainland, desiccated boulders stretch east. Combined with the distant fire's paling of the sky, I can't help wondering if the Bomb has dropped, if June is gone and the southern world as I knew it is now kaput. As I pull sunglasses back down and squint, I realize that the monotone quality of the landscape, seen through the haze of smoke, blurs all the edges. Shoaled islets, points, promontories, and rock outcroppings appear as one homogeneous, straight coastline. Yet the map shows it rife with nooks and crannies.

For the first time in my journey, I find rock cairns, or *Inuksuit* ("resembling a man"), piled on top of two long leglike rocks, placed to drive caribou down toward waiting hunters. Other cairns, lacking the round stone head on top, are *inuksuapik* used to mark campsites. An *inunnguag* (two piles of stones joined together by a sharp pointer stone on top) shows the way to ancient hunting grounds. The use of such cairns dates back to ancient times, even though The People may have maintained them in the last decade or two.

Stefansson in 1910 found Inuit here who had never seen *Kabloona*. Since he spoke their language and was an adept rifle hunter (even though he lacked the skill or patience to employ a harpoon), Inuit could not conceive of him as an outsider. Stefansson wrote that they "take me for an Eskimo." Since he found several men with light hair and bearded faces like his own, Stefansson set out trying to prove that these Eskimos were descendants of the Vikings.

In the winter these people lived in snow *iglus*—which Stefansson said the Eskimos to the west could no longer build—on the sea ice, hunting seals. But in the summer it's hard to imagine even the most skilled hunters surviving in such a moonscape as Cape Bexley, utilizing only spears, hooks and snares. Appearances are deceiving: The land might support hidden animal life, and maybe my isolation is making me jump to conclusions. It has been said before, but lonely explorers, pining for the easy hunting of non-migratory regions, similarly dismissed this great southern sweep of tundra, periodically rife with caribou migrations, as the Barren Lands.

On August 6 I paddle into Bernard Harbor. After the sterility of Cape Bexley, this harbor must have seemed like an oasis to Inuit. A sandhill crane calls out, like a man screaming into a long metal pipe. Geese honk. Sandpipers frolic and bob their tails in ponds, green with animal feces, that are weirdly elevated several feet above the tundra. Acres of avens gone to seed

*Red-throated
loon chick*

wave their fuzzy white wand heads beside orange-lichened rocks. Caribou run off in zigzagging patterns, as if running from rifle fire.

Herds of muskox growl in prolonged burps alongside my tent as I try to sleep, but it is better to leave them alone than to stand up and photograph them, inviting a charge. From the north-facing tent window, the orange sun lowers into a cloud bank. Then, at 11:15 p.m., it inflates into a red kickball and bounces into the sea.

In the morning I poke through a collapsed cabin. Outside, incredibly, an old Model T collects rust as a testimony to this harbor's former life as an RCMP outpost and a Hudson's Bay Company trader's camp. I walk in a dizzy circle, close my eyes, and feel overcome with separation anxiety. This tranquil harbor, now deserted, was once alive with hunters, broken into a dozen bands of a thousand people. These so-called Copper Eskimos were named after the green and blue ore that they found washed up on beaches and under cliffs, from Cape Bexley to Bathurst Inlet, four hundred miles away.

During the Copper Age in Europe, people discovered that copper ore could be heated to high temperatures and crafted into a substance stronger than stone. Copper Inuit technology was much simpler. They hammered the pure copper—stronger than chert, flint and bone—into hard but brittle arrowheads, harpoon points, adz blades, knife blades, ice picks, rivets, sewing needles, pins and spearpoints.

These people, according to the renowned anthropologist Franz Boas, were ripe for study as a pure hunter-gatherer culture. Unlike other Inuit to the east and west, they had no direct trade or commerce with Europeans, with the exception of several brief *Kabloona* visits.

Much of the iron lofted by these remote Inuit came from Captain Robert McClure's HMS *Investigator,* wrecked on Banks Island in 1853. One crewman noted that these "Esquimaux" lacked the mercenary spirit of Alaskan natives, already despoiled by "evil" civilization.

McClure abandoned twenty thousand pounds of salted meats, peas, tea, chocolate, sugar, potatoes, flour, rum, brandy and tobacco, none of which interested Inuit. For the next half century Copper Inuit dumped out English food (tentatively tasting biscuits and sugar). They broke apart iron barrel hoops for tools and cut the softwood crates into arrows and spears, rather than work with inferior driftwood. The *Investigator's* iron and wood were distributed for hundreds of miles, irrevocably changing Copper Inuit culture.

The women had previously toiled over skin clothing. After the influx of iron sewing needles (the flexible, unforged copper needles broke easily), stitching a caribou parka or sealskin kamik became quick work. By the time Diamond Jenness studied them, in 1914, they had already abandoned copper for iron and other trade goods.

At Bernard Harbor, Jenness lived with these people and learned their language. He too was short, modest and soft-spoken. He began smoking a pipe. His patience won his subjects' cooperation as he measured and charted the size of their skulls, teeth, foreheads, faces, height, weight, eye color (mostly brown), hair length and eyebrows. He summarized that bushy eyebrows were rare (confirming the origin of the word *"Kabloona"*). Jenness also found that their hands were too small for bushy eyebrowed men's mittens. Inuit weighed the same as Europeans, women tended to be bow-legged and pigeon-toed, men lacked facial hair, and their narrow noses and close-set eyes made it difficult for them to use wide-lens *Kabloona* binoculars. In the winter, snow cleaned their unwashed summer faces and made them look like different people. One day Jenness made the mistake of mentioning that they smelled objectionable.

An elderly *Inuk* replied, "That is not strange, for we noticed the same thing about you."

After measuring every conceivable color in their eyes, as well as uncommon eye folds that protected them from snow blindness, Jenness dismissed Stefansson's theory that the Copper Eskimos' blue eyes came from Viking intermarriage, a nod to Stefansson's own Scandinavian roots. Jenness, in one of his first publications, carefully proposed that old age, snow blindness or genetic anomalies caused the strange eye color. As for blond hair, the anthropologist respectfully demurred that he had never met such an Eskimo.

He drew and documented eighty-three cat's cradle games that depicted vulvas, hunters, kayakers, dog anuses and various animals. Because Inuit believed that these figures invoked evil spirits, Jenness was never shown them in sunlight. His resulting book, *Eskimo String Figures,* filled two hundred pages.

On the basis of his work here, he became Canada's most distinguished anthropologist. What made Dr. Jenness extraordinary—particularly as a former British subject, educated in a less humane and Victorian era of science—was his *compassion* for the Copper Eskimos. Rather than place them beneath Europeans on the conventional ladder of creation, he respected their separate culture, shared their food and customs, and eventually began to think as they did.

After three years living, traveling and hunting with The People, he began to see them more like family than fascinating subjects of study. He was adopted by Ikpakhuak (the Dirty One) and his wife, Higilak (the Icehouse), who anxiously looked after him. Higilak sewed him skin clothing. Ikpakhuak prevented him from losing face in front of other Inuit. Their daughter Kanneyuk (Little Sculpin, whom Dr. Jenness named Jennie) became his sister and favorite companion.

When he tried to record Inuit songs on his Edison wax phonograph, the adults of Bernard Harbor shrank away in horror, thinking that an evil spirit hid inside the machine. Jennie came to his rescue. By replaying her silly laughter and singing, she convinced her people that recordings were a game. Jenness eventually took away 150 songs. He also filled his ship with thousands of cultural artifacts—harpoons, bows and arrows, clothing, snares, spears, kayaks—in exchange for gunpowder, lead and steel traps.

During his time with the family Jenness was put on trial for murder by Inuit who believed that he had killed an *Inuk* man a hundred miles away by stealing his soul. Jenness had never even met the man. The anthropologist shrewdly enlisted a shaman, who convinced everyone—more through flim-flam gibberish than sorcery—that the *Kabloona* was innocent. Nonetheless, the dead man's family, according to local customs, could have killed Jenness.

Jenness wrote about leaving the Copper Eskimos:

> Even as we sailed away traders entered their country seeking fox furs; and for those pelts so useless for real clothing they offered rifles, shotguns, steel tools, and other goods that promised to make life easier. So the Eskimos abandoned their communal seal hunts and scattered in isolated families along the coasts in order to trap white foxes during the winter when the fur of that animal reaches its prime. Their dispersal loosened the old communal ties that had held the families together. The men no longer labored for the entire group, but hunted and trapped each one for his family alone.

Inuk *spearing char*

The anthropologist became the spokesman for Copper Inuit, but his position may have derived partly from guilt. After all, Dr. Jenness initially accompanied Stefansson to the Arctic to further his own career and to accomplish agendas of science that may have compromised Inuit, even though his later writings popularized their plight. He also took twenty-five hundred of their culture's tools (to be displayed in an Ottawa museum). On April 18, 1916, he made his last trade, according to his methodical journal, "for services," giving a 30-30 rifle to the Dirty One, formerly a great bow and harpoon hunter.

Jenness also noted that the RCMP and southern Indians had shamed Inuit into giving up infanticide, especially of girls. Before his departure, little Inuit girls suddenly seemed to be everywhere. The rifle replaced the bow. Caribou populations declined. Iron replaced copper, and Western dress replaced skin clothing.

In 1920, Jenness received a message from his adopted mother: "Higilak has heard of your marriage, and she longs for a picture of the strange white woman who is now her daughter. She wants, too, a bowl, a large agate bowl. But the picture she desires more than all."

His aging "father," the Dirty One, cabled Dr. Jenness to come visit quickly before Ikpakhuak could die. Also, the Dirty One mentioned, he no longer had the rifle that his "son" had given him. He had become poor.

The anthropologist now fully understood the undoing of this ancient culture. Seasoned in World War I, and turning from the cold regimen of anthropological quantification, he wrote a nonscientific book, *The People of the Twilight*. One sentence of this popular work summarized his philosophy and took personal responsibility for his well-intentioned actions with the Eskimos: "Were we the harbinger of a brighter dawn, or only messengers of ill omen, portending disaster?"

Dr. Jenness's warning about stopping the onslaught of white culture and disease was largely ignored. Shortly afterward his "mother," Higilak, and others began dying from influenza.

In 1929 a wrongly accused murderer, Uloqsaq, was returned to the present-day site of Kugluktuk, "place of falling waters." His imprisonment in southern Canada with tubercular Indians had left him wheezing and limping with an incurable form of the disease. While taking his last breaths in a stuffy skin tent filled with his relatives, Uloqsaq infected several villagers. On September 25 the newly arrived Catholic priest wrote in the Coppermine Codex Historicus kept by all Catholic missions: "We've finished putting on the roof. Death of Oulouksak [*sic*], one of the killers of Fathers Leroux and Rouvière."

As the priest watched the disease infect numerous adults and children, many of them related to the two Inuit who had killed Fathers Leroux and

Rouvière in self-defense, he wrote in his codex that tuberculosis was God's punishment.

A resident doctor repeatedly asked the territorial government to send a sunlamp to help cure tuberculosis. Numerous planes arrived from the south, but none carried a sunlamp. The doctor, who worked in Kugluktuk's "hospital," finally flew back to Ottawa to argue with his superiors about sending him proper support—sunlamps and various medical supplies and manpower—to combat the epidemic. For all his efforts they refused to send supplies, let alone him, or any doctor, back.

When Jennie Kanneyuk's "galloping consumption" spread, her vertebrae collapsed, compressing the spinal cord and bending her back as she lost control of her bladder and bowels. Onlookers could hear air wheezing through a hole in her back. Since Jennie thought that a sunlamp was coming, she kept up hope. On a wireless, she cabled her "brother," Diamond: "When are you coming? Maybe I will die before you come. I do not know. When you come bring me some pretty calico. Now I am a little better. In the summer it was otherwise. Kanneyuk."

Dr. Jenness knew how grave the epidemic was and responded: "I shall never forget my father and my younger sister. Though I would like to see you, it cannot come to pass. It is too far way. I am getting old. Do not be frightened. When we die we will meet each other. We will be happy all together."

The Anglican and Catholic priests fought over giving Jennie last rites. After losing to the Anglicans, the Catholic priest wrote that she was "a poor, sick, fantasized woman."

She gulped one last time, fighting for air, then pronounced herself dead: "I cannot live anymore."

Tears streamed down her husband's and father's cheeks. Lacking the wood for a coffin, Kekpuk, her husband, sewed his wife's body into a canvas bag, as their two-year-old son, Aime, looked on from where he was being carried in the *amautiq* (hood) of an aunt. The Protestant burial was performed by digging a shallow grave in the thin layer of topsoil above permafrost ice. Kekpuk then followed his wife's last request and built an open box over the head of the grave so that Jennie could breathe, out on an airy island of the Coppermine River delta, washed by breezes from the Coronation Gulf.

Tuberculosis and its shortness of breath are a nightmarish disease to Inuit, in a way that *Kabloona* administrators were hard pressed to understand. English-speaking people knew that it was a tiny germ forming lumps in the lungs that caused tuberculosis. For those people who spoke Inuktitut, the cause of the disease meant little. They mostly knew that the verb "to breathe" is derived from an Inuktitut root that means "the soul, that which is eternal." The way Inuit saw it, dying without breath would prevent them from entering the afterworld.

The disease took Kekpuk and the Dirty One two years later, perhaps mercifully, before the Copper Inuit lost their nomadic ways and moved into village squalor. Jennie's son, Aime, became part of this new survivors' culture: part Christian, part traditionalist. Bernard Harbor and various other outposts were abandoned for the hundred-mile-distant Kugluktuk, which *Kabloona* renamed Coppermine after the lodes of pure copper plucked off the land. In 1946, sixteen years after the government had withdrawn its medical support, Kugluktuk got its first nursing station. Dr. Diamond Jenness died in 1969, having spent his retirement writing the five-volume *Eskimo Administration,* criticizing inept and cruel government policies in the Arctic. Pensive until the end, this overlooked anthropologist stood alone among his colleagues who studied "the Eskimo." While Stefansson moved from Canada to the United States, actively promoting himself, denying his bastard son (like the fraudulent conquerors of the Pole, Cook and Peary), Jenness remained in Canada, trying to protect The People.

In 1990 Jennie's sickly great-grandchild Ikpakhuak (named after his great-grandfather) was sent to a southern hospital. Following the grandfather Aime's idea to invoke tradition, his grandson was renamed Diamond Jenness as a means of taking on a sturdier *atiq,* to give him longevity and good health.

Since then, even with modern antibiotics, tuberculosis infects scores of Inuit each year—mostly boys, fifteen to twenty-four years old—at a rate thirty-five times higher than that of nonaboriginal Canadians.

Protected Waters of Coronation Gulf

Aurora *with* Inuksuit

East of Bernard Harbor, where Jennie was so sick that she lay in her sled as her parents hunted caribou, I paddle around Cape Lambert and point south toward Kugluktuk. It is August 8. I haven't spoken to another person since leaving Paulatuk, three weeks and 330 miles west. One week of food remains in my kayak. I have taken to wondering if I'll ever come out the other end, still 100 miles away.

The memory of my June makes me dizzy. I wish there were some way for her to know that I'm okay. Every night at ten I have been channeling my thoughts to try to tell her that I am alive and well.

The headland is a series of olive-colored ledges, indented with hollow chambers, sucking in the swell of waves, accelerating the water and forcing it up and outward in a steamy, oceanic cough. A tricky reef is marked by a three-foot high symmetrical *Inuksuit,* built with white boulders and a round black headstone. I swing wide. Black-fuzzed rocks blur below my keel.

Dolomite cliffs rise behind the ledges. In between the ocean's spitting up through the rocks, a pair of nesting peregrine falcons swoop past. Their high-pitched keening is disturbing, but princelier than the rattling of arctic terns diving on my head.

I find drinking water by paddling in toward five unusually inattentive female common eiders and a troop of semipalmated sandpipers, chubby and black-legged, preening in a bed of kelp, damming a freshet. They splash up into the air, relinquishing their bath with silent reluctance. Upstream from the birds is a large puddle that tastes of bittersweet sedge and dwarf birch. I lie down in push-up position, funnel my lips and slurp up a liter before filling my bottles.

For two days a storm traps me on the lifeless and boulder-strewn Cape Krusenstern. I make notes about birds and memorize their Latin names. In the afternoons I wander the lifeless landscape and realize that because of prolific seal life, Inuit could survive here—but only out on the sea ice in their *iglu*s, not on these bouldered and sterile shores.

At dawn on the third day, I sit on a sheet of Arctic dew formed on my kayak and paddle a mile out before the wind can pick up. I follow a fifteen-foot-wide band of quiet water, dampening a cross swell created by opposing currents. For two hours I stop staring at the surf beating against distant cliffs and focus on following this eerie sidewalk of still water toward Locker Point. From somewhere nearby the sky grumble of a small plane upends the stillness and reminds me that I have not seen or talked to people for twenty-three days.

Out in the deep water I hear garbled talking. When I look toward the shore, I imagine men with spears in their hands. Being accustomed to the watery visuals of mixing land and sea airs, as well as my need for company, I have learned to write off these visions as mirages. Still, I can't explain the talking noises and the distinct feeling that I'm not alone as I pull toward shore and figure out how to get around the surf.

On Locker Point, Kugluktuk is so close I can almost smell it. Now the land curves straight south into tranquil Coronation Gulf waters. I shout with relief, then turn on the video camera and begin talking to it as if I had finally found companionship.

For two more long days I stop in at hunting shacks in hopes of finding someone to talk to, but all the camps are empty. I am surprised to find them immaculately clean, without litter and built with attentive detail to the position of the surrounding landscape (as if Inuit missed their nomadic past and still sought inspiration from the sea and earth). Miniature garages house four-wheelers. Plexiglas windows all aim toward the sea.

The tundra is speckled with crowberry and blueberry, freckled with glacial boulders and mostly untussocked. Late-afternoon clouds stack blackly up into the stratosphere as the heat kites off the land above the cool gulf air, allowing me to run under a reefed sail until deafening thunderclaps and cold rain send me cowering to land. Every few miles fifty-five-gallon drums dot the seashore. Turns out that they all are placed upright as giant trash cans, stenciled PLEASE DON'T LITTER. Campsites are neatly stacked with drift firewood; convenient anchor ropes await boats.

By Cape Kendall, a dozen miles from Kugluktuk, the water has turned murky warm from the sediment load of the Coppermine, Rae and Richardson Rivers. I can feel the current pushing against me at several knots, so I paddle in the lee of cold limestone walls until the sound of an approaching outboard engine all but shouts to me across the silence. I kick the left rudder pedal and let the current pull my bow seaward, then paddle out to meet the first person I will have talked to in twenty-five days.

Isaac Klengenberg is surprised to meet a lone kayaker all the way from Paulatuk. He wears a tattered blue gasoline attendant's jumpsuit. His dark and angular features, along with his poor dress and grammar, might make

After twenty-five days alone, outside Kugluktuk

him fit some urban stereotype. Out here, however, Isaac is the master of his own destiny as well as a fast friend. He offers me a beer, but I decline it in favor of soda because, as I manage to enunciate slowly so that the words come out clear, "My system is so cleaned out right now I'm not sure I can handle any alcohol," at which he guffaws.

As I clutch the skiff's gunwale, he reports photographing a walrus on a nearby beach, even though walrus are supposed to live more than a thousand miles away. His brother talked Isaac out of killing it because the animal was too big for their boat. I ask no questions and accept his sighting because the movement of wildlife in these horizons has infinite possibilities. Nor do I ask for details because I can easily imagine seeing the same walrus, then nod back at Isaac to show understanding. Although I am trying to shed a mind-numbing isolation, I am not yet ready to talk. We continue drifting, content with each other's company. For the first time in a month I stop worrying about the position of the shore until my new friend points out that we have drifted west in the current.

There is something new inside me. We are not talking with *Kabloona* pontification and explanation and verbose banter. Mostly we are smiling at each other, comfortably, without the least embarrassment, because Isaac understands that I have been alone out on the sea and that it has been hard. We sit in our respective boats, bobbing along, reveling in each other's company without the nuisance of complicated talk—or much talk at all.

Finally, as if we were both emerging from a dream, he offers to tow me in. I refuse with a shake of my head, then push off and paddle several strokes east as he yanks his engine to life.

I wave with a single finger, carefully dipping in the right, then the left blades of my paddle and bracing for balance against the wake.

He shouts out, "The People will know you are coming. I will tell them on my radio."

As the wake subsides, I film Isaac fading to the west, and with no warning at all I suddenly break down and cry. To make myself stop, I face the hand cam and tell it that I've been holding myself together so tightly for the last twenty-five days that I had forgotten how important people were.

Sailing in sight of Kugluktuk—dozens of square, brown-profiled buildings gumming up the distance like a surreal mirage—I realize what the last 420 miles alone has demanded of me. Like a traditional *Inuk,* I have hardened my heart, traded in linear thought and lived by instinct. In this state of intuitive awareness, I have slipped from the normal thought process of using words to form ideas. Mostly I have been making pictures of things in my head and relying on memory and sensory input. Every day I spontaneously dealt with challenges—aggressive bears, tricky surf and weather changes—relying upon inner workings and gut reactions that seem as distant and inexplicable as Venus.

The celebrated anthropologist Claude Lévi-Strauss described this state of being as "a greater intellectual mobility" because "the native is a logical hoarder, he is forever tying the threads, unceasingly turning over all the aspects of reality, whether physical, social or mental. We traffic in ideas, he hoards them up."

Now that I am confronted by the prospect of civilization and talk, I am filled with an ache. I have hardened my heart toward June to survive, so maybe if I invite her to join me on the way to Umingmaktuuq, she will come to understand how I needed to shut the world out to make it this far.

As I wipe off my tears on a shirtsleeve, I realize how the journey has twisted me. I cannot be alone anymore. It is not just the selfishness of isolating myself from June. Inside somewhere, like a light tripping a fuse, is the illumination that continuing alone would eventually have me speaking in Inuktitut and seeing the world as if I were a shaman in flight. I would feel such a connection to the Earth and Its Great Weather that I would stop trying to verbalize it in favor of simply feeling it deep inside as I do now. It is a wonderful state, being so outwardly possessed, feeling so connected to the land and sea and animals.

For the first time I finally understand the specific sorrow of Inuit: their intuitiveness is lost on the modern world.

Kugluktuk, Place of Falling Waters

Kugluktuk's beach is protected from northerly wind by a ring of limestone islands. The dirt streets and houses hold a sixty-six-foot hill, tucked against the brown rush of the Coppermine River. Four-wheelers buzz back and forth, dodging a shiny-tanked water truck. Boats ply the harbor, and Inuit wave. Unlike the western Arctic, all drivers here wear helmets and life vests. Paulatuk seems small in comparison.

For the last day I have been practicing the words for joining people again: "This is a beautiful place you live in" and, "Hello, how are you?"

Mostly I worry about forgetting how to talk. Before I can reach shore, there is an elder waiting for me in a small boat. His engine won't start, so I paddle over. He is lantern-jawed and calm, clad in studious-looking wire-rimmed glasses. He beams as if he knew me.

"Welcome to *Ker-luck-tuk*," he pronounces it.

"Thank you," I reply with difficulty, and since I can't say the part about how beautiful it is here, I don't want to appear unfriendly, so I say again, all I can manage, "Thank you."

He introduces himself, in workable English, "My name is Aime Ahegona."

I can't believe it. Everywhere I go in the Arctic, history is up and walking around. I ask, "You're not the same Aime, I mean, son of Jennie?"

"Yes, I was two when they buried my mother out on that island." He nods over his shoulder. "Are you the one who came all the way from Paulatuk?"

I nod, smiling.

"That's a mighty long way. You must have seen some things."

I look at him and nod, thinking about driftwood stick figures, the sensation of human forms hunting along the shores. Like seawater thrown from the Cape Lambert chambers, I spit out, "Yeah, you get pretty crazy after being alone for a while."

Aime smiles and corrects me. "Anything happening to you out on the land's not crazy, and most of The People understand this."

He recommends that I go check into the nearby inn to rest. Like most Inuit, he is lost trying to verbalize directions. So he gives up and simply points at the Coppermine Inn, *Kabloona* style, then fingers his clean-shaven chin to refer to my long beard with a smile. He uses the local colloquialism for a shave: "Looks like you need to lose some weight."

*Aime Ahegona of
Kugluktuk*

After I have had plenty of sleep, a few meals and a long soak in a tub, Aime takes me to an elder's home so that I can witness the dying art of throat singing. We doff our shoes by the door, and inside, in front of a television, Aime introduces me to two octogenarians who speak only in Inuktitut, so I bow. The elders, Walter and June, are dressed in traditional kamiks and parkas, and they begin an Inuktitut song. Aime translates. Again, I am meeting living history, because these songs were recorded by Diamond Jenness eighty-seven years ago:

> Whence pray have they always come
> The bull caribou stamping hard on the ground
> I then watching eagerly for it
> The arrow too because I did not want to let it fly
> Whence pray have they always come
> Katainaluk stamping hard on the ground
> ai yei yai ya na
> ye he ye ye yi yan e ya qana

Spit drools down Walter's chin. His eyes are closed, and his body is wracked with gentle shaking as he loses himself to the magic of the song:

> I then after having a desire to go
> The big dog too I did not to let it loose
> Whence pray have they always come
> The sickness after withering me up
> I then in my weakened condition
> My blood too down here sickness not wishing to leave

Several middle-aged women crowd the kitchen. They smile and join in for the soulful chorus chant, produced in wavering notes, from deep within their throats:

> ai yei yai ya na
> ye he ye ye yi yan e ya qana
> ai ye yi yai yana

A three-year-old looks on wide-eyed at the harsh beauty of her grand-mother's voice, riffling back and forth like the beat of surf on a beach. They finish, seemingly exhausted. Aime tells me that they will take no money, so I arrange for gifts to be sent to them and shake their hands as I leave.

Wandering through town, I learn about the March tragedy, which most Inuit would rather not discuss. Steven Ayalik, thirty-one, went on a drunken rampage while his wife was vacationing in British Columbia, sticking a shotgun barrel into his thirteen-year-old stepdaughter's mouth as he shoved her down into a bathtub, blowing her brains out. He then walked into the master bedroom and shot his sleeping seven- and four-year-olds in their faces. Another son came to the front door, but Ayalik waved him off, closed the door and turned the gun to his own head and finished his sad life.

In previous years Ayalik had thrown his infants across rooms, repeatedly beat his wife and tried to rape a neighbor who intervened. After the triple murder the investigating coroner blamed chronically inept social workers, as well as the RCMP for not exercising gun control after the earlier attacks. Ayalik had seven years of arrests, assault convictions and jail sentences. In 1994 a social worker wrote a character reference that allowed Ayalik, despite his previous acts of violence, to buy the murder weapon.

I find Shakespearean graffiti scrawled on a wall that speaks to suicide here: TO BE OR NOT TO BE?

At the hamlet office I meet Dave White, the senior administrative officer (SAO), who oversees town operations. Like most Arctic SAOs, White interfaces well with those southern bureaucrats allocating funds, but like most *Kabloona,* he does not fit in with The People he is serving. He works with a titular *Inuk* mayor, who will leave town at a moment's notice if the hunting is good, along with numerous other Inuit. Most Inuit hamlet workers will find someone to replace them if they leave town or get tired of working, and although it's not exactly irresponsible, it doesn't match the southern work ethic.

Like most SAOs, Dave is overworked and originally from Alberta. In his words, he "only served a year and a half's sentence yet in Coppermine."

Like many *Kabloona,* he prefers calling Kugluktuk by its temporary name, Coppermine. In fact, he complains about how what he thinks are the old names—Spence Bay, Bay Chimo, Pelly Bay and Cambridge Bay—are being retrofitted with new native names. Under a tight-fitting white windbreaker, his belly is as round as a salad bowl. He offers me a cup of coffee, remarking, "How can Inuit drink gallons of this and still go to sleep at night, eh?," then apologizes for not offering me a room in his house; he has other guests.

"How are people dealing with the triple murder and suicide?" I ask.

"Doesn't bother me one way or another. We have a lot of suicides here."

"Really?"

"It's a traditional thing, eh? The Eskimos have been killing themselves since time immemorial whenever times got bad or food ran dry or whenever they were too old and in the way."

"I never knew that the kids traditionally killed themselves."

"Sure, they left them out on the ice all the time."

"I thought that was infanticide?"

"Yeah, same net effect, you bet!" He laughs.

The suicide rate for Inuit is seven times higher than it is for *Kabloona* Canadians. It is different from traditional suicide, when people grew old and hanged themselves, or when food fell short and family members sacrificed themselves in order that others could survive. Modern Inuit suicides are usually teenagers hanging themselves. They see little or no hope for their future, are abused by alcoholic parents, or are following peers who took the same escape. History shows that there is nothing in traditional Inuit culture—Dave White's opinion to the contrary—about young people seeking suicide as a solution for depression.

As for crimes like Ayalik's, during the previous year in the Northwest Territories, assaults occurred at a rate of 5 percent (the rest of Canada experiences one-fifth that many assaults). The local RCMPs, all under thirty and serving out their early careers in Inuit villages, will typically enter more than half the local homes to settle domestic and alcohol-related disputes. But it is rare for RCMPs, unlike their colleagues in southern provinces, to be injured during drunken melees.

As Dave White explains, whenever alcohol seems to be getting out of control, the locals put prohibition back on the ballot. But so far the six hundred-plus voters here have not seen fit to repeal the present "unrestricted" drinking law. Even social workers believe that the restriction of alcohol brings in illegal drugs, encourages bootlegging and distillation of alcohol from other products, or prompts further use of inhalants.

The Coppermine Inn owner has considered serving beer or wine, which would earn a tidy profit and better serve his guests. But he believes that

Inuit would break down the doors and gut the inn if they smelled alcohol inside. Even the RCMP has tried storing confiscated alcohol, yet Inuit broke down the doors and drank it, quickly, lest the alcohol be confiscated yet again.

Although there are still Anglican, Catholic and Pentecostal churches, most Inuit here declare themselves Protestants. The Roman Catholic Church fell out of favor for a few years as the result of revelations of sexual and physical abuse against Inuit children by unnamed priests in the 1960s. One Churchill bishop issued a formal apology to Inuit in 1995, even though charges were never leveled against specific *Kabloona* abusers.

At night the Roman Catholic church of Kugluktuk sometimes shelters lovers. Since *Kabloona* construction workers cannot bring Inuit women and girls back to their inn rooms, word is that the altar within the Catholic church hosts the new consecrations. It strikes me as fittingly ironic.

As a passing kayaker I cannot shed light into all the dark corners of Kugluktuk's cultural assimilation. The most disturbing story comes from a longtime *Kabloona* resident who prefers to remain anonymous and tells me that AIDS among Inuit will soon make tuberculosis look like the common cold. He has no figures to prove this, and the local health care workers will deny it because I am just a passing stranger, but this man, who cares about Inuit, feels certain that the disease is going to devastate Nunavut.

It is not a stretch to imagine AIDS reaching epidemic proportions among Inuit, simply because it would fit a long-standing pattern of neglect. If the Canadian government proceeds as it has in the past—with its relocations, its inept social programs and its indifference to epidemics—the future of Nunavut could follow that of Africa, where most of the population is destined to die young.

It is helpful, as a foreign visitor, to forget cultural differences and simply appreciate The People and their strategically placed hill town, overlooking a diverse and bountiful ecosystem. Kugluktuk is nestled in a corner of Coronation Gulf that freezes over every winter with pan ice rather than multiyear icebergs. The ice melts by July, and then the beach opens for swimming. Eighteen miles east, the warming waters of the Rae and Richardson Rivers hit the far corner of the icy gulf. The tree line is barely a hundred miles away, beside the banks of the Coppermine River. Numerous Canadian canoeists finish their trips at the inn—$125 a night (an extravagance that makes one *Inuk* whistle when I tell him how much I'm paying).

At 10 p.m. a curfew alarm like an approaching freighter's foghorn signals anyone under the age of twenty-one to go home. Consequently, the local sport is staying up all night and outrunning the three harried *Kabloona* constables referred to as "bylaws." They drive their hamlet pickup truck back and forth during curfew, taunted unmercifully by the adolescents. The three RCMPs—also *Kabloona,* but federal employees and generally liked—stick to peacekeeping and leave the nitpicking offenses to the unpopular bylaws.

The town library is staffed by a taciturn twenty-something mother, tending a baby and two squalling children. The three cramped rooms are usually empty of readers and impressively full of mass-market paperbacks. Commercial best-sellers have been checked out mostly by *Kabloona,* while titles with useful information—the *Shotgunners Bible, Drying Fish* and a sewing manual—are rarely checked out.

There are fewer than 150 people in town who still speak Inuktitut, and half of them are bilingual. Yet Kugluktuk is largely illiterate, with less than 10 percent of its Inuit graduating from high school or learning how to read. According to the local census, 50 people here have university degrees, but these are mostly *Kabloona.*

Summer offers plenty of construction work, because of housing shortages, but the warm weather is also the best time for being out on the land. So *Kabloona* carpenters, painters and laborers are flown up from Edmonton or Yellowknife to take the jobs that Inuit don't want. Most Inuit have figured out that being on the dole brings in better income, less stress and more hunting time than any job in town. Nunavut's Hunter Support Program also

The average Inuit consumes twenty-four cases of soda per year.

buys rifles, snowmobiles, four-wheelers and outboard engines for those men who bring the village country food for the elders and nonhunters.

Food is not cheap in the two grocery stores. A box of cornflakes costs $5.15; a pound of bacon, $4.85; a gallon of 2 percent milk, $11.95; a pound of cheese, $8.50; a head of iceberg lettuce, $2.29; and a loaf of Wonder bread, $4.86. The soda aisles do brisk business at $1.75 a can.

Passage of the Swans

So Much to Talk About

June arrives on the plane from Yellowknife, and suddenly I am catapulted out of my numbness and into laughter and openhearted emotion. As we shelter in the tent, rain pours out of the sky. The black sea is rimmed with whitecaps. I read my journal aloud to purge the weeks alone. June is so horrified by my hands—cracked, grimed and swollen—that I get a manicure.

On August 19 we sail for Umingmaktuuq in a tandem kayak. Among the cognoscenti, it's commonly known as a divorce boat. Couples have to match each other's arm movements perfectly to avoid clanking paddles and arguments. I already know that being alone is no longer an option, and readjusting to the cramped confines of a tandem kayak seems a small compromise in exchange for sharing this seashore and culture with my soulmate.

June is five eight, and twenty-nine years old, but so fresh-faced that liquor stores still card her. She was raised amid a tradition of southern gentility that she has overcome by questioning authority and her intolerance for accepting the status quo. She is not an adventurer but loathes being without me, while I have offered to cancel the trip if it would cause me to lose her. In a compromise she has come north to join me to Umingmaktuuq. I also have an ulterior motive: If she learns to love the Arctic, maybe she'll stop worrying as much when I have to leave again next year to finish my trip.

Behind every successful adventure there is often an unseen intimate who instills the adventurer with both a sense of safety and a home-tilted compass. Initially Homer might have made Odysseus marry Penelope so that he could have a son. If Penelope has remained the symbol of faithfulness since the sixth century B.C., it is, I believe, because she gave Odysseus the freedom to take his extended adventures on the sea. Homer sent his hero almost everywhere, sometimes alone, often against overwhelming odds, but never north to the unknown, to what the Greeks called Arktikós, Land of the Great Bear.

Without June, there were times that I might not have beached on rough days or placed caution in the forefront of my actions. I am familiar with those adventurers who didn't make it home, many of whom did not have loved ones providing the necessary sense of gravity. In the end it's a lot harder to stay home and believe in the judgment of the adventurer than it is to traverse the Northwest Passage.

Fall comes with a sudden frost, lining the mornings silver. In the afternoons the distant sun warms the tundra, afire in crimson and saffron fall colors. The land is redolent of the tart pungency of rotting sepals and ripening berries.

Brants honk southward, as mergansers begin flocking along the shore. Lilac-colored river beauties have dried up, creating localized snowstorms of seed fur that tickles our faces. During one midday stretching break we find a whitened caribou skull and backbone, trapped upside down in a boulder field by its antlers, its torso picked clean by hungry predators. Beneath us, *Falco peregrinus* slides out of the sky toward *Somateria mollisima.* An instant before the blurred peregrine's talons can strike, the eider plops into the water and disappears, reminding us, now more than ever, that nothing is permanent here. Winter, like death, is always a heartbeat away.

Although the coming of winter should draw us closer together, our renewed relationship is not easy. June is cold, scared and uncertain about exactly what has happened to the man who is twenty pounds lighter than the last time she saw him. One day, after a disagreement in which I cannot explain myself, she tells me that she doesn't know whom I've become. This frightens me so badly that I begin talking, loquaciously, throughout the days. Also, for the first week her arms hurt so much that she can scarcely paddle. I pick up the slack and happily push us forward as she rests.

After a week I learn to give up compulsive mile making. At the same time, she learns to pee over the side like a man, rather than take the obligatory ten minutes to land, pull off the spray skirt, debark, urinate and reboard. Soon enough she learns that the Arctic can be respected rather than feared. She also gracefully defers to me despite my difficulty in explaining my often intuitive reasons for the myriad of route-finding decisions. Eventually we find a synergistic energy the equal of several paddlers.

She sets up the tent while I cook dinner. We paddle for each other to keep the kayak moving during rest breaks. She massages my sore shoulders and back, and we keep each other warm as the nights go dark again.

One hundred and ten miles out from Kugluktuk a pair of tundra swans trumpet into our cove at sunset. We sit listening to their cooing, watching the furling and unfurling of their long necks, coppery with mud. As my camera lens clicks, they beat the water for twenty yards, lumber up into the sky and fly past our tent with air soughing through their wings and their necks whistling expelled breaths. The male and female mate for life with a practicality similar to Inuit: Staying together equals survival. If there is beauty in the swans' passing, it lies in the streamlined and unlikely grace of Paleolithic animals conspiring against gravity and winter, pushing a dozen pounds of grass-fattened flesh up into the sky through the wonder of hollow bones and seven-foot-wide wings.

Later that night I am awakened by a noise outside our tent. I grab the cold shotgun and jump, half naked, out into a chill evening. I look for long minutes, sweeping my eyes left and right, waiting impatiently for my pupils to dilate and show the rustling intruder. June is awake and frightened. "Hello, Mr. Bear, where are you?" I loudly ask, informing the bear—if that's what I heard—that we're not silent prey. The water lies still in our protected cove, yet the unchanged rhythm of surf against the distant cliffs is not the same as the rustling that woke me up.

The weeks alone have taught me how to awaken at the slightest disturbance. I have also learned how to fall back asleep instantly, a lucky adaptation for long days that demand a good night's sleep. Most of the time I wake up to wind noise, a change in surf volume or a seal flippering water. My night alarm has not yet failed me. So I wait for my vision to fill the space around me with shapes. I sniff the air, but there is only my own vinegary body odor.

I am shivering by the time my pupils are dilated enough to inspect our campsite. I drop to the ground to profile moving animals, but the only break against the darkened horizon is the outline of the kayak. There are no new tracks in the sand. Before I can fire the gun as a scare tactic, I look upward and find the aurora borealis billowing overhead as a gossamer curtain of light. Then, in full brilliance before my dilated pupils, it morphs into hundred-mile-wide beams that undulate back and forth across a sea of stars. I strain to hear something, as mercury and oxygen ions slam back and forth across the heavens, and wonder about the Inuit myth of the man of the northern lights, shooting flaming arrows across the sky, about the alien beauty and marvels that The People ascribed to the heavens. June comes out, and we stand in each other's arms, lost in the clamorous silence of this solar light trembling across the night sky. There are possibilities up there, I know. If June and I believed in the Inuit afterworld, in flying polar bears and a goddess beneath the sea, who knows what wonders we might find here in this lifetime?

· · ·

After waiting out two days of northerly wind, we sail toward Agiak Headland in a muscled southwest wind blowing off the shore. Summer is holding, and we are now halfway to Umingmaktuuq. We round the headland at ten knots, leaning windward to counteract the boat's heeling. As our hull slices water, I close my eyes and imagine our slipstream as air *whoosh*ing against wings.

Grays Bay opens up to the south. I grimace as I stare across five miles of wind-furled white water. Suddenly we are trapped. We can't go back against the wind into the cliffs of the headland, and going forward means crossing an open cauldron of water, broadside to the wave fetch. June is either unaware of the danger or invigorated by it. She whoops as we accelerate into the bay.

I try to tack back toward the cliffs. After a few minutes of our moving slowly, bouncing dangerously to and fro, June talks me into tacking back east. I tighten the spray skirt against waves sloshing over the deck. I loosen gusts out of the sail by releasing the sheet. I rudder downwind when waves threaten a capsize.

Our pants go sodden below the spray deck. Since June is still reveling in our speed across the bay, there is no sense telling her how long we might last after a capsize. Instead I say, "I love you, honey," making her whoop even louder.

My mouth goes dry from the tension of not knowing if we will make it to shore (now three miles off). My back is arched tightly into the wind. Adrenaline keeps my hands from numbing, even with my arms soaking wet from hugging the starboard hull. A gust rolls the kayak up onto its port side, burying the sponson and outrigger pole; June and I lurch out onto the four-foot starboard outrigger to prevent the boat from flipping. As she leans out, she sees the fear wrinkling my forehead. I reef the sail down. June yells, "Steer toward the sun. Toward the sun!"

I reluctantly rudder south. The course puts us through the worst of the waves. We hold tight. Minutes pass like half hours.

After an interminable hour of riding perpendicular to the waves, our survival seems assured. Still, I can't help thinking that there will be a price to pay for this risk taking. We sneak through the surf by cheating straight up into a river channel and paddling the last fifty yards toward a cabin. I am exhilarated both for surviving and for covering twenty-six miles with only a half hour of paddle work. But the tension of the day has tuned all my muscles and nerves to piano wire tautness.

June jumps out and pulls the bow of the kayak ashore. I lever myself up and out of the cramped cockpit, feeling like a creaky old man, until an implosion of fire lights my spine. I yell in pain, "Help me, June!"

While I limp up to the cabin on June's shoulder, a gyrfalcon—the first

June Duell enjoying the ride (note lee board on sponson arm)

I've ever seen—glides past as silent as a cloud. Although my back is too tender to lift the binoculars from around my neck, I can see the gyrfalcon adjusting its height with its tail feathers to scout the rolling hills of sand and tundra. It beats the air rapidly, like a self-possessed gull. Then, just as suddenly as the gyrfalcon appeared, it disappears into the southern horizon. I look north, and the islands are swallowed by the descending white curtain of winter. For a brief moment I am so moved by the falcon that I forget what I have done to my back.

June fires up the cabin's kerosene heater while hail and snow shake against the walls. I lie flat on my back, wondering, yet again, if winter has finally come. Now I am as much follower as leader.

"Isn't it true," I ask June, "that the best leaders are always followers?"

It could just as easily be my own frailty as June's that halts our trip. If I don't heal soon, June will have to paddle out to get help. The battery on the personal locator beacon has gone dead.

The consequence of an injury out here, without a radio, would squash my idealism about self-sufficiency. Yet my dependence upon June also solidifies our relationship. Until now I had never imagined that *my* vulnerabilities would stop us from getting to Umingmaktuuq. So for the first time in more than fourteen hundred miles, I relax and let June care for me. She rubs my back with lotion, plies me with tea and reads to me.

The cabin is a haven, light-years beyond our tent. Foot-long sealing hooks hang inside, accorded the requisite care of Inuit hunting tools; hammers, screwdrivers and a saw are spread haphazardly outside. A tar-papered cooking table and benches, crookedly built with two-by-fours and plywood, stand inside beneath double-paned windows. Cotton sweatshirts hang from shelves of old antibiotics and cold medicine. *Snowmobile* magazines lie in their usual proud profusion, while a *Newsweek* lies hidden under the bed mattresses as if the owners did not want other guests to see any *Kabloona* propaganda.

On the plywood wall, above 1970s red-and-white-checkered counter paper, is a month-old note:

> Jimmy, Had a wonderful time. Saw lots of wildlife. Caught some fish at the rapids. Saw a couple of bears. One went right by the shore here. Can't wait to retire so I could enjoy the land too. . . . You are so lucky to have a place here in Kugluktuakyuk [Inuit name for the river].
>
> Koanakpiak [Thank you]
> Etokana, Derrick, Akana

After two days the muscle spasms subside, and I can walk and paddle again. My thankfulness manifests itself in a new and appreciative boyishness.

As we kayak east, every ten miles we find ancient stone tent rings, bookmarks of a people who had permanently retired upon the land. The rings are usually about ten feet wide, and the stones were used to hold down caribou skin tepees that housed families of nomadic hunters. Some may date back two thousand years, when the Paleo-Eskimos wandered east toward Greenland.

Inuksuit stand above mud shores rife with caribou hoofprints, like dogs marking wet cement sidewalks. Bones poke out of boulder-strewn graves. In a boulder field of brown slate, a shaman's abandoned pile of magic stones—quartz, chert, yellowed fossils, blond sandstone and pink granite—blazes in stony light.

The hundred-mile-deep Bathurst Inlet is studded with Tolkienesque islands, bristling with high walls, velvet green coves, rambling brooks and crystal-clear tarns hidden above the shoreline. As summer crumbles into that short Arctic interlude before eight months of blizzard, the ankle-high dwarf birch trees turn golden on the hillsides, and the sun disappears for days. The wind blows constantly, and our paddles become too cold to push without neoprene gloves. I think about John Franklin, passing down this same sound in 1821, having unlocked the middle of the Northwest Passage, destined for a winter of hunger. At night I read the stunning inventions within *Arctic Dreams,* while June is gripped by stories of huge waves in *The Perfect Storm.*

While we contemplate how to cross the seven-mile-wide Arctic Sound,

June's stomach is burning with anxiety, as it has for two days now. She is not entirely wrong that it is dangerous to be kayaking in such stormy waters or that smart kayakers would paddle two more days around the sound. But it is hard to convince her that calculated risks always yield new insights or that our instincts will tell us how and when to make the crossing.

Several miles down the western shore of the sound it simply feels right, so I nose the bow straight east in a headwind. For a long time we don't talk. We push our paddles like a well-synchronized machine, aiming toward a distant yellow patch of shoreline. An immature and slate gray glaucous gull leads the way, circling us, then flying off ahead to land in the water, waiting. Hundreds of button-size jellyfish hang suspended like claret constellations in the black water below. An unseen loon moos, barks and then quacks. We hold our gazes down so the distant shore doesn't hypnotize us with separation anxiety.

Halfway out, the wind dies, and we feel a current caressing the hull. Three and a half miles down, three and a half to go. We should be paddling at a rate of three miles per hour, but wind and current conspire against us. We rest our paddles on the gunwales and listen to the distant beehive pulsing that I still cannot identify. Ten miles away Wilburforce Falls drops 160 feet out of the Hood River and into the sea, but if we are hearing the falls, it sounds the same as the mysterious and inexplicable noise that has accompanied me ever since leaving the Mackenzie River in April. June believes it to be the sighing of the sea against its longed-for shore.

June is still fearful about being out in the middle of this expanse of cold water. Her eyes flit to the north, checking for rogue waves or bands of whitecaps. It doesn't help that she has just finished reading a book about people drowning at sea in sudden storms. I explain that I was never a great guide because I was always too sensitive to the fears of my clients.

"Is that why you like going alone?" she asks rhetorically.

The young gull beckons us onward, squawking raucously, as if we have spent too long resting. By our third hour of paddling the yellow patch has become fields of dwarf birch, and our bow grinds up onto empty black mussel shells on the eastern shore of Arctic Sound. June leaps out to pee, rather than rock the boat, and lofts a giant rack of caribou antlers above her head while prancing on the shoreline.

If there is any lesson for me about the crossing, it is never to underestimate those tasks that I invariably psych myself into doing. For the woman I plan to marry, the lesson is simply that open crossings aren't worth a stomachache. I think she got in touch with something out there, a glimmer of the infinite that draws most adventurers onward. Although the Arctic is not for everyone, June is beginning to discern its magic.

The sunset lights a narrow tangerine strip along the dirty western horizon. We have lost three hours of daylight in the last twenty days. Dew shimmers against reddening tundra; there is the indelible knowledge of the land having an absolute permanence. It is silent yet wholly alive. June might have called this a lonely place several weeks ago. Now the dearth of people and the time for contemplation have given her a feeling of belonging, a feeling that she has a place here.

"You're right," she says.

"About what?"

"About insights. And that this place is really not so hostile at all."

"And one more thing, sweetie," I ask, "this is *not* a divorce boat, right?"

On September 10 we paddle into Umingmaktuuq just as the barge arrives, unloading a year's worth of supplies for three dozen residents. Halogen beams flood the decks with a ghastly white light, while local aluminum skiffs whiz back and forth across the bay, to and from the barge. This annual delivery is a pivotal event in these people's lives. Unlike the rest of North America, most Arctic villages are disconnected from roadways, blocked by sea ice for nine months and prohibitively expensive for flying freight to.

Onshore no one moves to greet us. An *Inuk* bargeman in orange coveralls is surrounded by a bevy of villagers, like fans crowding for an autograph. No one stands still. At first the locals seem unfriendly, avoiding our gazes or greetings while bent over their numerous new supplies. After introducing ourselves, we learn that they are also reserved from lack of outside contact.

Gwen Tikhak takes us across the bay to the small Co-op store. Her husband, George, is so shy that he cannot look back at us. Holding the engine tiller in reverse, trying to avoid our gazes, he thuds the aluminum skiff against a boulder. A quick push from several arms gets the boat back into the bay.

From out on the water we can see that town has two dozen cabins ringing the bay. On the rocky ground between these four-hundred-square-foot dwellings are communal meat racks, strung with bloody caribou, footlong and sinewy white ground squirrel flesh and carrot-colored slabs of char. A snowmobile smokes its way across the gravel, hauling a *kamotik* loaded with crates from the barge.

White granite domes, carpeted with gray lichen, hump back against the horizon and reflect the seared orange autumn light down into the mile-wide bay. A gyrfalcon traces the waterline as precisely as a cartographer's pen, following the ten-foot contour above sea level. Sedges and willows are still golden, but somehow snow is holding back, as if giving the locals time to finish storing away the boxes stacked along the shoreline. Outside the Co-op store, burdened men and women lumber back and forth with boxes in their arms. The People move with an unhurried grace, laughing as a teenager with a club darts through their ranks chasing a ground squirrel. Locally knit wool hats cover their heads.

An ancient woman, carrying a skin rucksack with a leather tumpline across her withered forehead, meets our boat on the sand. She bows to June, speaks a few indiscernible words in Inuktitut, and then hunches beneath her load. When June introduces herself, the woman, older than snowmobiles and four-wheelers, says in precise English, "June is not a name; June is a month," smiling beautifully into the sun.

We follow Gwen to the store. She explains how she left Cambridge Bay twenty-one years ago, and now, if anyone asks where she is from, she always says Umingmaktuuq.

"Too much alcohol. You have got to be careful over there in Cambridge Bay."

There are no other *Kabloona* within 150 miles. People glimpse at us, quick and bashful, and then look away as we mumble introductions. I have the impression, now that I understand their shyness, that Umingmaktuuq ("like a muskox") is the utopian ideal of Nunavut. There are no scheduled flights, no television or telephone cables, no RCMPs or bylaws, and apparently no crime.

Gwen proudly walks us up three short aisles, fingering different packages of food and dictating prices, until her hand comes to rest on a shelf holding canned tuna and stew.

"We don't eat much of this white man's food here," she says. "We prefer caribou and ground squirrel."

She is just over five feet tall, pushing her early fifties, with a lithe and girlish face hidden behind her oversize black-framed eyeglasses. Her raven-colored hair is pulled into a waist-length braid, and when she smiles, we laugh with her. Then, inadvertently, Gwen shows us her preference of Inuit egalitarianism over *Kabloona* capitalism. Holding up a can of Coke, Gwen giggles sweetly and explains that there are two different prices for the soda: $1.50 a can for the soda that is barged in and $3 per can for the soda that was flown in. "It's your choice," she says.

We walk the spongy trail a half mile back to the village. Two boats stop and offer us rides, since no one walks if he can help it.

The schoolteacher, Peter Kapolik, talks us out of setting up our tent and walks us to the largest and only uninhabited building in town. Although hunters pay $150 a night to stay here, Peter will accept no money from us. The Hunters and Trappers Office (HTO), he explains, is powered by solar cells, a Honda generator and a half dozen car batteries.

Standing on the soggy tundra outside, Peter picks up a tiny and rusted cog, then holds it out for me to see. "This would make a very small starter for a very small engine," he says, and places it back on the ground where he found it, leaving the piece of metal for someone else to discover. I don't ask if the rest of the litter rustling across the tundra has any purpose. But as if reading my thoughts, Peter sweeps his arm around to the other bits of trash lying about and says, "We like winter here because snow cleans things up."

He leads us inside the HTO to a set of maps, a woodstove and several large tables.

"Please make yourself at home."

Peter begins to jiggle his hands nervously as soon as he sees that I will act like most *Kabloona* and ask questions instead of just silently listening. In a hurry now, he lines a portable toilet with a garbage bag, shows us how to use the satellite phone at $3 per minute and then agrees to answer a few questions.

"But just a few." He grimaces.

He scarcely hesitates when I ask him how many children are in his class-room (eight), but he falls silent when I ask how many children there are altogether in town. Surely, as the teacher, he can answer this question.

I look away rather than rudely ask him again. He is handsome, neatly dressed in a chamois shirt, and tries to give the impression that the school-children await his return, even though school let out several hours ago. Peter comes from a tradition that has little to do with the numeric values that I have been raised with. Quantitative things have so little bearing on his daily life that he has to carefully review each family in Umingmaktuuq, think about whether the children are in town, consider whether or not each child is of a certain age that would qualify him or her to be children (rather than an adult), and then consider why anyone would even ask such a nosy question.

He replies several minutes later, "There are eleven children in Bay Chimo [the temporary village name], but I can't be sure."

Sensing his need to be gone, I ask another question quickly. "I saw these stone rings." With my foot I draw a five-foot-wide circle. "Do you know what they are? They're smaller than normal tent rings."

Peter shrugs and closes his eyes.

"Could they be old enough to come from the Dorset Culture?" I ask.

"Must be."

Then June steps in, understanding Inuit literal-mindedness, narrowing my question down.

"Have *you* ever seen any stone rings?" she asks.

Peter responds enthusiastically, moving his hands slowly to describe a huge slab south of here, being held up by three rocks. He cannot say exactly what the slab was used for and gives us only the facts, bare of speculation or assumptions.

When Peter and I were first introduced, he asked the only original question I will hear from him: "How was your trip?" A *Kabloona* would have
asked how many miles I traveled, how strong the wind was, or how cold
it got.

Having too much momentum to stop my questioning and seeing that he
is squirming to be gone, I quickly ask, "Do you ever go out to the island ten
miles north of Umingmaktuuq?"

"You mean the island of lots of birds?" he replies, oblivious of the miles.

His wife comes to his rescue, taking off her boots and walking across the
room. Since Peter is uninterested in introductions or desperate to be away
from us as quickly as possible, I introduce myself to Martina with a handshake.

He motions her toward the door, where I politely ask what month the sea
ice goes out. Peter shrugs and looks at Martina. They confer in Inuktitut for
a minute. She nods. Then he answers, "July."

Now I have lost them both. They turn to go.

"Thank you very much," I say.

He waves from over his shoulder, hustling to get away. "*Kabloona*," I hear
him mutter. Neither of them looks back. I suddenly realize, to my great
embarrassment, that I have committed an unpardonable sin, like taking
photographs without asking permission: I have asked one question too
many. Our isolation and my curiosity have loosened my sense of Inuit etiquette.

In the morning, after a dozen phone calls to Yellowknife looking for a
flight out, we charter a three-seat floatplane to come pick us up: $1,900
(U.S.) for a four-hour flight south. We search for Peter to say good-bye and
thank him, but in all probability he is hiding from us.

The pilot ties the Cessna 180 up against some boulders. We cram our
folding kayak inside. Gwen comes by to say good-bye, apologizing for not
spending more time with us and agreeing to store the rest of my gear—shotgun, food and sundry supplies—until I return in the spring.

As the plane banks above the bay, circling for altitude, I feel as if we have
cheated winter by making it this far. June meanwhile is violently airsick.

Within two hours we are flying over the green glow of white spruce forests,
followed by a yellow sea of tall birch trees, dazzling in their autumn finery.
June prays for the airplane to land soon. From her motion-sick perspective,
this is the most terrifying crossing of the last month.

At first, the artifice of Yellowknife is almost too much. I am not happy to
be back among throngs of automobiles and people again. June and I visit a
department store because our clothes have become so ripe that they can't
easily be cleaned. Stacks of food, clothing and material goods, mostly inaccessible to Inuit, seem unnecessary and gross. The checkout clerk says

merrily, "Have a nice day," and I stop and stare to see if she really means it. June nudges me onward. Even the relatively diluted traffic stream of this northernmost city has my eyes wide open in fear.

During my first weeks back in Colorado, I cannot drive my pickup truck more than forty-five miles per hour. Any speed faster than that with which the wind propelled me seems unnecessarily dangerous. I also constantly note which way the wind hits the grass. If a cold wind comes out of the north, I feel briskly rejuvenated. Even weather reports assume a new importance to my life, as if I am unable to let go of the connection to living outside, under the Earth and Its Great Weather.

There is so much to be happy for. I could have been born into the Thule Culture, with no ties to the southern world. Instead I have a privileged life in a modest A-frame at the end of a dirt road beneath twelve-thousand-foot peaks and a national forest. Being with June and our three dogs is all I could ask for, at least before I started this trip across the Northwest Passage.

As winter comes, there is a crack in our comfortable life together. I spend my time conspiring about getting back to the Arctic and journeying on beyond the white granite drumlins of Umingmaktuuq. The shores of twenty-four-hour daylight call to me like sirens. June and I both fill with anticipation about the Arctic. She dreads my departure. While I'm not excited to leave her, I am happily consumed by trip logistics and research into Inuit culture. We disagree about one thing only: my leaving again. We disagree so badly that we decide to put off our wedding until next fall, when I will quit this Northwest Passage.

PART THREE

The Polar Bear

Gjoa Haven Winter

Tunniq

In February I go back north for two months to live in the village of Gjoa Haven, on King William Island. I arrive at 3 p.m. and the sun has already set. While I walk a short mile into town from the airport, a 70-below-zero windchill shows that I will be confined indoors.

Even my winters in Alaska have not prepared me for this sort of omnipresent cold. Just walking next door is desperate if the wind is blowing; many locals' faces are blackened with frostbite scars. Idle weeks fly past in which I can see how important family—and now television—are during the long and darkened winters. Although I learn a lot about Inuit culture, it is much too cold to travel on the land. The only polar bear that I see is dead, shot by a *Kabloona* sport hunter.

I make several friends. More than in any other place I have traveled, it is easy to talk to strangers, and curious adults and children often join me. I learn that *Kabloona* homes in Gjoa ("Joe") are decorated with soapstone carvings, paintings, scenic photographs and books. Inuit homes, even carvers', lack artwork and books. Framed photographs tend to be portraits, expressing the binding gravity of family.

I meet many people, including the region's new MLA. Uriash Puqiqnaq was recently elected to this office (the equivalent of a senator) in the upcoming Nunavut government. His platform is to bring back the Inuktitut language and original culture to disenfranchised Inuit youth. I ask what MLA means, but he shrugs his shoulders, uninterested in English-language acronyms. His thirty-year-old son, lounging on a couch watching cartoons on television, answers in a California accent, without turning his head, "Member of Legislative Assembly. Dad's one of seventeen guys who travel to the capital and make the new laws for us."

Uriash is missing two bottom teeth and explains that he was born in an

Chopping up frozen bearded seal for an iglu *lamp*

iglu in 1946, a remark that a more skeptical *Kabloona* mind might dismiss as an idle brag among Gjoa residents. Then, as if Uriash knew how southerners' minds work, he immediately explains in his soft singsong, "All my generation was born in snow houses. First time I saw buildings was 1959 in Joe. My family moves into town maybe ten years after."

Until he was elected, Uriash made his living as a carver. Like several other elders in the village, he uses a power grinder to create over a hundred thousand (mostly tax-free) dollars' worth of carvings per year.

Arctic Canada has produced carvings for the last four thousand years, beginning with the Arctic Small Tools tradition (ASTt). Mostly these people chipped intricate small arrowheads from multicolored flints. As this nomadic ASTt gave way to the Dorset Culture in the first millennium B.C., shamans began to develop their religion. The people built permanent settlements. This new life encouraged their expression: abstract carvings of spirit people and animals. Shamans attempting sympathetic magic carved ivory or wood carvings of bears with holes in the chest, holding tiny spears of wood.

Equally stylized carvings of bears show remarkably accurate "X-ray" depictions of the animal's skeleton and joints. Uriash explains that such miniature carvings were often worn in amulets around hunters' necks. The first evidence of soapstone carving was found in northern Quebec, where whole cliffs of soapstone were carved into distorted human faces, similar to those that Uriash carves.

After expanding north to Greenland and west into Coronation Gulf, the artistic Dorset period (Uriash calls these former people giants, or *Tunniq*) reached its zenith at about A.D. 1000. The ancestors of the modern-day Inuit, the Thule Culture, drove off, assimilated, or starved out the *Tunniq.* The invading Thule Culture learned about the soapstone quarries from the *Tunniq,* who carved lamps and cooking pots from the stone. The new Thule expressionism carved dolls, amulets or charms, or simple silhouetted figures in wood or ivory. They carved snow goggles or harpoons out of bone or wood, often incised with decorative and spiritual lifelines, and camp scenes of people and animals on antler tines or ivory.

The onset of the Little Ice Age between A.D. 1650 and 1850 changed Inuit art entirely. Europe experienced catastrophic crop failures, while the Arctic saw shorter summers, severe sea ice blockages around the Northwest Passage and a decrease in sea mammals to hunt. Uriash's forefathers broke up into small nomadic bands and began utilizing kayaks for hunting caribou on lakes and rivers, rather than seals on the sea. Consumed by day-to-day survival, they found little time for art. The insecurity of this new lifestyle may have changed The People, making them as obdurate as the stone they once carved. At the same time, contact with European metal tools and weapons led to a decline in traditionally decorated implements. From Uriash's standpoint, *Kabloona* of course took full advantage of trading with these desperate people. For three centuries their art all but disappeared.

In the 1950s Inuit carving came back to life as a commercial enterprise. James Houston, a southern artist, was given a kneeling caribou, carved out of soapstone by a starving hunter living in Hudson Bay. Houston was so impressed by the anatomical accuracy of the carving, as well as its resonance with early Dorset art, that he began organizing sales outlets in the south. Like others, Houston had the idea that Inuit needed a new economy. The Canadian government, in collaboration with Houston, printed a soapstone manual for Inuit. Houston arranged for the Hudson's Bay Company to accept Inuit carvings as viable trade items, to be sold to a nonprofit organization down south. Carving soon took off.

Inuit in Gjoa Haven were also trained to make totem poles, blanket scenes, pottery, traditionally sewn clothing, and prints. Most of these government-prompted enterprises failed, but sewing dolls and clothing now tithes a dozen Gjoa women (sewing in a shack where everyone splurges her social assistance check on the Arctic version of the lottery, "Nevada" bingo cards). On Victoria Island, Inuit printmakers do booming sales in traditional print scenes, learned from Japanese printmakers and based on Siberian designs.

One of Uriash Puqiqnaq's beautiful carvings

Uriash wants to teach carving to young people in Nunavut. He believes that letting the work come out of the soapstone is one more way of getting the bored young people to connect with their rich past.

Still, Uriash is hard pressed to explain his work. When I ask about the health dangers of carving (the famous and gifted Judas Ullulaq died in Gjoa two months ago from lung cancer, caused by breathing in soapstone dust), Uriash waves this off and says, "Most will probably die from cigarettes first."

Carving, Uriash mumbles, might be what penmanship or singing is to me. Then he looks over his coffee cup at me.

"Inuktitut has no words for artists or art, only the word for people, Inuit. I am just an *Inuk*. I am not an artist. And this"—he holds up a half-carved black boulder that looks like a flying polar bear—"it is not art, it is soapstone becoming a polar bear. And the polar bear can protect you."

He offers me another finished carving, for one thousand dollars; it will sell in a southern gallery for several times that much. Unlike the more commercial carvers in the western Arctic, Uriash is fond of carving the traditional, distorted Inuit faces. The agonized-looking, wide-eyed faces constitute a style compared with German Expressionism, more brutal than beautiful, and I have the impression that the facial carvings—missing teeth, frightened, or simply *dark*—are expressing the quintessential pain of the Inuit psyche, showing those abuses that most people keep to themselves.

By the time I fly home in late March, I have learned about despair from the faces of people walking the glacial streets of Gjoa. Feeling beat up, I greet June. The cold and darkness have confirmed that I will never be more than a visitor to the Arctic. To shake this torpor, while staring at the terrorized faces of the carvings I brought home, I organize a donation of clothing from two outdoor stores near my home. In May I ship several boxes of kayaking gear and clothing to Pelly Bay, where Inuit have recently relearned how to kayak. Also, one of my trip sponsors generously donates $4,000 worth of fleece clothing. I fly north on May 6 to give the clothing to The People of Umingmaktuuq and then dogsled back to Cambridge Bay, continuing my Northwest Passage.

Cambridge Bay, Nunavut

I am disappointed as I fly into the newly created territory of Nunavut, across the mainland to Victoria Island. It is 30 below outside the windows. I had been expecting spring.

Cambridge Bay is choked down in the southeastern maw of Victoria Island. Seen from the air above, as some elder hunters still claim to see the land, it is an openmouthed shark seining the frozen waters of Dease Strait. Elders still call Cambridge Bay Ikaluktutiak ("Good Fishing Place"). The mainland is thirty miles south, and nearly ten degrees warmer, away from early May's thick crown of sea ice.

Less than a century ago Stefansson ducked into low-slung skin tents here and sought blue-eyed, blond-haired Inuit. Today the progeny of those mythical Viking children bob in and out of six-foot double doors, into the Royal Bank of Canada, Kentucky Fried Chicken, Nunavut College, two large grocery stores, three hotels, the hamlet office and a meat-processing plant.

On one of several dozen frozen dirt streets a plump ten-year-old sticks his hand into my pocket and asks, "Mister, can I have yur money?"

With a population of thirteen hundred, Cambridge Bay is the biggest community in the surrounding Kitikmeot region. A fifth of The People here receive treatment for sexually transmitted diseases. Dr. Colin Irwin's 1988 government report *Lords of the Arctic: Wards of the State* fits Cambridge Bay. Speaking of the entire Canadian Arctic, Irwin refers to the lack of data and studies on this "sexually active and partially isolated population." He concludes, "I cannot say with any confidence that AIDS will not have a devastating effect on Inuit population."

Health Canada recently echoed Irwin's opinion. Despite allocating millions of dollars to prevent the spread of AIDS, the government admits that it has been "ineffective" except for possibly raising The People's awareness of the disease.

There is a grimness here that, at least to me, seems to leach up out of the snow and onto the faces of the shoppers in the Co-op and Northern Store. Alcohol has its usual tragic repercussions. The middle-aged, obese *Kabloona* electrician staying at the hotel receives nighttime visits from a lithe Inuk girl barely fifteen. The faux friendliness of people on the street is as fleeting and token as the distant green summer. If you spend enough time looking around and asking questions, the contradictions abound, to the point that it feels as if Cambridge Bay were hiding something.

Last summer three kids burned down the local high school while playing with matches. Whatever education falters at this level of schooling is recycled by Nunavut College. Like most of the adult education programs across Nunavut and the Northwest Territories, these optimistically named colleges are a stopgap for high school dropouts who need to learn how to read or earn equivalency degrees. The teachers are all *Kabloona* because the job requirements demand the college degrees held by less than 2 percent of Inuit. Both here and in Gjoa Haven the teachers say that their students are mostly oblivious of learning or that they can't conceptualize the future by saving money, planning for a family or figuring out what last month's inauguration of Nunavut has to do with their lives.

Most students are paid by the federal social assistance program to be in Nunavut College. The attendees often turn into "professional students," milking the system for their $300-per-month paycheck, flunking their courses and showing attendance records or a lack of curiosity that would doom them in any southern community college. The teachers have no choice but to lower the grading curve and accommodate the students, even if they're not learning much. Fifteen years ago, tests indicated that these adult education students scored 2.4 grades lower than what they had completed in earlier schooling. Today little has changed.

Dr. Irwin referred to these baby boomers as "a lost generation, whose education and enculturation provides them with little more than the skills required to live out their lives as wards of the state. If filling out a form is considered to be an essential skill for living in such a society, then many Inuit would fail to meet even this most modest of expectations."

Recently all government *Kabloona* employees were required to hire and train Inuit assistants so that Nunavut meets its mandate of becoming 80 percent Inuit governed. *Kabloona* still largely govern Cambridge Bay.

The population is nearly 20 percent *Kabloona*. This is unusually high for any Arctic village. Locals believe that this abnormal ratio causes job competition, and it is not stretching the truth to say that many Inuit are tired of *Kabloona* taking home the good money.

The highest-paying noncollege-degree job, guard duty, exists because Cambridge Bay is a "damp" town. But Inuit can't last at guard duty. The employees, presently all white, are called from a sign-up sheet whenever Inuit are arrested for fighting or drunken behavior. Guard duty pays $21 per hour, requiring that the guard periodically peek into the cells to see that the arrestees aren't choking on their vomit. The few Inuit who have taken the job quit as soon as it becomes apparent that no *Inuk* here can pull guard

Sewage truck pumping out home

duty without having to coddle or illegally spring their friends, in-laws, or family members.

"The Cambridge Bay gene pool," as one guard tells me, "does not run very deep."

Irwin, a *Kabloona* anthropologist married to an *Inuk,* referred to the white man's education and employment plopped into Inuit villages as "structural racism." His controversial report to the government was excerpted in the *Toronto Globe and Mail,* appearing throughout Canada. It was mostly denounced. But an Inuit representative wrote a six-page response asking why the southern press had never previously covered these social problems, which Inuit had given up on pointing out.

To southerners, the report might seem alarmist. In the decade following the study, several of Irwin's ideas—land reform, a hunter support program and educational monitoring—have been implemented. But here in Cambridge Bay, post-Nunavut, it seems clear that change will take years.

Dr. Irwin's short-term forecasts of gloom and doom have come to life, notwithstanding Nunavut. "If current trends continue," he forecast, "most of the Inuit living in the Arctic in the year 2025 will be second-generation wards of the state, whose society, economy, and culture may have more in common with an urban slum than with the life their grandparents knew."

Yet there are many prosperous Inuit here. Part of the misunderstanding in *Kabloona*–Inuit relations might have to do with those false expectations of The People's adopting the southern work ethic. Also, they seem hobbled by English communication; Inuktitut is spoken only by elders and those who spend time on the land.

On my first day in town, I befriend a thirty-year-old whom I'll call Jason Aguklaruk. Our communication falters because of my lack of Inuktitut and his limited grasp of English, despite his logging forty hours a week in front of American-programmed television. Initially, he appears to be fluent in Inuktitut because he speaks the language, albeit haltingly, around elders. Yet as I spend more time around him, he can't explain the meanings of his father's language. He thinks that *Kabloona* means "blond guy." It turns out that Jason, like many Inuit baby boomers, is hampered in both languages.

After visiting nine Inuit villages from Kaktovik, Alaska, to Pelly Bay, Canada, I have found that the dialects and spellings of everyday Inuktitut words shift like the weather. Polar bear, *Nanuq,* can also be called *Nänoq, nanuk, nänuvak, nanoq, nanuq, nannuraluk, takoaq, pisugtooq* or *ayualunaq.* Part of the confusion is that the regional dialects are lumped together in places like Cambridge Bay because Inuit are so transient. But the real issue is that Inuktitut, a mostly oral language, was not designed to be written. Poems, stories and songs are spontaneously recited, since their power is thought to be lost by locking them onto paper.

More than a century ago James Evans put the Cree language into syllabics. Then John Horden and E. A. Watkins adapted it for Inuktitut, but the Anglican missionary Edmund Peck took all the credit by promoting syllabics so that Eskimos could read the Bible. The Arabic-looking script, which is, moreover, the Word of God, spread quickly because it was easy to learn. Although syllabics are now found in prayer books, on stop signs and in phone books throughout the Arctic, this orthography ultimately showcases the *Kabloona* God. Hence missionaries quelled pagan superstition, toppling much of the specific grace and tradition of a forgotten culture.

In the western Arctic the Inuit goddess Nuliajak has now been anglicized into Sedna. Missionaries successfully distorted the name by confusing it with the Inuktitut word *sanna* ("down there"), showing Eskimos that their important Nuliajak was little more than a devil.

Today there is no real comprehensive Inuktitut-English dictionary, or so Jean Briggs informs me. Briggs, an anthropologist from the Memorial University of Newfoundland, spends her northern time shuttling among different Inuit households, vigorously recording the various spellings for her Roman orthography dictionary in progress. It's now at thirty thousand words, many of which include whole sentences when translated into English.

One of Briggs's previously published books is a fascinating study of Inuit

Gospel church in Gjoa Haven (note syllabics)

family life out on the land in the 1960s. *Never in Anger* depicts a utopian family from whom modern civilization would do well to learn.

In Gjoa Haven I met an *Inuk* woman (given a pseudonym in the book) who says that her family always gets a laugh at the anthropologist's misunderstanding of such simple words as "table." These confusions apparently lead even the best linguists astray because of the differing Inuktitut dialects.

Furthermore, I learn that a father sexually abused the girls with whom Briggs lived. The anthropologist writes obliquely, discoursing on language rather than sex, about how this father loved his fourteen-year-old "too much." Although the book is a college anthropology text published in 1970, sex is mentioned just once, and in a footnote, as being "completely inaudible" and not talked about.

The new joke, fondly told by Inuit, is that their average family has 6.5 members: wife, husband, 3.5 children, and one snooping *Kabloona* anthropologist. It has occurred to me that adventurer could now be added to that statistic.

Every day, despite answering the same cultural questions that they are bombarded with by anthropologists and researchers, Inuit become my gracious hosts. By being patient, I begin to meet the more prosperous people within this community. They invite me to the KFC and to their homes and offices for yet another cup of coffee. In the morning it is poor form to refuse a cup of this heavily processed and weak brew. In the afternoon it is acceptable to say, "I am coffeed out."

If your guest agrees to being poured another cup of coffee, he raises his eyebrows in lieu of saying yes. If he is coffeed out, he squints his eyes no. I realize, with no small chagrin, that this eyebrow signaling goes on throughout the Arctic. In the past, when I missed Inuit silently moving their eyebrows in answer to my questions, most of them politely filled in the silence for outsiders like me with a yes or no. *Kabloona* living in villages say that this habit derives from hunters' maintaining strict silence during long vigils over seal holes or caribou migration paths, but it's not that simple. Inuit, like many northern cultures, have a fundamentally different way of communicating with one another because of their community ties. Much of it is intuitive, utilizing body language and eye contact, and much of it may be lost in modern villages, particularly when a *Kabloona* like me tries to interpret it.

Over another coffee "mugup," I meet a garrulous and pock-faced Canadian Broadcasting Corporation radio announcer. He invites me to come to the station for an interview if I'm willing to talk about how I perform my adventures without using drugs. Since it is approaching late afternoon and the hour of being coffeed out, the cups jiggle in our hands and coffee sloshes onto the floor.

I meet a soft-spoken Adlair Air mechanic who pulled himself together after his mother's death from cancer and moved from Holman to Cambridge Bay to start over again. While camping out on a frigid May night, he repeatedly checks up on me in my "fragile" nylon tent (Inuit prefer canvas). He offers me his Sorel boots, caribou robes and, of course, more coffee. Trying to explain that drinking more caffeine would make me cold by constricting my capillaries would only be considered rude, even heretic.

I meet a facetious Renewable Resources employee who dresses meticulously, talks slowly, and sips his coffee even more slowly. His *Kabloona* companion on a trip to the mainland was amazed at how quickly he jumped on a snowmobile to chase a nearby wolf. If this government conservation officer had succeeded in shooting the wolf, the pelt would have fetched at least $200. No Inuit would find the *Inuk* wildlife officer's moonlighting abnormal.

The quickest study of them all is a wired twenty-eight-year-old who started a satellite Internet service—PolarNet—for the central Arctic. Next month he is closing on a two-story house built around a hot tub. He will pay $1,600 on his mortgage per month, and he's now paying $1,700 in rent. While turning left into the door of his office, visitors risk colliding with a coffeepot, the handiest accessory of his workplace. This computer jockey has also mounted a spy cam through his window, aimed at the airport, accessible through the Internet, to see if fog will cancel his flight home to Cambridge Bay.

I listen to all their stories. As with Inuit everywhere, Ski-Doos are their passion. The spring breakup sport, among the young at heart anyway, is called skimming: hydroplaning on snowmobiles at fifty miles per hour across leads of open water on the ice. No one has died from skimming here yet.

These mechanically minded and caffeinic sportsmen are the movers and shakers of Nunavut, the folks with their eyes on the future. It is apparent that they are a minority among an illiterate nation not yet weaned from alcohol, social assistance, illiteracy and disease.

To find out what remains of former traditions, as well as the cultural role of machines, I arrange for Jason's father, Billy Aguklaruk (I have changed both of their names), to meet me in four days, 150 miles south in Uming-maktuuq. From there Billy will carry me back along the same route by dog team. His guide fee is $150 per day, half the price of his *Kabloona* competitor.

In twenty-five years of adventuring, I have never hired a guide. I prefer to travel on my own or with friends. Here, amid this foreign culture, I am prepared to let go of my ego and pay someone to teach me about being out on the land, a phrase full of romance to Inuit ears. The idea of men working together out in the cold is so central to Inuit survival that the mere notion of traveling alone across the Northwest Passage, particularly without engines, dogs or a radio, strikes them as ridiculous.

Billy is fifty-seven years old, young enough to still be a good hunter and old enough for people to listen to and respect. He is one of only several dozen elders still actively going out on the land.

While growing up in tents on the Back River, he escaped starvation by snaring rabbits. Dwindling caribou herds made hundreds of his people starve. At fifteen he moved his surviving family to Cambridge Bay to take advantage of its health center. He married a woman he claimed to have fallen in love with. He raised his family by working monthlong shifts at the Lupine gold mine on the mainland and then at a lead mine on northern Victoria Island.

He is a hard man, not given to sharing his feelings, and it will take days to prize up his philosophy. At first our conversations are halting because of my lack of Inuit enculturation, his guttural pronunciation of English words and his deafness. The more time I spend with him, however, the more apparent it seems that he does not want to be understood.

Billy has a round face that lights up like a bucktoothed pumpkin carving when he smiles. While we sit over coffee, it strikes me how similar his culture is to that of the Nepalese: Laughter and smiling cover awkward pauses or embarrassment. Making fun of one another, in uncomplicated slapstick tomfoolery that transcends language, is considered high art. Since Billy is the elder, it is improper to tease him about his shortcomings, so I let him make me out to be the bozo—aka *Kabloona.*

We walk down the street back toward his house from the KFC, smiling at each other and our newfound friendship. My head is bald to the sub-zero May wind so that I can acclimatize to the cold, until I feel the no-turn-around nip of frostbite weighing against my ears. Then I will put my hat on. I have practiced this technique without frostbite for years, initially with a biofeedback technician and a digital thermometer and, eventually, in places much colder than springtime Cambridge Bay.

Billy's head is swathed with a wolf fur cap. He points at my head and says, "Need hat."

"That's okay. I have one in my pocket for when it gets colder."

He smiles. "Ohhhh, *Kabloona* very stupid and has much to learn. Much to learn."

"Yes, I do." I smile back at him and then pretend to trip over a frozen divot of motor oil, which makes Billy roar with a cackling laugh, prompting another *Inuk* walking by to burst out laughing, as if we all were players in some cosmic vaudeville act.

I keep my adventuring background brief and try to be humble by telling Billy that I walked and kayaked a thousand miles from Tuk to Umingmak-tuuq. "But I made mistakes," I add, "and Inuit have a lot to teach me about their way of living outside."

"Why do something so foolish?" he says.

"Because I like being out on the land," I reply, and with this all-important catchphrase, Billy grants a grunt of recognition as he guides me toward his house.

He stands several inches over five feet tall, his legs bowed from years of straddling Ski-Doos. He first rode an "autoboggan" in the early 1960s and promptly fried the single-cylinder engine because he couldn't read the instructions about adding motor oil. He signs his name in a cramped child's hand, and feigns rage—"Do you take me for a stupid man, *Kabloona*?"—when I ask him if he wants me to read aloud the invoice that I write for him to give to me. His face is as dark as Victoria Island limestone, while the skin below the tan line under his Adam's apple is as white as spring sea ice.

Inside his eighteen-hundred-square-foot home we pore through a shoebox full of faded and out-of-focus photographs. As we both begin to sweat in the 90-degree heat, he curses at the faulty thermostat and opens a window to a sub-zero breeze. I put on my jacket.

We spend another hour picking through the shoebox. Above the television—broadcasting *Miami Vice*—is a stereo and VCR, bristling with wires. Both are so frequently repaired that Billy has left their covers off to have quicker access to their circuitry. There are no books. A caribou haunch thaws on the kitchen linoleum. The obligatory guest book, a hundred-page pad of multicolored construction paper, has three *Kabloona* entries. I learn that Billy dogsledded these clients twenty minutes from the hotel to the airport. Our trip together will last a couple of weeks. I take a deep breath, hoping that we'll get along.

Qimmiq, the Eskimo Husky

Moving from One Inland Lake to Another

We harness up Billy's dogs on the afternoon of May 7. He will dogsled south to Umingmaktuuq, and to keep his load light, I will snowmobile there tomorrow so that I can return with him over a hundred-mile section of Northwest Passage without resorting to engines. Mostly I hope to learn more about Inuit culture by using both snowmobile and dogsled.

While Billy talks to each dog endearingly, his son stands by with the whip, far enough away that the dogs can't defend themselves.

Billy bellows, "DON'T HURT MY DOGS!"

Jason is smiling broadly, seemingly enjoying himself.

I try to show them that I have run dogs before by harnessing the dogs that Jason is afraid of. To show some authority, Jason yells at me, telling me I'm doing it wrong.

Jason's outburst is part of an ongoing game of complex Inuit pecking orders. Elders bark orders at youngsters. Youngsters bark orders at *Kabloona.* No one seems particularly ruffled by being bossed around.

Most of the dogs' necks are caked with blood. Two of the dogs, I note, cannot be trusted with my back turned. Four of the dogs are only eleven months old, too young to be hitched to a four-hundred-pound *kamotik.* Since protesting to Billy would merely be an insult, I jump right into the barking fray. By grabbing their collars and lifting them up off their front feet, I hop them on their hind legs to their trace positions and avoid being knocked over or getting bitten. Unlike many race dogs, these thick-furred canines will never become house pets, although some will accept petting— in a simpering fashion. Billy hasn't had these dogs for long, but he clearly bought a well-raised and obedient team. To judge by the way they cower from my hand actions, however, something is terribly wrong.

As we harness up, a *Kabloona* researcher stands by, photographing us. She and her boyfriend happened to adopt one of this team's newly weaned litters, more fur than claw, then brought it home to British Columbia. They were determined to prove that proper training and love could break the Eskimo husky's wildness. But after her boyfriend was twice bitten and stitched up at the hospital, they gave the young pup away.

Billy's dogs are thick-furred enough to sleep chained out on the bare ice with no shelter through 40-below temperatures and insect clouds. Ordinary sled dogs would die without being able to dig into a drift or shelter in a house. While it is not uncommon to see Inuit teams fed irregularly, Billy insists he feeds this team almost every day while they're traveling. As with most Inuit dogs, snow substitutes for drinking water, but during the summer thaws Billy chains them near puddles so that he won't have to haul water.

After a few shouts, several cracks of the whip, and a maniacal baying of bent backs, Billy yells, "Yah, yah, yah!" and pulls the cast-iron snow hook out of the sea ice just as the *kamotik*—weighted with caribou meat and all manner of supplies—scuffs away at ten miles per hour. The team is hauling a load suited for draft horses.

Jason is at my side, smiling crookedly. A wad of Copenhagen substitutes for a missing front tooth. "It sure is fun to be beating my old man's dogs. Hee-hee-hee."

Canadian Eskimo huskies, Qimmiq, on the sea ice with their master

I give Jason the benefit of the doubt. I guess that he means we will pass or *beat* the team tomorrow, Jason on the Polaris, me clinging on to the *kamotik*.

The Canadian Eskimo husky, or *Qimmiq*, is a light-colored bruiser that has lived with Inuit for two millennia. Legend has it that *Kabloona* and Inuit are offspring of a woman who mated with *Qimmiq*. Since dogs were skulking about the Arctic long before *Kabloona* came sailing in, the legend was emphasized to those missionaries who preached of even more preposterous origins.

Inuit are averse to the myth of *Qimmiq*'s being bred from the wolf. Wide shoulders and a broad stance show that the dog is an entirely different species. Because of *Qimmiq*'s ferocity, most *Kabloona* persist in making the wolf connection anyway, particularly when the dog is growling, clicking fangs and gulping down its dinners. *Natiq, tuktu,* char or muktuk is thrown, rather than handed, to these dogs from a safe distance.

Their ruffs surround them in a thick halo while their eyes follow every movement with the predatory wariness of an animal accustomed to Arctic winters and raw meat. Their white and red coats are shiny from eating fish, and their fur is so thick and often matted with dried blood that it's difficult to part it and check for skin abrasions. While their lower legs are furless, consisting of mostly cold-resistant cartilage, their splayed-out and white-furred paws resemble well-insulated polar bear feet, allowing them to withstand the sub-zero ice surface. *Qimmiq* are so accustomed to the cold that they overheat if the wind stops blowing or the temperature warms to above freezing. If a *Kabloona* dog lover brought such a dog into a heated house, it would pee on the furniture, shit in the kitchen, jump up on the counters and stand at the door panting to be let out.

Try to get these dogs play biting and they'll rip open your parka. Billy's adult huskies can jump up and box a man to the ground. Inuit children can often be seen throwing rocks at these dogs. Every winter in the Canadian Arctic children are killed or mauled by chained-up Eskimo huskies. *Qimmiq* are half wild, and once they've chewed open a caribou or muskox belly and gorged on fresh blood, they cannot be trusted near youngsters.

Some *Qimmiliriji* ("dog men") claim that their *Qimmiq* come from the Russian Chukchi polar bear dogs. Others say it is a relative of the Norwegian spitz breeds. *Qimmiq* origins predate most North American breeds, probably to several thousand years ago, when nomadic hunters walked the forebears of *Qimmiq* across the land bridge to Alaska. Less friendly than the big malamute, raised by an Alaskan subtribe called Mahlemutes, it bears little resemblance to the more urbane and quick-footed Siberian husky, which appeared on the Alaskan racing circuit after the turn of the century. The compact American Eskimo lapdog is the antithesis of the fractious Eskimo husky.

Before 600 B.C. the Arctic Small Tools tradition used dogs for hunting muskoxen and polar bears. Sometime after A.D. 1000—before Plains Indians made half-breed dogs pull travois—the Thule Culture became the first North American people to train dogs for pulling snow sleds, as their ancestors had done in Siberia. *Qimmiq* strode hundreds of miles across sub-zero snow and ice, allowing The People to adapt to the cooling trend. *Qimmiq kamotik*s were the next crucial adaptation, because the sea ice didn't melt for many summers, so this marine-based culture learned to rely upon dogs as much as boats.

During the Little Ice Age, The People were driven south, in pursuit of retreating wildlife. This Thule Culture was now reduced to surviving as small bands of nomadic hunters. European explorers and whalers arrived begging for Inuit help, while The People grew more and more dependent upon *Kabloona* for his iron and steel tools. Thus began the modern era of Inuit.

Like all periods of privation and setback, a cultural regression occurred. Inuit may have become callous. It was not until after the Little Ice Age that any written record appeared about the treatment of their dogs. In the pre-contact era, Inuit record was oral, and with scant tools for precise recollection, it was probably dramatized. If the ensuing era's written record can be believed, dogs were brutalized.

In 1860 *Anecdotes of Animals* (written just after Britain's RSPCA banned dogs from pulling carts) described Eskimo women getting *Qimmiq* to pull sleds: "A word from the female will excite them to exertion when the blows and threats of the men only make them obstinate."

Yet Diamond Jenness found an island of dog lovers around Ikaluktutiak (later named Cambridge Bay). In 1915 the anthropologist observed that they used the word *kia* (who) for only dogs and people, while calling most animals *huna* (it). Pups were reared in skin tents or *iglu*s with The People, on a bed of sealskins, tied to a stake so that they would not defecate on the hallowed Inuit sleeping platforms. Jenness thought that Inuit were not cruel and would never inflict pain for pleasure, even though the game animals they wounded might writhe for hours before being butchered. The anthropologist believed that Inuit's link with dogs was naturally close. People were given their dogs' soul names.

The scant number of whales for food around Victoria Island could not support more than two or three dogs per family. Typically an eight-foot-long *kamotik* was loaded with all the family's possessions. The woman and older children pushed from behind, while an infant was carried in the woman's hood and the head of the household hitched in with the dogs. All heaved together toward the next hunting camp. In summer the women sewed packs for both men and dogs.

The Eskimo husky can pull several times its seventy-five pounds but is ignored by modern sled dog racers since it overheats and cannot run as fast as the Siberian husky. Its real skill is in finding and cornering polar bears. The dog remains fearless enough to attack animals ten times its size. *Nanuq* hunters have to keep their dogs in check, because polar bears can pick them up and throw them across the ice, breaking their backs. *Qimmiq* were also useful in rounding up muskoxen, holding the herd still in a defensive circle as the hunters speared the fattest cows.

When trapping boomed, from 1915 to the 1960s, dogs had a new purpose. Inuit used *Qimmiq* to pull loads of fur to the trading posts. For several decades it was as if the balmy cornucopia of the Thule Culture had returned. *Kamotiks* were built longer. Dogs multiplied. But as the RCMP and various explorers began introducing other breeds, the gene pool of the pure Eskimo husky was compromised.

After the first snowmobile—called an autoboggan—arrived, *kamotiks* were built even longer, and Eskimo huskies quickly lost their purpose. Autoboggans allowed well-paid Inuit trappers to push farther out from their villages as fox, wolverine and wolf populations dropped. Finally, fur prices fell in the 1960s, and people could no longer afford the $700 "motorized dogsleds" (now priced over $10,000). Canine distemper finished the job that snowmobiles started. Barely a hundred of the original Eskimo huskies remained.

Beginning in the early 1970s, Bill Carpenter bred and registered several thousand "pure" Eskimo huskies in Yellowknife. For years Carpenter, with government help, sent the dogs north to Inuit *Qimmiliriji* for only the price of air transportation. Like the muskoxen and bowhead whales, the Eskimo huskies recovered. But now that The People have found some jobs, accepted social assistance and embraced the Nunavut Hunter Support Program, the Ski-Doo has made *Qimmiq* a mere ornament in most villages. Except for guided polar bear hunts (it is illegal for tourists to shoot *Nanuq* from a snowmobile) and a few clients like me, *Qimmiq* mostly serves to remind Inuit of their romantic past.

Dogsleds Versus Getting Nowhere Without Engine

Under the blinding mid-May sky, Jason and I prepare to snowmobile to Umingmaktuuq. He shows me his dad's twenty-foot-long *kamotik*. Thick iron runners are screwed into two two-by-sixteen-inch legs, spanned by two dozen one-by-fours, tied down to the legs with cord. To the uninitiated, such lashed-together lumber might appear jury-rigged. After all, the materials are cheap and the *kamotik*s themselves are strewn throughout villages, littering the coastlines like shipwrecks. Jason, who has the classic hundred-mile stare of a lost generation, says his neighbors have offered his family several hundred dollars for the sled.

"It's ten years old, and everybody in town wants it because it's biggest sled anywhere around," he explains.

A twenty-foot sled will bridge wide sea ice leads, which the driver (after unloading the *kamotik*) rides over, without resorting to skimming. Jason says that their long *kamotik* rides more comfortably than most fifteen-footers. But I have been warned by a local *Kabloona,* who recommended a free seat on an empty government plane to Umingmaktuuq, that riding a *kamotik* at twenty-five miles per hour over the bumpy sea ice is akin to a nonstop carnival ride.

"By the time you get to Umingmaktuuq," a woman told me, "be ready for a wicked backache and a case of whiplash."

I get down on my knees and see that the lashing holes for the one-by-fours are all carefully predrilled. The sharp ship's prows of the legs have had another wedge piece of two-by-sixteen screwed on, blunting the edge to prevent a runaway sled from goring bystanders. The feet of the legs holding the iron runners have been planed on the inside corners, to minimize chances of the *kamotik*'s tipping over and crushing its riders.

At the agreed-upon 8 a.m., I wake up Jason, still sleeping after a long night of television. Several hours later he has the sled packed. I make sure not to rush him, because he needs plenty of time to pack twice that of what southerners throw into their SUVs for a long weekend of car camping. He loads on several caribou skins, a two-burner Coleman stove, a thirty-pound tent, twenty-five gallons of gasoline, five liters of motor oil, twenty pounds of lumber for pitching the tent, a ten-pound, circa 1960s–era sleeping bag, a battered rifle, plenty of ammunition and sundry tools. All are heaped high upon the *kamotik.*

I carefully review the route on my maps. In a last-minute realization of Jason's spaced-out behavior, I pack my own tent, fuel, skis and food so that I can survive and walk back to Cambridge Bay in case something goes wrong. No telling what Jason might forget. My fifty-pound duffel, with padded shoulder straps, can be carried on my back or dragged behind me. Jason's gear is ten times as heavy, minus the sled and snowmobile.

"Is that all you're taking?" he asks.

Under Jason's guidance, it would be easy to disappear from the face of the planet. One lead of thin ice, slightly longer than the *kamotik,* would swallow the two of us as quickly as astronauts sucked from their protective capsule into the void of oceanic space. It takes five minutes of cajoling to convince his mother that it's okay for us to leave without a radio; most Inuit wouldn't be caught dead traveling without one, but Jason doesn't seem to care that his dad has the lone family set on the dogsled. I manage to convince Mrs. Aguklaruk that we will survive because other snowmobilers are following us toward the mainland and we will catch her husband in no time.

Jason repeatedly refers to his interest in world affairs gleaned through television, so I ask his opinion of Slobodan Milosevic. He replies, "It's fucked-up Finland's taking over that country." Jason's ego won't permit me to correct him. I can only imagine how growing up in the Arctic—without education, guided by the belief that circumpolar countries constitute the world, and bombarded by confusing twenty-four-hour news—would have changed my perspective of geography.

It's no secret that Jason has an arrest record for stalking women, that he freebases cocaine and that he is one of many professional students at Nunavut College. He repeatedly refers to his "investments" down south, where he keeps a pickup truck and drives all over the continent, picking up hitchhiking strippers and, to the best of anyone's knowledge, parcels of cocaine in Miami and Texas. In another month he claims that he is buying his own house. But he rarely works. He has a habit of standing too close and smiling up at me. Then, as suddenly as a storm cloud blocking the sun, he turns surly and reprimands me for pulling too tight on the *kamotik* lashing line. In this moodiness he is the spitting image of his father. Or an edgy drug addict.

His father's old Polaris at first refuses to start. After enough cranks to leave Jason covered in sweat, it belches out a black cloud. While squeezing the brake caliper, he guns it hard enough to score the cylinders. Oil spits from the exhaust. I cover my ears.

I jump on back, give him the thumbs up, and we're off at about the same

Repairing an overturned kamotik *before a journey*

speed at which his father's dog team left. Ten minutes out we climb a hill-side, then accelerate south into a milky bright suspension of land, sea and sky. It is not a friendly place this time of year—like falling into an overlarge frost-hung freezer and being blinded by a bare lightbulb—but it has a reluctant beauty all its own. Wind whips around my hood and up onto my forehead like an ice compress. As I squint with my sunglasses down, sit backward and peer away from the slipstream of our passage, the reclusive sky blushes with the same cobalt that lies five feet beneath the *kamotik* runners. A seal the size of my leg sways into an *aglu* fifty yards away, leaving the sea ice an uncluttered field of sparkling white.

In forty-five minutes, the clutter of Cambridge Bay's greenish buildings fades out, spilled over by the glowing milkiness. While holding on tightly, trying to assume an athletic stance with which to absorb the bumps, I remember those stories that made Arctic culture so intriguing to me: how Inuit forge through a landscape of such immense and indiscernible proportions that they must possess internal radar. Or how Inuit position themselves in the landscape by wind-drifted sastrugi or other unknowable minutiae, gathered in their cortices as wisdom that defies all linear definition. After no small amount of research, I am confused by these *Kabloona* storytellers, authors of well-known books that constitute our northern literature. Maybe they lacked winter survival skills. While shepherded around the North by Inuit snowmobilers or standing inside the heated bridges of icebreaker ships, these writers may have fanned modern Inuit route finding out of all proportion. Although Inuit came from an age where intuitiveness equaled survival, today it seems that most hold less sixth sense than a *Kabloona* can glean after careful training and deliberate solitude. I may be deluding myself about Inuit intuition of the land.

The three-foot-wide snowmobile tracks we're following are spider-webbed with outgoing hunter trails. The main trail—like that of a giant's Vibram footprint, walking heel to toe—will climb up out of the ocean in another twenty miles, onto rolling tundra, following a chain of lakes across a ten-mile-wide skein of mainland. Inside this portage is the ten-mile-wide fjord of Elu Inlet, stretching sixty miles east into Bathurst Inlet. Here the trail swings back south, heel-toeing it another forty miles along the coast to Umingmaktuuq.

I have come to realize that most Inuit travelers trace the sort of snowmobile trail that we are following today, a highway created by ribbed steel rototilling the ice. But Inuit snowmobilers regularly lose this path when it drifts in or whites out. Dogs still retain a sense of orientation that prevents their owners from getting lost. Most Arctic villages regularly perform rescues when snowmobilers lose their bearings, get lost and run out of gas. From the place where I sit, holding tightly to the lash lines on the best *kamotik* in Cambridge Bay, bouncing hard over hummocks of ice, I can see it is likely that Jason's premature deafness has a lot to do with two-cylinder-engine noise. His hands cramp on the throttle as our eyes sting with exhaust. If he loses the trail or the engine dies, he is ill conditioned and mentally unprepared for a long wilderness trek. It would be unfair to suppose that Jason's time indoors as a modern *Inuk* would equip him for leadership, let alone for making the right decisions in an emergency. If I should accidentally bounce off and be abandoned, the four-ounce GPS safely stashed in a vest pocket of my down parka will be my ticket out.

An hour and a half out Jason shuts down the Polaris so that we can relieve the pressure of badly jostled bladders. He mumbles that he has forgotten all the food that his mother had set out for him. I toss him a Clif Bar. He swallows it in several bites, then pushes more chewing tobacco into the void of his missing front tooth. We stand straddled in our own separate universes. I can feel the space pushing down on me as we sway imperceptibly on the deep waters of Dease Strait, interrupted only by the ringing of unhealthy snowmobile decibels.

The limestone mainland rises to the south like a row of nicotine-stained teeth, biting through the mirage air of the snowy Kent Peninsula. An island stands alone to the west. Aside from the giant's steel-ribbed tracks, there are no birds or bear scat or any sign of wildlife. Cigarette packages, urine stains, abandoned *kamotik*s and several snowmobiles are all destined to become underwater reefs once the sea ice melts.

Jason brings the Polaris back alive in only four pulls, as I ask him to try to take it easier on my back. He grins lopsidedly, guns the engine and the sled lurches and slams through convoluted sea ice. No man or machine can take this sort of abuse for long.

Several hours later, sixty miles south of town, we pass early flocks of birds—I am too shaken to make any identification. Then we spy his dad. Fifteen minutes after Billy and dogs first appear as a line of dots out in Elu Inlet, his body comes into focus, bent over the snow beside his dogsled.

He grunts at me as the Polaris shuts down. Our eardrums are still ringing from the snowmobile. Billy draws "1063" into the snow with his finger,

"Caribou I have counted," he says, thinking to impress a linear-minded *Kabloona*.

"Tracks or live animals?" I ask.

"Both," he replies. Then he gazes out over the horizon, straining to see more *tuktu* through his wire-rimmed glasses.

When I point out the distant seal that Billy seems to have missed, he laughs and quips, "No dead muskoxen."

His son mumbles the Inuktitut word for meat: "*Niqi.*"

Billy pulls out a bloody cloth wrapping a chunk of uncooked caribou meat (*quaq*), then sets out three cups for coffee, pours himself one and lets Jason and me fend for ourselves. *Quaq* is like eating bloody sushi, with crunchy bits of ice between the layers, but the ice crystals and blood make it easier to chew than cooked wild game. Billy reminds me, "No clog arteries like barnyard cow."

In my former meat-eating days I avoided eating raw meat, like most people, because of internal parasites. Nonetheless, I eat three finger-size bites, feel a rush of warmth and see that my hosts are satisfied.

Billy refuses a Clif Bar by gargling a quick puking noise. When I ask if he can still build an *iglu,* he glares back at me. He wouldn't believe me if I told him I have built dozens, let alone that I have run dog teams across the wilderness for weeks at a time. It's better to remain silent and learn from him, rather than speak of my own experiences. When I ask him the word for snow, he picks it up in his hand and replies, "This *aniu.*" No doubt he can recite a dozen more depending upon whether it falls from the sky, is icy, wet or frozen.

The popular idea that Eskimos used an untold number of words for snow is a myth. One of the most experienced Inuktitut linguists, Duncan Pryde, said in the 1960s that they used twenty-five to thirty different terms. Today that number may have been halved—less spectacular than a modern *Kabloona* skier's vocabulary. In Cambridge Bay, with all its government housing, fewer than a dozen Inuit can still build *iglu*s. Snow has lost a lot of meaning in their modern lives. Since caribou are still actively hunted, Inuktitut employs as many different words for *tuktu* as a southern rancher does for cattle. *Tuktuluit* means caribou fur around the hood; *tutalik,* caribou boots; *tuktuyaq,* daddy longlegs spider; *tuktoyaqtoq,* signaling by waving your arms about your head; *tutouk,* a caribou-shaped star constellation; *tuktukiuk,* flyblown caribou meat; and *tuktoyuktuk*, resembling a caribou. And so on.

The richness of Inuktitut used to be about The People's intimacy and understanding of animal life. Now the word bank seems to be overdrawn, as Nunavut scrambles to reinvest in the language. If I had been able to ask Billy's grandfather to identify a species of loon, he would have answered *tullik* (yellow-billed), *maliriq* (Pacific), or *qaqsrauq* (red-throated). Inuit had been practicing this precise identification long before Carl Linnaeus's disciples arrived in the Arctic with Latin name tags. Today most elders simply lump together all three loon species as *qaqsrauq,* substituting the red-throated and most often seen loon's name for their ancestors' knowledge of the birds. And among those younger Inuit who pretend to speak Inuktitut, Jason has already identified two loons to me as *amaulegeroq* (an eider) or by simply saying in English, "duck."

Suddenly his father yells, "YAH-YAH-YAH!," pulls the snow hook out of the ice, and the dogs are running.

The *quaq* falls and falls and falls in my stomach below. My digestive juices boil bloody flesh so hard and lean from running across tundra that I might as well be metabolizing my own biceps. It is the first meat, cooked or raw, that I have eaten since last summer. It takes all the discipline of a seasoned poker player not to show Billy or Jason how sick I feel.

We let the dogsled go first. For the next couple of hours we catch up, stop, then catch up again.

Billy finally halts his dogs in the lee of rocky ridge. He hooks a two-hundred-foot chain into chopped-out sea ice holes and clips each dog twenty yards apart to prevent fights. Jason and I pitch the white canvas tent, line the snow with animal furs and dig a cooking pit by the front door. It takes the three of us two hours to pitch camp.

As Jason takes potshots at snowshoe hares, Billy declares, *"Tuktu."*

I jump onto the *kamotik,* and after a five-minute chase behind a nearby herd of white caribou, Billy stops the snowmobile and looks for the choicest meat. He aims and fires his father's old rusted Winchester 243, but no caribou fall, so he aims and shoots the remaining four cartridges, until the *tuktu* run out of range.

Billy restarts the Polaris to continue the hunt. This *Inuk* and the fleeing caribou—several dozen bleached-out and large-dog-size ungulates—are enacting an ancient ritual. Billy drives the snowmobile alongside rather than directly into their midst, which allows him to select the whitest back (black splotches show warble fly infestation). It is as if the *tuktu* were letting themselves be hunted. The lack of tension here makes it feel like complicity just shy of shopping in a grocery market meat section. The caribou don't even seem flighty or frightened. It is as if they have accepted the reciprocity of being killed for other beings to survive.

Billy cuts the engine, glides to a stop, then braces more carefully on his snowmobile seat. He fires repeatedly at a nearby cow, until a liquid wallop brings her front legs skidding down flat onto the ice.

He then tows the *kamotik* directly up to the small caribou, lifts the hundred-pound-plus animal and ties it down, deftly flipping the rope over and under the cow's legs. The caribou is still alive. She shivers and stares up with glassy spins of big brown eyeballs at the *Inuk* who is wiping his hands clean of her blood; then, in the strangest and most unexpected ritual I have beheld, he leans down to petulantly return her stare. I had never witnessed an adult enjoying an animal's death throes.

"Let's go, *Kabloona*," Billy says.

Back at the tent Billy and Jason make quick work of quartering and skinning the caribou. Billy jabs his knife up through the stomach lining, reaches

Caribou calf fetus removed from the cow

in, then pulls out a two-foot-long calf, perhaps a week away from dropping out and running on its spindly legs. He holds the wiggling calf high in the air for my education, placenta fluid running down his arm, while he gaggles crazily for a photograph.

It is my camera, I think, that allows me to step outside these scenes to try to see the world anew, from their perspective, slowing down time and capturing moments that I neither understand nor try to judge from the stilted view of my own upbringing in an agrarian society.

I aim as carefully as Jason did at the arctic hare that he shot and broke in two with a high-powered rifle. The animal will remain uneaten on the snow as a pile of matted red and white fur beside the now dead and quartered caribou, its fur pulled inside out. I aim at the decapitated cow's head lying alone on the sea ice.

Billy interrupts my reverie and calls my attention to several pinkish warble fly cysts upon the skinned caribou's back. He pulls one off, saying, "Taste mushroom!" and holds it up for me to examine.

I am reminded of the time *Hypoderma tarandi* ("under the caribou skin") homed in on my carbon dioxide emissions like a buzzing hummingbird, then touched down on my arm. If I had not brushed the bumblebee-size fly off, the parasite might have laid its sticky eggs. The highly adapted fly took off in search of hairier prey.

Although humans, muskoxen and moose are not immune, and warble fly maggots have been extracted from behind children's eyeballs, its preferred host is the caribou. Unlike the southern species of warble or gadflies (*Hypoderma bovis* or *lineatum* are hosted in cows), the caribou warble can fly continuously for thirty hours, covering up to five hundred miles, allowing it to trail its wide-ranging host species. The powerful wings of the fly allow it to penetrate even windswept coastlines, where caribou shelter from the more pedestrian mosquitoes. Entomologists theorize that the warble fly arrival, known in southerly climates to cause "gadding" (stampeding) of cattle, is the trigger for huge herds of caribou to begin migrating.

Billy reminds me that he has sometimes mistakenly shot *tuktu* with thousands of *kamangit* on their back, softening the meat into a bacon-flavored pulp, *tuktukiuk,* which makes Billy turn up his nose.

"Mushroom okay but not *tuktukiuk,* rotten meat," he says.

"Billy what is this mushroom you keep talking about?"

"You no like mushroom, *Kabloona*?"

The adult warble fly lives for less than a week. Since the fly has no mouth, its mission in life is to breed, then (for the female) to lay eggs. Once landed upon a *tuktu* belly or legs, the fly lays up to a hundred sticky eggs, then drops off and dies, desiccated as a spent salmon. Most animals would inadvertently brush the tiny warble fly eggs off, but a large ungulate does not have the luxury of grooming its inaccessible underparts. Within a week the eggs hatch out as tiny and transparent maggots, which immediately burrow into their host's skin. Maggots then spend the summer tunneling up and around to the back, next to the spine. Once arrived at their winter's home, they cut out a one- to three-millimeter-long breathing hole through the hide, causing, as may be imagined, considerable agitation and itchy backs. For up to nine months the maggots grow a centimeter wide, feeding off their host's fatty flesh to support their eventual mouthless and egg-laying incarnation. Throughout the winter its host is continually roaming, pawing the ground for sedges and, if badly infested, rolling on the ground in obvious discomfort.

Watch enough caribou, even without shooting them, and you can see the effects of the warble. Black abscesses and infections line the parasites' breathing holes. A self-defense mechanism in the host's circulatory system crusts over the maggots with a spiny armature that does little to slow the warble feeding. Sometimes a whole caribou herd may be spied collectively wriggling their backs, like a wave breaking down a long shoreline. Combine enough maggots with deep snows, and the caribou will simply drop in exhaustion as the parasites continue to wriggle-feed in ecstasy.

If this cow had lived another month, the two dozen maggots would have tunneled out their breathing holes and dropped to the tundra at about the same time as the caribou calf.

While the calf is born running, the warble fly maggots tunnel into the earth to become inactive and slowly developing pupae. A month later, like butterflies crawling from their former caterpillar beginnings, the orange, yellow and black–striped warble fly pops out and hums through the air. Then the cycle begins anew, with the caribou playing out its central role, feeding insects, Inuit, bears, wolves and dogs.

Billy continues to shake the marble-size warble cyst in front of me. Keeping my composure, I focus upon the warble fly maggot, ensconced in a crusty shell not unlike that of a pink snail. Through the camera lens, it could be an inverse knuckle growing out of Billy's palm.

Then, to my horror, Billy plops it into his mouth like a ball of gum. "*Tuktu kamangit,*" Billy says, "caribou lice. Taste mushroom. Have one," he commands.

"No, thanks, but it's kind of you to offer."

"You must eat," Billy says.

I walk away. From a safe distance I watch the pandemonium.

The Aguklaruks cut the meat into eleven softball-size chunks and loft it underhanded to the dogs, from a cautious and distant pitcher position. Dogs bay impatiently; Billy barks out directions to his son. The din must be scattering wildlife miles away.

Manny, the biggest dog, is a tireless puller and a lion-maned 125-pound miscreant. He is adorable, to me anyway, at least until he begins eating. Jason repeatedly justifies whipping Manny because he has seen him pull down and eat caribou. But Jason is not stupid. His real reason for the abuse is simply his fear that Manny, like the abused dog Buck in *Call of the Wild,* will someday turn on him.

For dessert, Billy pitches Manny an entire lower leg bone since he inhaled five pounds of dinner in seconds flat. If Billy runs shy of bullets and needs a caribou, Manny would do the job. He cracks the thick bone open, macerating it like an ordinary biscuit, all the while growling as if the leg were still alive and might attempt to run loose from his throat. Manny knows how to eat still-moving animals. Jason screams at me to move away from the dog.

Inside the tent Billy pumps up both two-burner Coleman stoves, lights them up along with another cigarette, then turns his shortwave radio up to a maximum pitch of crinkling static and human voices bent onto radio waves. Within minutes, I am dizzy from carbon monoxide fumes. I strip down to a T-shirt and try to lift open the floor flap of the tent for oxygen.

Billy throws on a five-gallon pot filled with snow. As it melts, he plops in ten pounds of the choicest caribou backstrap, ribs and tongue. I steel myself for dinner.

Half an hour later Billy reaches into the boiling pot with his fingers and lifts the meat onto a large plate. After serving himself, he pushes the plate and motions me to try the kidney-colored pieces of tongue. "Delicacy, *Kabloona.*"

I pick one up tentatively and put it in my mouth: a rubbery gasket that does not lend itself to chewing. I swallow my small piece of tongue whole, barely getting it down.

"Whatsa matter, you no like Eskimo food?" Billy asks, as his son breaks into another fit of giggling.

"No, no," I insist, picking up a remarkably lean-looking rib with my fingers, "it's just that I'm not used to tongue."

With his mouth full of backstrap, Billy says, "Caribou meat make you feel light."

As he looks away briefly, I slide the three remaining cubes of tongue to Jason. His eyes brighten. I then try to separate what little meat clings to the rib bone with a dull knife. If there is any consolation here, the meat should have boiled long enough to kill any parasites. Thinking of Manny, I lift a pound of flesh to my face and assault directly with my teeth. Billy smiles back at me. For half an hour there are only aggressive chewing noises, belches, *niliqs* (farts) and omnipresent radio static. From everything I have heard and read, sharing *tuktu* should bring us closer together.

Billy shakes some salt into the pot and pours me a bowl of the leavings. "Caribou soup *good.* Make you sleep *warm.*"

Father and son pull their ten- and fifteen-pound sleeping bags out of their three-foot-long duffels, then pull their bundles of cotton and eider-down up to their chins.

"*Kabloona* be coming in with me tonight to stay warm?" Billy jokes. He can't suppress his cackles as he buttons up the sides of his 1960s flannel-sheeted sleeping bag.

"No, thank you," I say as I worm into my mummy Polar Guard 3D Fiber-fil bag like a newly hatched warble.

His humor is probably an ironic poke at his Eskimo glory days, mixed with a bit of redneck homophobia pinched from working with *Kabloona* gold miners in the Lupine mine.

All night long he pumps the two stoves, burning a gallon of naphtha, to stay warm. I sleep soundly, albeit covered in sweat.

In the morning I awake to Billy blowing cigarette smoke and lifting my double cross-country ski boots over the stove where he might burn them up. "Garbage," he says, smiling.

"Maybe heavy, but they're warm and work good for skis," I reply.

He reaches over and fingers my synthetically filled sleeping bag. "More garbage," he says.

"Do you know that cotton and down are no good when wet?" I finger his sleeping bag, covered, like everything else in the tent, with the morning beard of stray caribou hair.

"Bullshit, this *five-star* best bag made."

"You would know, Billy," I say.

By midmorning the dogs are all harnessed up, and Jason and I agree to wait for Billy ten miles out. After only an hour of waiting, Billy catches Jason and me, but he sounds ready to kill. He screams at his lead dog, Tunok, to go left—"HAW, HAW, HAW!"—and Tunok goes right (gee) around the Polaris, tangling the traces. From where I stand on a hillside a quarter mile away, it is not an insurmountable tangle. None of the dogs are fighting. Yet Billy is having a bad day, to judge by the edge in his voice. He throws in the snow hook, bangs his shin against the *kamotik,* and grabs a suspiciously handy-looking two-by-four from his load. He strides forward, clubbing and kicking dogs left and right, and arrives in a state of rage next to the leader. Tunok, an otherwise intelligent and calm animal that has earned its place in front of the team, knows what's next. She lies down and whim-pers. As Billy raises the two-by-four, I run as fast as I can down the hill. Billy clubs with all his might. The beating goes on for several minutes, hard pine walloping mere flesh and blood, protected only by a dense and woolly fur, crying out for mercy. Then Billy sees me arrive and pulls up short, giving the dog a final kick.

"Tunok, you cunt," Billy says.

This time I have no camera in front of my face. This time there is no distancing myself from the man. He looks as if caught with one hand in someone's pocket. All my interests of remaining objective have slowly been crumbling in the face of Inuit social despair and Western assimilation. Now, as I witness this new cruelty, all that I have known and read about their graceful culture has left me confused.

Does Billy beat his dogs because *Qimmiq* does not respond like his well-oiled machines? Or is this the underlying pain that Billy feels from losing his cultural bearings?

As Jason and I speed another ten miles down the sea ice to wait for his father, I know that I can weather insults that Billy heaps upon me. I can forget his cavalier style of harvesting caribou. I can overlook Jason's firing upon most every nonhuman being in sight. Yet when Billy turns and beats *Qimmiq,* the cornerstone animal of his culture, I am really sad for the man. Surely the Aguklaruks are not representative of an entire culture, and their words and actions are theirs alone, even if it all seems a familiar pattern among other Inuit I have observed.

While we wait for Billy to arrive, I remember readings about Inuit dog abuse. In Gontran de Poncins's book *Kabloona,* he describes hiring a *Qimmiriji* in Gjoa Haven for a 150-mile trip. The dogs should have spent only a week to run the *kamotik* to Pelly Bay, but it took them seventeen days to walk the twelve-foot-long, thirteen-hundred-pound *kamotik.* Poncins writes about that 1939 trip:

> Algunerk beat his dogs out of the impulse which made him, from time to time, beat his wife: he had worked himself up to a pitch of anger. . . . He would pull a dog towards him by the individual trace to which it was harnessed, the beast meanwhile crawling and resisting his pulling, and howling with terror. Once he had the dog at his feet he would take the sock of the whip to it and beat it over the loins and kidneys as hard as he could. Eskimo dogs must, as a matter of evolution, have backs specially built against these beatings, for when the horrible scene was over, the dog would rise with no ribs broken and go back to its place. But Algunerk's fury was not sated by a single beating. He would run alongside and continue to slash and hit even after we had started up again, bounding among the traces with an agility astonishing in a man of his years (for he was by no means young).

Two decades later, Jean Briggs describes in *Never in Anger* how a man at the Back River broke a tent pole over the back of a howling and hungry dog.

Or how a poker-faced woman repeatedly threw a boulder onto a thieving dog's ribs. Briggs writes about how Inuit beat their chained-up *Qimmiq* with any object they could hold in their hands: boots, frozen fish or hammers. It went beyond mere training, because The People smiled at their dogs' pain.

When Billy arrives two hours later with several dogs bloody from more beatings, I can no longer look him in the eye. He is shouting, "Fucking cunt dogs!"

He throws in the snow hook and then pulls out the two-by-four. This time I am ready, reaching for my camera, but not to distance myself. I make sure Billy sees me focusing in on him, then wait for his ego to take over. He predictably stops. He drops the two-by-four so that I cannot photograph him beating his dogs. It is a technique, no doubt, that I will use again with Billy.

He limps back to his granddaddy *kamotik* and slumps down next to me. "Leg hurts."

"Would you like me to look at it for you?"

"No." He reaches inside my open parka and snatches out a flask that I am keeping warm in an inside pocket. "Ah, whiskey, *Kabloona* smarter than he looks," he says.

"Whatever, Billy, help yourself."

As the water hits his mouth, he spits it out. "I going to get drunk soon as I get Umingmaktuuq," he complains.

"We'll meet you there tomorrow then," I suggest.

"Okay." He scuffs two inches of snow from the surface of the sea ice. "Too soft for dogs. No good."

"They seem to be running pretty good to me, Billy, but if you want to go back to Cambridge Bay, that's okay, because I'm prepared to walk back from Umingmaktuuq."

He is obviously insulted, his ego again on the line. "Maybe take me two days. Maybe leg heals."

"Your call."

That afternoon it's Jason's turn to grow angry. He conceded to take his turn riding the bucking *kamotik*. Although I drive it more slowly than what he subjected me to the previous day, Jason learns that Inuit backs are no more shockproof than *Kabloona* backs. After half an hour he has had enough and waves me down to stop. He jumps off the sled in remarkable mimicry of his father, jumping up and down in rage.

"You are not good traveler," he says.

"I'm probably not."

"You have broken our *kamotik* with all the up and down!" He kicks it once for good measure.

"It still looks intact to me."

He changes the subject. "We need more fuel to make Umingmaktuuq."

"We've only got twenty miles to go, and we've got a quarter tank left. Are you sure you want to dump more in?"

"You are bad traveler and know nothing about how we go."

"I admit I'm not much of a motorhead," I say.

He bristles at the implication, growing angrier by the minute. "We would be nowhere without engine," he insists.

"It's just interesting to me, Jason, how your people have evolved into a society incredibly adept at all things with motors, but you can't hear and see what's around you, and man, it's blinding you."

"But I can go much faster than you on foot, and we would be nowhere without the engine." As Jason picks up the 243 from the sled, checking to see if it's loaded, I'm tempted to tell him that I could have ridden the plane for free while his gas and services will cost me several hundred dollars. This seems too negative to articulate and maybe even dangerous. Jason takes quick aim at a sleeping seal, sixty yards off. He has shot, lost or wounded a dozen seals over the past two days. The seal slips away as the bullet whistles past. Judging how Jason's face is wrinkled into a set of furrowed lines, like waves of sastrugi rippling the sea ice, I know that further discussion will not be well received. Jason considers himself the boss, and the subject is closed. He refuses to catch the ball of reciprocal conversation and throw it back again.

I give it a try anyway. "Jason, I agree that the machine is a necessary evil. Still, we would hear a lot more, see a lot more, and no doubt cover a lot less miles, but we would know a lot more about what's around us, without it."

"We would be nowhere without engine," is all he can say.

"Then let's go." I add, "You drive, since you're the expert."

That night in Umingmaktuuq we sleep in Jason's uncle's house. John Kuptana regulates the diesel stove up at its maximum register, over 90 degrees. Although sixty-one-year-old John speaks no English, his gestures and smiles show us that we are welcome, even though Jason tries to kick me out. That evening John's snores suddenly stop vibrating the Sheetrocked walls of his tiny cabin. I wake up. John then breaks into subconscious Eskimo chanting, "Ai ya ya ya, Ai ya ya ya, Ai ya ya ya ya ya," as he has for the past twenty years, every night since his mother died of some unnamed disease. There is no stopping the ghostly chant, short of waking John up.

The next morning, as a privileged *Kabloona* guest, I find it most appropriate to appreciate my own good fortune and wonder why he and his people are so unlucky. I am invited into several different houses for tea.

In small communities throughout the Arctic, Inuit habitually drop their differences. Living in such close proximity to one another—formerly in *iglus* and now in cramped government housing—demands it. Since forgiveness is one of their most endearing traits, I too must learn to put whatever misgivings I have about dog beatings and the sheer quantity of violent videotapes (Jean-Claude Van Damme is a favorite here) and Honda generator–powered VCRs and televisions. Although this is the only village in the Canadian Arctic without electricity or telephones, Western civilization has found its inexorable entrance.

A mother and her son here have the HIV/AIDS virus. Children are playing bingo instead of learning how to read in school. Another one of my favorite couples, recently diagnosed with both heart and lung problems, frequently do drunken battle with fists and forks. Last fall, while trying to figure out how to fly out of the village before winter came, it escaped my attention that a sixteen-year-old had committed suicide just before I came; his surviving family moved back to Cambridge Bay. So the tiny enclave of traditionalists whom I perceived last fall as living in Shangri-la are in the same state as the villages they claim to be escaping.

In the morning I unzip a huge duffel, recently flown in and full of donated Polartec fleece clothing. I hand over a sweater in John's size. He puts it on (and will probably keep it on for the whole summer), bowing and saying, "*Cowanna*."

Jason takes the pick of sweaters for himself and then demands another for a Mother's Day gift back in Cambridge Bay. Since I have more than enough to outfit the village, I let him have his way.

Over the next three days no one is interested in why I am handing out clothing, only that I am giving it away. I learn not to explain or expect anything in return. For my part I am happy that they'll be wearing more than their inadequate cotton clothes. (Billy is one of the few men I have met with a caribou skin jacket.) If this were a town in southern Appalachia, I would arrange a seminar on proper dressing techniques, demonstrating how the fleece clothing stays warm when wet, can be wrung dry after a soaking, and ideally is worn in layers to prevent sweat from getting your skin wet. But such a seminar would be perceived as rudeness to Inuit. They will have to learn the clothing's benefits on their own, through experience.

Most locals seem to remember me from September. Clarence Klengenberg stomps off in mystified silence as I give him a photograph of the polar bear carving I bought from him last fall.

The three boys of the village take turns stealing my only boots. In exasperation, I take them for walks on the hills above their tiny harbor town, but as they become more familiar, they only become more unruly. Quaho is an outspoken twelve-year-old, named after the kayaker whose rubber boots protrude from the burlap bag covering his corpse, in a lidless casket on the tundra outskirts of town. Quaho has dirt rimming his mouth and a Nunavut cap perched at a jaunty angle on his head. He has become familiar enough that he feels comfortable reaching into my pockets for money. I continually explain to the children that I don't like their reaching into my pockets or stealing my only pair of boots.

Billy arrives that night exhausted. As we chain out the dogs, I ask about his leg. He waves it off, then limps up to his brother-in-law's house.

John discreetly breaks out the home brew. The two elders steadfastly refuse to let me share, so I sit and listen. I interrupt as little as possible so that Jason might translate for me as Billy joshes John about the water stain on his pants being a pee stain. Then, over the radio, there is the voice of the woman that they would like to bed. Billy's *niliqs* smell like *tuktukiuk*.

Quaho and his sister, Beckey, walk in without knocking, as all people do in this village. If people want to nap or undress, they simply lock their doors. If they're serving tea, they whistle out their windows. Billy begins a "coochy-coo" tickling of the young girl, and something distinctly raw fills the cabin, as if a window had been opened to a storm wind. It's a transformation in Billy's laugh, as well as a speeded-up and giddy relief from the listlessness of everyday life in this village. If I didn't know better, I would say that the alcohol has made both men into strangers.

"Is it good home brew?" I ask, thinking that they might share or at least give me an idea of where the night is headed. But Billy replies to my words with an Inuktitut joke, something foul and unrepeatable enough that Jason refuses to translate. Billy and John laugh, maniacally. The two children sit in their chairs wide-eyed about what might happen next.

As if to affirm that the mood has changed, their young mother shoves open the cabin door. Billy and John chatter on without saying hello. The mother, Irene, still standing outside, demands that her children come out immediately. Quaho and Beckey leave. The door slams. John and Billy make fun of the distant radio voice.

I open up my rapidly dwindling duffel, hand Billy a brand-new fleece jacket, then grab my sleeping bag to find some peace. As I open the door to wish them good night, Billy holds up this new gift.

"Jonnn!" he says, looking at the jacket.

"Yeah, Billy?"

"Cowanna."

"You're welcome."

"Jon?"

"Yes?"

"Eet's garbage! Hee-hee-hee-hee."

"Next to your caribou jacket you might be right. Sleep well."

I take shelter in the Hunters and Trappers Office I stayed in last fall. Three *Kabloona* grizzly bear clients now inhabit the building. Terry, Steve,

Leonard and I have little in common, yet their company is a chance to compare notes and see how other men perceive Inuit. The outspoken leader of the group, Terry, has already shot his trophy, which was skinned (courtesy of his *Inuk* guide, Noah) and laid out on the floor. Over the years, he has killed five grizzlies during a dozen different hunts, but in this instance he claims, "I had no choice when it started coming after me."

Terry is jowled and bursting at the seams, nearly six feet tall and perched upon stick legs. His lower belly is distended. His voice is an astonishing deep growl, punctuated by earsplitting laughter for his frequent jokes. To shoot his eight-foot bear, Terry never changed his sitting position from his padded shooting box, pulled behind the snowmobile. He merely pushed off the safety on his 300 Magnum, looked through the scope and then squeezed the trigger. His guide had pulled so close to the bear that even a poor shooter would eventually have hit it after emptying the chamber. If Terry's rifle had jammed and the bear had charged, the guide would have driven his client to safety, because no bear can outrun a snowmobile.

As the men roar off in different directions each morning, reclining in their padded plywood boxes, loaded down with cold cuts, radios, stoves,

Kabloona *bear hunter being hauled in a* kamotik

thermoses and sleeping bags, they evoke Indian mahouts atop elephants. They spend most of the day being pulled countless miles on riverbeds and sea ice, hoping to cross fresh grizzly tracks.

"Hunting with Eskimos here in the Canadian Arctic," Terry is not ashamed to say, "is the only place in the world where you can shoot a grizzly from a snowmobile."

"Really?" I ask, surprised because this can't be done with polar bears.

"It does not take much skill," he adds, needlessly.

His words seem so unlikely and self-condemning that I actually find myself, at least momentarily, in sympathy for him. But I can't keep my eyes from going back to his skinned bear, built remarkably similar to Terry. The hide is still bulging with fat, naked on the floor. The resemblance is chilling as Terry poses next to the naked body for a photograph.

If Terry's skin were scraped off with an ulu, would his fat be whiter and thicker than the grizzly's? I wonder.

Steve and Leonard still have another week left on their permits to shoot a bear, if their Inuit guides can find one. Although the Americans claim to be avid outdoorsmen, none can show me on the map wall where they have spent their days hunting. That night Terry, chagrined, gets his guide to grease pencil the kill site. If all three hunters succeed in killing a bear, the total will expend this year's quota, imposed upon Umingmaktuuq's HTO by Renewable Resources.

No hunter is guaranteed a bear, even after paying $7,500. The only real guarantee here is that 75 percent of the fee goes to this village, 15 percent to the agency that booked the hunt and the rest to the government for administering it. Additionally, each guide (if he finds a bear) is tipped another several hundred dollars.

Although Inuit come and go from the HTO building at will, these *Kabloona* sportsmen, dressed in the sort of expensive suits that alpinists wear for ascending into the death zone, talk as if their guides did not understand English. While Terry's guide, Noah, stands in earshot, bent over the bear with an ulu, tediously scraping off fat from the hide, Terry growls out in his baritone, "The Inuit aren't particularly good hunters. Mostly because of all that time roaring around on their snowmobiles."

"Really?"

"But neither are we either, huh?" Terry lowers his hands to graphically support his belly and then laughs uproariously at his own self-deprecation.

Jason walks into the room and, after a short round of introductions, sits down to thumb through a hunting magazine, seemingly disengaged from Terry's vaunting.

"I've measured my bear here, and it's definitely a record for a barren ground griz. They don't get any bigger than eight feet."

He then launches into a detailed story about his hunt last year in Paulatuk, watching kids crawl in and out a neighboring window to fuck a retarded girl and how the whole town got so wasted that he had to punch out his drunken *Inuk* guide, then quick call a charter plane to get out of Dodge.

Terry might be indifferent, but he is not a racist. He is not terribly observant either, and ultimately he epitomizes those attitudes of our colonizing roots. He has spent a lot of time with Inuit guides in the Arctic, and although he claims that his cultural experiences are the best part of the hunts, he cannot remember, aside from Paulatuk, the names of the other villages or his previous guides.

He turns to lambasting Noah's silences and incomprehensible route-finding decisions in a half whisper. Then he shouts across the room, "Want some more coffee, Noah?"

Noah silently squints his eyes and lowers his thin brows into a no.

Terry grumbles, "Gawd, the guy never says anything." Then, with another bout of inspiration, he shouts, "Noah, you didn't want to drink out of this cup anyway, because I haven't washed it and you'll get white man's disease; you'll go bald and gray! Haar, haar, haar!"

Noah manages a weak smile but doesn't laugh.

Terry turns to me, several feet across the table, and blares out, "That Noah is a shitty hide preparer, and he better not accidentally cut off another paw because I won't be able to *bear* it! Haar, haar, haar!"

Noah is silent and built as low to the ground as a wolverine, his rear end flowing out the top of his pants. He mostly thinks of his clients as dumb, rich and impatient—in short, *Kabloona*. To Noah, the word is laced with meaning. Since most of Umingmaktuuq's income is derived from such sport hunts, constituting the bulk of Inuit-*Kabloona* interaction for the year, the local guides have formed their own opinions about their clients and southerners in general. Inuit are much keener observers of culture than are their clients.

At that afternoon's feast, held in a local's cabin, I am invited, if only because I am an outsider bearing gifts. Since everyone is curious about what I might say, two dozen ears perk up as I pose a question. While Noah is picking up a haunch of boiled caribou from a serving platter on the floor, I ask him what he thinks of Terry, who has been left alone in the HTO.

Noah replies, without prejudice, shaking his head, simply "*Kabloona*," bringing the house down with laughter. The word explains all that needs to be said about such a man: his money, his rudeness and how much he resembles his wasted bear, which he doesn't care to eat.

I spend the rest of my time in Umingmaktuuq politely requesting stories from the locals. They initially respond with an inexpressive weariness, as if they were long used to complying with anthropologists and biologists about those tales that data could never confirm.

Joseph Tikhak tells me about seeing a killer whale in the bay, scared off by the arrival of a *Kabloona* airplane. John talks about watching *Nanuq* out on the local fishing island, skinning ringed seals with more skill than any *Inuk* seamstress. Finally, a third *Inuk* relates how the walrus often came to Bathurst Inlet. Two of the men, I notice, exchange quick smiles with their family while looking back to me with the serious smiles of wizened elders. The impression I come away with, since none of these animals have ever been found within several hundred miles of Bathurst Inlet by biologists, is that Inuit enjoy pulling *Kabloona* legs.

I leave on my fourth evening in Umingmaktuuq. The guided sportsmen think I'm crazy and ask where I will go and how I'll survive.

Billy refuses to leave town for another few days, and since he expresses no interest in getting on his *Qimmiq kamotik* ever again, it seems that he might have to fly his dogs out. He stands and watches me leave, certain I will come whimpering back by morning. After all, I have nearly 150 miles of walking to reach Cambridge Bay. Quaho trails me for a half mile with a penknife, trying to cut the rope attached to my duffel sled.

As I turn the corner of the bay and put the village out of sight, I am relieved. I'm happy to be alone, using only my own wits and muscle fiber for progress and trying to absorb that which a whining two-cycle engine has already denied me. Also, after the last few nights of Eskimo chanting and Terry's ursine snoring, I need to catch up on lost sleep.

I bivouac on a shore beyond the sea ice, not yet ready to trust a surface that will soon be water. I fall asleep to a flock of geese singing like sled dogs, uninterrupted by any bears or roaring generators.

The next day at noon I'm worried. The temperature has risen to 60 degrees. While the ice is five feet thick, seawater is pooling on the surface. Nothing to do but head far out from shore and try to make some miles. Sandhill cranes rattle through the sky above my head. Bands of caribou skitter and splash across the sea ice.

Every few hundred yards I come to a lead, split up to three feet wide, five feet thick and running as far as I can see out into the ocean. The water is as black as tar. After a quick ski pole probe of jumping and landing surfaces, I leap across. The sled follows, splashing and tugging.

By late afternoon the sharp and melting ice has ripped up the tarp wrapped around my duffel. I lash my skis together with two halves of a ski pole and bundle the duffel onto the ski sled. The load is not nearly as heavy as last spring, but walking through pools of water is disconcerting. The horizons stretch so endlessly that my own fragile, antlike life seems a mere blip amid the big picture. Limestone cliffs hang between a tapestry of snow and sky, and the sun is haloed with a bright-orbed parhelion, a hundred miles across, as if God were looking down with his own yellow eye to consider swallowing me into this continuum of earth, sea and sky.

By early evening, after scant progress, I have pitched my tent beneath a twenty-foot-high boulder and called it quits. Out beyond the water, blurring from north to south at the horizon, I spy Clarence hauling Leonard in his shooter's box. But bear guide and client are too spent by a day of two-cycle fumes and bumpy, wet sea ice to wave back at me.

Shortly after, appearing as jet skis throwing spumes of water, Jason comes splashing along with several companions. They expect to make Cambridge Bay this evening. Their snowmobile hoods are lashed down upon their *kamotik*s so that their engines will not burn out in the thaw. I still don't know if Billy will show up, but asking his son about Dad's plans will only earn me a shrug.

Jason excitedly says, "Jon, I saw a barren ground grizzly. I could get those bear hunters their bag in no time. Double big."

"How big?"

"Eleven feet tall." Like the other storytellers of Umingmaktuuq, he delivers this news deadpan. But unaccustomed to the elders' carefully nuanced techniques, Jason blows it: "And there were two of them!"

In the morning the clouds burn off, and the air falls cold again. Thin ice puddles crack out in thirty-foot-long honeycombs under my weight, and the wind comes into my face. I walk all day and manage to put fifteen miles behind me, reaching a dozen-mile-long sea corridor, pinched between an island and the mainland. It is the place that I instructed Billy to look for me should he change his mind and dogsled home. It takes me another hour to find a windbreak for my tent, fifty feet above the sea ice, on a ledge in an island cliff. The trail lies directly below, so Billy shouldn't miss me.

While cooking dinner, I hear the nails-on-a-blackboard scrape of overloaded iron dogsled runners on hard ice. I yell out Billy's name, knowing that I will have to walk another hundred miles if he passes me by. In all likelihood he will not backtrack to find me. I am standing up in my bright yellow tent door and waving my arms, but Billy is prostrate like a couch potato across the top of his *kamotik*, smoking a cigarette and staring forward; he is oblivious. So I shout, "WHOA!"

Although Billy still doesn't hear me, the command is unmistakable to his well-trained leader. Tunok, predictably, stops on a dime. All the other dogs cross lines while skidding to a stop. It is a small but quickly resolved tangle, part of the business of owning a leader that pays attention. But since Billy heard nothing and issued no command, he is rabid with anger. He throws out the snow hook. He grabs his two-by-four. Then he runs forward to beat his dog. Since Inuktitut lacks the effective level of crude fury, he screams in English, "Fucking cunt, Tunok, I teach fucking lesson!"

I yell, "Billy! Billy! Billy!" horrified at what I've done. But short of jumping off the cliff in my socks, I can't get his attention, so I point the shotgun behind and, just as he raises the club, squeeze a round into the sky.

KER-PUGHHHHHHH!

Billy looks right. Then left. Then up at me in the cliff. He lowers the two-by-four along a leg in hopes that I am as blind as he is deaf. Then he yells up, "*Kabloona!* Garbage campsite."

(In the days that follow, we meet Inuit wolf hunters and Umingmaktuuq bear guides hauling clients, lumped into shooting boxes, in circles. Billy repeats one story, with the requisite pauses and nuances, concerning how he chipped *Kabloona* out of the ice from a ledge in the cliff and saved his life. The more he tells his story, the harder I laugh.)

I join Billy on the back of his sled. I am exhausted from a long day of walking, but his sled offers an effortless perspective of the land around us. Given the lack of visual cues, the whiteness, and one-dimensional appearances, there is the impression as we pass through the narrow channel that the dogs are climbing up a mountain pass. It is ten degrees, cold enough that we must turn our faces backward and away from the chill wind.

Billy has unharnessed one of the sub-adults. The dog has a nasty infected leg abscess, preventing him from keeping a tight trace line. When the dog runs up alongside the team, struggling to keep up, Billy points his index finger out in a pistol shape and in effective and silent mime shows a recoil blowing his hand back, then splays out his hands, showing the dog dying on the snow. Billy giggles so inappropriately that I gather the snarling forty-pounder and lash it on top of the sled, away from its owner's reach.

Caribou run up around us, as though curious about some remnant memory of men pulled by dogs across the sea ice. From his position in the middle of five pairs of harnesses, Manny sprints left, V-ing the whole team out of kilter toward fresh meat. Tunok, always a leader, or maybe just in fear of being beaten, straightens the team before the *Qimmiliriji* can throw the snow hook and grab the club.

Billy has the *tuktu* parka fur up against his own skin, absorbing perspiration. The white hide blocks the wind and, if necessary, keeps out the rain.

I stay one step ahead of hypothermia by false shivering for warmth and wiggling my toes. I also refuse to drink the capillary-shunting thermos of coffee that Billy keeps pushing in my face.

"Don't worry. I take care of you now. You safe with me."

Sometime around midnight, jagged by the coffee, he decides to let me in on his wisdom. Billy is accustomed to soft *Kabloona* clients, half frozen after twenty-minute dogsled hauls to the airport. By now he expected me to beg him to stop and pitch the tent and fire up the stoves. Since I have temporarily risen above the average *Kabloona,* Billy figures it is a good time to begin teaching me the way of Inuit. The revelation begins with Billy regaling me: "When I was forty-two, I think I know everything and no one could tell me anything. But I wrong. I know nothing then! Nothing! I am so stupid then."

I take my cue. "You're so right, Billy. I'm an ignorant man when it comes to understanding many things. At what age did you reach that state where you got it all figured out?"

"Maybe fifty-five. Now that I am fifty-seven I know many things. Many things I never thought I would understand when I was forty-two. Like beating dogs. It does not seem to be a good thing to beat my dogs, and I know this is not a good thing, but I also know that good will come and my dogs will maybe be smarter and more well trained. Who knows how the world really works, eh, *Kabloona*?"

I try to forge a new understanding with my guide by admitting, "I know there are many things I don't understand, so that's why I ask questions. I know it's rude to ask too many questions, but I hope you won't mind, because I do this so that I can better understand things."

Billy, having already made a confession of sorts, has no choice but to accept my confession. Since his head is turned, like mine, out of the wind, I cannot see him lifting his eyebrows.

"Ah, *Kabloona*," he continues, "my father is ninety-nine, and now he tells me what's going on. I walk into his house and see him watching TV, always watching girls on Playboy channel, and when I say, 'Why you doing this?' he says, 'Go away. I know what I doing.' "

Billy drags the hook in the snow and brings the dogs to a stop at the entrance to Melville Sound. The ice yawns ten miles north to the Kent Peninsula and Turnagain Point, where John Franklin turned around in 1821. The immensity of this fjord stirs me behind a dog team in a way that would be incomprehensible on a snowmobile. If we break a leg or get sick, we will spend days crossing the sea ice, a hundred miles back to Cambridge Bay. On a snowmobile I became indifferent if only because the miles were no longer an obstacle. Tonight, like the last few nights, far from the sound of any motor, the Arctic shows its enormity.

I help Billy pitch the tent, and while he stakes out his team, I crawl inside, chew on a bit of raw caribou and fall sound asleep. Once, in the middle of the night, I awake to my companion cursing and pumping his stoves. In the noxious fumes of his tent I realize how much I miss my own cold tent.

In the morning Billy drags his hand across the snow and asks me to look closely. "Snow getting better. Yesterday no good. Today it melt smooth and fast for my dogs. You see it? Shine no good."

"Yes, thanks for pointing it out."

We mount the *kamotik* like two seals curled above their *aglus*. For hours we say nothing, watching the distant jawline of cliffs shrink inside the sixty-mile-deep fjord.

"Here I kill fourteen wolves."

"Trap them?"

"No. Got 'em on my Ski-Doo. Just ran 'em down."

A hundred yards from a sleeping seal, Billy stops the team and grabs his battered rifle. He fires, wounding the seal, then crouches down to wait above the *aglu* for it to reemerge. Standing patiently above the hole, dressed in his caribou parka, he could be the quintessential Inuit hunter—except that traditional seal hunters spent all day over a seal *aglu* without moving a muscle. Billy desperately needs another smoke. Within fifteen minutes he is back at the sled, dogs warily eyeing him as he fishes through the fifty-gallon Coleman cooler for his Exports.

That night he disappears from camp with his rifle. An hour later the dogs begin baying as they smell him, a few hundred yards out, dragging four caribou quarters with a rope. Since I heard no rifle fire, I can't help but wonder if his son had shot and cached the caribou two days earlier with their Polaris. Even if this were true, Billy would never confess; it's as if he needed to propagate the old myths about his people's hunting prowess. He has now assumed the habit of answering all my questions facetiously.

"How far out did you shoot *tuktu*?"

"Ten miles west," he replies, deadpan.

"Will you feed the dogs tonight?"

"No, in morning." (He feeds them a few minutes later.)

"Do you see that seal out there?"

"No, *Kabloona*, dead muskox."

As he prepares dinner, groaning that his son is not around to help fill the stoves and boil the water, he grows merry as he hears a familiar woman's voice, slurring out over the radio from Cambridge Bay.

"She very good fuck."

"I thought you said you were in love with your wife."

"Yes, but this woman fucks all the men that want her. I introduce you when we get back to town." He picks up a boiled rib from his pot and rips off a bite.

"That's okay, Billy."

"But, *Kabloona*," he says, incredulous at my refusal, "you ever have Eskimo pussy?"

It seems a question better left unanswered, but Billy won't let it go.

"Eskimo pussy is best. White woman no good, like falling into big cave. I know this thing. If you try Eskimo pussy, you no more like white woman."

"Thanks just the same, Billy."

He waves me away in disgust. "You strange, *Kabloona.*"

The next night, thirty miles farther down the trail, Jason arrives with his mother on the back of the Polaris, which is belching out a suspicious cloud of black smoke. Husband and wife kiss like long-lost lovers, and Mrs. Aguklaruk jumps aboard the sled, where they coo to each other for the next few miles to camp.

I yell over to Jason, who is following along: "Hey, I saw a twelve-foot barren ground grizzly. Three of them." I keep my face serious. But as Jason breaks into a smile, we both know the animal tales have ended.

The Aguklaruk family sets up camp inside the Kent Peninsula portage, where I plan to continue kayaking in July, when the ice melts. Since Jason has also ferried out his handicapped aunt and the family's adopted ten-year-old, there is no longer any room for me; it doesn't matter that they are supposed to be taking care of me. I happily pitch my own tent in the lee of an upturned *kamotik* a hundred yards off. I sleep the soundest and least claustrophobic sleep of several nights.

In the morning Billy is retelling the story of my rescue from the cliff in Inuktitut. I smile and laugh at the requisite pauses, just as everyone else smiles and laughs. Outside, the horizons are bleak and gray, and the wind is picking up—forewarnings of a low-pressure system. If Billy is concerned, he isn't showing it.

"How will you be getting everyone back to Cambridge Bay?"

"You and I take dogsled, everyone else on Ski-Doo and big *kamotik.*"

"That's a big load for your Polaris."

"*Kabloona,* don't worry, we take care of you."

"Should we try to beat this storm?"

"No worry, *Kabloona,* we rescue you if we have to!" His wife and Jason laugh, and the other elder woman goes out to try to catch more lake trout. While the Aguklaruks spend their day drinking coffee and tinkering with the Polaris—being out on the land together, as they say—I ski tour across miles of high lakes, hidden amid the glacier-scraped hills of the portage. It is a bitter cold May day. I try to imagine paddling these lakes in my kayak, but the land is so cold and inhospitable, it seems that summer will never come.

Grizzly tracks parallel my own. Caribou run on the eskers above. As I spin in circles, my arms held above my head as antlers, a dance called *tuk-*

toyaqtoq, the nearsighted caribou run down to me and tag along for a hundred yards.

By 4 p.m., when I arrive back in camp, the family is pulling down their tent. Cambridge Bay is only forty miles off. Since I don't consider this leg a part of my Northwest Passage, it doesn't matter whether I ride a snowmobile or a dogsled.

Billy and I leave an hour later, left behind by the snowmobile. The wind has increased, whirling around us in miniature white snow devils. Several miles north, we catch the family, standing over the wrecked *kamotik,* which Jason crashed into a rock. Billy is uncharacteristically silent. He spends an hour lashing it all back together. I start up my stove to melt some drinking water.

The two-cycle engine contingent finally roars off. Two miles later we catch the Polaris yet again, now running on only one cylinder and coughing as pitifully as *Qimmiq* choking on a whalebone.

Since it is Sunday night, Inuit are returning from their weekend of shooting geese and caribou on the mainland. No fewer than a dozen men stop to offer Billy advice and tools. Visibility has dropped on the northern edge of the Kent Peninsula, thirty miles from Cambridge Bay and Victoria Island. Jason gives his father ten yards of space, knowing the foul mood that has descended upon him, like the clouds now hitting sea ice.

Young Gary, a white boy, whips the dogs with a cord. Since no one else seems interested in either the nine-year-old or the dogs' welfare, I ask him if he knows that the dogs are dangerous and how it would be better if he were kind to them. Billy shouts back to Gary (one of many orphans of the recently dead Duncan Pryde—Hudson Bay trader, Inuit rights advocate and best-selling author).

"Don't listen to *Kabloona.*"

Gary asks me, "What's *Kabloona?*"

"It means a person with bushy eyebrows. And just remember, whatever people call you, *Kabloona* or *Inuk,* be sure to tell them that you're proud to be both."

I walk back to Billy and watch him exchange spark plugs and wires given to him by other snowmobilers, since Jason forgot to pack a tool kit.

"*Kabloona* want me to pose for photograph now with hands covered in grease?" He has the same leer that he gave the dying caribou.

I step back. "No thank you, Billy."

The family seems marked by disaster. Billy has no more food or fuel. There is nothing that I can do for them. Since several days ago, when, aside from facetious rejoinders, Billy stopped communicating with me, I can learn no more from him. If a storm hits in the middle of Dease Strait, when some other piece of jury-rigged gear breaks down, Billy won't be able to help me. I will only further burden his responsibilities to his family. So I throw my duffel on the *kamotik* of a snowmobiler returning to Cambridge Bay. I say a quick good-bye.

Billy shouts angrily, "*Kabloona,* where you go?"

"You're overloaded, so I'll be one less person for you to worry about."

"All right, *boss,* you the *boss.*"

I give my favorite dog, Manny, a quick pat, then leave Billy to his new tantrum, knowing that by the time I see him and pay him tomorrow, he will forgive and forget. In Cambridge Bay, Billy will exit the land and once again assume deferential and humble habits. Although most Inuit are naturally polite, there are simple men and there are complex men. So it is important for me to remember that Billy's Jekyll and Hyde behavior and cruelty to animals are not necessarily representative of his community.

"*Kabloona* always the boss," he spits out.

I watch the family shrink to the south. They stand with insect ambiguity against the immensity of sea and sky. I suddenly realize that they are no more comfortable out on the land than I am. Although I thought it would be a pleasure to travel with others, the last ten days have been an awkward social epic. Covering a mere hundred miles by dogsled has been the single most expensive leg of my Northwest Passage. Yet I have learned more about The People of the Arctic than all my solo traveling combined. It is half tempting to believe that all the Inuit animal tales and respectful hunter stories I have heard were romanticized and disconnected myths of the past. But cultures are never as simple as they appear. If there weren't some confusion, some gray area of change, between graceful myth, assimilation and humorous exaggeration, then the anthropologists would be wholly correct with their black-and-white theories. Inuit culture, let alone the world, would be a simple place indeed.

As for the future, who can say? Inuit live, like most people, in the memory of some former glory.

Summer Gone Winter

Spring Arrival

At first, the satellite sea ice maps imply that summer will not come to the Arctic. Even by late June, when it is 70 degrees at our home high in the Rockies, Cambridge Bay is still frozen. Finally, by July 15, it appears that leads are opening up along the mainland sea ice.

At the Denver airport June and I say an awkward good-bye. She is upset because I forgot to get her a card. I feel terrible. For the last few weeks I have been subconsciously distancing myself in preparation for this day. Explaining this to June only makes things worse.

Flying north, I wonder how it would be possible to leave the one you love without mentally preparing yourself for the adventure of a lifetime. Although I have repeatedly told June that I would support her own adventures, if that was what would make her happy, I am secretly relieved that I don't have the task of staying at home and worrying.

Two nights later, while I am staying in the ramshackle Co-op Hotel, Billy comes to visit. Two months have passed since I last saw him. He wears a motorcycle helmet, and his round wire-rimmed glasses are steamed from walking in out of the cold. I brace myself for some verbal abuse. But Billy is in his docile village demeanor, apparently glad to see me. After a stilted handshake and a comment about how he likes the weather hot, he announces in non sequitur that he had to kill his dog Manny, the best puller on the team. I ask why.

"Fighting. Always fighting."

"You didn't lose your temper and get mad at Manny, did you?"

"No, noo."

"How did you kill him?"

Billy pantomimes a handgun with his thumb and index finger and says, "BOOM." He smiles at the memory.

I try to hide my anger. "It's a good thing that you don't have the SPCA up here, you know?"

"*Kabloona,* you so strange! What the SPCA?" Billy asks, his innocence so complete that the differences between our cultures are clearly poles apart.

I charter a floatplane, along with two companions: a cinematographer, Kees 't Hooft, and his *Inuk* canoeist, David Amagainik. Since positioning and repositioning my tripod and cameras take a lot of time and energy away from the effort of making miles, Kees's presence will allow me to concentrate on getting across the portage without having to film myself.

Between Victoria Island and the mainland, Dease Strait is still covered with the white skin of winter, bleeding out blue seawater through a myriad of jigsaw puzzle pieces. Up above, an army of cumulous clouds falls into alignment, marching in chilling mimicry to the frozen ocean below. My heart sinks as I see that even the protected waters of Elu Inlet, where I stopped my eastward journey with Billy two months ago on the Kent Peninsula, are still frozen white.

The last thousand miles of the Northwest Passage have haunted me all winter. If it was hard for me, it was more difficult for June, if only because I was forthcoming about long and exposed crossings, huge tides and multi-year icebergs instead of flat pan ice. If and when I can make it to Hudson Bay, I told her, I would be camping among polar bears, putting all my paci-

Portaging from Elu Inlet to Labyrinth Bay

fistic ideas about respect to the final test. But now that I'm here, plunged into the wonderful creativity of route finding, I can relax. This is what I do best.

Giving the sea ice another few days to melt, I decide to begin portaging twenty-five miles across a chain of lakes, planning to hit the ocean again at Labyrinth Bay. The ever polite Kees and the gaunt-looking David trail me in a canoe. I am glad for their company because statistically three people (versus one) are less likely to be harassed by grizzlies.

Matching the fear of bears is the knowledge that I must adopt the same coping strategies as last year. Along with talking to myself, imagining people on deserted shores and perceiving animals as sharing human souls, I am concerned about sacrificing some vital part of myself to solitude. It is not so much a fear of going crazy as it is knowing that I have to learn how to rely totally on myself. Too far down that road, I know, will make it really hard to share myself with June, to resume routines, to get excited about going to the grocery store or living indoors again. I have to hold myself together, tightly, so I don't disappear into a world inhabited only by me. After all, we plan to be married in October.

By traveling with Kees, for even a few days, I'm hoping to shift into isolated wilderness more gradually. You can afford to make mistakes while traveling in a group. Also, with others to double-check your actions, you can get properly reacclimated to the vast horizons and joke about the mosquitoes. Once we reach the other side of the portage, Kees and David will turn around and leave. After being photographed from every conceivable angle, night and day, as well as trying to explain myself to a microphone (held by the laughing David), I will be more than ready to be alone.

White seashells carpet the beaches. Cranes and swans feed along the lakesides, rimmed with rich green mats of tundra and short limestone cliff bands. It is no surprise to David or me that the legendary biting birds of the Arctic hover about us in thick clouds, but Kees, who has never seen anything like these mosquitoes before, is horrified. I try to reassure him that we have a bit of a reprieve because the air is staying cool enough to wear thick protective clothing and that the strong north wind quells the insects. Still, his discomfort reminds me how much I, let alone the stoic David, have simply learned to look past the mosquitoes.

When I first shook David's hand, with the customary Inuit gentleness, our hands held high, he says, "I know you, Jon."

"From where?"

"I know you."

I get the feeling that David is not being facetious. Still, I am on guard, weary of the *Kabloona* jingoism that I experienced with Billy.

David watches me assemble my kayak with an indefinable air of knowledge. When I hesitate at snapping in a seat rest and stand back to stretch, he politely asks if he can help. His bony limbs leave spaces in his clothes, the cuffs and seams carefully mended with brown thread. He uses deft hands and the sort of instinctual engineering knowledge often attributed to his ancestry; he gently lifts, pushes, then locks together the seat on my folding Klepper.

"Have you used this boat before, David?" I ask.

"Eskimo *qayaq*?"

"No, German kayak that they took from your ancestors."

He doesn't answer the question, but it's as if he understands that I will properly fill in the blank. His earthy brown eyes are flecked with the same blue cloudiness that prompted Stefansson to tell the world that The People were descended from Vikings. For our weeklong outing he has a World War I rucksack, bleached white by the Arctic sun, its disintegrated shoulder straps replaced with half-inch polypropylene.

I begin lugging *Swims with Bears* on my shoulders across the first portage. It's almost too much weight, and during one of several rest stops, as I crouch with the bow tilting down to tundra, David tries to help. I refuse, explaining that it's important that I do this trip under my own power. Still, he looks hurt.

As I grunt along under the weight of a month's worth of food and gear, David is traveling incredibly light, undoubtedly so that he will not be a burden while helping Kees. In this way he is the opposite of Billy, laden with so much superfluous and heavy gear that his dogs could barely pull the sled. Most striking of all, David carries no rifle, because, he says, "bears no need guns."

That night Kees and I watch David neatly pull all his belongings from the rucksack: a matted down sleeping bag, several packs of cigarettes, a peculiarly smoky-smelling map, a trapper's radio, which he uses to call his wife in distant Cambridge Bay every night, spare batteries and an anorak—"in case snow," he explains.

The next day, while Kees positions the big camera, David and I drag and paddle our respective boats, then backpack our loads across quarter-mile stretches of tundra between lakes. When I study my one-to-fifty-thousand-scale maps, David takes out his one-to-one-half-million-scale jetliner pilot map. I ask him if his smoke-scented map has enough detail to show where we are. It is so crispy and old with age that it flakes apart in our hands, but David instead draws a circle beside his temple, saying, "It's all here, no need maps."

I am more than tempted to believe him. Again and again David hangs back and allows me the courtesy of leading, showing me that he understands that I don't need or want a guide. I use my GPS and maps to unravel the maze of lakes into a coherent pathway toward the ocean, while David walks to the high ground to double-check my route finding with his eyes. Once, when I walk too far south and later correct myself by walking back east, he patiently offers no criticism.

At night David often crouches outside the tent, surrounded by a brown cloud of mosquitoes. Once we convince him to come in, he says please and thank you. He races to wash the pots before I can do it. He smokes cigarettes downwind of us. He listens politely as Kees and I discuss books that we have read, the abolishing of English lordships, or the U.S. economy. We don't know if David has discussed these things before, but it is clear that like a deaf man who remains aware with other senses, he is incredibly discerning. He watches me light a stove he has never seen before, then expertly lights it himself for the next meal. I have not spoken a word about my fear of bears, but he tells me that I might have been such an animal in another life. Although he has never used an autofocus camera, after being shown once, he is adept at picture taking.

David adds nothing to our conversations. Nor does he ask what time we would like to get up, eat or go to sleep, but we include him in all our decision making. His intelligent and kind manner demands no less of us, but we also have the feeling that he intuitively understands all that is said. Kees and I agree that if he ever offers us advice, we should act on it immediately.

There is something immeasurably wise in the way that he watches everything, his hands folded neatly behind his back. If he doesn't understand our conversation, filled with those quantitative things and linear ideas that Arctic culture has patently avoided, he listens so that he might see a greater context that we might be missing. After all, Kees and I agree, isn't true intelligence the ability to find context?

David never complains about the lack of meat in our meals. Or how badly the Gore-Tex tent leaks in the rain. When the clouds of mosquitoes build intolerably, I look to him to see if he is okay, and he laughs his hearty chuckle: *A-huh, a-huh, a-huh!*

"Bugs are our friends, right?" I ask, half-jokingly.

"Even the bugs, Jon," David replies without sarcasm.

When I ask David if it is fair for Kees to be paying him $200 a day, he only smiles and thanks me.

He says he is fifty-five, but his ropy jaw and sunken eyes make him look fifteen years older. While he drags his loaded canoe across mosquito-hung bogs, as fast as I can drag my own kayak, he mentions that he used to be stronger. But in contrast with other middle-agers who sing this familiar praise, I don't doubt him. Hiring a guide for this sort of work anywhere else on the continent would get you a beefy young stud; David's age and build are a testimony to the toughness of Inuit.

We frequently stumble past old stone tent ring campsites, which David attributes to his ancestors. One night I catch him grunting at a swan, so I ask what he is doing.

"I telling swan he has nothing to fear."

On July 20 I get ready to continue alone. I have 360 miles left until my next resupply in Gjoa Haven. I will not be seeing people for several weeks. After saying my good-byes to Kees, I shake David's hand.

"Thank you for your help."

"Thank *you*, Jon." Without any prompting, he knows exactly what I need to hear: "You will do well, Jon. I know this, I know you. You find your bear." He touches me lightly on the shoulder with his other hand. I will not see David again, not in this life, but I now have the distinct impression that I have met him sometime before this trip.

I turn, step into the kayak and paddle away as hard as my tendons will carry me toward cove's edge. I take a quick delight in the power behind my strokes, knowing that this will fade as I get tired and lonely. The bow sends up a small wave rippling over the white seashells. Ice water trickles lightly off the paddle blade and splashes fiery cold on my cheek. I wiggle my hips

Kees 't Hooft filming the Kent Peninsula portage

several times before leaving the shallows, until I feel the boat's balance point. I brace a paddle blade to prevent capsizing.

I turn to wave good-bye. Kees is fiddling with the camera on a tripod up on the hill. David stands still on the beach where I last shook hands with him, nodding his head. I wonder what he meant about the bear: Will it pull me sleeping out of my tent?

A breathless feeling wells up somewhere beneath my solar plexus that they could be the last people I ever see. With this sudden shock of departure into companionless wilderness, I realize that my dogsled trip with Billy had misled me. Billy was simply taciturn and unhappy; it would be wrong to try to understand his culture through him alone.

David has reaffirmed what I have felt about Inuit all along: that they live rich spiritual lives, imbued with animal myths and a patient generosity toward all sentient beings. He is also only one man. But he has clarified my confusions about his people. It seems likely that if others like David learn to speak Inuktitut, spend plenty of time on the land and retain their graceful humility, Inuit culture will serve as a model for us all.

As I spin the kayak out of the cove, the full force of the wind buffets me, blowing the ball cap off my head and dangling it from its neck keeper strap. I look back one last time, and just before David disappears from sight, his hands neatly clasped behind his back, he bends from the waist and subtly nods in a gentle bow.

Now it's just me and my kayak. Man, I'm already talking to myself again.

Every day the wind is refrigerated as it passes over unmelted ice floes to the north. To make progress, I have to ride out into the surf on a regular basis, swamping the boat and sailing across the wind at reckless speeds through whitecaps and ice. It will take me weeks to pass through the Queen Maud Gulf Migratory Bird Sanctuary, stretching fifteen million acres to the south and more than two hundred miles along the coast. Although it is too remote for most human visitors, thousands of white birds fill the water and appear as avalanches moving down distant hillsides. I am looking at both Ross' geese (the gulf is the nesting area for most of the world's population) and lesser snow geese.

While rounding peninsulas and entering bays, I constantly surprise birds. The lesser snow geese, formerly classified as blue geese, are either dark or snow-white, with red bills and ocher-stained faces. Biologists have counted as many as two thousand of these birds nesting in each square mile of their brood areas. Unlike the disappearing Eskimo curlew, lesser snow goose populations have exploded since the 1970s. Because of their crowding and their unique habit of violently pulling up grasses and weeds by the roots,

Queen Maud Gulf's lush tidal flats and tundra plains appear to be browning into a desert. The same biologists who once fought to conserve the species are wondering how to thin its numbers before irreparable damage is done to habitat and other nesting birds. Open season has been extended to Canadian hunters, who continue to shoot as many birds as they need, just as they had done with bow and arrows before biologists existed. *Kangut's* uniquely bitter taste is preferred over other geese, even though midwestern farmers often observe the migrating geese pecking "recycled" corn out of cow manure.

While threading my boat through vast colonies of lesser snow geese herding their young away, I avoid the surf by snaking through river channels and riding tidal currents through semiprotected bays. But holding tightly to land, I get stuck repeatedly in pluff mud. Trying to walk in this quicksand, covered by a few inches of water, is impossible. So I stand up in the kayak, balance hands on the mast, stick a leg out behind the sponsons, and push the kayak, scooter style, until I reach deeper water. These enormous copper-scented tidal flats, deposited by uncountable rivers, are also the summer feeding grounds for over a half million caribou, Canada geese, white-fronted geese, brant, arctic terns, sandhill cranes and tundra swans.

On my third night alone, fifty-five miles east of the portage, I crash through wind and surf onto a several-acre-wide island in Campbell's Bay. Since the wind is building and arctic terns are dive-bombing, I jump back in and sail a half mile south to another island. Although it's only an acre wide, there are no terns, and having a bigger island to windward will protect me from the surf.

Translucent ships of ice bob and splash around my reddish atoll. A gull screams, nipped in the head by an angry tern, then rejoins the family feast, plucking finger-size herrings out of the sea. The fingerlings swarm as thickly as mosquitoes.

I have to push my tent and kayak back from the sea twice. By the second night only a half acre of island remains above the storm. The rain comes down in sheets, and during the middle of the afternoon, drunk on sleep, I roll over and wake up as my head lands in an inch-deep puddle. The Gore-Tex tent is filled with quarts of water, and rather than try to sponge it dry, I knife four drain holes in the floor, then fall back asleep.

By my fourth morning trapped on the island, the wind slows enough for me to leave. It takes two hours to pack the tent and food into the boat and then squeeze into the dry suit. I kick off my boots. I force feet through ankle gaskets. I pull the suit up over my waist, then wedge hands through the wrist gaskets. Finally, I slide my head up through the neck gasket, then zip the chest zipper all but the last foot up to my shoulder. I stretch to touch my toes, let the air finish hissing out of the top zipper, then seal myself inside.

I push off from shore with the sail popping tautly against the north wind. If I capsize again, the dry suit is my best hope of making it to shore without succumbing to hypothermia.

After last summer's sufferings, I have improvised and improved my gear. Along with a larger sail, the most important addition is a two-foot-by-eight-inch padded plywood seat bridging the cockpit. Hiking out over the water from the seat, without a spray skirt, necessitates the dry suit. (Little did I know that the constant wind and cold would make the dry suit doubly important.) Since I can't reach the rudder pedals while hiking out above the kayak, I installed a hand tiller behind the seat.

Whistling along at nearly ten miles an hour, I scoot my rear end out to the side so I can face away from the cold wind. From this high position, I can spy hull-ripping boulders, counteract heeling by hiking out and taking pressure off the leeward sponson now dipping under like a sounding dolphin, and generally feel more confident about waves. While I am sunk low in the cockpit paddling position, my eyes only two feet above the water, my confidence is eroded by waves splashing over my chest.

A colony of long-tailed jaegers dart to and fro, silently and swiftly as thunderheads. Even though I am busy dynamically leaning and hand steering my kayak, bird-watching gives me such peace inside that I give my full attention to *Isunngaq,* hovering and soaring like the superhero of all birds, so unperturbed about the surf on their island that I try to carry this fearlessness with me.

I give the Ellice River's surfed shoaling a mile of leeway. But the waves are even more terrifying out beyond the delta, as the three-foot-long sponson arms creak and groan, threatening to rip my kayak apart every time a wave washes over me. After only a half dozen miles, I surf onto an island no bigger than a traffic cop's lectern raised several feet above the thoroughfare. If I can't make headway in the wind, which shows no sign of stopping, I will never reach Gjoa. I have to somehow seize this summer's bad weather as an opportunity. It is simply too rough to be paddling. I also need the stability of the sponsons. So, while blowing on my cold fingers, I unlatch the outriggers and reset them closer to my body, at the gunwale's widest point, to prevent the boat from ripping apart. I push off anew, determined to make progress.

I practice sailing in the wave troughs as long as possible, then quickly rudder out, downwind, before each wave breaks over me. I hunt for smoother water by setting a course to the lee of islands. In the calms I can compose myself before plunging back into the fray. I take a few deep breaths. I chew a chunk of dried fish. Then I unzip the drysuit's custom-made pee zipper and relieve myself. When the heeling gets bad, submerging the lee sponson, straining the outrigger arm and threatening a capsize, I lean half out of the boat to windward for correction: seesawing the sponson back onto the surface and flattening out the hull. When I get cold, I open up the thermos and sip hot herbal tea. Half an hour later, shivering again, I have no choice but to jump out on an island beneath Whitebear Point. I run in place until the shivering stops.

It's July 26. I'm two weeks out. Queen Maud Gulf stretches on through another 150 miles of deep bays, labyrinthine peninsulas and silted deltas. I wonder if I'll ever get out.

Later that afternoon, with no island in sight, my toes go numb, but I'm willing to try anything to make progress. So I bite the sail sheet, pry off my boots to expose neoprene socks, undo the lower dry suit zipper, then urinate into my boots and pull them back on. My wet feet warm immediately.

All this to gain only nineteen miles, blocked by an ice pack on another islet. At least I'm safe from grizzlies. A blond-headed common eider flies off with a faint whisper of wings, abandoning a clutch of green eggs in a gray nest of down. I want to feel their temperature, knowing that the eggs are as warm as I would like to be, but I leave them undisturbed.

I pitch my tent several yards away, in a sheltered hole. The hen flies back, as silent as the wind, and spends the night beside me, warming her brood, clucking as I move, sleeping as I do. This comforts me.

By morning the tide has pulled the bone-colored ice pack just far enough out that I can sail along the shore. As the sun is enveloped by another bank of storm clouds, the ice steams like a misty cloud over the water, going from cobalt to the same cloud-colored white as the ice.

Snow geese bleach the hillsides. A black-headed Sabine's gull cries melodically. Troops of gray-shouldered jaegers sit like shamans on red, rocky atolls. Every time I think it's time to quit I spy another bird flying with such verve through the wind that I can't help but be inspired.

Finally, my nerves strung tightly, I drive my kayak up onto boulders padded with scarlet seaweed. Rain pours from the sky. Walking fifty yards up the bouldered hill winds me. Potential tent sites are all rocky, so I close my eyes and dip my fingers into a jar of emergency peanut butter, hoping to figure out what's next. In this state, beyond rational thought, I suddenly sense the presence of another being. It is here somewhere, smelling me, approaching steadily. Down the hill I suddenly see it, lumbering toward my kayak: a fat barren ground grizzly.

I run down the hill, racing the bear for the prize. Twenty feet from the kayak, I chuck the peanut butter jar onto the seaweed in front of the bear, then dive onto the sailing sponsons and push the boat through a breaking wave. I flip the boom against the wind and take the next wave in my lap, half filling the cockpit. As this big black bear works the last of my peanut butter, holding the jar between his forepaws, I drop the sail and suck out the water with the bilge pump. Bouncing out in the hilly chop, I try to concentrate. I need to send my respect shoreward.

I avoid speaking as I leave. Pulling the sail eight feet up the mast, I make a slow Zen bow, from my head down to my waist. The bear does not swim after me.

It takes another two hours to put enough distance between the bear and me to consider camping again. Adrenaline buzzes in my fingers, but my toes are so cold I am forced to pee in my boots again. I stay alert, weaving in and out of big breakers and whooping with exhilaration, while thinking about my new sense of connection. Whether it was smell or intuition, I had sensed the bear's presence before seeing him. I'm both scared and elated because being alone out in the Arctic is sharpening some long-dormant level of awareness. I feel invulnerable. Unstoppable.

Hudson's Bay Company on Perry Island

Sledding in Springtime

All my cockiness disappears when I get trapped on Perry Island. The north wind has jammed the ice tight against the land and as far as I can see in the gulf. If it was chilly before, now it is too cold to consider sitting in a kayak. Even with clouds hiding the sun, the ice pack is so bright I have to wear sunglasses. Waves lick the windward side of the floes. Silence creeps over the land like fog.

I sift through several Hudson's Bay Company buildings. Clothing is abandoned in the drawers, as if people had left wearing what was on their backs. Black-mudded grizzly paw prints mark the whitewashed stone walkways, past the *Elementary English for the Eskimo* booklets and Inuit invoices scattered about the buildings, and into the fur warehouse. Because of the lack of humidity, the forty-year-old booklet that I hold in my hands is still intact and readable. The steel leghold traps at my feet are free of rust. The scene is so eerie and the silence so complete that I feel like a time traveler pulled back into history upon a deserted earth, to a time when fur traders ruled the world.

According to the booklet, the Hudson's Bay Company (HBC; employees called it Here Before Christ) became incorporated in 1670. During one typical century of business, HBC shipped its furs to London and auctioned a quarter million bears, a half million wolves and five million beavers—to name only a few. For more than two centuries, fur trapping in northwestern America flourished, until the animals were so widely trapped and hunted that many faced extinction. HBC became one of the richest and most powerful monopolies in Canada. Almost single-handedly it changed environment, politics and native cultures. Like other smaller fur-trading competitors, HBC relied upon Native American hunters who killed wild animals for food. Trading goods, rather than paying cash (as it did with white entrepreneurial trappers), meant that HBC could realize incredible profits. As the British Admiralty threw itself at the Northwest Passage, the privatized company realized that the other side of the rainbow offered no more than what Inuit already had access to. By the early 1900s, as fur harvesting diminished in the sub-Arctic and the Arctic became more accessible, HBC went north and opened up shop.

At first, Inuit elders and shamans tried to thwart HBC. Inuit were wary of jeopardizing their own power, ancient value systems and the delicate dance of human and animal souls. But these egalitarian old men, seasoned by cold and hunger, were no match for capitalistic traders who knew how to fill their own pockets and bellies. Managers seduced would-be Inuit trappers with addictive tea, sugar and tobacco. Rifles turned even mediocre hunters into great providers. Canned meats were handed out as a substitute for hunting wild meat, while Inuit were cajoled to spend their time trapping fur-bearing species.

Although HBC claimed that it was feeding The People, Inuit on the Belcher Islands and west of Hudson Bay were still dying of starvation in the 1940s. In 1959, Diamond Jenness, who had lived among Inuit before and after HBC, wrote that trading "made life harder instead of easier, more complicated instead of more simple. The commercial world of the white man had caught the Eskimo in its mesh, destroyed their self sufficiency and their independence and made them economically its slaves."

Traders also gave Inuit alcohol. Once Inuit were addicted to various *Kabloona* vices, furs flew over the counters. Traders at Perry Island and elsewhere were often forced to lock themselves indoors—among people who had never seen locks before—to protect themselves against the violent binges that uprooted communities.

In one sense, these traders were merely finishing the job of exploitation and assimilation that whalers had first wrought two hundred years earlier. After the turn of the nineteenth century HBC teamed up with police, missionaries and government to force Inuit into what one ethnologist described as economic serfdom. The Anglicans, whose Aklavik church featured an altar painting with the Three Wise Men—an HBC trader, a missionary and an RCMP—had taught much of the pagan population syllabics and English. HBC then began publishing books and pamphlets of propaganda like those left behind on Perry Island.

Elementary English for the Eskimo is cannily written by a Ph.D. and teaches just enough language, including two sample invoices of food purchased in exchange for furs, so that the HBC traders can train the remaining illiterates. In drafty warehouses scattered every few hundred miles along the Northwest Passage, Inuit were given their numbered Eskimo disk "dog tags." The first page of *Elementary English for the Eskimo* explains how to have "your pupil . . . be sure that he knows his number and can write it from memory." Once the number was presented, Inuit were given food, ammunition and other goods and then billed for payments, which they

Fox trap and Elementary English for the Eskimo *inside abandoned Perry Island building*

could make with fox, bear or wolverine furs. The Canadian government, working in concert with HBC, published this 1950 booklet.

I still feel transported in time. As the light slants back through the windowpanes, I can't shake the tone of condescension that fills the pages.

The Eskimo Book of Knowledge, published by HBC in 1931, was the high-water mark of Inuit assimilation and colonialism. The foreword of the book states, in uppercase type: "BY WHAT MEANS CAN WE RETAIN IN OUR CAMPS THE FORMER HEALTH AND HAPPINESS OF OUR FATHERS? AND FULLY ENJOY THE PROSPERITY WHICH COMES FROM OUR TRADING WITH HBC?" It continues with biblical overtones and inducements toward law and order. The People are warned not to become fat and slack, with a metaphor on how sled dogs have to be whipped when overfed, and how traders can't be "easy-going" because "then the people become easy-going." By page 237 the author, George Binney, an HBC trader, concludes: "Many White men will explore your lands in search of precious rocks and minerals. These traders and these wanderers are like the drift-ice; today they come with the wind, tomorrow they are gone with the wind. Of these strangers some will be fairer than others, as is the nature of men; but whosoever they be, they cannot at heart possess that deep understanding of your lives through which our Traders have learned to bestow the care of a father upon you and your children."

Binney could have been writing about an orphaned Scot to come, named Duncan McLean Pryde, author of a best-selling and controversial book about Inuit. I sleep in Pryde's bedroom (after pulling inside a spring cot, savaged by a grizzly) and try to imagine him living alone. Pacing through a half dozen rooms during the dark winters. Reading a book a day. Drinking his rum. Courting Inuit wives (and then locking both the doors here). Since the ice has prevented me from leaving, I am looking for further insight into Pryde's time in the Arctic.

His P. G. Wodehouse novels and English whodunits (filled with enough death to keep a trader's imagination spinning) have been pawed down to the floor by a grizzly. The massive radio set, underlain by a bank of two dozen car batteries, is still intact. I drape one of his red and yellow Hudson's Bay blankets over my sleeping bag to ward off the winter chill.

For such outposts as Perry Island, HBC traditionally hired down-on-their-luck Scotsmen seeking adventure in the North. In 1955, Pryde, an eighteen-year-old warehouse worker, orphaned when his family was bombed in World War II, read an HBC ad in the *Glasgow Sunday Post*: "Single, ambitious, self-reliant young man required. . . . Far north of Canada . . . Must be prepared to live in isolation. . . . $135 per month." By 1961, after learning Inuktitut and working at other company posts in the Arctic, Pryde was put to his final test at Perry Island, whipping unruly Inuit trappers into shape. He was frightened by their violence after they drank lantern fuel. He wrote that "many Eskimos were blinded and killed in this stupid way," mentioning nothing of his predecessors who had introduced them to alcohol then taken it away. Pryde was a natural storyteller and a showman, fond of displaying the lurid tattoos covering his body and occasionally sharing his rum. These traits helped in his dealings with Inuit as much as his proclivity for numbers fulfilled his accounting obligations to HBC.

Pryde housed Inuit a half mile away on the opposite side of the island. Six of their plywood shacks are miraculously still standing, and except for their placement in a muddy, mosquito-ridden slough, these tiny houses are more easily heated and comfortable than the large, drafty white and red shuttered building that Pryde lived in.

In his book *Nunaga: Ten Years of Eskimo Life,* Pryde writes of the eighty Inuit with whom he traded: "Not only were they supposed to be a tough bunch and drink a lot, but primarily they were known as killers." He claims that most of the murders (he is vague about numbers) were committed because the shortage of women caused men to kill husbands in order to steal their wives.

Pryde describes how to get permission properly from Inuit husbands before sleeping with their wives. He also details several drunken and violent melees (undoubtedly after not obtaining permission) that forced him to radio for Cambridge Bay RCMP reinforcements. Through the caroming static of distorted radio waves, the police counseled Pryde only to kill his drunken attackers in self-defense. He wrote: "Young Eskimo women are at least as eager as young white women. A man isolated in an environment where there are only native women, where he never sees a white woman, doesn't take long to adjust to native standards of beauty. He will soon find that he appreciates their striking looks, and he can always find a girl to sleep with. The problem is which one."

Pryde began siring what modern-day Inuit in both Gjoa Haven and Cambridge Bay have told me to be no fewer than one hundred bastard children throughout the North. Most were raised by their mothers alone and then given their last names. Today you can't find a Pryde in village phone books. The final irony is seeing youngsters like his ten-year-old grandchild Gary, temporarily adopted by Billy in Cambridge Bay, orphaned just as Pryde had been.

In 1961 an MLA dropped in on a floatplane to Perry Island and handed the trader his first mail in eight months. Pryde replied in a Scottish burred double entendre: "You didna bring a fe-*mail?*"

Pryde was emblematic of HBC's colonizing superiority. He succeeded in substituting his own culture's dogma by trading guns, ammunition, food and tobacco. By becoming fluent in Inuktitut and being curious about Inuit customs, he ultimately took all that he wanted from both the culture and the land. Utterly unabashed, he wrote about the intimacy of nose rubbing with another *Inuk's* wife. A journalist described him as having the Arctic "reputation of a Don Juan on runners." His *Kabloona* cohorts still smile and wink about his money and women problems, knowing that Pryde's sexual exploits with Eskimos had to be edited from the *Nunaga* manuscript because the publisher found the book "too sexy."

He describes killing twenty-five polar bears (including four cubs) in one trip to Victoria Island. In another place he tells about Inuit teaching him how to shoot and wound caribou in one leg, so that they could be herded, rather than carried, to a distant boat and then dispatched. His tone is one of first disbelief and ultimate acceptance of efficient killing methods. Elsewhere he details how his favorite sled dog killed "thirty or thirty-five dogs" and how half his team died of hunger and cold during a trip from Bay Chimo to Coppermine. In the larger context, it might not have occurred to the author, who says he was proud to work for HBC for eleven years, that his employer was plying Native American people with alcohol and firearms and stripping down their culture in return for enormous fur profits.

HBC's best weapon, allowing it to work without military intervention, was the devastating effect of diseases. Traders unknowingly introduced tuberculosis, typhoid and even the common cold, which often killed Inuit because of their lack of antibodies. If Inuit at Perry Island and elsewhere weren't crippled by alcohol, they were sick in bed, begging for medicine, and forced to accept missionaries over shamans. Since Pryde's narrative glosses over disease, he was either inobservant or deliberately omitting HBC's ill effects.

Like *The Eskimo Book of Knowledge, Nunaga* served the author's agendas and mythmaking. Pryde had just finished a second term as a roving council member for the Northwest Territories when he wrote the book. He claimed responsibility for introducing the quota system in hunting muskoxen and polar bears, as if atoning for his earlier massacres.

Kabloona remember him as a compassionate spokesperson for Inuit. He stood up without notes in front of the Yellowknife council in 1969 and delivered a two-hour plea for the government to develop a new attitude toward the North. "It sometimes seems to me," Pryde said, "that the United States defeated their Indians by warfare. In Canada, the Government is defeating the Indian and the Eskimo by a process of attrition, and the weapon is inaction." He asked rhetorically where the Inuit police or nurses were, then answered that they all were down at the social assistance office drawing relief. Finally he prophesied, "Economic disparity between native and white is our biggest problem. It is an economic problem, but it will become racial if we don't act."

Pryde was one of those Europeans, like dozens who have passed through Inuit villages over the last two hundred years, who are fondly remembered by their *Kabloona* contemporaries. Yet I found that the many Inuit who knew Pryde have a different opinion. Like most Inuit oral tradition, their story has a resonance and durability that may outlive *Nunaga.* Andy, a middle-aged *Inuk*, told me how the Scotsman had abused Inuit for a decade, convincing husbands to leave the village to hunt, then borrowing their wives; running for political office with the slogans suggested by *Kabloona* supporters and the councilman himself ("Every Eskimo woman ought to have a little Pryde in herself" and "Vote for Daddy"); leaving fatherless children across the land and justifying it by citing adoption as an old Inuit tradition; growing rich by telling The People's stories as his own.

One day, Andy said, The People grew choleric about their Duncan Pryde problem. Since they did not dare kill him, for fear of reprisals, a shaman put a curse on him as he left on a dogsled trip in 1968. Two weeks later Andy found the lone *Kabloona* starving to death in an *iglu*, believing himself to be in a storm (which Andy said was caused by the shaman and surrounded only the *iglu*). He fed Pryde and guided the shaken trader back to Cambridge Bay. Pryde's journal records this event, describing how his dogs were so hungry that they were eating their own feces and how he would have had to kill them the next day. But if Andy rescued him with food, the event was omitted in Pryde's version, printed in *Time* magazine, which mentions only his brief contact with a rescue plane.

He moved to Yellowknife and married a Cree, enemy of all Inuit, who had recently been named Miss Northwest Territories. In 1969 his photograph peered out through the ruff of his wolverine hood, on the cover of *Time Canada,* with the caption "Northwest Territories' Duncan Pryde." Pryde finished his book, which became an immediate best-seller in Canada. He began touring the continent, appearing on television and in various newspapers, speaking with authority on Eskimo life.

However, as Andy explained, the curse apparently stuck to Pryde. By 1974 he had got the young daughter of a prominent Edmonton surgeon pregnant, so his wife, the former Miss Northwest Territories, divorced him. The judge, a close friend of the woman's family, awarded all of Pryde's assets to his wife. Since Pryde had been having trouble paying his taxes, Canadian Revenue had already claimed these assets. Pryde fled.

He resurfaced in Barrow, Alaska, suffering from an old eye injury, reinjured during a fistfight with an Anchorage prostitute. He was given a job at the Barrow high school teaching Iñupiaq to Iñupiat children who mostly spoke English. Within a week, after he had smoked pot and had sex with students, parents demanded his dismissal. Since he was well liked by the superintendent and principal—burly northern men enjoyed living vicariously through Pryde—he was allowed to stay on as a janitor so that he could continue working on his English-Inuktitut dictionary. Soon enough U.S. Immigration was on to him. Pryde abandoned Inuit life.

He moved to the Isle of Wight, in Cowes, England. Although he chose to live out his final years below 52 degrees north, his address was 6 Arctic Road. He remarried and quietly opened up a newsstand ("Pryde of Cowes"). *Nunaga* was reprinted in England in 1985, but since neither the publisher nor his family could find him, they could not send him the royalties. On November 15, 1997, at sixty, Pryde died from cancer. Shortly before his death a linguistics professor from Copenhagen congratulated him on the excellence of the several-hundred-page first volume (the A's) of his Inuktitut dictionary, listing two dozen dialects. He never finished a second volume.

At the end of *Nunaga,* Pryde writes: "There will never be a job such as the one which enticed me as a dreamy-eyed young man all the way from Scotland with romantic notions in my otherwise empty head. There will never be another fur trader in the old tradition, just as there will never again be an Eskimo in the old image."

By the late 1980s trapping fox and seal furs had gone bust, and HBC sold its fur trade department. Now the North West Company has taken over the

Hudson's Bay building on Perry Island, surrounded by sea ice

monopoly of selling groceries at exorbitant rates at the Northern Stores in Inuit villages. It was no small coincidence that traditional northern culture had crashed by the time HBC left. Today, down below the Arctic Circle, HBC has consolidated into the largest and most profitable chain of department stores in Canada.

Former Scottish traders still live in most Inuit villages, having intermarried and joined Inuit communities, but the heyday of rapacious trading and trapping has passed. Perry Island is now listed in the Nunavut government's Resource Report as one of those eyesores in need of cleanup; hundreds of diesel fuel drums adorn the landscape.

Humming Through Queen Maud Gulf

On the first day of August a warm wind replaces the cold northern breeze, and the ice pack silently crawls back out to sea. Within hours Duncan Pryde's refrigerated bay warms to 50 degrees. The smell of a garbage dump behind the outpost perfumes the air, as arctic terns stall gleefully through clouds of mosquitoes. After three days of being stranded on Perry Island, I am happy to leave Pryde's novels and the sleeping cot to the barren ground grizzlies.

I sail past Perry River, at the bottom of Queen Maud Gulf—67 degrees and 40 minutes North. Past the delta's warmth, a northern breeze usurps the tail wind. I sail this chilly air by rigging a jib onto the front deck, sliding off my hike-out seat and down into the cockpit, so my body won't block the breeze. The GPS shows that the jib produces an extra knot of speed.

When the breeze drops, I paddle to a nearby island. It takes fifteen minutes to disassemble the sails, outriggers and sponsons. Then, wasting no time, I slide back into the cockpit, stiffly wrapping my fingers around the double-blade paddle. The ache in my back and the tightness in my right shoulder capsule recall a litany of paddling grievances.

My fingernail cuticles are inflamed with salt and cold water immersion injury. This electric jangle courses through my nighttime dreams of dropping vital items such as my lone paddle or map case. Fortunately, the dreams have replaced nightmares of being eaten by the bears.

The cold has also prevented me from bathing. Although I am now adjusted to solitude, I worry about running into people again and grossing them out with the acid stench of unwashed clothes and body odor. Every night when I zip out of the clammy dry suit, a smell not dissimilar to a compost pile pervades the tent. I write in my journal:

> Breaking the solitude, for me, threatens to reduce life to predictable banality again. Where my senses don't need to be razor sharp for the bear/ the wind shift/ the hidden island in the fog. Where—amid the clamor and routines of people going about their everyday lives—it will be difficult to visualize life as it is here (birds as icebergs, humming that could be the quintessential breathing of the earth). Where I can live through actions, not words. Where my interactions w/ wild animals are necessarily filled w/ the same respect accorded to fellow humans. And where I have to accept that my time here on

the planet is sometimes bound by the same societal conventions and political wrongheadedness that savaged Inuit.

Ever since I was a young boy, I thought the lone wolf's movements were guided by a more divine light than that of the flock. This notion, however, is now gilded by my life with June. Her presence changes Everything. Without her, I might just have let myself disappear up here.

I miss her terribly.

As I put my journal down, the humming from outside the tent becomes so loud that my ears seem to be vibrating. Just like innumerable other times over the last few years, I zip down the door to try to identify the source of this noise: *Oyyy-oyyy-oyyy-oyyy-oyyy-oyyy-oyyy-oyyy . . .*

I have heard it in midwinter out on the sea ice (when most birds have migrated south), miles offshore, and at all times along the shore. The closest natural sound like it is the hooting of a grouse, even though that bird is not found north of the tree line. Perplexed, I get out of the tent and walk, watching some silent old-squaw ducks through binoculars, as the sound speeds in intensity to a continuous hum, then stops as a pair of nesting loons quack past and the rain begins. Some things in the Arctic, I think, are best left unexplained. So I let it go.

I grow confident, even relaxed, until the next morning out on a windswept island outside the delta of the Simpson River. I finish packing away the tent into the beached kayak, then haul the mainsail and let it luff in the wind. While I walk away to don my dry suit, the wind catches the jiggling sheet line and jams it against a cleat, filling the sail and pulling the kayak off the beach and into the water. Just as I bend toward my suit, I see the boat, with all my food and gear onboard, sailing out to sea. I run out into the 39-degree water until it laps up over my waist (thinking: *If only I had my dry suit on*). Then I dive in and begin crawling for my life. With the rudder stuck to starboard, the kayak miraculously circles back toward me, and I catch the trailing stern rope with fingers gone to hypothermic claws.

Back onshore, I tether the kayak to a boulder and try to wring the water out of my pants. I stomp my neoprene socks dry against granite ledges warmed by the sun. I am shivering with cold. I can't make this sort of mistake again.

As I dry off, I begin teaching a class on how to minimize bear conflicts. A semicircle of imagined people surrounds me, and since no one asks questions, I am forced to be thorough, continuing with a methodical session on how to put on the emergency brake while parking kayaks on beaches. As I sail off an hour later, my pants still wet below the knees, I teach kayak navigation techniques. Later I discuss how to sail with a trailed safety rope that the sailor can grab in case he falls overboard. The students are always faceless, but by the time I finish each step-by-step class, my safety seems assured.

Day after day I eke out anywhere from ten to twenty-five miles across the vaguely charted islets of western Queen Maud Gulf. Recently the Canadian Hydrographic Service admitted that some of the charts in this region were as much as a mile in error because of primitive mapping techniques. So I get to apply all my hard-won, dead-reckoning skills and navigate by what I can see, rather than what the GPS and charts suggest. I often find myself consulting David's jetliner map, trying to put myself into a bird's-eye context with all that surrounds me. His smoky-smelling gift makes me smile.

On August 5 I am forced to sail a wide bay in a hard breeze, so I teach an imagined class on heeling techniques. Halfway across, an ice fog blows in from the sea. I try to steady myself by teaching another class on GPS navigation, but I give up the lesson plan when the islands no longer match the chart. I am forced to sail blind, passing a twenty-yard-square island thrumming with surf, defended by angry arctic terns and bristling with ancient marker cairns called *tammariikkuti,* for pointing to earthly and spiritual places. I steer south, taking the cue from the *tammariikkuti* markers, until an island looms up out of the gray fog like a cargo ship confronting a Hobie Cat. I perform an abrupt tack by flipping the sail and pushing the tiller and land broadside on a steep steel-gray beach. I stagger out of the boat to study the map and GPS, but I can't place the island. So I rope the kayak up by both stern and bow to boulders, then wander uphill. I figure my sense of direction will return when I warm up.

On the two-hundred-foot-high brow of the island, I find an ancient stone fox trap. It is chinked waist high with interlocking boulders into an open cone so that the fox can crawl in, jump down, and grab the caribou leg, now disintegrating and molded bones. I reach in for the bones and nearly break my hand when the hidden kill stone falls and smashes into the flat stone floor.

Twenty yards away, half hidden by the fog, is a human skull sitting below a boulder. I sit down next to it, keeping my hands in pockets and imagining its view out over the fogged-in bay. Suddenly taken by the fragility of life here in the North, I put my head in between my knees and begin weeping with the knowledge that sooner rather than later, my bones are destined to go the same green-molded and worm-channeled way of those Inuit and caribou shards surrounding me. Maybe I have been alone too long, but I have the feeling that I am not alone, sitting here in this prehistoric camp with the ancient ones.

Above the beating surf, I hear the humming again, coming from the very bowels of the earth, like a long and pervasive mantra from the afterworld.

Old stone fox trap baited with molded caribou bones

I run back to *Swims,* shove off and jump in. All afternoon I sail through fog and big breakers, stopping twice to run in place until the shivering goes away. I sail blindly through blackened seas, using the lee of islands to shelter me from the waves, unable to hear the humming through the wind and surf. Humanoid stone forms blur past through the fog. Thousands of molting old-squaws gabble and croak like frogs, ducking under my bow. By sheer luck, unable to study the map long enough to match my position with the GPS, I hit a protected cove.

For the first time since leaving people on the Kent Peninsula portage seventeen days ago, I pitch my tent on the mainland. I am tired of cold-ocean island camping. Even a barren ground grizzly visit would be better than being alone and listening to the creepy humming.

Unable to lie still and listen any longer, I pull my dry suit back on and walk in the rain. A caribou and calf spook me and disappear into the fog. Ghostlike snowshoe hares spring behind boulders. Fox traps and ancient stone rings that once held down caribou skin tepees line the stony eskers. I can imagine the ancient ones checking their fox traps, throat singing and lofting spears as they returned each spring from *tuktu* grounds down south. No doubt The People built these walkways so that they could find their fox traps in times of light-headed hunger or fog. I stroll inside these ancient, stone-fenced walkways, and each time the route changes direction, *Inuk-*

suit marker cairns steer me. These *inuunnguaq* ("giver of direction cairns") are built cleverly in profile against the skyline, but I have to crouch to see them, as if I were a five-foot-tall Inuit rather than a six-foot-two-inch *Kabloona*.

Some of the tent ring stones press old rotted caribou skin. Other more recently used stones hide tattered bits of canvas tent, recycled .440 bullet casings, or 1930s cigarette wrappers, their owners now coughing tubercularly instead of throat singing.

I am guided back to the cove by the disconsolate cry of a yellow-billed loon. As I zip open the door to go to sleep, I notice that I have inadvertently pitched my tent inside a stone ring campsite, half-buried by sand.

My spirits rise when the humming stops, along the Klutschak Peninsula. It now seems likely that I will be able to reach Gjoa, a week away, before my food runs out. Instead of feeling anxious, I think it oddly irrelevant that the blustery winter weather might prevent me from reaching Hudson Bay, six hundred miles away. It might be smart to settle for Pelly Bay, two hundred miles closer.

I have gotten used to these extended periods alone over the last few years and have come to look forward to the spaciness that I float into. While paddling, I mouth James Joyce's words, gleaned from his time along the Irish

Examining a stone tent ring and imagining the past

Sea: "He was alone. He was unheeded, happy, and near to the wild heart of life. He was alone and young and willful and wildhearted, alone amidst a waste of wild air and brackish waters and the seaharvest of shells and tangle and veiled grey sunlight."

On the evening of August 8 it is too warm to start the stove in my tent. The shores hide inch-high dwarf birch trees, bedded in sand so soft that I am compelled to linger in my sleeping bag the next morning. Even the north wind is forcibly warmed over the dunes, before recycling to the sea and blow-drying my wooden fingers warm for the first time in weeks. As I slide in and paddle north, the clear waters magnify the sand corrugations fathoms below, while the kaleidoscopic swirl of pink polka-dotted char appear more Caribbean than polar. I stop and play with this thick sand, sifting it as though my hands were an hourglass ticking away these precious few days of Arctic summer. The grains are the consistency of unrefined brown sugar. Even wet, they won't stick to my clothes, frost my cold pancake lunches or clog up the stove. While sleeping on this sand, I wiggle my hips and feet into a customized mold.

Muskoxen continue to wake me in the morning, growling near my tent, their underwool dreadlocks flying soft as cotton streamers in the wind. Filmy tentacles from the venomous *Cyanea arctica* jellyfish tangle in my paddle blades.

At 10 p.m., on a swale atop an island several miles from shore, I sip water with a pair of peach-lit swans. Four flightless cygnets emerge from the tall grass, murmuring as innocently as the day that we all emerge from our respective wombs. I photograph them while lying in a cloud of mosquitoes, impervious to their bites, then bow good night as the sun showers its final gold light, glowing in the swans' eyes. I stare at my own alien-lit hands, wondering if we have all gone radioactive. I need sleep.

Remains of the Franklin Expedition

The next day I found human bones. A cairn, suspiciously larger than the traditional *Inuksuit,* led me to climb up to the center hill of the island, surrounded with ancient stone ring campsites. It was clearly a *Kabloona* cairn, piled four feet high in the bulky, inartistic style of nineteenth-century explorers. Along the cairn were two shallow, oblong piles of boulders, and by removing one, I was shocked by five unmistakable finger bones, covered with green mold and a rotting mitten. Chills ran down my spine. I backed away, quickly.

Now I sit, listless, wondering what to do. I pour a cup of tea.

Kabloona last saw Sir John Franklin in July 1845, sailing off the west coast of Greenland with 128 men and several years' worth of food and supplies. Franklin had been the fourth choice for this command (the other three refused its dangers). Lord Barrow was skeptical of the leadership of "the man who ate his shoes" because cannibalism and starvation had been a recurring motif in his travels. Barrow provided a trusted second-in-command and explicit orders. Franklin had merely to fill in the holes on his previous maps to resurrect the pride of the Royal Navy in peacetime.

The fifty-nine-year-old was traveling with all the regalia befitting an English lord. He had become portly and balding, with jowls and huge, outturned ears. For a knight in his twilight years he had settled into an appropriately sedentary lifestyle, dependent upon the whims of God and scrounging by on half pay. Still, he was driven to leave his wife, Lady Jane, for one last success after his bitter failure governing Tasmania. He was not prepared to live off the ice; his men were dressed in useless Royal Navy–issue leather boots and thin wool sweaters. Only two of the officers had had Arctic experience; a third of the sailors were newly conscripted.

Their rounded-hull bomb ships, *Erebus* and *Terror,* had originally been built to absorb the recoil from firing mortars. For the ice-choked Northwest Passage, their hulls were reinforced with iron plating and extra planking, scant protection, it turned out, against the untold pressures of a frozen and shifting sea.

They wintered at the eastern entrance to the Northwest Passage, on Beechey Island. By April, Franklin had buried three men. One died from tuberculosis, one from what they thought was scurvy, and one from God knew what. That spring of 1846 Franklin's ships beat and bumped through a maze of ice, hoping to unlock the secrets of the fabled route to the East.

After navigating several hundred miles south through the ice, *Erebus* and *Terror* were held fast off Cape Felix, north of King William Island, for two winters. All hands suffered in the sub-zero cold and blinding whiteouts, punctuated by two months of nearly continuous night, and were terrified by the creaking and splintering of ship's timbers. The tremendous pressures of six-foot-thick ice shifting with the tides, the wind and summer breakup stove in at least one ship.

Franklin's men had rations of lemon juice and other antiscorbutics, yet these were not enough to prevent scurvy. Gums swelled, and teeth began loosening in the sailors' mouths. Their bones grew brittle; some men began hemorrhaging. If Franklin had not dismissed local knowledge (his predecessor, James Ross, survived scurvy in ice-locked ships for several years by hunting and eating with Inuit), he would have seen that an Inuit diet of raw or lightly cooked meat prevented scurvy. The British sailors' heavily salted beef lacked vitamin C.

Although lead poisoning from a newly patented solder closing their food cans probably didn't kill sailors outright, it caused lethargy, depression and loss of lucidity. Botulism from improperly canned meats was thought to have killed some of the men. At first the afflicted became dizzy, and their speech grew slurred; diarrhea, then paralysis set in; and within three days the deadly spore hit the respiratory system, stopping the victims' breathing. Sailors also weakened from pneumonia. As the pallor of defeat settled over the ships like an ice fog, their dreams of glory slipped away. Since no one survived the trip, the rest of their story is a combination of anecdotal evidence, speculation and, perhaps most telling of all, Inuit oral history.

By 1850 the expedition was two years overdue. Several rescue ships left England. Lady Jane bankrolled numerous rescue expeditions and then toured the United States, soliciting help. Eventually she compelled the Admiralty to send still more ships and offer an enormous £20,000 reward for artifacts showing Franklin's fate.

After discovering Beechey Island's graves, searchers worked their way south for more clues. In 1854 Inuit told an HBC surveyor, John Rae, about a party of forty *Kabloona* sailors who had starved to death and resorted to cannibalism. (A recent exam showed postmortem cut marks on ninety-two of three hundred bones scattered on King William Island. The bones, many pitted with scurvy, were expertly cut, often between joints. Some experts theorize that the dying men were dispatched so that the others could continue. The lead content showed as much as 83 parts per million; normal is 18 to 50.) As a final irony, the dying sailors, plagued with scurvy and too

A daguerreotype of Captain Sir John Franklin, just before leaving England

weak to walk, received no real relief or vitamin C from eating their dead, sinewy shipmates. While most animals produce ascorbate from glucose in their livers—Inuit had long taken advantage of this by eating raw animal meat—humans lack the enzyme to produce the ascorbate that prevents scurvy.

Rae offered Inuit a reward for evidence, so The People gathered up the dead sailors' equipment, including one of Franklin's medals, and presented it to Rae, who collected the reward from the Admiralty. Lady Jane, along with most proper English society, was scandalized that cannibalism was suggested and that Rae did not push farther to look for survivors.

In 1858, a dozen years after Sir Franklin had sailed from the Thames, another expedition to King William Island was horrified to find decapitated bodies in and around an abandoned dory. They also found scattered human bones (the first support of Rae's cannibalism tale), shallow graves, pewter silverware and all manner of clothing. Alongside a high cairn at Victory Point, a note was discovered from Franklin's second-in-command: "25th April 1849. H M Ships Terror and Erebus were deserted on the 22nd April 5 leagues N N W of this, having been beset since 12th Sept. 1846. The officers and crews consisting of 105 souls under the command of Captain F.R.M. Crozier landed here in Lat. 69° 37′ 42″ Long. 98° 41′. . . . Sir John Franklin died on the 11th June 1847 and the total loss by deaths in the Expedition had been to this date 9 officers & 15 men. [signed] James Fitzjames, Captain H M S Erebus, F.R.M. Crozier Captain & Senior Officer, and start on tomorrow 26th for Back's Fish River."

Franklin's duplicate and sealed ship's papers would have told the whole story, but no one could find them. Six more ships were lost in efforts to uncover something new. More than forty expeditions found little more than scattered bones and gear and a few more blotted and laconic journal entries. Along the shores of King William Island, more than one hundred miles north of where I sit, Petty Officer Harry Peglar's diary was found, with a cryptic message written backward: "Oh Death whare is thy sting, the grave at Comfort Cove for who has any doubt how . . . the dyer sad." Peglar's remains, along with those of half the other men, were never found.

Charles Dickens composed a play based on the vanishing (vilifying Eskimos). Lady Jane all but immortalized Sir John and spent the rest of her life traveling the world and writing letters, beseeching foreign governments to turn the Arctic inside out until her dear husband was found. She died unhappy and heartbroken, never learning what killed her husband.

Franklin's nephew Alfred, Lord Tennyson, wrote on his uncle's tomb in Westminster Abbey:

> Not here! the white North has thy bones; and thou
> Heroic sailor-soul,
> Art passing on thine happier voyage now
> Toward no earthly pole.

A century later the search for Franklin's mortal remains and papers continues. Several Inuit, informed by oral tradition, told me that Franklin would have made it through the Northwest Passage if he had listened to their advice and gone east around King William Island in ice-free waters, instead of west through permanently clogged ice. The 1879 testimony of an *Inuk* named Puhtoorak stated that the *Terror* had escaped the ice and beat west of *tikerqat* ("two fingers," which describes the two points of mainland directly beside me, here in eastern Queen Maud Gulf). As the story goes, Inuit did not know how to enter the abandoned and ice-locked boat, so they chopped a hole in the side (later causing it to sink as the sea ice melted). They found a huge dead man, so heavy that it took five Inuit to pick him up and move him, implying, of course, that they had found Franklin's corpse. They took all the food stores, twisted the rifle barrels into tools and used planking for firewood.

Since there have always been an abundance of Inuit stories about the fate of Franklin, most *Kabloona* paid little attention to this tale. Previous searches had mostly concentrated on King William Island. Until several years ago.

In August 1997 a team decided to follow up on Puhtoorak's testimony. They searched within sight of this finger-boned island, utilizing tundra radar and side sonar and walking across islands—but not this one. They found a nineteenth-century Caucasian skull (the team archaeologist, Margaret Bertulli, believed it was that of a twenty- to thirty-year-old man from the Franklin expedition), various pieces of an old boat and a perfume box. Bad weather sent the team's ship and helicopter packing.

Since Inuit did not build cairns like the one above me, the phalanges leaking from this grave could be from one of Franklin's men (old Inuit remains were always more discreetly buried, and the other Royal Navy corpses recovered have all been remarkably preserved by the dry climate). If I am right, this rocked-in sailor would have abandoned the nearby frozen-in ship and, while trying to escape south, would have died from scurvy, lead poisoning, botulism or starvation. Several other men, in a proper British ceremony, would have buried him, without wood for a coffin or tombstone.

Then the party would have walked downhill, across the sea ice, and headed south on their own funeral march (their long-strided and heavy-heeled footprints on a nearby beach were also described by Puhtoorak). Their pitted and scurvy-brittle bones, like a hundred others from this voyage of epic bungling, have become part of the Arctic's greatest mystery. Mostly these bones are covered with a new skin of mold beneath boulders. Those men who withstood scurvy the longest and walked the farthest, as yet undiscovered, have been assimilated by the humming and bleached by the sun, like all the other bones lying about.

I have no intention of probing any further. I am alone and already harried enough by the enigmas of this huge landscape. Although my imagination suggests that digging up the grave or knocking down the cairn might yield a vest pocket diary or even the lost papers of Franklin, for now I am too strung out to linger. Winter is coming, and the thought of being stuck in such a place might prove too much for my fragile psyche. Like Franklin's men, I need fresh food and warm shelter. I miss my Lady June. My gums also feel swollen from eating only freeze-dried food for a month.

My kayak waits. I screw the cup back onto my thermos and leave this wind-washed grave with a swift bow.

I paddle northeast, against the wind, counting the time that it will take me to reach Gjoa—perhaps a week away—balanced by the few days' worth of food remaining in my dry bags. It would be easy to feel overcome by the presence of both Inuit remains and Franklin's fate. If I have learned anything about being alone over the last few years, about preserving my own sanity, it is to look for points of light amid the darkness.

The waves force me over onto a narrow spit of sand, dotted with huge wolf tracks. I try not to look around too much. Keeping a tight focus on camp tasks is merely another coping tool, like my imagined teaching sessions, to avoid feeling swallowed up by the wilderness. But as I pitch the tent, I can no longer help myself: The sunset above is burning the clouds char-belly pink. This contagion eventually adheres across bare blue air. It spreads and spreads, until I look down at my feet to see that the sand, my favorite sand, has gone roseate. Suddenly the ocean ebbs, stills and then fluoresces into sky. I feel so suddenly sated, so light-headed, that I vault into the tent and close the door. I zip all but my head and hands into the sleeping bag. Then I force myself to write a single entry, pulling it from memory, off the Plaque over the fireplace mantel of the great naturalists Olaus andMardy Murie, and placing it in my journal:

> The wonder of the world, the beauty and
>   the power, the shapes of things, their
>   colours, lights, and shades; these I saw.
> Look ye also while life lasts.

Sailing Along King William Island

At the tip of the Adelaide Peninsula, poking up into Simpson Strait, I am twenty-three days and 350 miles out from Elu Inlet. I am overjoyed to see the browned mass of King William Island. The land spills so far over the horizon that I can *almost* understand why Ross mapped it as King William *Land*. If Ross had paid a bit more attention to Inuit, his party would have learned that King William Land was called *qikiqtaq* ("island").

Gjoa is only a few days away. As I lie in my tent, caribou graze nearby. I fall asleep to the gurgling of sedges in their stomachs, dreaming their vision as my own view of the world: a floodlit, watery orb that whooshes against sugar-grained sand, alive with bad-breathed grizzlies and crepuscular wolves.

In the dawn I sail east across Simpson Strait in a gentle northern zephyr, reveling in the last placid waters of summer. Beneath the bluffs of the Malerualik River, I spy a camp of Inuit hunters, the first people I have seen in twenty-four days. At first I look away, panicky about resocializing, and consider a bivouac alone on the other side of the river, until I recognize the ursine profile of Paul Iquallah, a friend from my visit last winter. He is running down the beach to greet me. I rudder north and sail upwind the last fifty yards to shore, then splash into the water and across the boulders. We embrace each other.

"Paul, it's great to see you!"

"And you too, Jon!"

We walk the boat upriver, then sprawl together on the tundra amid a clutch of white canvas wall tents. Although it is August 12, normally too late for bugs, the first island mosquitoes of summer land sluggishly on our cheeks.

"It's been freezing all summer," Paul says.

Kids tug on my shirtsleeves. An elder hands me a cardboard soda box filled with dried char. Someone starts to pluck the snow geese that Paul had shot. For the first time in a month I laugh out loud, pausing to listen to the sound of my voice registering against other people's eardrums.

Paul's wife, Rebecca, sees the exhaustion in my slow movements, so they put me to bed early on a muskox robe in their tent. At midnight Paul wakes me, holding out a plate full of boiled snow goose legs, still bristling with quills, and filling the tent with a steaming manure stench that I hope will mask my own foul presence. I blink, slowly, for a better look at my dinner: The goose flesh is the color of a cancerous mole.

Paul says, "You don't really *know* an animal until you eat it. And I love snow goose."

The Iquallah family eats with a knife in one hand, a leg in the other, paring off chunks of meat that their jaws cannot dislodge and spinning the legs under their teeth like corn on the cob. I try to look enthusiastic, mimicking Paul's aggressive, breathing-through-the-nose, head-down eating style. The rubbery flesh tastes of liver mixed with seaweed and licorice roots and sulfuric marsh grass. There is something else too, an unmistakably fecal taste that makes me think of the bird pecking through midwestern cattle lots. Twice I spit out pieces of lead buckshot. After ripping off all I can from three legs, as their young children work on their fourth and fifth, I set my plate down.

A sudden silence fills the tent. Paul is staring at my plate. I look at his: The goose flesh has been stripped clean, down to the bone. Meat still clings to the bones on my plate. Before an insult can be given to either goose or hunter, I pick up an unfinished leg with both hands, lift it to my mouth and say, "Don't worry, I'm just getting warmed up."

That night, in between Paul's ratcheting bouts of snoring, I dream of brazenly sledding down Mount McKinley's West Rib, a steep ice climb that I climbed with my eyes wide open eighteen years ago. In the dream the ride kills two of my companions. Somehow I survive, dusting the snow from my sleeves after a nine-thousand-foot sled ride, knowing—in that not altogether unconscious intelligence within the dream—that the odds of surviving what I just did were slim. When I wake up, before dawn, I consider the dream a general omen for all the risks I have already taken this summer. If I interpret the dream as a premonition, it will prevent me from leaving for Gjoa and taking a well-earned rest. So I pack quickly and creep out while Paul is still snoring, figuring I'll catch up to him in town.

Outside the tent a toothless elder accosts me. His gaunt skull bristles with white stubble. He speaks little English, and looks somewhere past my corneas and down into my frontal lobe, as if to harpoon his Inuktitut words home. He offers me some char from a ten-inch slab on his slate plate. I refuse, so he says something violent in Inuktitut and looks behind my eyes again, jiggling his rock plate. Central Arctic Inuit prefer to leave their fish out on a rack, unlike the smoked char to the west. As soon as the weak sun and strong flies crust up the outside, keeping the inside soft and chewy, the char is ready to eat. I plop a several-inch-long piece into my mouth and suppress a gag. Then the elder, knowing that I have enough fish fat to keep me warm for the morning, is ready to give me a weather forecast. He looks up at the sky, pries his gummed-together lips apart with his tongue and says, "Big water Douglas Bay. Maybe big wind, snow."

"Yeah, looks bad." I detour around him and stride down to the water.

"Long time alone?" he asks my back.

I turn around and lift my eyebrows yes.

Then he adds the age-old wisdom that has propelled me through my passage, nine months over the last three years. He says, "Being alone out on the land open our minds." He taps his head and smiles cavernously. "You know this thing?"

"Yes, I do, but I have to go, *cowanna*." I thank him all too briefly and push my kayak out into the river current, haul the sail and steer east, hurrying to beat the snow and this elder's disarming prescience. He keeps his hands at his sides and smiles with a wink, as if he knows me. The wind luffs the sail, catches it tight and violently shoves me out toward Simpson Strait. I lock my rubber-booted toes around the mast foot to hang on.

Molar-shaped tooth clouds rake the sky, while the black delta water riffles with the fins of Arctic char. It's time to be alone for two more days to Gjoa Haven, and I turn to emphatically thank the elder, worried that my restiveness might have offended him.

There is only a field of boulders, a drying rack of reddened char meat and a sleeping camp. He has vanished. I wonder if I have just met a shaman. I look up as a snowflake tumbles down from the fading stars, settling on my cheek like dry goose down.

As I tack around Tulloch Point to investigate the bay, my dream and the elder's words are already haunting me. Douglas Bay is so deep that I cannot see land inside it. I could disassemble the sails and paddle around the bay—that would take all day—or I could sail five miles across the end, out in the widening waters of Simpson Strait. I decide to test the big bay by sailing a mile east in a brisk north wind.

The waves are manageable. The wind seems steady. The far shore that I am aiming for appears less than an hour away. So I go for it.

Twenty minutes later the wind shifts strongly. I am forced to change my point of sail so that I'll rejoin King William Island farther east than I planned. Since I'm already halfway across, it seems a waste to retreat and sail back west. Then the waves increase. I reef my sail. Water foams over the cockpit coaming, so I lean hard to windward as panic tightens my chest.

In desperation I drop the sail and try paddling into the wind toward shore, two miles off. Every paddle stroke forward I lose back in the current. I haul the sail up again, and holding the kayak as close to the wind as it will sail, broadside to the whitecaps, I aim east. If the wind or waves pick up anymore, I will be swamped and blown out into the eighteen-mile-wide strait.

I hold on tightly, quickly steering downwind as waves threaten to break over my chest. Now the only thing left is to pray. I'm helpless. A slight increase in the wind will kill me.

I pray that my life should be spared for June's sake, for the sake of our upcoming marriage and so that we can raise a family together. I humbly invoke God or the Supreme Being or Buddha or Sila or Whoever or Whatever cares to listen. I close my eyes and lift my face to the sky, then down to the water where Nuliajak dwells. I promise that our future children will help make the world a better place, and that I will publicize the plight of Inuit however I can, and that there *is* a purpose to my life. Therefore, I argue, I should be spared. When I am through, several minutes later, I whisper, "Thank you."

I hold on, feeling as infinitely small and stupid as I have ever felt in my life. As the shore draws closer, and I know that I will make it, my relief begins ebbing away. My boat plows up onto the bouldered James Ross Point at six miles per hour; a muskox bull gallops away. I jump out and kiss the first dry rock. I repeat my thanks. In the absence of any sign of divine intervention, let alone any feeling of mastery about having crossed Douglas Bay in dubious conditions and not paying attention to my dream and the elder, my loss of relief gives way to shame.

Starting across the mouth of a big bay

For the last month I have taken one risk after another and gotten away with it. More than the preceding two summers, I have blindly trusted in an ill-defined intuition and my own elevated sense of mastery. Somehow, somewhere, the siren call of danger in my vision quest has subsumed me. I have had too many friends, more talented athletes than I, who have been killed taking fewer risks. Franklin, who was accompanied by 128 men in state-of-the-art ships, found an early grave when he chose not to consult Inuit elders. So why have I made it this far?

Luck? Intuition? Or skill?

It is a question I'm not ready to answer. I still have miles to go. The mosquitoes are gone. Snow geese are honking southward in cloud-colored chevrons. Blowing snow is sticking to my beard, tickle-melting on my wind-reddened cheeks. I have to reach Pelly Bay somehow. I have to do it without risking so much.

I shelter in an Inuit hunting shack, protected from the shrill night wind. It is likely that I will reach Gjoa tomorrow—due cause for celebration. But it is going to take all my willpower not to retreat south to June on the first scheduled plane. I put my head down on my pile jacket pillow feeling more broken than elated for having survived Douglas Bay. For all I know, in the lonely obsession that settled over me for the last month, like seeing swooping gulls through an eider chick's translucent eyelid, I have risked too much. I have become a gambler. My last thought before blessed sleep steals me off is the horrible knowledge that I have placed too much stock in bald luck. This was not my intention.

Summer's End in Gjoa Haven

Seen through March snows, Gjoa appeared pale and scrubbed. Now, in mid-August, litter glides through the windy streets. Stray dogs pick at random piles of garbage too heavy to fly. Empty fuel drums in front yards read KEEP GJOA HAVEN CLEAN.

Despite the triumph of Nunavut, Gjoa is in a slump. It's partly because the new government has frozen spending while figuring out how to allocate all the money properly, but it's mostly due to unemployment. The hotel, normally filled with southern construction workers, has been empty all summer. Even the fishery has shut down; no one paid attention to the "empty" oil gauge during a rescue last fall, and now the only fishing vessel is broken.

As the snow continues to fly, my frustration grows. I can't paddle in this cold. Some *Kabloona* schoolteachers generously share their house with me. They refuse my proffered rent money with typical Arctic hospitality and share my amazement about the less-than-luxurious hotel's $150 rooms. Like most teachers here, they hail from southern Canada.

Since I last visited, Gjoa has been rocked by a sex scandal in the high school. After more than a hundred former students were interviewed, two of their former teachers—Inuit men now in their early forties—have been charged with twenty-eight sex crimes toward their students. All but one of these alleged crimes occurred inside the school from 1977 to 1988. Most *Kabloona* in town find the news shocking. But most Inuit in Gjoa (as in other Arctic villages) seem to silently shrug it off, long accustomed to suicide and abuse and social dysfunction.

Kabloona who last more than a winter up here often attribute their longevity to "tolerance." RCMP, hoteliers, researchers, nurses or teachers. Gontran de Poncins, the French count, wrote about trying to make this cultural adaptation in 1940 Gjoa: "There was no getting on with the Eskimo except on his own terms; and as I was not a tourist concerned with externals, but a man concerned to find himself with the aid of the Eskimo, I had to get on with him. . . . Again and again the European in me would protest, would rage; and particularly when the physical strain seemed too great to be borne, would refuse abruptly to accept the need for the adoption of the Eskimo view of life—and would suffer certain consequences."

I am invited to lecture at the junior high and high school, in front of several dozen students. One teacher dressed in a white lab coat claims that he is paid *not* to teach, because so few of his students show up for class. None of his seven students has woken up for the ten o'clock English lesson.

He sits down with a groan, unfolds his legs beneath a small student desk, and says, "No Inuit adult in town will wake their kids up for school. This is because when they were growing up in *iglu*s and it was cold outside, they would never get out of bed all day."

Another teacher laments that his lessons are a wash because the seventh graders can't read above comic book level. That day, a half hour into a journal-writing assignment, most kids get no further than copying the date off the blackboard. This same seventh-grade class is being taught the equivalent of fourth-grade math.

When it's time for me to try to inspire them, I look around the classroom. Few students will meet my eyes. When I'm through with a thirty-minute talk on photography and adventure, no student will ask a question. When I ask a few questions of my own—about bears and where the carvers obtain their soapstone—the teachers answer for me. The two Inuit and a dozen *Kabloona* teachers are dedicated despite their frustrations. Along with required lesson plans, they use an Inuit syllabus in hopes of showing the youngsters their roots.

The kids spend a lot of time staring up at space somewhere beneath the ceiling, sleeping or chatting with one another as I try to engage them. Finally I look out a window, trying to imagine their perceived lack of future, their torpor. Their thoughts drift across the upcoming World Wrestling Foundation match on television, or playing hockey, or sex, to which no boy or girl in the Arctic is a stranger.

Gjoa Haven students in high school classroom

As the kids file out at the bell, the teachers assure me that the students really listened, that they never forget their visitors.

Later on I resolve to test the intelligence of three curious kids who surround me out on the street. It is a friendly meeting, for Gjoa, a dry town, is still free of the alcoholism and racist anger simmering in Cambridge Bay, Paulatuk and Tuk. One boy points to the sun, sinking as a huge orange ball into the southern ocean. I have the sensation of floating in the saffron sunset light, somewhere between the darkened sea and nighttime clouds.

The sixteen-year-old asks my age. He is innocence personified, ball cap on backward, smiling and interested enough in the outside world that he might have a chance to join it. For a fleeting moment I can imagine Gjoa's future through these children. I reply that I graduated from high school in 1974 at eighteen years old and then turn the question back on them: "So how old am I?"

They don't answer, so I give them a hint that I graduated twenty-five years ago. After several minutes they still appear to be stumped. Thinking that they are merely shy, I jest: "Okay, I'll tell you. I'm twenty-one."

Only the girl doesn't believe me. I quickly realize, with a flush of guilt, how easily these guileless people are taken advantage of. As they walk off, the ten-year-old yells back to me, "Want me to be your slave, Jon?"

Given the closed-door abuses of these villages, the terror of darkened rooms and abusive guardians, I can only wonder where the boy gets his sense of humor.

After a few days Paul returns. I am still trapped in Gjoa by winter weather. It appears that my trip is ending, but rather than quit, I pace the streets.

Since it is no longer considered a total shame to have *Kabloona* blood, Paul and his stepbrother and sister all have recently confessed that Roald Amundsen is their grandfather. Their father, Luke, who died in 1974, was mostly closemouthed about being Amundsen's son.

I am shocked. The uncelebrated Amundsen is one of my role models.

Amundsen, unlike Franklin, spent two winters here studying Inuit. Unquestionably, Inuit living practices allowed him to complete the first Northwest Passage. He later became the first to reach the South Pole (using Inuit-style dogsleds). Shadowing his footsteps a month later, the Englishmen led by Robert F. Scott—disdainful, like Franklin, of Inuit methods—all died from starvation. As much as anything that I admire about him, Amundsen took only carefully calculated risks. Throughout Amundsen's life, in his memoirs, and in Roland Huntford's impeccably researched biography of Scott and Amundsen, *The Last Place on Earth,* the famous Norwegian hid the knowledge of his son, born before Amundsen sailed out of Gjoa in the summer of 1905.

Paul has no resemblance to the sled-nosed Amundsen. The explorer's bronze bust is displayed in a rarely visited section of the hamlet building, next to a model of his ship, the *Gjoa,* and photographs of the crew. Paul's fifty-six-year-old stepbrother, Bob, shares the explorer's distinctive nose, a profile unlike most pug-nosed Inuit. The brothers beam proudly for photographs next to the bust. While it is difficult to say where the Iquallahs fit into the complex village hierarchy, which still disdains non-Inuit blood, both men claim to have been born in *iglu*s and are deeply attached to being out on the land.

The bilingual Paul, recently flown to Japan to give an *iglu*-building demonstration, is a garrulous and self-effacing delight. He suggests that I take advantage of the bad weather by meeting as many Inuit as I can.

He guides me to the house of a village elder, who may be able to impart some wisdom for my trip. We walk inside the Arctic entryway without knocking. I place my North Face running shoes next to the pile of Nike runners. Greeted by the smell of boiling meat, Paul yells for Louis Ameralick.

Louis, seventy-nine, a smiling and narrow, elfin figure, half toothless, is trying to make us out through his thick-lensed glasses. He seats us at his kitchen table, beside a wall magnet rack holding eight ulus instead of

Paul Iquallah and Bob Konana with bust of their grandfather, Roald Amundsen

knives. He lights up a new cigarette from the stub in his left hand. With Paul translating, Louis tells me about his first polar bear.

In March 1940, alone and miles from his village, Louis was surprised by *Nanuq*. He had one recycled .22 bullet in his long-barreled rifle, and he shot true, but the bullet glanced off the bear's thick skull. *Nanuq* rushed Louis, picked him up by the chest and rear end, then threw him onto a cliff's edge. Louis tried to stand up, but the snow was too soft, and the bear appeared to be making its final lunge, jaws opened wide (he holds the base of his palms together and pantomimes an alligator mouth as Paul laughs). Then Louis pulled out his snow knife and plunged it in between *Nanuq*'s ribs. He knew that he was thinking clearly because he pulled the knife back out in case he had to stab it again, but *Nanuq* started running, until it finally dropped down onto the snow and died. It was a shame, he said, to have killed such a powerful being. I can only wonder at the fear that Louis, no more than five feet three inches tall, would have felt beneath such an animal.

Louis's caribou parka had been torn open, and his body ached all over, but he was otherwise unhurt. Today, even in the modern-day village hierarchy, Louis Ameralick remains revered, but it was not because of his bravery. He had respected *Nanuq*. In turn the bear had given him something. While many villagers his age are stooped over and ill, Louis has lightness to his steps and a youthful grin. "It would be unwise," Louis says, in a long and breathless guttural utterance, "to ever speak poorly of such a magnificent animal."

In a surprise question, the only one of the afternoon from Louis, he asks, "Do you know that polar bears fly?"

I shake my head no, slowly. Louis is grinning so widely that I have no choice but to dismiss his comment as a joke.

Louis Ameralick with ulus in his kitchen

. . .

I go to the beach beneath the RCMP quarters and pick up an abandoned polar bear skull. It weighs maybe ten pounds and is twice the size of my own head. Just holding it makes me feel taller, somehow less vulnerable. With pliers, I pry out two giant teeth and then zip them into my pocket. I bow deeply before leaving.

After ten days stalled in Gjoa, I have become surly about the wintry north winds and big seas that have prevented me from paddling across to the mainland. I am freaked out about the fourteen-mile crossing, eight miles longer than any crossing I have ever attempted. To make matters worse, bronchitis has settled into my chest, and I have a fever. Just walking through the chill streets of town becomes an effort.

Reaching Pelly Bay, or even the village of Taloyoak, 120 miles away, seems a lost cause. Already I have hung it out too far. Still, every morning I have awoken hopeful. There's got to be a solution.

That night I coerce Paul and Rebecca to eat dinner with me at the Amundsen Hotel, since sharing food is the easiest way to understand culture. "We have our own food," Paul protests.

It occurs to me that they have never been taken out to dinner. I reply, "It would make me happy to buy you a meal and share your company."

We sit in the hotel's vinyl-backed chairs beneath the new Nunavut flag. It also flies above the post office. No one in town seems happy about the stark *Inuksuit* cairn in front of bright red and yellow stripes.

Paul knows that I am itching to leave Gjoa. He chides, in his high-pitched, melodic voice, that I could ride an Inuit motorboat to Taloyoak. I change the subject. Paul is fond of a good jest, like most Inuit, and knows that I would despise becoming a passenger in a motorboat instead of earning my miles.

"When are you leaving, Jon?"

"Yesterday. I had hoped."

He runs his palm across his face and wipes the sweat across his black crew cut. "Jeez, Jon, where's your patience? Didn't you know that my grandfather spent two winters here before conditions allowed him to complete the first Northwest Passage?"

As the cook shouts out the specials, I finally understand the Iquallahs' reluctance to eat out with me. Hamburgers and chicken are *Kabloona* food. Fortunately, the cook has some muskox steak. But *omingmak* is eaten, albeit boiled or raw, only by starving Netsilik, people of the seal. Rebecca looks away, embarrassed.

When the sautéed steak is placed on the table, Paul manages to eat half of his. Then, after seeing me look at his plate in curiosity, he pretends to eat the rest of his *omingmak* with relish. Rebecca pushes her uneaten plate of food away.

It comes as a sudden revelation that the only restaurant in this village eschews traditional boiled or raw meat. This is the same scenario, in reverse, that I experienced while eating snow goose in their tent. I ask, "Is the food okay, Paul?"

He replies, with a shy, downcast look to the floor, "It's maybe a little more overcooked than we like to eat our food."

Then he brightens and lifts his head up, happy to give me another lesson: "Jon, we are *Netsilik.*"

I have to try to make the crossing before winter makes me pull an Amundsen, so I pack up early on August 25. It is June's birthday; I keep this foremost in my mind because I am sick. Victoria Jason hit this same sort of weather several years ago, and on August 22 she wisely stopped paddling here in Gjoa.

The raw north wind forces me to keep my gloves on while packing the kayak. Out beyond the harbor the seas appear to be whitecapped. Just as I begin pulling into my dry suit, two Frenchmen row ashore from their forty-foot cutter. I had paddled out the night before and knocked on their transom, but they were too exhausted to wake up. I try not to get my hopes up because even if they are going east, it's unlikely that they'll want a passenger.

Olivier Pitras, the captain, is tall and lanky with angular features and oversize glasses. His partner is Jean-Michel Guillevic, stout and silent and bearded. They have sailed from Alaska in a mere month. When I announce that the same distance has taken me six months over the last three years, Olivier merely laughs and says, "Yes, but uhh you air on zee kayak following zee shore while we air sailing at ten knotz out on zee ocean."

"I'm afraid I'm going to have some difficulty making this fourteen-mile crossing to the mainland"—I gesture to the northeast—"but I'm going to go and have a look anyway."

Olivier doesn't bat an eye before saying, "*Mais,* why don't you lettuse take you acrozz?"

"Are you sure?"

"Zat would be no prob-lem, Jon."

"Well, it might be, because I have gone without motors for the last two thousand miles, and to accept your kind offer I have to ask if you could try without your engine."

Olivier quickly confers with Jean-Michel, then turns back and says, "*Je comprends,* and zat eez no prob-lem."

Peace of the Arctic

While hanging from a bosun's chair halfway up the mast, I photograph Olivier hauling the fore jib in big swells outside the harbor. The *Ocean Search*—a fourteen-ton aluminum cutter, its hull reinforced with steel plates for pack ice—bounces and rolls gently, stalled into the wind. Spray blasts the foredeck. As wind fills the third sail, Jean-Michel eases the tiller. The boat shudders, heels and then finds its slicing course across the waves. I whoop with exhilaration. I am back on the sea at last.

The Frenchmen smile. A troop of jaegers wheels to starboard. Gjoa shrinks beneath fang-shaped cumulus, raking the sky and leading us toward polar bears and ice packs.

I hang from the rigging, then stand on the bowsprit. Once under sail, I stop worrying about my chest cold and where I'm going and just let myself go, the exquisite luxury of dry sailing in a brisk wind. A distant purple strip of mainland beckons to the west. At the area I had planned to paddle across, most of the icy rollers that we are effortlessly plowing through would swamp my kayak. I call out bits of opaque ice to Jean-Michel and Olivier.

In the cockpit Olivier serves us red wine and cheese sandwiches. I ask about their lives. He answers slowly and modestly. Olivier was chartering sailboats in the Caribbean, and after rounding Cape Horn, he wanted to sail across the top of Russia on the Northeast Passage. After weeks of waiting for permission in Kamchatka, the Russians refused to let him through. So he and Jean-Michel, a French ship engineer who learned how to sail on Windsurfers, spontaneously sailed to Alaska, picked up some charts and bolted east on the Northwest Passage.

After dropping me off, they plan to sail to Greenland, down its west coast, then across the North Atlantic—at the height of hurricane season. They hope to reach France by mid-October. (They will become the first sailors to complete the Northwest Passage in a decade and in a single season to boot.)

It's easy to relax between two such skilled seamen. As we raise our glasses in a toast to our hoped-for successes, I silently resolve to end this trip without taking any more risks. I am strangely light-headed and exhausted, and I realize that even if the sea was calm, I no longer have the strength to attempt such a crossing. Something is wrong with me.

Jean-Michel Guillevic, the author and Olivier Pitras toasting June Duell's birthday with red wine on the Ocean Search

That evening the wind falls off, and Olivier is forced to crank up his forty-horse diesel engine to cross the last miles to the mainland.

"I am sorr-ee, Jean," he says.

"That's okay," I reply. "After all, Amundsen once said that his ship *Gjoa* would never have made it without the auxiliary engine."

As Olivier motor sails toward a bight on the mainland, I reassemble my Klepper on the foredeck. I can't help but remember the words of Billy's son, Jason, while we were snowmobiling to Umingmaktuuq. Jason had screamed that we—meaning human beings—would be getting nowhere without engines. At the time it seemed a motorhead philosophy at odds with my whole reverence for wilderness earned by muscle power. Isn't it true, I had argued, that the speed and noise of engines kill our appreciation of the natural world? But here on the *Ocean Search* foredeck, moving forward under the throaty growl of a diesel engine, I know that the words of Inuit will return to haunt me again and again, ringing as clarion bells of wisdom.

I shake hands with my French friends, lower the Klepper into the water and begin paddling, sad and slow.

"Good-bye," they shout.

"*Bonne chance,*" I reply.

As the *Ocean Search* sails north along the eastern edge of the Boothia Peninsula, I steer east toward a narrow isthmus. Taloyoak is only two days away.

Befriending Olivier and Jean-Michel was the most pleasurable part of my summer, but this only hides a new and depressing thought: Everything Inuit have taught me shows that the world, even the remote Arctic, is a different place from what I would like it to be. There is no time left for a people who espouse patience and animal spirituality, because these beliefs collide with the high-speed dogmas of modern Western culture. Nor is there much room left for wilderness adventurers (versus today's legions of performance-driven athletes), because we are aided by technology and linear know-how.

I have submitted to all too much technology. High-speed aircrafts will take me home. A Gore-Tex dry suit seals my body, while I clutch a carbon-fiber paddle in my hands. I stow all matter of technology on my rubber-molded kayak: a PLB, a GPS, foil bags of vacuum-sealed and freeze-dried food, a barometer watch and two dozen maps.

I am no closer to the wilderness than an *Inuk* clutching an Evinrude throttle.

Within mere hours of my leaving *Ocean Search,* my sickness hits like a saffron meteor shower bursting out across my vision. I black out in the midst of a cold headwind; when I awake a half minute later, I stroke the air in terror with my paddle. I try to right the spinning shoreline by sucking down a few deep breaths. It is only luck that I have not capsized. It takes all of my concentration to get the boat ashore and set up the tent. The cold and windy summer has used me up; I collapse into unconsciousness.

In the morning I awake with a splitting headache. I stumble out to break the ice from a nearby pond for my drinking water, then force myself to leave. I paddle into a headwind, determined not to take any chances or abandon the shoreline in case I pass out again.

At noon three boatloads of Inuit whale hunters beckon me over to a beach for lunch. Each takes out his GPS, and we compare notes about how much safer their lives have become since satellites started circling the Arctic.

After a few racking coughs, bent over the cockpit, I pull out several pounds of smoked char as an offering. One of the elders slices me a slab of raw muktuk from a beluga they killed two hundred miles north, on Prince of Wales Island. With all five men watching me, I smile, place the gray blubber in my mouth like a communion wafer, then begin working the nutty and rubbery flesh. Everyone smiles. Someone slaps my back. Inuktitut words are exchanged, and we all laugh.

Suddenly a gyrfalcon swoops down onto a snowshoe hare along the shoreline, one aerial white blur falling atop another blur bleaching across the rocky tundra. The hunters all turn their heads, distracted just long enough for me to spit out the unchewable blubber and cover it with my boot. The gyrfalcon's talons clutch at empty sand as the hare mews and ducks under a boulder.

The oldest hunter pours me a cup of hot water from his thermos and hands me a packet of presweetened instant cappuccino. I turn it over, wondering if they have acquired Italian tastes or if the Northern Store is just capitalizing on their sugar cravings.

"You okay?" the elder asks.

"Just something in my chest, but I'll get better in Taloyoak." I don't mention that my stomach is cramped with nausea, trying to digest the concentrated Omega 3 muktuk oils.

Another younger man cuts me a foot-long square of muktuk from under a tarp in his boat. "Eat this Inuit energy bar, and you feel better."

I try to refuse, explaining that muktuk scent will draw in polar bears, but they only laugh. Already in too deep, I accept the gift. No sense seeming ungracious about their favorite food.

"We will be looking after you in *Tell-your-lo-rock*." They all start their engines, sated from their weeklong vacation, not a little bit sad about having to make the transition back to the routines of village life.

"*Cowanna!*" I yell.

As soon as their boats disappear around Cape Isabella, I fling the muktuk beyond my kayak and out into the water, where it skips, floats for a second, then sinks through clear water like a feather falling through air. Glaucous gulls fly in, lowering their bills to sip whatever whale oil remains on the water, while ogling the unreachable slab of raw alabaster energy on the ocean bottom below. I bend over and begin scrubbing the stinky oil off my hands with sand and seawater. A minute later I look up beyond my kayak. A mirrored whale oil slick stretches out an acre. It speaks so precisely to the calamity within my stomach that I drop down to catch the shore on my outstretched palms, open my mouth wide and retch onto the beach.

I paddle several more miles, looking to the landscape for enlightenment. An eider slinks off low in the water with three chicks riding her back. Long banners of white seaweed, appearing at first to be paper towels, drape the shorelines. Snowy owls swoop past with swift and powerful wingbeats, scattering ground squirrels.

By sunset I am close enough to watch Taloyoak's lights wink on like trembling green leaves from across the blackened waters of Spence Bay. Since I am probably far from the sensitive noses of bears, I torch up a driftwood campfire for warmth. An immense rose-colored moon comes out of the sea and bathes me in its light as the clouds continue blushing with sunlight. As the campfire wanes, drowned out by the fire in the sky, I wander across the tundra, lost in rapture.

I decide that everyone should visit the Arctic, if only once. For the moonbeams, midnight sun and aurora borealis. For the weird downy or winged creatures. For a humming that resembles the breathing of the earth. Even if technology and engines have irreversibly altered culture, the Arctic environment remains unspoiled. In these days of cultural homogenization, as the world merges toward a single market, it is essential to know where and how we fit on our home, our lovely earth. Maybe this, I think, truly defines what my vision quest is. If everyone could know this peace—the specific soft swish of snowy owl wings overhead, as well as the sense that *if* God exists, it is in the light—then the world might someday clean up its act.

I continue tiptoeing over the tundra and casting my moon shadow across the furry-looking poppies and river beauties gone to seed. When I hear the padding of an animal from behind a nearby knoll, I run back to the tent, trembling, hoping that it's only a snowshoe hare. Nevertheless, I am happy that there are still places wild enough to fear animals other than men, where our imaginations, for better or worse, are set free.

In the calm before sleep I know that the only important thing left in this passage, aside from surviving, is to meet a polar bear. That's all I want.

At dawn a gale springs out of the west, and just as I raise my kayak sail and bounce out into the waves, a burly white pony runs across my field of view. I turn to leeward. I wipe the wind tears from my eyes. I look again. It's a polar bear cantering away! My campfire must have drawn it in.

It hits the blur of wind and water, then disappears into surf. I look left and right, as jumpy as an American pipit, not knowing where the bear might reemerge. Although the wind is lifting the water into small hills, I steer over and around the breakers. I debark at every sheltered nook to look around and plot how best to avoid the waves. To stand up on hilltops, I have to brace a leg out to the side so that the wind doesn't blow me down.

In one cove, I stop breathing when I see *Nanuq* a stone's throw away, stalking me like a seal, swimming with only its black nose above the water. I blink my eyes and see that it's a black rubber line buoy, bobbing in on the current. I jump back in the kayak. I can't see over the waves until I crest them, but the polar bear still has me more spooked than the sea.

Finally I make my commitment to rounding into the protected Stanners Harbor. I reef the sail down to several square feet and pull it to the deck to minimize torque on the mast.

This is the biggest water I have ever sailed in. If the boat swamps, I can swim to Taloyoak's shore and sprint into a warm house quicker than hypothermia can kill me. First I pry my boots off. Then I time the five seconds between each breaker, pick the biggest wave I see, and turn and sail downwind in its wake. Several seconds later, as the kayak is jerked up onto the next wave, I cut across the wind and steer into the calm water behind a cliff. The bow crackles as I surf down the wave. I throw all of my 185 pounds against the wind and ride the breaking waves, hydroplaning out at twenty miles per hour across still water.

I scream to release the fullness in my head.

A crowd of people awaits me onshore. Most of them couldn't see my half-submerged kayak over the waves and, having never seen one sailed before, thought that I was riding a Windsurfer. Some of them heard about me from the whale hunters and want to make sure that I'm okay. The RCMP wants to borrow my kayak.

One elder asks why I am kayaking in such big seas. I confess that I'm fleeing a polar bear that appeared to be stalking me. But he doesn't believe me.

"*Tôrnârssuk* never come to town," he yells, holding his arms calmly at his sides. "But if you see *Tôrnârssuk*, never look him in the eye. Never talk to him. And never show your gun unless you mean to kill him."

No one laughs. The elder is obviously respected. Somebody adds that it is bad luck if the bear comes into town from the rear, but since it might be following me in from the front, it is okay. After I ask what *Tôrnârssuk* means, everyone hushes.

The elder answers, "One who gives power."

I finger the teeth in my pocket; what I saw of the bear was much too distant, fleeting and fear-filled. I want something more.

Ken Boone, the RCMP, takes my kayak to his house so it won't get vandalized. Dennis Lyall, the mayor, drives me to his hotel. All the smiling faces and handshakes and kids tugging at me become a blur until my head hits the pillow in a strange warm room. I sleep for two days.

The Good People of Taloyoak

After World War II, Taloyoak ("place that caribou are driven") was renamed Spence Bay, only to be given its original name back a half century later. In 1948, Ernie Lyall relocated his *Inuk* wife and two dozen others (who had been relocated before) from the distant Arctic Bay. Moving Polar Inuit in with the indigenous Netsilik made them argue about where to place beacons for the annual supply ship and where to build their new town—until the two factions began to intermarry. Some locals still can't understand one another's dialects. For instance, Netsilik called the polar bear *Nanuq*. The newcomers called it *Tôrnârssuk*.

Lyall, a Hudson's Bay Company employee, fathered eleven children and became one of three *Kabloona* throughout Canada who received an Eskimo disk number. Like most HBC men, he defended his employer even after quitting and taking a government job for three times the pay. HBC had repeatedly relocated these Inuit to help with fox trapping in Spence Bay and elsewhere, but unlike other Canadian Inuit relocators, Lyall was looking after The People. Inuit here trusted HBC; all the talk about "ripping the people off" belied what Lyall believed to be an order that kept the "people's good at heart."

He was different from *Kabloona* traders like Duncan Pryde. Lyall's Scottish grandfather and father both worked for HBC. Ernie Lyall was born in the North and would die there. By raising a family in the Arctic and suffering the same setbacks as Inuit did, he showed his commitment to The People. When his children were sent away to school for five years and prohibited from speaking Inuktitut, Lyall protested to the government. If HBC looked after Inuit in Taloyoak, it was because Lyall made sure that the prices weren't raised and that medicine was flown in. When Lyall quit, things became strained between HBC and Inuit.

He protested that social assistance would destroy Inuit life. He pointed out that drinking was bad too, but he liked his scotch, and besides, The People had already been boozing a long time. Looking to the future, Lyall was convinced that Nunavut would not work. In 1979 he said: "The people never believed in times back that this was their land, as a property they owned sort of thing. They didn't think about the land that way, so how can they lose it? I know they couldn't run Spence on their own, not yet. And I feel that there's no way that the Eskimos can take over the Northwest Territories, not at this stage of the game."

On my third day in town, Ernie Lyall's son Dennis, born a half century ago as his mother squatted above the shores of an inland lake, ferries me and several others across the wide waters of Spence Bay to a fishing camp. He and his brother, Pat, are piloting $30,000 jet boats, purchased from southern Canada. By scooting across whitecaps at 45 miles per hour, regardless of the weather, the Lyalls can continue to catch fish as Inuit have done for centuries. The catch will barely pay for the price of fuel, never mind the cost of a jet boat. Their money comes from shrewd construction investments.

For the first time in three years I am invited to drink with an Inuit party. Dennis shares out generous portions from a plastic gallon jug of Cheney, which he lofts into the air and calls a cocktail. Soon the winter breeze feels warm. Even more impressive, Dennis has brought along a teetotaling friend as the designated driver. No one gets staggering drunk, but the whiskey is almost more than I can handle.

A dozen miles south we motor into a cove beside Ikaujatiak Point, long known to The People as a resting place for char, before they run up the Netsilik River to spawn. As two younger guys pluck the nets, I run in place to stay warm. The Lyalls wield their knives with incredible accuracy on the cutting table, slicing off heads, paring open bellies and surgically detaching green guts from orange meat. Two dozen *Larus thayeri*—thought to be a form of the Iceland gull—wheel above us, shrieking and pleading.

"Amazing how solid those gulls are," Dennis remarks with the matter-of-fact way of a man raised on animal flesh. "When you hit one with a twenty-two, it really makes a thud."

Dennis and Pat have suddenly turned to discussing "what a crock it is" that Columbus or the Vikings discovered North America. They look back at me, repeatedly, to make sure that I am on the same wavelength.

Continuing in non sequitur, Pat moves on to how the Franklin searchers got it wrong. If they would just listen to Inuit, searchers would find Franklin himself, "sleeping in deep water off the peninsula."

"Which peninsula?" I ask.

"I'm not saying."

I go for a walk to warm up. The land falls back to a range of stony hills, and in lieu of trees, ancient *Inuksuit* whisker the skyline. Even with binoculars, I can see no sign of life. To the north, across the blurry furl of salt air lashing Spence Bay, Taloyoak's water tanks and buildings are too far away to

Removing livers from char, Spence Bay

see. Coming out onto the land as suddenly as we did, after being in the village confines, is a shocking change. Here it is quiet, and the land's wholeness and amplitude offer up a myriad of possibilities to our imagination. Back in the village of seven hundred people, truck backup beepers and humming generators and revving engines are an assault to the ears. I am beginning to understand why it is so difficult for villagers to maintain their traditions.

I come back to the cutting table full of questions. Dennis replies that the land has always been his sanity, but he sees no contradiction about using engines while he is out hunting. I give it up and ask about the challenges of Taloyoak from his mayor's viewpoint.

"Housing, unemployment and suicide—there have been twenty in the last ten years." But like most proud Inuit, Dennis refuses to discuss suicide. Which only brings to mind the tortured and muted faces of soapstone carvings.

Pat unfurls white butcher paper from ten pounds of muktuk. Rather than eat it raw, he boils it in salt water over a Coleman stove. After ten minutes Pat peels off the gauzy skin, which he calls hair, then flicks it away. Hickory barbecue sauce is passed around so that we can drown the nutty-tasting flesh. Dennis dips his in vinegar. Everyone licks their fingers. As I watch their sixteen-year-old nephew substituting potato chips for traditional food, Pat suggests I photograph the new "Inuit dichotomy: junk food versus muktuk."

We jet back to town with several hundred pounds of char stacked in milk crates like cordwood. Pat and Dennis seem happy to be boating in these dangerous waters. The boats crash up and down, throwing a huge wake of spray and jumping out of the waves, causing the jets to peal and grind uselessly in the air. Since the chop is too frightening to look at any longer, I distract myself by talking with the taciturn thirty-three-year-old who came to pluck nets. Since Pat can't hear us over the roaring twin jet engines and since my new friend is drunk, he pours his heart out: "Living here really gets to you. Sometimes you just want to let loose, commit a crime, you know?" He uses direct eye contact, his mouth two feet away as he talks, his face lined with smallpox scars and airbrushed with a nihilistic yet feminine moustache. He has served two half-year jail terms for burglary and assaulting his "girl," with whom he has fathered three children.

"I wouldn't want anyone to think that I beat her up that often, but you got to know what it's like living here, man. It's not despair, it's hard to explain, it's more like sadness."

I stay focused on the dead fish bouncing in their boxes at our feet, rather than look out at the waves towering above. I wag my head to let him know that I am still listening, keeping my ear close to his mouth over the roar. He is reaffirming all of the troubles I have seen in other villages over the last three years. On some level he is also speaking to me, to everyone, about all those unknowable demons that we carry inside ourselves. He is asking me to understand the human condition, and he holds nothing back, because he believes we are all alike.

He is Netsilik and thin. He prefers uncooked char; he unabashedly rescued all their livers, which his family eats raw and considers a delicacy. The Lyalls are part Polar Inuit, part Scottish *Kabloona,* and they like their fish cooked. I have seen their portly worldliness before, from Prudhoe Bay to Gjoa Haven. I have seen it in the Elaniks, the Gordons, the Grubens, the Thrashers, the Klengenbergs, and the Porters, all descended from European traders. While the Lyalls have not hesitated to make money, they have stayed in Taloyoak. They have taken these young men and me out fishing and gotten us drunk. Tonight, as we sleep it off, Pat and Dennis will be giving out two hundred pounds of fresh char to neighbors and family.

In the morning, before I can begin portaging across the Boothia Peninsula, a gam of belugas makes the mistake of swimming into Stanners Harbor. Within minutes of the sighting, every able-bodied gunner and boat are out on the water. The gunfire is constant. One whale takes no less than three dozen bullets before Jimmy Oleekatalik thrusts a harpoon into it.

Admiring the beluga whale carcass in Taloyoak

Another whale is harpooned twice, then lost, as it sounds and mysteriously disappears from sight attached to two five-gallon gas can floats. The first whale is roped by its tail and dragged to the beach.

The whole town comes down. Even the school lets out so that the children can run down to the beach and stroke the whale. Blood ebbs and flows in the wavelets. No one seems to mind that their runners are soaked from standing ankle deep in mud. I stand inside the crowd, oooooh-ing and ahhhh-ing with the children jumping up and down beside their twelve-foot whale and running their fingers along its opaque dog-size teeth. Several elders are dressed in sealskin kamiks and caribou parkas. No one leaves. The whale is the cleanest white carcass I have ever seen.

Shoulder to shoulder with these people, jostled by the energy rippling through the crowd, I feel something special. I find myself transported yet again, despite my own cultural misgivings about the prolonged agony of the whales. From a distance I had mistaken The People's joy to be the gloating and vaunting that *Kabloona* hunters show over deer carcasses. What I had heard described yesterday as "the sadness" is no longer evident on any of the faces surrounding me. These traditionally minded people are lifted back to another world as they stroke the whale's soft skin and remember that it has given itself up as food and that it shares the same soul and cold waters and hard life that they all know. A life, some of them still believe, that is governed by the goddess Nuliajak from under the sea.

No one says anything disrespectful to the whale. I hear "beautiful" over and over again, even from the children. Taloyoak is not dry like other villages, and there are a couple of stumbling people here, but there are also more than a few elders who have not forgotten the old ways. Even those people too young to understand or celebrate at this evening's impromptu dance will learn the significance of this day. For one precious afternoon, both Netsilik and Polar Inuit have forgotten the rest of the strange world and danced alongside their beloved whale.

An elder on the beach sums it up for me: "*Kilalurak* chose to swim right here where we live. He did not have to do this. He could have stayed in Spence Bay or James Ross Strait. He came to us. Maybe Nuliajak sent him."

Ursa Major at Last

Power

Kees 't Hooft arrives on the afternoon plane to film me portaging the thirty-mile lake-dotted isthmus east, out into the Gulf of Boothia and on toward Pelly Bay. Lately I have been wondering if it is wise to be continuing in these wintry conditions. If I can get out into the range of Atlantic tides, and if I can meet my polar bear, the trip will feel complete. I have to hold myself back from going for Pelly if it doesn't feel right.

Is this what it's come to, protecting myself from myself? I wonder.

For transportation, Kees hires Jimmy, who harpooned the whale, his father, Simond, and their battered eighteen-foot skiff. The Oleekataliks know that I want to see a polar bear, up close, and although they seem to have some misgivings about this idea, they agree to help Kees however they can.

Jimmy wears his hair at shoulder length, in the old way. After several years of living in Yellowknife, he missed his people, and all the money he made got squandered on alcohol. At thirty-three, he has decided to stay in Taloyoak and help out—maybe someday as a politician. Since the Nunavut government has recently converted the new territory's three time zones into one central time zone, Jimmy announces that he is in favor of going to the thirteen-hour day.

Kees has the gentle, smiling way of his Dutch upbringing. Unlike most cinematographers, he seldom imposes on his subjects, and he always asks, politely, if he can film them. So he is the perfect and unobtrusive sort of filmmaker with whom Inuit feel comfortable. But he also has a restless mind, so he inquires, respectfully, about the logic of Jimmy's proposed time clock.

Jimmy replies, "Inuit need to solve their own problems, not southerners." He is careful not to ostracize Kees or me by saying white people, let alone *Kabloona.* He goes so far as to say that the word *Inuk,* at least to the Netsilik, means only a person, regardless of his skin color. His tolerance and his worldview could be a model for any culture.

He then tries to help us understand: "Since southerners use ice chests to cool their food, and Inuit use ice chests to prevent their food from freezing, how could southerners possibly know what we want?"

Despite the underlying air of trouble in his life (he is already a grandfather, while the unruffled Simond has adopted at least one of his children), Jimmy has a winning personality. He speaks in a pleasant singsong, repeating each phrase like a distant radioman trying to break through a faint signal, spinning his short, staccato sentences with accidental poetic charm. Self-deprecating jokes are his specialty.

He asks Kees, "Do ya know where do the Inuit keep their money? Do ya know?"

"I'm not quite sure," Kees replies in his English accent.

"In snowbanks."

It takes two days to backpack my kayak and its contents four miles to Middle Lake. I have lost the fever, but my vision still blurs whenever I move too fast. With the help of a collapsible four-pound cart, I wheel the Klepper around the town's water lake, walking just fast enough to stay warm, yet slow enough to keep the dizziness away.

As I paddle, two nesting peregrines repeatedly flush past in whistling, wedge-shaped blurs, crying *kreeee-kreee-kreee!* next to my ear.

A stone tent ring, salted with shattered caribou bone, looks over the distant electric plant and airport and telephone wires, showing the uneasy collision that has shaken the humble Inuit. I find stashed in a nearby grotto a huffer's thirty-pound tank of propane, stolen from town.

That rainy afternoon I catch up to Jimmy, Simond and Kees, camped in a big white wall tent. The Oleekataliks, whose name means "men with capes," use wind jackets in lieu of waterproof raincoats. Their leaking stove is a hodgepodge of misfitting parts, their lantern lacks a globe, and their leaky tent has been ripped open and sewed back together with four raised wounds that look suspiciously like claw marks. Each time they manage to crank to life their old coughing Evinrude engine, they whoop in celebration. Even by Inuit standards their gear is abused and neglected. Nevertheless, their cheerful optimism and sense of humor easily make up for their material unpreparedness.

Simond is a round-faced and cheerful soul whose rocking walk resembles that of an old rodeo rider. As a Polar *Inuk* he married a Netsilik, Nee, who made him rich with old stories. Simond tells us about a nineteenth-century shaman who communicated with a *Kabloona* priest on one of Franklin's boats, then went out to trade for forks, which The People converted into harpoons. The story seems leaky, a blurry sort of dream tale, but before we can dismiss it as myth, Simond patches it with bits of detail: the strange ship whose mast resembled distant forests, an *Inuk* trying to trade for a saw, people running away from the thump of gunfire and an Inuit dog sniffing the strange *Kabloona*.

The Oleekataliks cannot explain why they have hauled along a relative's dog, a pitiful and slight whimpering white cur, more American Eskimo lapdog than Canadian Eskimo *Qimmiq*. Since it has no name, Kees and I call it Hot Dog after its favorite stolen snack. Rather than speak to the dog as it slyly noses open the ice chest to gulp down yet another morsel of junk food that they are trying to keep from freezing, Simond and Jimmy hiss through their teeth at poor Hot Dog.

Simond tells us about sleeping in the tent with his wife, Nee, out in the Gulf of Boothia. In the middle of the night, while he was snoring away, a large and shaggy white paw ripped open the tent wall and woke them up. Before Simond could grab the rifle, Nee fired off a bloodcurdling scream. The paw retreated outside the tent. Simond cautiously peered through the ripped tent wall and watched three *Tôrnârssuk* running for their lives.

"On another campout with family," Simond says, slowly searching for the right English words, looking down at Hot Dog as if he had suddenly found a use, "*Tôrnârssuk* swim straight to camp, so I fire over head but keeps coming. Right up out of water and running up beach to eat us. I kill *Tôrnârssuk*. We cut *Tôrnârssuk* open and only seaweed in stomach."

"Do you regret having to kill the bear?" I asked.

"Maybe bad luck," Simond says, looking down at Hot Dog. "Maybe very bad. Maybe we no camp there."

In the morning Simond and Jimmy haul their aluminum Lund between lakes with a wheeled trailer and a series of plywood ramps equipped with plastic rollers and winches. I follow behind, first backpacking, then wheeling my kayak.

On the morning of September 3 I lift the Klepper through an ancient fish weir. Simond stops and pulls out some char, and Jimmy puts in a net for lake trout. While we wait for the nets to fill, Simond takes Kees and me to the remains of a baby's grave.

"*Tunniq*," Simond says, "giants long ago." He asks me to lie down in the stones above the baby's body, a perfect fit for my six-foot-two frame. I lie on the cold earth surrounded by yellowing crowberry leaves and try to imagine these people. Snow geese honk through the air above, and snow feathers down out of the sky. The *tunniq*, or Dorset Culture, disappeared from the face of the earth and left only its otherworldly carvings, objects of such great beauty that many modern-day Inuit think that they come from the afterworld. It would never occur to Simond to dig up the grave.

"It's not an old frame," I ask as we walk, "where people once rested a skin kayak for the winter?"

*Jimmy and Simond Oleekatalik
show me stone-outlined graves of baby*
Tunniq

"No, too short, kayak," Simond replies, with a solemn nod from his boat. "Grave only."

As I shoot down past the weirs on a rushing river and out into the brine of Lord Mayor Bay, the ocean has all the placidity of a calm before the storm. An eleven-foot Atlantic tide sucks and gurgles up against diorite cliff tapestries of orange and yellow lichens, clinging beside thick lime mats of moss. I am pulled down through salt-water rapids and out toward the gulf below the Parry Channel entrance to the Northwest Passage.

I paddle past migrating caribou, holding their racks high in the air as they funnel past ancient *Inuksuit* cairns and down into the bay, blood-eyed and snuffling beside me in the water. They emerge on the southern edge of the bay, panting and shaking off showers of water before disappearing south.

At that night's campsite, with no warning, while standing several feet outside the tent, Jimmy shoots three *tuktu* with the big rifle. I drop my macaroni and cheese dinner; my ears are ringing. Simond merely smiles and takes a last bite before rushing out to help Jimmy butcher the *tuktu*. They cover a hundred pounds of meat with boulders, for their return with an empty boat in the spring.

I wonder if it will be foolish to continue another day east. I miss my June, and I promised myself not to take any more chances. We will be married in just another month. But while studying the maps, I convince myself that I might still be able to somehow sneak through to Pelly Bay. Although I have essentially linked the tidal ranges of the world's two great oceans, I have yet to see an Eskimo curlew or come face-to-face with *Tôrnârssuk*.

The next morning Simond and Jimmy spend hours potting away at the big curious eyes of the ringed seal with their old, rusted .22 rifle. Their rounded heads appear, through my dizziness, like glistening brown stepping-stones across the ocean. I have never seen so many seals. Although *natiq* is the favorite food of the Netsilik, it is obvious that The People of Taloyoak rarely take the trouble to portage out here.

As Simond says, "Only *Tôrnârssuk* eat now."

Kees sits patiently in their boat, watching me paddle away into the distance as Jimmy fires dozens of rounds toward these shiny stepping-stones across the sea. Next to a whale tail–shaped iceberg, Jimmy finally puts a bullet through a seal's forehead. Simond motors over, and before the seal can sink, Jimmy grabs its rear flipper and drapes it over the transom, gushing blood and further encrusting their battered gear. Kees backs up to the stern, trying to keep his camera clean.

While Kees films the hunt, I manage to paddle twenty miles. I give icebergs wide berths in case they should roll, as frequent riflelike cracks and splashes attest. Also, polar bears keep cool by lying on these bergs. These tilting ships of ice now command half the ocean. As I paddle wearily through the sunset, blazing the sky and sea and ice into a great orange Popsicle, black wavelets begin to look like stealthy *Tôrnârssuk* noses.

That night, as seal boils in the pot, Jimmy explains that The People do not shoot or kill or get animals like *natiq*.

"We catch them," he clarifies. "To talk about it in any other way would be disrespectful."

"Why?" I ask.

Simond gives his son the answer in Inuktitut, while Jimmy replies, "Because the animals are giving up their lives to us, you know what I mean? They give up their lives to us."

The tent fills with a ghastly cloud of steam that smells of low tide along tropical clam beds. As I review my maps in the lantern light, trying to figure out how to cross exposed iceberg waters to Pelly Bay, I recall the Netsilik story of Kiviot, an ancient *Inuk* who set off on a vision quest alone in his kayak.

For months Kiviot battled storms and big waves. He was pulled far from home and loved ones, concentrating only on survival and the glory of crossing hundreds of miles through the Earth and Its Great Weather. Along the way, like a resurrection of Odysseus's vision quest, he was forced to battle and fornicate with giant insects. After taking too many risks, Kiviot fully understood what his life at home meant to him. A long-billed bird, which I would like to believe was the elusive Eskimo curlew, guided Kiviot back home in his kayak to the woman whom he intended to marry. It has come to my mind that Kiviot went home when the gods of the Arctic had spoken to him, rather than settle for any specific goal or destination.

Simond passes Kees and me a bowl filled with a steaming haunch of seal. "*Natiq* good." He motions us to eat.

Kees and I tentatively pick up the sliced meat, dripping with blood, and bite off small pieces that taste like a mix of undercooked beef and elastic lobster. I take another, larger bite. If I force myself not to smell the putrefied essence of old clams and sea mud, and if I visualize how this blubbery meat will help me sleep warm, *natiq* has a lot more to offer than mere sweetbread or chicken liver. But it will never be served in restaurants outside the Arctic.

Kees raises a flap to let more putrid steam out of the tent. Simond and Jimmy are licking their fingers, so I do the same. Then I ask the Oleekataliks if the famous Netsilik story of Kiviot's kayak trip has a moral.

"Jon," Jimmy explains patiently, wiping the ends of his crusted hair that dangled in his bowl, "Inuit stories have no morals; that is only what southerners want. A story is just what it is."

To offset his uncharacteristic seriousness, Jimmy tells us an apocryphal story, putting a modern-day spin on Inuit kayaking: "Just a few years ago two Netsilik Inuit who were not used to kayaking make a blubber fire in their kayaks to warm up. They lit the seal blubber on fire, and as their kayaks went up in flames, both of them sank to the bottom. When the priests bring their bodies back to Taloyoak, he warned us all, 'You can't have your kayak and heat it too.' " We all laugh. Yet it is an epiphanic moment for me. The Oleekataliks' self-deprecation—like that of so many other Inuit I have met over the last three years—has inadvertently shown me the specific grace of their culture: selflessness.

Simond abruptly leaves to drag the seal carcass fifty yards north from the tent. Then he ties Hot Dog up to the south. Behind our tent is a protective band of cliffs.

"*Tôrnârssuk* bait?" I ask Simond.

He lifts his eyebrows affirmatively. Simond doesn't want to shoot *Tôrnârssuk,* only to keep him away from the tent. When I ask if it would have been wiser not to shoot a seal in the first place, to avoid drawing in *Tôrnârssuk* with the smell, Simond seems insulted.

I walk back through the inky blackness with my shotgun slung tightly against my back. I can't decide whether or not to quit. If winter catches me between here and Pelly Bay, I could be locked into the ice like the frostbitten kayaker Don Starkell. While my heart says no, there is nothing in my head that says that I'm not capable of forging ahead.

I turn to the big dipper for direction, its cup pointing to the North Star, Polaris. At home in Colorado, I find it in the north, but here I locate it straight above, the cold breeze running down my throat as I gaze up into the heavens. This stationary star is supposed to be one hundred times bigger than the sun. I am gazing into distances that make all my own quandaries seem small by comparison.

Spinning around Polaris are the seven bright stars of the Big Dipper, forming part of Ursa Major, the Great Bear. I squint my eyes to see the handle as an imaginary polar bear tail, the cup as its torso and another half dozen dimmer stars as legs and muzzle extending west and north. Inuit too saw this Great Bear in the stars. Long before the time of transatlantic navigation, The People used Polaris for bearings while traveling. They believed that the stars were holes into the afterworld, and if people up there were moving around and the stars flickered, as they do now, it meant that snow would be knocked down through the holes. The other side of the stars held all their ancestors and the hunted animals, while the most powerful beings, such as polar bears or shamans, could fly in and out of the stars, commuting from one world into the next.

They believed that a falling star (*anoktok*) was star shit. I have stood here on the dome above camp for a half an hour, bouncing from one foot to another to stay warm. The stars have held their course, without falling, spinning almost imperceptibly around Polaris, pulsating with light. Ursa Minor, the Little Dipper surrounding Polaris, is pale and whitish; Ursa Major is blinking the outline of its body.

I know that the concept of *anoktok* truly encompassed Inuit theology because of a French anthropologist a half century ago. The Frenchman picked up off the ground an elegant inch-long polar bear, carved from shiny ivory. The piece held a honey brown patina of age. When he got back to the village and asked the first *Inuk* where the ancient work of art had come from, the elder immediately replied, "*Uluriak anoktok* ["star shit fallen from the sky"]."

Anoktok was no joke. Inuit believed that whatever came down from above held such otherworldly power that you could only marvel at it. The intricately carved bear, posed as if flying through the air, with its long and birdlike neck, was not only beautiful but a reminder from the afterworld of what this great being was fully capable of. The "one who gives power" could just as easily fly back and forth from its home beyond the stars as it could swim like a whale or run like a caribou.

I am shivering when I return to the tent. That night we all take turns peeking out the flap for *Tôrnârssuk*. For once Simond's snoring has stopped; he is lying awake listening for footfalls outside the tent. I am certain that Hot Dog doesn't sleep any more than we do.

September 5 dawns with a frost that cakes the ground with hard, opaque ice. I go for a walk to warm up, passing paw prints twice the size of my own large feet. Puddles have frozen solid. Even a half mile back from the shore I can feel the sea ice refrigerating the land. These shores of the Gulf of Boothia are glacial and desolate; the stony ground holds no ancient villages and is even avoided by *tuktu. Nanuq*—or should I say *Tôrnârssuk*—thrives here.

Walking back, I catch myself after losing my balance, planting my hands on cold stone to prevent hitting my head. A stone's throw from camp, Simond is nervously scouting with the rifle slung on his shoulder. He isn't looking for *tuktu,* because there aren't any.

As I push the kayak in for the day, wondering how to make it to Pelly, the wind is already frothing the sea. Out on the water, no one can stay warm in the Lund, so they motor ahead of me, then jump out and warm themselves by running in place until I catch up. I paddle as fast as I can move my arms, but I still lose the circulation in my fingers and toes. Stars flood my vision if I don't breathe slowly and regularly. I humor myself by thinking of this dizziness as *anoktok* in my eyes.

Simond offers me a ride and gestures back to Taloyoak, pointing to the ice pack blowing in from the open gulf. I ask him what he would do if he

Sun parhelion above me

were I, but the question is so nonsensical to his way of thinking that he only shrugs in reply. Above our heads a rainbow parhelion circles the clouded-over sun, showing moisture in the sky. Everything feels wrong, like the coming of some unfathomable disaster. From our small cove in the bottom of the Gulf of Boothia, looking out over the brown, burnished domes of the Astronomical Society Islands, I am torn. I don't know whether to continue or turn back. My head says go. My heart says no.

In the midst of this indecision, Jimmy points east to a sleeping polar bear. He hands me the binoculars. It looks like a hummock of dirty snow. Now my heart is pounding.

This might be just the sign I'm looking for.

Jimmy and Simond promise to let me go first, so they won't scare it away. As I run over and jump into the kayak, Hot Dog is cowering at the bottom of the Lund.

I shortcut beneath a long arching iceberg, stopping to catch meltwater in my mouth. From somewhere behind, a big berg collapses with another rifle shot explosion and splash.

I paddle straight out into open water and steer east toward *Tôrnârssuk*. As I crawl closer against the current, it dawns on me that I might have been asking for trouble by naming the kayak *Swims with Bears*.

I am ready to turn in case *Tôrnârssuk* should jump into the water and challenge me. I am mostly sure that I can outpaddle her (the curved face and slim profile show her sex), but I don't care to be given the chance. From half a football field away, she sits up and stares at me. The young female's neck and leg fur, gone piano key yellow with seal oil and sunshine, ripples in the wind. A dead seal lies at her feet. I paddle closer still.

From twenty-five yards off, she jumps into the water, swimming in circles, obviously unwilling to come after me. I'm relieved; my gun is correctly stowed away. I take care not to approach any closer to the seal carcass. I also avoid looking directly at *Tôrnârssuk* or speaking to her. While cupping and breathing into my hands to warm them, I trust she doesn't see it as weakness.

Looking east, I see the impassable ice pack blowing toward us. After I don gloves, my hands are still cold. Even wearing all my clothing—long underwear and pile jackets inside my dry suit—I can no longer stay warm. The ocean will soon slush up into grease ice.

Looking inside my head, I realize that the Northwest Passage has shown me that I don't care to be alone, because the richest parts of the trip were those moments when animals or Inuit or June reeled me back to lucidity. Even my ego has been supplanted by something more graceful and whole: a connection to the earth and its animals that I rarely experience. If I used to be brave, I am now craven. Never mind Pelly Bay. I am all but shivering.

Like Kiviot, I am ready to abandon the journey and go home to June. If there has been a single lesson to all of my efforts, it is just this: No one is meant to be alone.

Looking west, I have paddled, sailed, skied and dogsledded twenty-two hundred miles over ten months. Others could do it faster and go farther than I, but continuing to Pelly might be the last and most foolhardy act of my life. I know in a flash—more clearly than watching the stars, or trying to forecast a storm—that my journey has ended. There is nothing factual about this decision. Instead I feel the weight of risks—sailing across rough bays, being alone for weeks on end, capsizing in Franklin Bay, losing my kayak, blacking out, paddling through storms and being chased by bears— that have lifted me to this moment of truth with the polar bear. I have been turned back from summits before, with regret, but I don't feel disappointed here. I had schemed to find a physical destination to end my journey, but what I had dreamed of all along was a spiritual goal: the Great Bear. While backpaddling circles alongside the circling *Tôrnârssuk,* I feel empowered.

Tôrnârssuk clambers onto her ice floe. She senses that I am no threat. Ice water pours off her glossy fur like rain from a roof. Since I have never been this close to a wild polar bear, I am amazed to see that she holds her tor-pedolike head a couple of feet out from her body with a long neck—the effect is remarkably similar to that of a swan preparing to fly. Then she changes her mind and sits back on her haunches, sufficiently cooled off

Tôrnârssuk swimming toward me in the Gulf of Boothia

from her swim to appraise me, a mere boy ending his vision quest. She lofts her jet black muzzle to reach across the seawater and smell my clammy seal breath and acrid sweat and moldy nylon and, I hope, lack of aggression.

I am confronting the animal of both my dreams and my nightmares, an animal that has reared above me in the night sky for all my life. It would not be unheard of for this bear to shuck me out of my kayak, crack open my skull with her teeth and then pull me up alongside her seal dessert.

Yet I want to believe that *Tôrnârssuk* knows I have come only to gaze upon her. I have eaten the seal and the whale that she eats. Instead of a rifle, I lift only a camera. Somewhere between us in the still air is the indelible knowledge, almost a power, that we are the same, neither prey to each other nor preying on each other. She spreads her jaws, briefly, all snow-white teeth and gray gums. We keep our faces averted from each other. She doesn't hiss; I put down my camera.

She is implacable, as regal and self-sufficient as I had once wanted to be. She is alone on the isolated roof of the continent, attuned to the movement of all beings, adept at crossing land or water, undeterred by the cold and unafraid. She is merely curious about Arctic darkness and mysterious humming and steep-sided seas—all those things that unhinge me. There is something else too, something all knowing and alien about her, as though the ancients might have been right all along.

My quest has ended. I feel my own fragility—being cold and indecisive and so helplessly mortal—more than ever before. By envisioning this bear for the last three years, I have arrived in front of it only to find that I am terrified.

It is time to spin back west. I'm ready to go home. But there is still something left undone. I think of all the elders' advice and know that in parting I have to give a final gesture of respect. I finger the polar bear teeth in my pocket, then close my eyes and drop my head into a deep bow toward *Tôrnârssuk*. I bow out of humility. I bow for all the mastery that has got me through, and I also bow for luck. I keep my head down against the spray deck, clutching the gunwales for a few seconds more to let all the thoughts clear my head.

When I sit up again, a great calm comes over me. Seeing *Tôrnârssuk* is all that I ever wanted. I am going home.

As the wind comes into the cove, I need to look down and concentrate on keeping upright in the chop, balancing my paddle blades left and then right. As I look back up, *Tôrnârssuk* leaps nearly thirty feet off the ice floe onto dry land. My vision has always been normal, but maybe I am still a bit feverish or my tears have blurred things: I have the impression that her shaggy paws are not touching the earth. It occurs to me that once you reach that destination you have fought for and dreamed of for so long, perhaps your goal is as illusory and unattainable as an ice mirage. I'm also ready to believe that it's something about the Arctic itself, long understood by Inuit and so powerful that it cannot be rationally explained.

I watch, ever carefully now, holding my breath so I don't miss a step.

After her quick rush to shore, she runs across a jumble of loose boulders and tidal pools that somehow hold still—no noise, no clicking, not even a splash. Right before my eyes, the legs of *Tôrnârssuk* go blurry, her fur softens, and like a star reclaiming its own unearthly and pallid beauty, she takes flight into the vast Arctic.

Appendix A: *Wildlife Observations*

During three summers of solo travel I had a privileged perspective on animals. Most species are not preyed upon from the water, so by quietly kayaking along the shore at several miles per hour, I was able to approach elusive birds and fearless bears. I was able to contemplate my surroundings for hours, even weeks, at a time without interruption. One of the primal delights here was in training my eyes to detect animals by distant blurs of movement or color disparities against the landscape. Every turn brought the promise of meeting a new bird, sleeping seals or migrating caribou.

Those animals that I could not draw near to were brought into full view with a pair of powerful waterproof binoculars, then duly recorded with a 100–400 mm image-stabilizer lens that allowed me to expose sharp images on choppy seas or in low light.

The following bird and mammal lists begin with the least commonly sighted species. Notes include a variety of brief comments from my journals, including location, sounds, behavior and Inuit/Latin names and meanings for the species.

Birds

On my journey I saw a total of fifty-six species. An obsessive birder could have counted twice this number, but I was more content watching than identifying. Most of the birds are brief migrants; only a few winter in the Arctic. Although I had hoped to see an Eskimo curlew, the bird might be extinct. A highlight of my trip was sighting the great gyrfalcon, which numbers fewer than five thousand throughout North America.

Common Name / *Latin Name* / Notes

Horned lark / *Eremophilia alpestris* / Saw one inside abandoned Alaska building.

King eider / *Somateria spectabilis* / Male seen alongside wreck of Amundsen's *Maud*.

Wilson's warbler / *Wilsonia pusilla* / One singing along ocean bluffs in Alaska.

Merlin / *Falco columbarius* / Seen hunting common eider chicks.

Northern harrier / *Circus cyaneus* / In the Mackenzie River delta.

Whimbrel / *Numenius phaeopus* / Distinctive down-curled bill.

Spotted sandpiper / *Tringa macularia* / Mackenzie River local.

Golden eagle / *Aquila chrysaetos* / Seen north of known range, soaring in Franklin Bay.

Black-bellied plover / *Pluvialis squatarola* / Nesting on Parry Peninsula, often heard others.

Gyrfalcon / *Falco rusticolus* / An unforgettable and powerful, pale flier; saw several.

Red phalarope / *Phalaropus fulicaria* / My one sighting was of more than a thousand, migrating on Flaxman Island.

Lincoln's sparrow / *Melospiza lincolnii* / Not commonly an Arctic bird.

Thayer's gull / *Larus thayeri* / Saw several in Spence Bay, eating char with glaucous gulls.

Sabine's gull / *Xema sabini* / Mingling with colonies of nesting arctic terns.

Black guillemot / *Cepphus grille* / Inuktitut: *pitsiulaaq*. Nests at Herschel Island church.

Pacific loon / *Gavia pacifica* / Seen usually in pairs along Alaskan waters.

Lesser yellowlegs / *Tringa flavipes* / Conspicuous in Mackenzie River delta.

Pintail / *Anas acuta* / On Mackenzie River only.

Spotted sandpiper / *Actitis macularia* / Obvious underparts, seen on Mackenzie River.

White-winged scoter / *Melanitta fusca* / Distinctive whistling wings overhead.

Bald eagle / *Haliaeetus leucocephalus* / Saw several north of range, fishing on rivers.

Surf scoter / *Melanitta perspicillata* / In distant flocks out at sea.

Red-breasted merganser / *Mergus serrator* / Frequently mingling with common eiders.

Snowy owl / *Nyctea scandiaca* / Called *ukpik* by Inuit; not uncommon.

Black brant / *Branta bernicla negriaans* / Inuktitut: *nirliq*. Nesting on Anderson River, and often seen flying overhead.

Common merganser / *Mergus merganser* / Frequently seen, far north from its range.

White-rumped sandpiper / *Calidris fuscicollis* / Distinctive *cheet* call; uncommon.

Herring gull / *Larus argentatus* / Not nearly as frequently seen as the glaucous gull.

Semipalmated plover / *Charadrius semipalmatus* / Its *chuu-we* cry is unmistakable.

Long-tailed jaeger / *Stercorarius longicaudus* / Inuktitut: *isunngaq*. Throughout Arctic.

Lesser golden plover / *Pluvialis dominica* / Call like semipalmated; fakes broken wing.

Bank swallow / *Riparia riparia* / Mostly on warm river deltas darting among insects.

Solitary sandpiper / *Tringa solitaria* / Seen alone, as its name implies.

Sandhill crane / *Grus canadensis* / Hard to approach, but conspicuous and noisy.

Rough-legged hawk / *Buteo lagopus* / Frequently seen nesting along coast.

Red-necked phalarope / *Phalaropus lobatus* / Fond of bathing in tundra ponds.

Common redpoll / *Carduelis flammea* / Not as common as name and supposed range.

Greater white-fronted goose / *Anser albifrons* / Often seen with goslings on muddy shores.

Ruddy turnstone / *Arenaria interpres* / Common and seldom solitary.

Parastic jaeger / *Stercorarius parsiticus* / Seen in colonies on islands in Queen Maud Gulf.

Peregrine falcon / *Falco peregrinus* / Often seen hunting ducks. Throughout Arctic.

Yellow-billed loon / *Gavia adamsi* / Discoverer: Edward Adams, Franklin searcher.

Hoary redpoll / *Carduelis hornemanni* / Common.

Tundra swan / *Cygnus columbianus* / Inuktitut: *kugyuk*.

Raven / *Corvus corax* / Believed to be messengers from the spirit world and of bad news.

Red-throated loon / *Gavia stellata* / Only loon that can take off from tundra.

Rock ptarmigan / *Lagopus mutus* / Its stomach is considered a delicacy eaten raw.

Common eider / *Somateria mollissima* / Female barely distinguishable from king female.

Snow bunting / *Plectrophenox nivalis* / Inuit believe that its arrival shows spring has come.

Least sandpiper / *Calidris minutilla* / Prolific.

Arctic tern / *Sterna paradisaea* / Most aggressive Arctic bird; Inuktitut: *imiqqutailat*.

Glaucous gull / *Larus hyperboreus* / Inuktitut: *nauyaq* is the name for gulls in general.

Old-squaw / *Clagula hyemalis* / Inuktitut: *kivgaluk.* Saw most everywhere in Arctic.

Canada goose / *Branta canadensis* / Inuktitut: *uluagullik.* Prolific.

Ross' goose / *Chen rossii* / Saw thousands, only in Queen Maud Gulf.

Snow goose / *Chen caerulescens* / Saw tens of thousands lesser and greater.

Mammals

The animals that I did not see on this journey were the bowhead whale, the narwhal and the wolverine. Most of the large land animals follow the caribou herds, and once these herds migrate south in late September, only muskoxen remain.

Common Name / *Latin Name* / Notes

Wolf / *Canis lupus* / Inuktitut: *amaruq.* Rarely seen, because its fur is valuable.

Arctic hare / *Lepus timidus* / Uncommonly seen.

Arctic lemming / *Dicrostonyx torquatus* / Swimming offshore in Coronation Gulf.

Arctic fox / *Alopex lagopus* / Seldom seen, probably because of rabies and overtrapping.

Bearded seal / *Erignathus barbatus* / Inuktitut: *ugyuk.* A playful animal.

Polar bear / *Ursus maritimus* / The three I saw were curious, perhaps, but not aggressive.

Red fox / *Vulpes vulpes* / Seen only in Alaska.

Grizzly / *Ursus arctos* / The barren ground grizzly is remarkably aggressive and prolific.

Beluga / *Delphinapterus leucas* / Seen in western Arctic, then again in Spence Bay.

Muskox / *Ovibos moschatus* / Rarely seen alone.

Ringed seal / *Phoca hispida* / Inuktitut: *natiq.* Much shyer than bearded seal.

Caribou / *Rangifer tarandus* / Aggregate herds as large as three hundred thousand (by Bathurst Inlet).

Ground squirrel / *Spermophilus undulatus* / Its call, *sik-sik,* is also its Inuit name.

Appendix B: *Canadian Arctic Cultures Timeline*

ARCTIC CULTURES		OUTSIDE WORLD
Nunavut/Inuvialuit Agreement (1999/1984)—	A.D. 2000	—(1907) Amundsen's first transit of NW Passage
Tuberculosis/diseases (1900s)—		—(1847) Franklin dies
	1800	—European–Inuit contact in Arctic
200-year Little Ice Age begins—	1600	—Matchlock rifle invented
		—(1492) Columbus reaches New World
Kayakers reach Scotland (1420)—	1400	—Bubonic plague
	1200	—European Crusades
Kayaks/dogsleds introduced—	1000	—(1000) Leif Ericsson reaches New World
	800	—Dark Ages of Europe
	600	
	400	
	A.D. 200	
	0	—Copper Age in Europe
Toggle harpoons—	B.C. 200	800 B.C.–A.D. 400 **Romans**
Stone/ivory carvings—		—Bronze, gold sculptures
Umiaks (skin whaleboats)—	400	1450–100 B.C. **Greeks**
Snow *iglus*—		—Belief in Arktikós, Land of the Great Bear, inhabited by northern Hyperboreans
Rectangular stone/sod houses—	600	
	800	—Homer writes *Odyssey*
		—Galleys (wooden warships)
	1000	
	1200	
Chipped stone drill bits,	1400	3000 B.C.–A.D. 4 **Egyptians**
with wood/bone handles—	1600	
Dogs used for hunting—		—Horses introduced
Bows and arrows—	1800	
	2000	—Shipbuilding
Skin tents with stone partitions—	B.C. 2200	—Domesticated cats
		—Pyramids
		—3000 B.C. Mesopotamia invents wheel

Inuit (Thule until 1600s)

Paleo-Eskimos Dorset (*Tuniiq*)

Arctic Small Tools Tradition (*Pre-Dorset*)

All dates are plus or minus 200 years, depending on Arctic region.

Appendix C: *Inuktitut Syllabics*

Inuit language is written with these symbols representing the different language sounds:

	i	ii	u	uu	a	aa	
	△	△̇	▷	▷̇	◁	◁̇	
	i	ii	u	uu	a	aa	
p	∧	∧̇	>	>̇	<	<̇	<
	pi	pii	pu	puu	pa	paa	p
t	∩	∩̇	⊃	⊃̇	⊂	⊂̇	⊂
	ti	tii	tu	tuu	ta	taa	t
k	ᑭ	ᑭ̇	ᑯ	ᑯ̇	ᑲ	ᑳ	ᒃ
	ki	kii	ku	kuu	ka	kaa	k
g	ᒋ	ᒌ	ᒍ	ᒎ	ᒐ	ᒑ	ᒡ
	gi	gii	gu	guu	ga	gaa	g
m	ᒥ	ᒦ	ᒧ	ᒨ	ᒪ	ᒫ	ᒻ
	mi	mii	mu	muu	ma	maa	m
n	ᓂ	ᓃ	ᓄ	ᓅ	ᓇ	ᓈ	ᓐ
	ni	nii	nu	nuu	na	naa	n
s/h	ᓯ	ᓰ	ᓱ	ᓲ	ᓴ	ᓵ	ᔅ
	si/hi	sii/hii	su/hu	suu/huu	sa/ha	saa/haa	s/h
l	ᓕ	ᓖ	ᓗ	ᓘ	ᓚ	ᓛ	ᓪ
	li	lii	lu	luu	la	laa	l
j	ᔨ	ᔩ	ᔪ	ᔫ	ᔭ	ᔮ	ᔾ
	ji	jii	ju	juu	ja	jaa	j
v	ᕕ	ᕖ	ᕗ	ᕘ	ᕙ	ᕚ	ᕝ
	vi	vii	vu	vuu	va	vaa	v
r	ᕆ	ᕇ	ᕈ	ᕉ	ᕋ	ᕌ	ᕐ
	ri	rii	ru	ruu	ra	raa	r
q	ᕿ	ᖀ	ᖁ	ᖂ	ᖃ	ᖄ	ᖅ
	qi	qii	qu	quu	qa	qaa	q
ng	ᖏ	ᖑ̇	ᖑ	ᖒ	ᖓ	ᖔ	ᖕ
	ngi	ngii	ngu	nguu	nga	ngaa	ng
ɫ	ᖠ	ᖡ	ᖢ	ᖣ	ᖤ	ᖥ	ᖦ
	ɫi	ɫii	ɫu	ɫuu	ɫa	ɫaa	ɫ

Appendix D: *Differing Inuktitut Dialects*

The Lord's Prayer in Syllabics (across the Arctic)

(9) ᑏᒪᐃᒪᑦ ᐃᒪᖕᖓᓕ ᑕᖅᑫ ᑐᒃᓯᐊᓕᖀᖕᒐᑦᓯ ᑐᒃᓯᐊᕐᑐᒃᓴᐅᕗᓯ:
ᐊᑖᑕᕗᑦ ᖅᑭᓚᖕᒦᑐᑎᑦ: ᐊᖕᒋᓂᖅᐸᖕᒍᓃᑦ ᐃᒃᐱᒋᔭᐅᑦ –
ᑎᐊᕐᓕ;
(10) ᐊᑕᓂᐅᕚᑦ ᖅᑮᓚᐅᕐᓕ; ᐱᔪᒪᔭᐃᑦ ᐊᑐᖅᑕᐅᓕ ᓄᓇᒥ
ᓲᖅᓗ ᖅᑭᓚᖕᒥ ᐊᑐᖅᑕᖕ ᒪᑦ.
(11) ᐅᕝᓗᒥ ᓂᖅᑭᒃ ᓴᑉᑎᓐᓂᒃ ᑐᓂᓯᕙᑎᒍᑦ.
(12) ᑕᒻᒪᖅ ᓂᑉᑎᓐᓂᒃ ᐃᓱᒪᒃᑲᖅᑲᕙᕆᔪᖕᓃᖅ ᓗᑕ ᓯᒪᐅᑎᑎᒍᑦ,
ᓲᖅᓗ ᐃᓘᖅᑲᑎᑉᑕ ᐅᕗᑉᑎᖕ ᓐ ᓄᑦ ᑕᒻᒪᖅᓂᕆᑦ.
ᓰᒻᒪᐅᑎᔭᖀᖕᒐᑉᑎᒍᑦ ᐃᓱᒪᖅᑲᕙᕆᔪᓐᓂᖅᐸᒃ ᑲᑦᑎᒍᑦ.
(13) ᐆᒃ ᑐᖅᑕᐅᑎᑦᑏᓕᑎᒍᑦ ᐊᔪᖅᑕᑉᑎᒍᑦ, ᓴᐳᑎᑎᒍᓕ
ᓭᑖᓇᓯᒥᑦ.

The Lord's Prayer in English (known throughout the Arctic)

9. Our father, which art in heaven: hallowed be thy name.
10. Thy kingdom come. Thy will be done on earth as it is in heaven.
11. Give us this day our daily bread.
12. And forgive us our debts, as we forgive our debtors.
13. And lead us not into temptation, but deliver us from evil. For thine is the kingdom and the power and the glory for ever and ever. Amen.

The Lord's Prayer in Eastern Inuktitut

10 Nâlegauvît kailaule. Pijomajat piniataule nuname sorlo kilangme.
11 Uvlome piksaptingnik tunitjivigitigut.
12 Idluinivut issumagijungnaikit, sorlo uvagut idluitulivigijivut issumagijunganaivigigaptigik.
13 Oktortaulungnermut pitinata. Piulitigulle ajortomit. Nâlegaunek, pitsartunerlo, ânanaunerlo pigigangne issokangitomut. Amen.

The Lord's Prayer in Copper Inuit Inuktitut (which includes MacKenzie River)

Imaatun kengakpagluhi.
Angutikput kilangmiitutin.
Atkin nagugiyauli.
Atanguvin kaili,
Ihumatin taimaliullit nunami kilangmi-iliyutun.
Uvlumi nekikhaptingnik aituktigut
Huinekutiptingniglu ihumagiyunaeglutin,
Huinekiyigiyavut ihumalutigihuigaptigit,
Uktuktaunegmun hivulliuktailuta tupilagminlu annautitigut.

The Lord's Prayer in Iñupiaq (Alaska)

9 Anaayyuscitchaiasii inna. Aapavut qilangmiittuatiin, iñuich qiksigilisin.
10 Ilivich atanniqsimakkich iñupayaat. Iñupayaat pilich pisuutignik nunami, qilangmi pisuutignik piruatun.
11 Aitchuqtigut uvlupak niqiksraptingnik.
12 Suli suliqutigingaikkich itqaumayumiñaigglugich piluutivut, Uvagat-tauq suliqutigingaiggmatun itqaumayumiñaiqtlugich tamatkua piluk-siruat uvaptingnun.
13 Suli iktligutchaktinniaktinnatigut, annautilutalu piluktuamiñ. Qanuq ilivich umialgurutin suangngatiqaqtlutin kamanautiqaqtlutillu isuitchu-amun. Amen.

Bibliography

Because the literature of the North is vast, this bibliography should in no way be considered comprehensive. It mainly includes works of nonfiction. These books, articles, films and Internet pages constitute the research—in addition to my observations while traveling—that this book is based upon. The information from many of these works has informed my narrative, often without direct quotes. While my book often names authors and titles with original ideas or cultural insight, it rarely mentions the historical works below. The list also shows some inspirations for my own journey.

Adney, Tappan, and Howard I. Chappelle. *The Bark Canoes and Skin Boats of North America*. Washington, D.C.: Smithsonian Institution, 1964.

"AIDS and HIV in Canada," a report from Health Canada, Ottawa, 1998.

Alunik, Ishmael. *Call Me Ishmael: Memories of an Inuvialuk Elder*. Inuvik: Kolausok, 1998.

Ambrose, Stephen E. *Undaunted Courage: Meriwether Lewis, Thomas Jefferson, and the Opening of the American West*. New York: Simon & Schuster, 1997.

Amundsen, Roald E. G. *The Northwest Passage. Being the Record of a Voyage of Exploration of the Ship "Gjoa," 1903–1907,* vols. I and II. New York: E. P. Dutton, 1908.

Anawak, J. "Inuit Perceptions of the Past." In *Who Needs the Past,* ed. R. Layton. London: Unwin & Hyman, 1988, chap. 3.

Anderson, Sarah. "Obituary: Duncan Pryde," *The Independent* (London), December 30, 1997.

Anderssen, Erin. "Nunavut to Be a Welfare Case," *Globe and Mail,* June 5, 1998.

Arima, E. Y. *Inuit Kayaks in Canada: A Review of Historical Records and Construction*. Ottawa: Canadian Museum of Civilization, 1987.

Babcock, William H. "Eskimo Long Distance Voyages," *American Anthropologist* 15 (1913): 138–41.

Baker, Dr. Robin. *The Mystery of Migration*. London: Macdonald Futura Books, 1980.

Barrett, Andrea. *The Voyage of the Narwhal*. New York: Norton, 1999.

Béland, Pierre. *Beluga: A Farewell to Whales*. New York: Lyons & Burford, 1996.

Berger, Thomas. *Northern Frontier, Northern Homeland.* Report of the Mackenzie Valley Pipeline Inquiry. Ottawa: Supply and Services Canada, 1977.

Bergman, Brian. "Dark Days for the Inuit: Tuberculosis Outbreaks Revive Memories of an Earlier Epidemic," *Maclean's* 109:10 (1996): 66–68.

Berton, Pierre. *The Arctic Grail: The Quest for the Northwest Passage and the North Pole 1918–1909.* Toronto: McClelland & Stewart, 1988.

Bethune-Johnson, D., D. C. G. Conner, and E. Elias. *Our Arctic Way of Life: The Copper Inuit.* Scarborough, Ontario: Prentice Hall, 1986.

Bielawski, Ellen. "Dual Perceptions of the Past: Archeology and Inuit Culture." In *Conflict in the Archeology of Living Traditions,* ed. Robert Layton. London: Unwin & Hyman, 1989, 228–36.

Binney, George. *The Eskimo Book of Knowledge.* London: Hudson's Bay Company, 1931.

Boas, Franz. *The Central Eskimo.* U.S. Bureau of American Ethnology, Sixth Annual Report, 1884–1885, Washington, D.C.: Government Printing Office, 1888.

Bockstoce, John. *Arctic Passages: A Unique Small Boat Voyage in the Great Northern Waterway.* New York: Hearst Marine Books, 1991.

———. *Whales, Ice, and Men: The History of Whaling in the Western Arctic.* Seattle: University of Washington Press, 1986.

Bourgeois, Annette. "Inuit Carving 'Industry' Ground Down to Dust," *Nunatsiaq News,* September 24, 1998.

———. "Kugluktuk Residents Reeling from the Shock," *Nunatsiaq News,* April 1, 1998.

Briggs, Jean. *Never in Anger: Portrait of an Eskimo Family.* Cambridge, Mass.: Harvard University Press, 1970.

Brody, Hugh. *Living Arctic: Hunters of the Canadian North.* London: Faber and Faber, 1987.

———. *The People's Land: Inuit, Whites and the Eastern Arctic.* Vancouver: Douglas & McIntyre, 1991.

Brower, Charles D. *Fifty Years Below Zero: A Lifetime of Adventure in the Far North.* London: Robert Hale, 1944.

Burch, Ernest S., Jr. "Muskox and Man in the Central Canadian Subarctic, 1689–1974," *Arctic* 30:3 (1977): 135–54.

Calamai, Peter. "Chemical Fallout Hurts Inuit Babies: Researchers Link Vulnerability to Prenatal Exposure," *Toronto Star,* March 22, 2000.

"A Canadian Territory Celebrates Its Creation; but Nunavut Already Faces Social Problems," *International Herald Tribune,* April 2, 1999.

Carpenter, Edmund. *Eskimo Realities.* New York: Holt, Rinehart and Winston, 1973.

Chance, Nancy-Fogel. "Commentary," *Arctic* 47:4 (1994).

Chance, Norman A. "Alaska Eskimo Modernization." In *Handbook of N.A. Indians,* vol. 5: *Arctic,* ed. D. Damas. Washington, D.C.: Smithsonian Institution, 1984, 646–56.

———. *The Inupiat and Arctic Alaska: An Ethnography of Development.* New York: Harcourt Brace, 1990.

Condon, Richard G., Peter Collings, and George Wenzel. "The Best Part of Life: Subsistence Hunting, Ethnicity, and Economic Adaptation Among Young Adult Inuit Males," *Arctic* 48:1 (1995): 31–46.

———. *The Northern Copper Inuit: A History.* Norman: University of Oklahoma Press, 1996.

Cookman, Scott. *Ice Blink: Sir John Franklin's Last Polar Expedition.* New York: John Wiley & Sons, 2000.

Courcol, Christine. "A Frozen Land Is Born in Canada: Nunavut, the Size of Western Europe, Has 25,000 Residents," *USA Today,* April 1, 1999.

Cowper, David Scott. *Northwest Passage Solo.* London: Seafarer Books, 1993.

Crantz, David. *The History of Greenland: Including an Account of the Mission Carried on by the United Brearen in That Country.* 2 vols. London: Longman, Hurst, Rees, Orme & Brown, 1820.

Delgado, James P. *Across the Top of the World: The Quest for the Northwest Passage.* New York: Checkmark Books, 1999.

DePalma, Anthony. "A New State for Inuit: Frigid but Optimistic," *New York Times,* January 29, 1999.

———. "New Capital Struggles with Boom," *New York Times,* April 1, 1999.

Dewailly, Eric, Pierre Ayotte, Suzanne Bruneau, et al. "Susceptibility to Infections and Immune Status in Inuit Infants Exposed to Organochlorines," *Environmental Health Perspectives* 108:3 (2000): 205–12.

Diamond, Jared. *Guns, Germs, and Steel: The Fates of Human Societies.* New York: Norton, 1998.

Dorais, Louis-Jacques. "Inuit Identity in Canada," *Folk* 30 (1988): 23–31.

Draper, H. H. "The Aboriginal Eskimo Diet in Modern Perspective," *American Anthropologist* 79:2 (1977): 309–16.

Duffy, R. Quinn. *The Road to Nunavut: The Progress of the Eastern Arctic Inuit Since the Second World War.* Montreal: McGill-Queen's University Press, 1988.

Eastcott, John. "Still Eskimo, Still Free: The Inuit of Umingmaktok," *National Geographic,* November 1977, 624–47.

Elliot, Ian. "Ex-IRC Execs Back in Court in July," Northern News Services, May 1, 1998.

———. "Healing the Survivors," Northern News Services, April 17, 1998.

Finnie, Richard S. *Lure of the North*. Philadelphia: David McKay, 1940.

————. "Stefansson's Mystery," *North/Nord,* November–December 1978, 2–7.

First Nations and Inuit Community Youth Solvent Survey and Study. Vernon, B.C.: Kaweionnehta Human Resource Group, 1993.

First Nations and Inuit Health Programs—Alcohol and Drug Abuse. Health Canada: http://www.hc-sc.gc.ca/msb/fnihp/drug_e.htm.

FitzGerald, J. M., L. Wang, and R. K. Elwood. "Tuberculosis: 13. Control of the Disease Among Aboriginal People in Canada," *Canadian Medical Association Journal* 162:2 (2000): 351–55.

Flaherty, Robert. *Nanook of the North*. A 1922 documentary film about Inuit hunters. New York: Kino International Corp., 1988.

Floyd, Timothy. "Bear-Inflicted Human Injury and Fatality," *Wilderness and Environmental Medicine* 10 (1999): 75–87.

Foote, Don. "Remarks on Eskimo Sealing and the Harp Seal Controversy," *Arctic* 20:4 (1967): 267–68.

Fraker, Mark. "Status and Harvest of the Mackenzie Stock of White Whales," *Thirtieth Report of the International Whaling Commission* 30 (1979): 451–58.

Francis, Daniel. *Arctic Chase*. St. John's, Newfoundland: Breakwater Books, 1984.

————. *Discovery of the North*. Edmonton: Hurtig, 1986.

Franklin, Sir John. *Narrative of a Journey to the Shores of the Polar Sea in the Years 1819–22*. London: John Murray, 1824.

————. *Narrative of a Second Expedition to the Shores of the Polar Sea in the Years 1819–22*. Rutland, Vt.: Charles E. Tuttle Co., 1971.

Freeman, Milton M. R. "Polar Bears and Whales: Contrasts in International Wildlife Regimes," *Issues in the North* 1:40 (1994): 1–8.

————. "Social and Ecologic Analysis of Systematic Female Infanticide Among the Netsilik Eskimo," *American Anthropologist* 73:5 (1971): 1011–18.

Freuchen, Peter. *Book of the Eskimos*. New York: Ballantine, 1983.

Friesen, T. Max, and Charles D. Arnold. "Zooarcheology of a Focal Resource: Dietary Importance of Beluga Whales to the Precontact Mackenzie Inuit," *Arctic* 48:1 (1995): 22–30.

George, Jane. "Global Warming, Inbreeding Threaten Nunavut Muskoxen," *Nunatsiaq News,* April 14, 2000.

————. "How to Stop the Spread of Tuberculosis," *Nunatsiaq News,* April 23, 1998.

Gollop, J. B., T. W. Barry, and E. H. Iversen. "Eskimo Curlew: A Vanishing Species?," Saskatchewan *Natural History Society Special Publication,* no. 17 (1986): http://www.npwrc.usgs.gov/resource/othrdata/curlew/curlew.htm.

Halifax, Terry. "A Widow's Wisdom: Survivor of Triple Murder/Suicide Offers Advice to Government," Northern News Services, April 19, 1999.

———. "Coroner's Report Slams Government Inaction: Says Triple Murder/Suicide Was Preventable," Northern News Services, April 5, 1999.

Hall, Sam. *The Fourth World: The Heritage of the Arctic and Its Destruction.* New York: Vintage, 1988.

Harper, Kenn. "Duncan Pryde—An Appreciation," *Nunatsiaq News,* November 21, 1997.

———. *Give Me My Father's Body: The Life of Minik, the New York Eskimo,* 2d ed. South Royalton, Vt.: Steerforth Press, 2000.

———. "Writing in Inuktitut: An Historical Perspective," *Inuktitut,* September 1983, 3–35.

Harper, Ray. *Coppermine: Consequences of Contact with the Outside.* National Film Board of Canada, 1992. A documentary film about tuberculosis in Kugluktuk.

Harwood, Lois A. "Distribution and Abundance of Beluga Whales in the Mackenzie Estuary, Southeast Beaufort Sea, and West Amundsen Gulf During Late July 1992," *Canadian Journal of Fisheries and Aquatic Sciences* 53:10 (1996): 2262–73.

Herscovici, Alan. "Forgotten Story: The Impact of 'Animal-Rights' Campaigns on the Inuit," Native Americans and the Environment, http://www.conbio.rice.edu/nae.

Hickey, Clifford. "An Examination of Processes of Culture Change Among 19th Century Copper Inuit," *Études/Inuit Studies* 8:1 (1984): 13–36.

Houston, James. *Confessions of an Igloo Dweller.* Toronto: McClelland & Stewart, 1995.

Hulen, David. "Polar Bear Mauls Mechanic: Bloody Attack at North Slope Ends with Two Shotgun Blasts," *Anchorage Daily News,* December 2, 1993.

———. "Victim of Polar Bear Mauling Files Lawsuit," *Anchorage Daily News,* August 16, 1995.

Hunt, William R. *Stef: A Biography of Vilhjalmur Stefansson, Canadian Arctic Explorer.* Vancouver: University of British Columbia Press, 1986.

Huntford, Roland. *The Amundsen Photographs.* New York: Atlantic Monthly Press, 1987.

———. *The Last Place on Earth: Scott and Amundsen's Race to the South Pole.* New York: Random House, 1999.

"An Inuit Response" (to "Lords of the Arctic"), Tungavik Federation of Nunavut, 1988, http://www.carc.org/pubs/v17no1/4.htm.

"Inuit Win Compensation, but No Apology, for Arctic Ordeal," Associated Press, Toronto, March 29, 1996.

Inuuqatigiit: The Curriculum from the Inuit Perspective (draft). Yellowknife: Department of Education, Culture and Employment, 1995–96.

Irwin, Colin. *Lords of the Arctic, Wards of the State: The Growing Inuit Population, Arctic Resettlement and Their Effects on Social and Economic Change.* A Summary Report. Ottawa, Ontario: Health and Welfare Canada, 1988, http://www.carc.org/pubs/v17no1/2.htm.

James, Geoffrey, and Ed Ogle. "In the Great Tomorrow Country, Tomorrow Is Now," *Time* (Canada edition), May 2, 1969, 10–15.

Jason, Victoria. *Kabloona in the Yellow Kayak: One Woman's Journey Through the Northwest Passage.* Winnipeg, Manitoba: Turnstone Press, 1995.

Jenness, D. *The Life of the Copper Eskimos; Report of the Canadian Arctic Expedition 1913–18,* vol. XII. Ottawa: F. A. Acland, 1922.

———. *Eskimo String Figures: Report of the Canadian Arctic Expedition 1913–18,* vol. XIII. Ottawa: F. A. Acland, 1924.

———. *Comparative Vocabulary of the Western Eskimo Dialects: Report of the Canadian Arctic Expedition 1913–18,* vol. XV. Ottawa: F. A. Acland, 1924.

———. *Eskimo Administration,* vols. I–V, Alaska-Greenland, technical papers. Arctic Institute of North America, 1965–68.

———. *The People of the Twilight.* New York: Macmillan, 1959.

Jenness, Dr. Stuart E., ed. *Arctic Odyssey: The Diary of Diamond Jenness, Ethnologist with the Canadian Arctic Expedition in Northern Alaska and Canada, 1913–1916.* Hull, Quebec: Canadian Museum of Civilization, 1991.

Joyce, James. *A Portrait of the Artist as a Young Man.* New York: Random House, 1996.

Kenney, Gerard I. *Arctic Smoke & Mirrors.* Prescott, Ontario: Voyageur Publishing, 1994.

Klein, David R. "Wilderness: A Western Concept Alien to Arctic Cultures," *Information North* (Arctic Institute of North America) 20:3 (1994).

Klengenberg, Christian. *Klengenberg of the Arctic.* London: Jonathan Cape, 1932.

Knudtson, Peter, and David Suzuki. *Wisdom of the Elders.* Toronto: Stoddart, 1992.

Kofinas, Gary. "The Costs of Power Sharing: Community Involvement in Canadian Porcupine Caribou Co-management." Ph.D. diss., University of British Columbia, 1998.

Kulchyski, Peter, and Frank James Tester. *Tammarniit (Mistakes): Inuit Relocation in the Eastern Arctic, 1939–63.* Vancouver: UBC Press, 1994.

Lander, Karen. "Son of a Sailor: Descendants of Explorer Roald Amundsen Share Memories," *News/North Nunavut,* February 15, 1999.

Lansing, Alfred. *Endurance: Shackleton's Incredible Adventure,* ed. Martin H. Greenberg and Charles G. Waugh. New York: Carroll & Graf, 1999.

Lantis, Margaret. "American Arctic Populations: Their Survival Problems." In *Arctic Biology,* ed. H. P. Hanson. Corvallis: Oregon State College, 1957.

Larramendi, Ramón Hernando de. "Perilous Journey: Three Years Across the Arctic." *National Geographic,* January 1995, 120–38.

Larsen, H. *Ipiutak and the Arctic Whale Hunting.* New York: American Museum of Natural History, 1948.

Lentfer, Jack. "Agreement on the Conservation of Polar Bears," *Polar Record* 17:108 (1974): 327–30.

Lindemann, Dr. Hannes. *Alone at Sea: A Doctor's Survival Experiments of Two Atlantic Crossings in a Dugout Canoe and a Folding Kayak.* Oberschleissheim, Germany: Pollner Verlag, 1993.

Loomis, Chauncey C. *Weird and Tragic Shores: The Story of Charles Francis Hall, Explorer.* New York: Knopf, 1971.

Lopez, Barry. *Arctic Dreams: Imagination and Desire in a Northern Landscape.* New York: Charles Scribner's Sons, 1986.

Lyall, Ernie. *An Arctic Man: Sixty-five Years in Canada's North.* Edmonton: Hurtig Publishers, 1979.

MacInnis, Jeff. "Braving the Northwest Passage," *National Geographic,* May 1989, 586–601.

———, and Wade Rowland. *Polar Passage: The Historic First Sail Through the Northwest Passage.* Toronto: Random House, 1989.

Mandeville, John J., et al., eds. *The Complete Dog Book.* New York: Howell Book House, 1992.

Mannoni, O. *Prospero and Caliban: The Psychology of Colonization,* trans. Pamela Powesland. Ann Arbor: University of Michigan Press, 1990.

Martin, Calvin. *Keepers of the Game: Indian-American Relationships and the Fur Trade.* Berkeley: University of California Press, 1978.

Mathieu, A. "Polycyclic Aromatic Hydrocarbon-DNA Adducts in Beluga Whales from the Arctic," *Journal of Toxicology and Environmental Health* 51:2 (1997): 1–4.

Matthiessen, Peter. "Survival of the Hunter," *New Yorker,* April 24, 1995, 67–77.

McGhee, Robert. *Ancient People of the Arctic.* Vancouver: UBC Press, 1996.

———. *Beluga Hunters.* Toronto: University of Toronto Press, 1974.

McGinnis, Joe. *Going to Extremes.* New York: Plume, 1989.

Melnbardis, Robert. "Canada Natives Prepare Controversial Whale Hunt," Reuters, Montreal, April 27, 1998.

Mikkelsen, Ejnar. *Conquering the Arctic Ice.* Philadelphia: George W. Jacobs, 1909.

Minor, Kit. *Issumatuq: Learning from the Traditional Healing Wisdom of the Canadian Inuit.* Halifax: Fernwood Publishing, 1992.

Mitchell, Alanna. "The Northwest Passage Thawed," *Globe and Mail,* February 5, 2000.

Morrison, David. *Arctic Hunters: The Inuit and Diamond Jenness.* Hull, Quebec: Canadian Museum of Civilization, 1992.

———, and Georges-Hébert Germain. *Inuit: Glimpses of an Arctic Past.* Hull, Quebec: Canadian Museum of Civilization, 1995.

Mowat, Farley. *The Desperate People.* Boston: Little, Brown, 1959.

———. *People of the Deer.* Boston: Little, Brown, 1951.

Müller-Wille, Ludger. "Cost Analysis of Modern Hunting Among Inuit of the Canadian Central Arctic," *Polar Geography* 2:2 (1978): 100–14.

Mulvad, Gerth, and Henning Sloth Pedersen. "*Orsoq*: Eat Meat and Blubber from Sea Mammals and Avoid Cardiovascular Disease," *Inuit Whaling,* June 1992.

Nelson, Richard. *Shadow of the Hunter: Stories of Eskimo Life.* Chicago: University of Chicago Press, 1980.

Nemeth, Mary. "Breaking the Silence: A Report Reveals Abuse Against Inuit Children," *Maclean's* 108:28 (1995): 15.

Nickerson, Colin. "Bear-Shaped License Coveted in Nunavut," *Boston Globe,* December 23, 1998.

"Nunavut Assembly Promises to Be 'a Good Mix' of Young, Old," *Globe and Mail,* February 17, 1999.

"Nunavut Government Must Act on Coroner's Report," *Nunatsiaq News,* April 15, 1999.

Ovsyanikov, Dr. Nikita. *Polar Bears: Living with the White Bear.* Stillwater, Minn.: Voyageur Press, 1996.

Parfit, Michael. "A Dream Called Nunavut," *National Geographic,* September 1997, 68–91.

Peacock, F. W. *Eskimo-English Dictionary and Eskimo Synonyms Dictionary.* Memorial University: Newfoundland, 1974.

Perkins, Robert. *Into the Great Solitude: An Arctic Journey.* New York: Henry Holt, 1991.

Pielou, E. C. *A Naturalist's Guide to the Arctic.* Chicago: University of Chicago Press, 1994.

Poncins, Gontran de. *Kabloona.* New York: Reynal & Hitchcock, 1941.

Powless, Richard C. "Native People and Employment: A National Tragedy," *Currents* 4:2 (1985): 2–5.

Pryde, Duncan. *Nunaga: Ten Years of Eskimo Life.* New York: Walker, 1972.

Pullum, Geoffrey K. *The Great Eskimo Vocabulary Hoax and Other Irreverent Essays on the Study of Language.* Chicago: University of Chicago Press, 1991, 168–71.

Purich, Donald. *The Inuit and Their Land: The Story of Nunavut.* Toronto: James Lorimer, 1992.

Qitsualik, Rachel Attituq. "The Problem with Sedna," Parts One–Six, *Nunatsiaq News,* March 5–April 15, 1999.

Rasmussen, Knud. *Across Arctic America: Narrative of the Fifth Thule Expedition.* New York: G. P. Putnam's Sons, 1927.

———. *The Intellectual Culture of the Iglulik Eskimo,* vol. 7. Copenhagen: Gyldendalske Boghandel, 1929.

Rasmussen, Lars Toft. "The Wrong Seal Hunt," *New York Times,* March 21, 1979.

Roberts, Helen H., and D. Jenness. *Songs of the Copper Eskimo: Report of the Canadian Arctic Expedition 1913–18,* vol. 14. Ottawa: F. A. Acland, 1922.

Sailing Directions: Arctic Canada, vol. 3. Ottawa, Ontario: Canadian Hydrographic Service, 1994.

Schaefer, Otto. "When the Eskimo Comes to Town," *Nutrition Today,* November–December 1971, 8–16.

Scott, Shirley L., ed. *Field Guide to the Birds of North America.* Washington, D.C.: National Geographic Society, 1996.

Sculpture/ Inuit. Toronto: University of Toronto Press, 1971.

Shackleton, Sir Ernest. *South: The Last Antarctic Expedition of Shackleton and the Endurance.* New York: Lyons Press, 1998.

Shweder, Richard A., and Edmund Bourne. "Does the Concept of the Person Vary Cross Culturally?" In *Culture Theory: Essays on Mind, Self, and Emotion,* ed. Richard A. Shweder and Robert A. LeVine. New York: Cambridge University Press, 1984, 158–99.

Simon, Alvah. *North to the Night: A Year in the Arctic Ice.* New York: McGraw-Hill, 1999.

Smart, Reginald G., and Alan C. Ogborne. "Drinking Among Aboriginal People." In *Northern Spirits: A Social History of Alcohol in Canada.* Toronto: Addiction Research Foundation, 1996, 101–12.

Smith, Lorne. "The Mechanical Dog Team: A Study of the Ski-Doo in the Canadian Arctic," *Arctic Anthropology* 9:1 (1977): 1–9.

Smith, Thomas G. "How Inuit Trapper Hunters Make Ends Meet," *Canadian Geographic* 99:3 (1979–80): 56–61.

Soublière, Marion, ed. *The Nunavut Handbook.* Iqaluit, Nunavut: Nortext Multimedia, *1998.*

Starkell, Don. *Paddle to the Arctic: The Incredible Story of a Kayak Quest Across the Roof of the World.* Toronto: McClelland & Stewart, 1995.

Stefansson, Vilhjalmur. "The Blond Eskimos," *Harper's Magazine*, January 1928, 191–98.

———. *Discovery: The Autobiography of . . .* New York: McGraw-Hill, 1964.

———. *The Friendly Arctic: The Story of Five Years in Polar Regions.* New York: Macmillan, 1921.

———. *My Life with the Eskimo.* New York: Macmillan, 1923.

Steitz, David E., and Lynn Chandler. "Increasing Greenhouse Gases May Be Worsening Arctic Ozone Depletion and May Delay Ozone Recovery," *NASA News* 21:12 (1998).

Stirling, Ian. "Habitat Preferences of Polar Bears in the Western Canadian Arctic in Late Winter and Spring," *Polar Record* 29:168 (1993): 13–24.

Storr, Carter B. *Elementary English for the Eskimo.* Ottawa: Minister of Resources and Development, 1950.

Strohmeyer, John. *Extreme Conditions: Big Oil and the Transformation of Alaska.* New York: Simon & Schuster, 1993.

Swinton, George. *Sculptures of the Eskimo.* Toronto: McClelland & Stewart, 1972.

Talaga, Tanya. "Tuberculosis Still a Threat: Disease Infects as Many as 140 Persons per 100,000 in Native Populations," *Toronto Star,* February 8, 2000.

Taylor, Glenn. "Former IRC Chair Under Investigation," Northern News Services, August 15, 1997.

Tener, J. S. *Muskoxen in Canada.* Ottawa: Queens Printer, 1965.

Terres, John K. *The Audubon Society Encyclopedia of North American Birds.* Avenel, N.J.: Wings Books, 1991.

Turk, Jon. *Cold Oceans: Adventures in Kayak, Rowboat, and Dogsled.* New York: HarperCollins, 1998.

Vanast, Dr. Walter. "The Death of Jennie Kanneyuk: Tuberculosis, Religious Competition, and Cultural Conflict in the Canadian Arctic," *Etudes/Inuit Studies* 15:1 (1991): 75–104.

Vancouver, George. *A Voyage of Discovery to the North Pacific Ocean and Round the World . . . ,* 4 vols., ed W. Kaye Lamb. London: Hakluyt Society, 1984.

Vollman, William T. *The Rifles.* New York: Viking Penguin, 1994.

———. "The Very Short History of Nunavut," *Outside,* July 1999, 56–64, 128–33.

Ward, Vincent. *Map of the Human Heart.* 1992. A feature film about a tubercular Canadian Inuit boy swept up into World War II.

Watkins, T. H. *Vanishing Arctic: Alaska's National Wildlife Refuge.* New York: Aperture, 1988.

Weber, Richard, and Mikhael Malakhov. *Polar Attack.* Toronto: McClelland & Stewart, 1996.

Weidensaul, Scott. *Living on the Wing: Across the Hemisphere with Migratory Birds.* New York: Farrar, Straus & Giroux, 1999.

Wenzel, George. *Animal Rights, Human Rights: Ecology, Economy and Ideology in the Canadian Arctic.* Toronto: University of Toronto Press, 1991.

———. "The Integration of Remote Site Labor," *Arctic Anthropology* 20:2 (1983): 79–92.

———. "Inuit and Polar Bears: Cultural Observations," *Arctic* 36:1 (1983): 90–95.

Wilkin, Dwane. "The Answer to Suicide: Land, Family and Community?" *Nunatsiaq News,* April 29, 1999.

———. "The Business of Renewable Resources: Cambridge Bay's Food Plant," *Nunatsiaq News,* September 3, 1998.

———. "Former Gjoa Haven Teachers Face Multiple Charges," *Nunatsiaq News,* July 2, 1999.

———. "Social Workers Helped Kugluktuk Killer with Firearm Permit," *Nunatsiaq News,* April 8, 1999.

———. "Some Chesterfield Survivors May Launch Lawsuit," *Nunatsiaq News,* April 15, 1999.

Wilkinson, Paul F. "The History of Musk-ox Domestication," *Polar Record* 17:106 (1974): 13–22.

Woddis, Jack. *Introduction to Neo-Colonialism.* New York: International Publishers, 1976.

Woodman, David C. *Unraveling the Franklin Mystery: Inuit Testimony.* Montreal: McGill-Queen's University Press, 1997.

Author's Note and Acknowledgments

I arrived in the North as a stranger, with no formal introduction or references, and I will never forget the kindness of so many people I met there. In Inuvik, the Canadian Coast Guard made me copies of charts and satellite sea ice maps. Mike Mueller was a thoughtful host and dropped off a cache of food on Herschel Island for me. Ron Morrison counseled me on sea ice conditions and breakup.

Eddie Greenland and then Reverend Chamberlain Jones and his wife, Irene, pulled me in from clouds of mosquitoes and fed me the Last Dinner and Breakfast in Aklavik, as well as graciously heard my ideas about finding religion in the wilderness.

The hunters of Shingle and Griffin Points and the wardens of Herschel Island Territorial Park—too many people to name—were kind to me. In Kaktovik, Merylin Traynor and Walt Audi, owners of the Waldo Arms Hotel, refused either to let me stay in my leaky tent during the monsoons or to accept money for my hotel room. The people at the Kikitat store were also generous.

The Elias family—Jim, Brian, Jorgan, Kurt, and Eleanor—were the kindest people you could hope to meet, especially while I was stranded in a spring thaw on the Anderson River delta. Rueben Green and his dad, Sam, were fine hosts at the hunting camp outside Paulatuk. Ken Thompson, former senior administrative officer of that village, gave me the use of his house and fed me, as he did for so many other passing adventurers. Sadly, he died suddenly several months later.

In Kugluktuk, Aime Ahegona is the sort of elder whom every skeptical *Kabloona* like me should meet and become enlightened by. The People of Umingmaktuuq were kind to me. In Cambridge Bay, Luke Cody and Natasha Thorpe were more than helpful; Darrell Ohokannoak donated the use of his Internet service, PolarNet. Charlie Cahill and Mike and Jan Ellsworth of Gjoa Haven were the personification of hospitality during my visits. Paul Iquallah instructed me well in the ways of his people, the Netsilik of Gjoa Haven.

I will long cherish the exhilarating day of sailing with Olivier Pitras and Jean-Michel Guillevic, who selflessly hauled me along on their cutter, *Ocean Search*. Pat and Dennis Lyall, then Jimmy and Simond Oleekatalik, became fast friends in Taloyoak.

Far from the hospitality of the North, I learned how selfless my own community of family, friends and peers are. Susan Golomb, my literary agent, helped bring the book proposal into focus. My publishers came on board after a chance meeting with Peter Andersen, design director at Knopf, on a train en route to Boston in October 1997 (this sort of cosmic serendipity also carried me safely across the Arctic). Peter thoughtfully looked at my maps and then introduced me to my superb editors. Gary Fisketjon, vice-president and editor at large at Knopf, and his former assistant, Rob Grover, have been kind, considerate and incredibly supportive. Peter—along with Karen Mugler, Amber Qureshi and all those other unknown, behind-the-scenes professionals at Knopf—have been discerning shepherds throughout the production phase. Sarah Davies, senior editor at Random House Canada, has also been helpful.

Mark Eckhart of Long Haul Products at the Klepper Service Center donated a lot of time, parts and labor to customize a super kayak, replete with zippered decks and expedition hull, out of my old, leaking Klepper. Mark Balogh of Batwing Sail Designs helped me with his superb sponsored sailing system. Steve Allen of Kyocera and Kevin Conlin of Solarcraft donated the solar panels and battery that allowed me to charge my notebook computer and accessories. Russ Sonneborn and Dennis Korn of Alpine Aire Foods generously provided me with seven months' worth of freeze-dried food.

The North Face became my main supporter in 1999. Of the various people there, Jordan Campbell made it all happen. David Schipper and Jason Olden customized a suit that kept me dry during the last wet summer. Conrad Anker, Joe Erlich, Jason Singer, Chris Eng, Jon Heinemann, Markus Hutnak and Robert Mackinlay (who conceptualized the book-jacket photograph) also looked after me most considerately.

W. L. Gore and Associates awarded me a Shipton-Tilman grant and donated the Gore-Tex immersion fabric for my dry suit. Polartec–Malden Mills awarded me with an Adventure-Challenge grant, supplied me with clothing and arranged for Polartec garments to be donated to the hamlet of Umingmaktuuq.

My other sponsors included Air B.C., Black Diamond, Clif Bar, Fischer skis, Kifaru International, Klepper, Magellan, MountainSmith, Natural Life Pet Products, Prijon / Wild Vasser, Sector, Stohlquist and Voyageur. Other friends and advisers—Landis Arnold, Jim Balog, Karen Barkley, Joe Blackburn, Jeff Blumenfeld, Dr. Ralph Bovard, Jeff Bowman, Patty Brink, Ruthann Brown, Adrienne Ciuffo, Carol Duell, Caroline Duell, Holland Duell, John Dunn, Paul Eckhart, Scott Gill, Rod Haenke, John Harlin, John Harrington, Kerry Horn, Mark Hrubant, Phil Huff, Victoria Jason, Stuart Jenness, Kara Klein, Marla Limousin, Jeff Long, Christian Mason,

Peter Metcalf, Jonathan Nettlefield, Chris Noble, Børge Ousland, Paul Parker, Jeff and Kellie Rhoads, Eric Robertson, Laura Saidler, Vince Savage, Patrick Smith, Sunniva Sorby, Eric Stiller, Andrew Thacher, Alex Thomson, Kees 't Hooft, Jon Turk, Paul Van Peenen, Stephen Venables, Ed Webster, John Wilcox, David Woodman and Len Zanni—rallied in too many ways to mention.

Steve and Marilyn Davis of Summit Canyon Mountaineering went to great lengths to outfit me. Sue and Don Edmonds of Bristlecone Mountain Sports were also helpful. Both stores, along with numerous employees, also helped collect donated equipment and clothing for the Pelly Bay Inuit.

American Adventure Productions of Aspen, Colorado, paid expenses for making a two-hour television film, *Odyssey Among the Inuit*, for the Adventure Quest series on the Outdoor Life Network. Learning Outfitters provided no small support in exchange for my weekly journals on my "Northwest Passage" educational Web site, adventureonline.com. John Rasmus of *National Geographic*'s *Adventure* magazine and James Mathewson of *Computer User* magazine helped with expenses and product support.

Christian M. Boissonnas and Laurie Stevens of Cornell University's Olin Library in Ithaca, New York, mailed me scores of hard-to-find books and obscure articles. Librarians at the Pitkin County Library in Aspen, Colorado, and the American Alpine Club in Golden, Colorado, were also efficient and obliging.

June Waterman, Susan Golomb, Michael Kennedy, Dr. Gary Kofinas, Kelcey Nichols and Claudine Wiley read drafts of the manuscript and provided invaluable advice. By being critical, these treasured friends and readers were performing a service above and beyond simple support.

Too many people to name—more than fifty—voted on title ideas. As for those I may have forgotten to acknowledge, they have both my apologies and my gratitude.

I cannot thank my wife, June—cum Penelope—enough. Her support and enthusiasm made the whole project possible. Without her, I'm not sure I would have even made it back from the Arctic. When all is done and said, she had to stay home and believe in me, often enduring weeks with no word of my well-being. I believe that any adventurer must consider who bears the brunt of his indulgences, as well as the true meaning of courage, empathy and suffering. In addition to the many hats she willingly wore, she helped me train, packed expedition food, photocopied proposals, dog-sat and paid the bills while I was gone, flew up to the Arctic twice to look after me, listened to (and critiqued) the entire manuscript being read aloud and provided understanding and needed terra firma for my free-floating time at sea. Odysseus never had it so good.

Illustration Credits

Over the course of three years, I exposed nearly a thousand photographs—scant documentation, because too much energy was expended self-filming my trip with a video camera. I used only slide film, Kodak E100 and Velvia (often pushed in low-light situations); some of the halftones were shot with Scala black-and-white slides. For self-photography, 15- and 17-millimeter lenses facilitated fitting everything in; a self-timer and a remote also helped.

Those few times I was not alone, David Amagainik, Jeff MacInnis, Olivier Pitras, June Duell and several anonymous Inuit snapped photographs with my camera. Kees 't Hooft, in particular, obliged me by putting down his video camera and picking up my 35-millimeter.

Elizabeth King and Gary Kofinas, of the Institute for Global Awareness, donated, respectively, the images of a bearded seal (page 154) and a caribou migration (page 94). Both pictures were shot during our 1989 trip across the Arctic National Wildlife Refuge.

All other photographs are mine. None were digitally enhanced or unnaturally filtered.

Grateful acknowledgment is made to the following for permission to use illustrations:

Germaine Arnaktauyok: pages 3, 34, 70, 82, 140, 182, 194, 205, 219, 265 and 320

Family of Sara Joe Qinuajua: pages 114, 119, 233 and 276

National Maritime Museum of Greenwich: page 292

A Note on the Type

This book was set in Fairfield, the first typeface from the hand of the distinguished American artist and engraver Rudolph Ruzicka (1883–1978). Born in Bohemia, Ruzicka came to America in 1894. He designed and illustrated many books, and was the creator of a considerable list of wood engravings, copper engravings and aquatints.

Fairfield displays the sober and sane qualities of the master craftsman. It is this trait that accounts for the trim grace and vigor, the spirited design and sensitive balance, of this original typeface.

Composed by North Market Street Graphics, Lancaster, Pennsylvania
Printed by Quebecor World, Fairfield, Pennsylvania
Endpaper maps by George Colbert
Designed by Peter A. Andersen